THE JEWS OF EGYPT

THE JEWS OF EGYPT

From Rameses II
to Emperor Hadrian

JOSEPH MÉLÈZE MODRZEJEWSKI

Translated by Robert Cornman
With a Foreword by Shaye J. D. Cohen

PRINCETON UNIVERSITY PRESS
PRINCETON, NEW JERSEY

Published by Princeton University Press, 41 William Street,
Princeton, New Jersey 08540
In the United Kingdom: Princeton University Press,
Chichester, West Sussex

Reprinted by arrangement with The Jewish Publication Society, 1930
Chestnut Street, Philadelphia, PA 19103

Library of Congress Cataloging-in-Publication Data

Modrzejewski, Joseph.
    [Juifs d'Égypte. English]
    The Jews of Egypt : from Rameses II to Emperor Hadrian / Joseph
Mélèze Modrzejewski ; translated by Robert Cornman ; with a
foreword by Shaye J. D. Cohen.
        p.   cm.
    Previously published: 1st English ed. Philadelphia : Jewish
Publication Society, 1995.
    Includes bibliographical references and index.
    ISBN 0-691-01575-9
    1. Jews—Egypt—History.   2. Egypt—Ethnic relations.
3. Egypt—History—To 640 A.D.   4. Rameses II, King of
Egypt.   5. Hadrian, Emperor of Rome, 76–138.   I. Title.
DS135.E4M6413   1997
932'.004924—dc21   97-33449
                              r97

Princeton University Press books are printed on acid-free paper and
meet the guidelines for permanence and durability of the Committee
on Production Guidelines for Book Longevity of the Council on
Library Resources

First Princeton Paperback printing, with corrections, 1997

http://pup.princeton.edu

Printed in the United States of America

10 9 8 7 6 5 4 3 2 1

FOR LYDIA

CONTENTS

FOREWORD

Shaye J. D. Cohen

Hellenistic Egypt. Islamic Spain. Renaissance Italy. These were magical times and places, "Golden Ages" in the history of Jews and Judaism. What makes an age "golden" in the Jewish memory is a vibrant cultural interaction between the Jews and their gentile hosts. Challenged by the attractiveness and magnificence of the culture around them, the Jews did not isolate themselves within the protective confines of Jewish law, nor did they withdraw from contact with gentiles and gentile ways. On the contrary. In these Golden Ages, Jewish creativity thrived, precisely because the cultural challenge from their environment allowed—compelled, perhaps—the Jews to enrich their Judaism with new ideas and new forms of literary and artistic expression. The adaptation to modernity, far from weakening or diluting Judaism, strengthened it and fructified it.

The two best-known Golden Ages occurred in Moslem Spain and Renaissance Italy. Under Arab influence, the Jews of Moslem Spain (tenth to twelfth century) read and wrote works of philosophy, belles-lettres, religious poetry, secular poetry, medicine, astronomy, grammar, scriptural exegesis, and much else besides. Their art and architecture were heavily indebted to Islamic models, as the synagogues of Cordova and Toledo spectacularly demonstrate. The Jews of Italy in the fourteenth to the sixteenth century were almost as well versed in Italian and Latin as their coreligionists in Spain had been in Arabic. Similarly, under Christian influence, the Jews of Italy read and wrote works of philosophy, belles-lettres, religious poetry, secular poetry, medicine, astronomy, grammar, scriptural exegesis, and more. Their art and architecture were heavily indebted to Italian models, as can be readily seen in the synagogues of Venice and Ferrara.

Hellenistic Egypt was the setting for perhaps the first Jewish Golden Age. From the third century B.C.E. to the first century C.E., Alexandria, the largest city in the ancient world, was home to a large and vigorous Jewish population. The countryside too had a Jewish presence, with Jews living in virtually all the large towns and many villages along the length of the Nile. Egyptian Jews abandoned Hebrew and Aramaic and produced a luxuriant literature in Greek. Roman literature begins with the translation of the works of Homer into Latin by Livius Andronicus; Hellenistic Jewish literature begins with the translation of the Torah into Greek by a group of sages imported for that purpose from the land of Israel (or, at least, so runs the story. For a discussion of this translation, known as the Septuagint, see Chapter V below).

Once the Torah became available in a language they could understand, the Jews of Egypt began writing works of philosophy, belles-lettres, poetry, and scriptural exegesis. All of these works concern themselves in one way or another with the Torah, but all of them were written in Greek, in Greek literary forms, and with Greek literary techniques. The greatest of these Egyptian Greek-Jewish writers is also the last, the philosopher Philo (first half of the first century C.E.). In his numerous essays, Philo attempted to show that the Torah is not (only) a book of stories and laws but a book of instructions for the soul. Philo's God is not the anthropomorphic and anthropopathic God of the Torah but a God more like Plato's. The goal of human existence is to "see" God by ascending through the spheres, escaping the world of matter, and arriving at the world of pure *form*. Philo's thought is a unique combination of the Torah, postbiblical Jewish thought, Platonism, Stoicism, and Pythagoreanism—a veritable fusion of Judaism and Hellenism.

This cultural effloresence was facilitated by the physical security, economic sufficiency, and social prominence of the Jews. Centuries earlier, under the Persians, the Judean community at Elephantine was the victim of a pogrom by the Egyptian populace, abetted by the Persian governor (see Chapter II below); and in the first century C.E., the Jewish community of Alexandria was the victim of a pogrom by the urban mob, abetted by the Roman governor (see Chapter VIII below); but under the Ptolemies Jewish life was secure. (Egyptian Jews had a legend that told of a Ptolemy [*which?*] who attempted to kill all the Jews [*of Egypt? of Alexandria?*] and almost succeeded, but he was thwarted by divine intervention. The historical event, if any, couched in this legend, is not evident; see Chapter VII below.) The Jews of Ptolemaic Egypt were soldiers, farmers, shepherds, artisans, policemen, tax-gatherers, government officials, and merchants. A few were rich, but the vast majority were not; the impression one gets from reading the papyri is that most Jews were able to support themselves by the sweat of their brows.[1]

It is striking that a few Jews were able to achieve high station in government service. In the third century B.C.E. there was Dositheus son of Drimylus (see Chapter III below), and in the Roman period (the first century C.E.) there was Tiberius Julius Alexander (see Chapter IX below). Both of them were "apostates"; the former was a high official at the Ptolemaic court, the latter the governor of Egypt. A papyrus document refers to an Onias who was a person of high rank in the Ptolemaic hierarchy in the middle of the second century B.C.E. (see Chapter VI below). At the end of the second century B.C.E. Cleopatra III appointed two Jews, Helkias and Ananias, as commanders-in-chief of her army. They served their queen well, although in one remarkable episode they counseled her not to invade the territory of Alexander Jannaeus because "an injustice done to this man will make all us Jews your enemies" (Josephus, *Jewish Antiquities* 13:354). These Jewish courtiers prefigure the Jewish courtiers of

Moslem Spain, the most spectacularly successful of whom were Hisdai ibn Shaprut, court physician and chief of foreign trade to 'Abd al-Rahman III (mid tenth century C.E.), and Samuel the Prince (Shmuel ha-nagid, or Samuel ibn Nagrela), commander-in-chief of the army of Granada (1030 to 1056 C.E.).

Of course, Golden Ages always contain a certain amount of brass, and they always come to an end. Jewish culture may have been enriched by contact with Spanish Moslems and Italian Christians, but the Jews remained outsiders in their host societies. They were tolerated, at best, and persecution was always a danger. The invasion of the Almohades in the twelfth century and the growing success of the Christian reconquest put an end to the Golden Age of Islamic Spain. In the sixteenth century the expulsion of the Jews from Spanish possessions in Italy and the increasingly severe treatment of the Jews in the papal states, largely as part of the Counter Reformation, put an end to the Golden Age of the Jews in Italy.

Similarly, the Jews of Hellenistic Egypt met with a certain amount of "anti-Judaism," even during the period of their greatest influence (see Chapter VII below), but things did not turn noxious until the Roman period. Ethnic strife and urban violence in Alexandria caused serious damage to the community from 38 to 41 C.E. Many of the details of the story are obscure, but the basic outline seems clear (see Chapter VIII below). The Jews in the city feuded with the Greek and Egyptian elements of the population, were defeated in a series of bloody confrontations (apparently with the connivance of the Roman governor), and would have fared even worse had the emperor Caligula not been assassinated and replaced by the more sensible Claudius. This conflict seems to have left emotional scars on the community; the literary fusion of Hellenism and Judaism comes to an abrupt halt at this point. Philo, an eyewitness to the painful events of 38 to 41 C.E., is the last known Greek-Jewish writer from Egypt. Seventy-five years later the community itself was wiped out in a massive and massively misguided uprising against the Romans. The Jews of Alexandria, the Egyptian countryside, Cyrene and Cyprus, several hundred thousand in number, were killed or enslaved. The Golden Age ended in a catastrophe that was, in large part, self-inflicted (see Chapter IX below).

There are many differences, of course, between the Golden Age of Hellenistic Egypt and the Golden Ages of Islamic Spain and Renaissance Italy (not to mention the many differences between the latter two); I shall discuss here two of the most important differences. First, as I mentioned briefly above, the Jewish culture of Hellenistic Egypt was linguistically Greek. Philo and his Jewish predecessors studied the Torah in Greek and pondered its inner truths in Greek. Philo may have known some Hebrew, but neither he nor any of his Egyptian coreligionists could read the Torah in Hebrew, let alone compose works in Hebrew. In stark contrast, the Jews of Moslem Spain were masters of both Arabic and Hebrew; under the influence of Arabic models, they composed Hebrew poems of extraordinary virtuosity and complexity. The study of Hebrew grammar had its beginnings with the Jews of Moslem Spain. The Jews of Italy knew Italian and even wrote some prayers, poetry, and philosophical works in Italian, but their literary culture was, of course, a Hebrew one.

Second, the Jewish culture of Hellenistic Egypt was nonrabbinic, or to be more precise, prerabbinic, whereas the Jewish cultures of both Islamic Spain and Renaissance Italy were decidedly rabbinic. Rabbinic culture first achieved literary expression in the Mishnah, a work that was redacted in the land of Israel in about 200 C.E., and then in the Talmudim of the land of Israel and Babylonia and in related works (400 to 500 C.E.). Rabbinic culture was a Hebrew culture, based on the recitation of Hebrew prayers, the study of the Tanakh (in Hebrew, perhaps with the assistance of an Aramaic Targum), and the study of the Oral Law (rabbinic lore and tradition). The authority figure in rabbinic society was, of course, the rabbi. The Jewish cultures of Golden Age Spain and Italy were rabbinic cultures. Virtually all of the important courtiers, poets, philosophers, physicians, and grammarians were rabbinic scholars. Many of them wrote talmudic commentaries, rabbinic responsa, or compendia of rabbinic law. This is not to say that all the Jews of Spain and Italy were exemplars of rabbinic piety—clearly this was not the case. But the communities and their institutions were rabbinic in character and were under rabbinic control.

Not so the Jewish community of Hellenistic Egypt; there were no rabbis, no rabbinic literature, and no rabbinic tradition. Scholars have written numerous studies of Philo and Philonic thought, attempting to distinguish the Jewish elements from the Greek and in turn to assess his relationship with the rabbinic traditions that would take shape in the land of Israel in subsequent centuries, but the connection remains unclear. Certainly, the Jews of Egypt, beginning with the Judaeans of Elephantine in the Persian period (see Chapter II below), often acted in a manner that would seem to violate not only later rabbinic law but even biblical law. Jewish marriage and divorce contracts were not distinctively Jewish, implying that the wife had as much right as the husband to initiate divorce; Jews occasionally displayed extraordinary respect for the pagan gods of Egypt, saluting them in epistolary greetings, making donations to their shrines, and even (according to Artapanus, a Jewish author) attributing the origins of Egyptian polytheism to Moses himself; the chief of a synagogue was honored with a statue;[2] it was permissible to charge interest on loans. All of these violations are discussed in this book.

Perhaps because of this prerabbinic (or nonrabbinic) character, Jewish scholars in the middle of the nineteenth century, who were looking for models of the integration of Judaism with western culture, passed over Hellenistic Egypt. These scholars instead glorified the Jews and Judaism of Moslem Spain, spoke glibly of Moslem tolerance, invented the notion of a Golden Age, and praised the accomplishments of a Jewish community that was allowed by its host culture, so it was said, to combine the best of Judaism with the best of Hellenism (as intermediated and interpreted by the Arabs). Golden Age Spain was to serve as a model of the hoped-for German-Jewish symbiosis. The Judaism of Hellenistic Egypt was less useful for these Jewish historians because, viewed rabbinically, it was less Jewish. The growth of secular, nonreligious varieties of Judaism in the latter part of the nineteenth century and the beginning of the twentieth paradoxically meant that the nonrabbinic Judaism of Hellenistic Egypt gained new relevance because now it could serve as a mirror for the nonrabbinic Judaism of modernity. Harry Wolfson's description of the Jews of Alexandria in the time of Philo, with its account of three types of apostates ("the weak of flesh," "the socially ambitious," and "the intellectually uprooted"), sounds remarkably like a description of the Jews of New York City in the 1930s.[3] Who can withhold a smile of recognition upon hearing Philo's description of the Day of Atonement: "On the tenth day [of the seventh month] is the fast, which is carefully observed not only by the zealous for piety and holiness but also by those who never act religiously in the rest of their life" (*On the Special Laws* 1:186, trans. F. Colson).

The theme of *The Jews of Egypt* is not cultural interaction and religious development but social change and institutional history. Professor Modrzejewski makes remarkable use of marriage contracts, petitions, affidavits, loans, and tax receipts. This material is usually dry and technical, hence often overlooked, but in the hands of a master such as Professor Modrzejewski, the scattered remains of a once proud bureaucratic society become fascinating and important sources of information. Without a trustworthy guide, these documents are inaccessible to the nonspecialist; Professor Modrzejewski is the model of a trustworthy guide.

While the intended audience of this book includes all those interested in the history of Jews in Egypt in antiquity, specialists too will learn much that is new. Particularly impressive are Professor Modrzejewski's discussions of Dositheus son of Drimylos, a Jewish apostate; of the Jewish *politeuma*, not an organ of the state but a voluntary religious association; of the Ptolemaic category of "Hellenes," which included Jews; of the "civic laws" (*politikoi nomoi*) of the Jews; of the contradiction between information found in 3 Maccabees and information in the writings of Josephus, regarding the identity of the Ptolemaic king who would have killed all the Jews; of Philopator's confusion of the Jewish God with Dionysus; of *anosioi Ioudaioi*—impious Jews—whose impiety consisted of refusal of emperor worship; of the destruction of earliest Alexandrian Christianity in the war of 115 to 117 C.E. These subjects have been treated by Professor Modrzejewski in numerous French publications, and we should all be grateful to Robert Cornman, translator, and to The Jewish Publication Society for making Professor Modrzejewski's scholarship more accessible to the English-speaking readership.

NOTES

1. See Tcherikover's survey in *Corpus Papyrorum Judaicarum*, 1:10–19.
2. This is how Professor Modrzejewski in Chapter IV interprets the text of the surviving inscription (the statue itself is lost); a more likely interpretation is that the head of the synagogue has donated the state [of whom? of what?] to the synagogue. It is very possible that the "synagogue" is not Jewish but Greek (an association or club).
3. Harry Wolfson, *Philo* (Cambridge: Harvard University Press, 1947, frequently reprinted; 2 vols.), 1:73–86; Leo W. Schwarz, *Wolfson of Harvard* (Philadelphia: Jewish Publication Society, 1978), 155.

INTRODUCTION

"And a stranger thou shalt not wrong, neither shalt thou oppress him,
for ye were strangers in the land of Egypt."

Exodus 22:20

From time immemorial, Egypt has exercised a singular power of attraction over the Jews. This is rather astonishing, in the light of the misfortunes they suffered in the service of Pharaoh, ritually evoked each year at the Passover Feast: "We were the slaves of Pharaoh in Egypt, and the Eternal our Lord brought us forth from there . . . with a strong hand and with an outstretched arm, with great terror, and with signs and wonders." Once delivered, however, they had no qualms about returning at the earliest opportunity. Was it because the "house of bondage" was also the land where the Sons of Israel had spent their childhood, where the bitter memories of bygone misery were intimately bound to tender recollections of the carefree days before the giving of the Torah, with all its exalting but demanding exigencies? The fact remains that the return journey of the Jews to Egypt was much shorter than the flight from Pharaoh. Given favorable circumstances, the Jews were to write new chapters in the book of their Egyptian adventures. The sages of the Talmud were to condemn their imprudent behavior, denouncing it as one of the principal causes of the great misfortunes that befell them under Roman rule. "Thrice has Israel been warned not to return to Egypt," Rabbi Simeon ben Yohai tells us, "and thrice has Israel disobeyed." When they disobeyed for the third time, a terrible punishment was called down upon the Jews: the destruction of Hellenized Jewry in Alexandria and Egypt.

There our voyage shall come to an end. In the last years of Trajan's reign, the annihilation of Egyptian Jewry in the wake of the rebellion of 115–117 CE marked the end of a period of four centuries, during which the Jews, in Alexandria and on the banks of the Nile, peacefully lived out their Jewishness in terms of Greek culture and the Greek language. Without having had to relinquish their religious practices nor their Jewish identity, they were, socially and culturally speaking, full-fledged members of the Greco-Macedonian community, the "Hellenes." It was a fecund experiment, rich with promise for posterity, especially for nascent Christianity, rooted in Alexandrian Judaism; but a perilous one for the Jews themselves, ending as it did in unmitigated tragedy: it was drowned in a "sea of blood" (we shall learn the aptness of this metaphor).

Notwithstanding, all was not yet over. The Jewish community as such had been destroyed, but some individuals or even small groups had managed to escape with their lives. We know next to nothing about them. It was only some two hundred years after the revolt had been crushed that the timid beginnings of a new community could be discerned on the banks of the Nile. It had little resemblance to the one that had been assassinated in 115–117, but was a harbinger of the Jewish presence in medieval and modern Egypt, under the rule of Islam. The days of Alexandrian Judaism were numbered, but a good part of its cultural heritage has survived. Invisible hands had preserved from destruction the Greek version of the Bible—the Septuagint—and the works of the philosopher Philo, both of which had become an integral part of Christian tradition. This spiritual continuity is undeniable, as is the radical cleavage between the collapse of Alexandrian Judaism and the emergence of the Church of Alexandria, toward the year 200 CE. These phenomena appear in the epilogue to our book.

The facts of history oblige us to end our inquiry at the beginning of the reign of Hadrian (August of 117 CE); its starting point is more difficult to determine. Aramaic documents discovered at Elephantine, near Aswan, afford us a glimpse into the life of a Judean military colony in the fifth century, when Egypt was a province of the Persian Empire. In the first part of this work, we shall cite a good number of them. In order to look further backward in time, we have only the biblical account to go on, on the one hand, and a few Egyptian documents supplemented by some rare archaeological data, on the other. Here, we are on more slippery terrain. But can one tell the story of the Jews in Egypt without beginning with Joseph and his brothers, without speaking of the infant Moses saved from a watery death, without evoking the Exodus of the Hebrews? By placing this latter event during the long reign of Rameses II, in the thirteenth century BCE (1270?), we may face the accusation of taking refuge in a comfortable hypothesis, but we shall nevertheless run that risk.

Our project is beginning to take shape. Its chronological limits are marked out by the reigns of an illustrious Pharaoh and an emperor, renowned for loving the land of the Nile and its marvels. Within this time span of some fourteen centuries, we shall concentrate our attention on the epoch that began with Alexander the Great and the foundation of Alexandria in 331 BCE, continued under the domination of the Ptolemies and that of the Romans after their conquest of Egypt in 30 BCE, and ended with the catastrophe of 115–117. Regarding this option, a few remarks may be appropriate here, concerning our sources and our methods.

In the absence of directly applicable archaeological data, this book is based essentially on written sources, which may be divided into two categories. On the one hand, literary texts; some are well known and easily accessible, such as the Bible, the writings of Philo of Alexandria and Josephus; others, such as the Apocrypha and Judeo-Alexandrian literature, are a bit more specialized. On the other hand, we have gathered a rich supply of information from Greek papyri, which have been unearthed, over the last hundred years, from the sands of Egypt and scrutinized by scholars from many nations.

In fact, toward the end of the nineteenth century, a great harvest of documents written on papyrus was reaped on the desert borders of the Nile Valley and in the oasis of the Fayyum, heralding the emergence of a new scientific discipline: papyrology. Strictly speaking, the first papyrological texts to come to the notice of Western readers were not of Egyptian provenance but were discovered in Italy. As early as 1752, the curiosity of archaeologically oriented members of Western society was aroused by the discovery, in the house of the Pisones family near Herculaneum and in several neighboring houses, of more than 1,800 scrolls of carbonized papyri, subsequently identified as a philosophical library. But Egypt promptly supplanted Italy. From the eighteenth century until the latter third of the nineteenth, sporadic acquisitions of documents and literary texts made their way into European libraries. Among these were the speeches of the Athenian orator Hyperides, lost for centuries and suddenly rediscovered in the form of copies made in Egypt. Then, during the winter of 1877–78, the market of Egyptian antiquities was literally flooded by hundreds of papyri in seven languages: Greek, Latin, Coptic, Aramaic, Syriac, Persian, and Arabic. Fortuitous purchases were obviously insufficient, and had thenceforth to be supplemented by regular excavations.

From the last decade of the nineteenth century up to our day, excavations and purchases have incessantly augmented the impressive inventory of ancient texts written on papyrus and discovered in Egypt. After having revealed Hyperides to us, the Egyptian sands have restored many other treasures of Greek literature: Aristotle's *Constitution of Athens*, the *Mimes* of Herondas, the *Epinicians* and the *Dithyrambs* of Bacchylides, the theatrical works of Menander, and the *Hellenica from Oxyrhynchos*, a historical work whose author has not yet been surely identified. But the bringing to light of these texts, however great their cultural value, did not suffice to earn papyrology its place among the other sciences of Antiquity. Its principal focus has been the discovery of the tens of thousands of documentary texts at our disposition today, documents in the literal sense: for example, legal rules and regulations, contracts, wills, fiscal receipts, accounts, correspondence both administrative and private. Their testimony allows us to reconstruct a lively image of all the aspects of everyday existence in ancient Egypt. We shall become intimate with their authors, learn their secrets, share their worries and their joys, as we accompany them in the humble course of their daily errands.

This documentation is of capital importance for our subject. It enables us to project onto the traditional sources of the history of Judaism the bright new light of these precious new sources. As has been mentioned, Aramaic papyri found on the island of Elephantine, near the Sudanese border of Egypt, have taught us the details of religious practices and family life among the Judean colonists in the service of the last Pharaohs and the Persian sovereigns. Since the conquest of the country by Alexander the Great (332–331 BCE), numberless Greek papyri dealing with the Jews and Jewish affairs have afforded us fresh insights into the world of the diaspora in Egypt under the Ptolemies, and later, under Roman domination. Without this documentation, we would know neither how the Jews in Egypt spent their days, what they hoped for, what they feared, how they dealt with their daily problems, what they desired, how they got on with the Greeks and the Egyptians, nor how the passionate adventure of the Hellenized Jews came to an end in Alexandria and on the banks of the Nile.

Our knowledge of the most ancient biblical manuscripts in Greek comes to us through the papyri, which have furnished fragments of the translation of the Torah elaborated in Alexandria at the beginning of the third century BCE (the Septuagint). On the authority of the papyri, the institutional realities of the Ptolemaic monarchy offer a proper field of research for the solution to the debate over the origins and the purpose of this translation. Thanks to the papyri, we can examine with a critical eye certain memorable episodes in the history of Egyptian Jewry, such as the foundation of the temple of Onias in Leontopolis, or the confrontations between Jews and Greeks in Alexandria at the beginning of the Roman epoch. To the papyri we owe our knowledge of the succession of events during the revolt of 115–117 CE and the attitude of the Romans toward the insurgents.

Because of their abundance and their historical value, I have given preference to these sources, and it follows that the bulk of the work deals with the Greek and Roman periods to which they pertain; secondarily, I have resorted to Greek inscriptions and ostraca, the shards of pottery the Egyptians used as receipts. The majority of the reading public is not well acquainted with this material. For many readers, this book will be their first contact with papyri and papyrology. So much the better, as one of my goals is to furnish the reader with first-hand knowledge of the papyrological testimony itself and, by occasionally expressing a personal preference, to appeal to his critical sense. The task has not been disagreeable to one who has spent more then forty years of his life in the company of papyrological documents, scrutinizing the horizon in three directions, standing now at the point of their intersection: ancient Egypt, Hellenistic civilization, and the history of Judaism.

The priority given to documentary sources is the reason why social and institutional history occupy the foreground of this work. The Septuagint, for example, is here envisaged from the viewpoint of the history of law and justice, and not in a linguistic or exegetic perspective. Literary sources, even where novel-like accounts are concerned, such as the story of Joseph and Asenath or the Third Book of Maccabees, find their place here only as historical testimony. In this respect, preference has been accorded to less well known authors, such as Demetrios the chronographer or the historian-novelist Artapanos, to the detriment of a personage as well known as Philo the philosopher, whose work has already been the object of a number of specialized studies. Philo, that veritable symbol of Alexandrian Judaism at the beginning of the common era, appears here, for the most part, as a Jewish notable of Alexandria, very much involved in the events of his time, which does not in any manner diminish the esteem he deserves as a great thinker. I hope the reader will not regret my choices, which may enable him to discover some aspects of ancient Judaism, neglected or barely touched upon by the historians of our time.

This book could never have been written without the help and advice of certain persons and institutions, who have afforded me the opportunity to treat the history of the Jews of Egypt in antiquity in the light of papyrological documents. First of all, I would like to mention the Martin Buber Institute for Judaic Studies in Brussels and its director, Willy Bok, under whose auspices I first tackled the subject in 1979 before a faithful and attentive audience. At the Rashi Center in Paris, another public, just as attentive and as faithful, followed the elaboration of the material that has gone into this book. Jacques Hassoun asked me to join him in the writing of *Juifs du Nil*, which he published in 1981; my contribution to that volume was the point of departure for the present work. Bernadette Menu has been kind enough to read the first chapter and to verify the Egyptological data. Gérald Finkielsztejn has shared with me the fruit of his archaeological experience, enabling me to flesh out a substantial part of the chapter on the synagogues. I am most grateful to Micheline and Henri van Effenterre, who not only invited me to write the book for their collection "Les Néreides," in which the first French version was published in 1991, but provided faithful encouragement during the long period of its gestation.

The present American version of my book differs in many respects from the French original. In order to bring it up to date, a great number of revisions and additions have been made; some passages have been entirely rewritten. The bibliography has been adapted for the English reader. The translations of the texts and documents quoted in this book have been prepared from existing material. Biblical extracts are quoted from the Masoretic Text (Jewish Publication Society, 1917). For the Aramaic papyri I have used, with the kind permission of the editors, Bezalel Porten and Ada Yardeni, the *Textbook of Aramaic Documents from Ancient Egypt* (The Hebrew University of Jerusalem, Department of the History of Jewish People). The Greek papyri appear in the translations of the *Corpus Papyrorum Judaicarum* (in which prior English translations are frequently reproduced), revised and amended if necessary. Greek and Roman authors are quoted in current translations, especially those of the Loeb Classical Library (William Heinemann, London, and Harvard University Press), which I have adapted.

I have attempted to resolve the difficult problem of the spelling of proper names— Egyptian, Hebrew, Greek, Latin—by reference to a dual criterion: the respect of established usage and of the original form. Thus the reader will find "Judah," "Cleopatra," "Heracles," when well-known personages are mentioned, but "Yehudah," "Klearchos," "Herakles" ("Herakleides," "Herakleia"), for persons whose names appear in original documents and more specialized texts (the transliteration of Hebrew and Aramaic names follows the conventions of the Jewish Publication Society). For similar reasons, well-known localities such as "Miletus," "Pharsalus," and "Tarsus" conserve their traditional form, while "Kaunos," "Krokodilopolis," and "Oxyrhynchos" are preferred to "Caunus," "Crocodilopolis," and "Oxyrhynchus." The Latin ending -us is generally restricted to

Roman names ("Aurelius," "Claudius," "Tiberius"), while the Greek ending -os is applied to Greek names ("Apollonios," "Aristoboulos," "Demetrios") and to Hellenized names ("Artapanos," "Josepos," "Sabbathaios"). However, the ending -us has been employed for authors ("Aeschylus," "Callimachus," "Diodorus of Sicily," "Herodotus," "Josephus," "Theocritus"), rulers ("Antiochus," "Hyrcanus," "Philadelphus," "Seleucus") or divinities ("Dionysus") whose names, Greek or Hellenized, are listed in all current dictionaries. Consequently, the Egyptian king "Psammetichus" and the Greco-Egyptian commander "Psammetichos," who bears the king's name, the queen (or the Jewish princess) "Berenice" and the priestess "Berenike," the historian "Cleitarchus" and the banker "Kleitarchos," the Jewish chronographer "Demetrios" and the Seleucid ruler (or the Athenian statesman) "Demetrius" are spelled in a slightly different manner. However desirable they may be, perfect coherence and uniformity in these matters is hardly an attainable goal.

This American edition would not have been possible without the unflagging interest and material support of Betsy and Ed Cohen, to whom I express my warmest thanks. I am grateful to Robert Cornman, not only for his elegant translation, but also for his unceasing help in amending and completing the French original with a view to the English version. I owe special thanks to Thomas Drew-Bear and Nicholas de Lange, who have contributed many valuable suggestions. Last but not least, I am deeply indebted to Shaye J. D. Cohen for his constructive commentaries and his remarkable Foreword, in which the topical importance of the "Alexandrian model" of Judaism for the contemporary world and its problems is brought to the fore.

Joseph Mélèeze Modrzejewski

Note to the Princeton Paperback Edition

Thanks to an initiative of Princeton University Press, this paperback edition of the present book is available two years after the original publication of the American version in 1995. During this time I have had the opportunity to discuss different aspects of the problems dealt with in this work with my colleagues, especially Bezalel Porten and Daniel Schwartz in Jerusalem, when I was a member of the Institute for Advanced Studies at the Hebrew University in 1995/1996, as well as Roger Bagnall (Columbia University) and Diana Delia (Brown University). If I could write the book again, I would modify the contents of some chapters to take into account their suggestions. The main points concern the interpretation of the Aramaic documents in chapter two and problems of Jewish communal organization (*politeumata*) in Ptolemaic Egypt (p. 82). Some additions might also be made to the bibliography (pp. 247ff.). But such changes were not possible in this edition, which simply reproduces the original text. All I was able to do, by kind permission of the Publishers, was to correct a number of misprints and factual errors. In this way, the book is once again accessible to an English-speaking readership.

J.M.M.
July 1997

THE JEWS OF EGYPT

THE DAWN: PHARAOHS AND GREAT KINGS

CHAPTER 1 ☙

Biblical Egypt

JOSEPH AND HIS BROTHERS

We all know how deeply the origins of Israel, from Abraham to Moses, are rooted in the Egyptian past. The long sojourn of the Hebrews in Egypt was the prelude to the three basic events in Judaic history: the Exodus, the giving of the Torah, and the Mosaic covenant. But should a historian attempt to bring the biblical account into correspondence with available historical and archaeological data, he would be hard pressed indeed, since the two are vastly dissimilar. The style and contents of the Pentateuch (the Greek noun for the first five books of the Bible) are not those of the royal hieroglyphs. The Egyptian archives bear no trace of a Abraham or a Moses. Conversely, neither Genesis nor Exodus contains the slightest reference to the great political events studding the remote epoch these books are supposed to treat. Biblical Egypt and Egyptological Egypt have few points in common, and the few they have are debatable ones. The part played by hypotheses and delicate choices is all the more considerable.

Chapter 47 of the Book of Genesis tells how Joseph was authorized by Pharaoh to bring his father and brothers to settle in "the land of Goshen." This marks the starting point of the Hebrews' sojourn in Egypt. In fact, the event probably accounts for merely one branch of the Israelites' genealogical tree. The patriarchal tradition of Genesis and the Mosaic tradition of Exodus are bound together by only the flimsiest of threads. The memory of the Egyptian sojourn and the Exodus, dominant in the latter, is practically absent from the former. The patriarchal tradition originated among groups of people who probably had never gone to Egypt. In the Pentateuch, the two traditions are combined in a comprehensive table: Israel appears as the people of the twelve tribes, descended from the twelve sons of Jacob. Thus was the classical succession established: the Patriarchs, the sojourn in Egypt, the Exodus, the conquest of Canaan. The actual experience of one group was expanded by Jewish memory into the recollection of a common adventure.

The Pentateuch is ambiguous concerning the length of the stay in Egypt. The number of generations oscillates between three for the descendants of Levi (Ex. 6:16–20 and

Num. 26:58–59), and seven for those of Joseph (Num. 27:1). One could be led to believe that the descendants of the former had a lifespan twice that of the latter. In absolute numbers, too, there is a discrepancy between the Patriarchal and the Mosaic traditions. In concluding the covenant with Abraham, the Eternal foretells 400 years of slavery for his descendants (Gen. 15:13). In Exodus this figure becomes 430 (Ex. 12:14). Rabbinical exegesis explains away this difference: the Egyptian sojourn lasted only 210 years; between Jacob's arrival in Egypt and the birth of his grandsons Manasseh and Ephraim, five more years had elapsed, bringing the total to 215; however, the Lord, in his desire to alleviate the sufferings of his people, counted the nights as full days, doubling their number to the 430 of Exodus. Simple arithmetic!

Whatever the figure one adopts for the period separating the Patriarchs from Moses and those who left Egypt under his guidance, one should not expect a corresponding evolutionary change in a few hundred years. We are dealing with one people, whose general lifestyle encompassed various independent traditions: the Hebrews.

Who were they? The word *'Ibri*, "Hebrew," occurs some thirty times in the Bible, a small number compared with the 2,500 appearances of "Israel." The two terms are not synonymous. *'Ibri* designates the people of Israel in their relations with the surrounding world. Foreigners used it in speaking of Israel, and so did the Israelites when they spoke of themselves to foreigners. Rather than denoting a national identity, it suggests a difference felt by those who dealt with the Israelites, a difference perceived as such by the Israelites themselves.

For more than a hundred years, orientalists have likened the word *'Ibri* to the terms *'Apiru*, found in Egyptian texts, and *Habiru*, its cuneiform equivalent. These terms, signifying "dusty" or "dust-covered," apply to western Semitic populations spread over a vast territory, extending from Egypt to Mesopotamia; they were semi-nomads roaming around the fringes of the desert, on the marches of sedentary society. Their identity is obscure; it may be approximated by an anthroponymic reference to a national divinity, *'Apir-Baal*, "the dusty one of Baal," or *'Apir-El*, "the dusty one of El." By vigorously sifting the "dust", these marginal people could occasionally be put to use and absorbed into the local population as workers or soldiers. But "civilized" society still looked upon them with fear and distrust.

In regard to the Hebrews, another Egyptian term should be taken into account: *Shosu*. It first appears in texts from the fifteenth century BCE, under the reign of Thutmosis III (1479–1425), where it applies to the turbulent nomads of the Negev, whose numerous incursions were countered by the Pharaonic troops of the New Empire. The *Shosu* were brave warriors, who could be conscripted into the Egyptian army or employed as forced laborers. Under the rule of the Ramesside dynasties, some became temple servants of the goddess Hathor or of Amon in Thebes. They were divided into clans, one of which bore the name of YHW, a word which naturally caught the eye of historians searching for the ancestors of the Israelites in Egypt, since it is the abridged form of the Divine Name, the Tetragrammaton, later to appear in the documents of the Judean colony of Elephantine.

This, then, was the Egyptian view of the "sons of Israel" and the "sons of Joseph," ancestors of the Israelites who came down to Egypt and settled on its frontiers, worked for the Pharaoh if obliged to do so, and sometimes even managed to make careers in the royal administration. They were not an ethnic group or a nation as such, but rather a social category with a common lifestyle. The ancestors of the Israelites were part of a larger marginal group, ambiguous but integrable, suspect but occasionally useful. Were not some characteristics of this distant past transmitted to their progeny? A day was to come when a few handfuls of these immigrants, no longer willing to lead lives of drudgery in an inhospitable country, would take leave of Egypt under the aegis of a certain Moses. For the Pharaonic government, it was a minor incident: the departure of one among several groups of *Shosu*. For the sons of Israel it was, on the contrary, a historic moment of capital importance.

Let us now attempt to situate the Egyptian adventure of the Hebrews in an historic framework compatible with the chronological parameters of the Egyptologists. If we accept the four-century span of biblical tradition, where shall we place these centuries within the 600-year period extending roughly from 1800 to 1200 BCE, which covers the so-called Second Intermediate Period and part of the New Empire?

During the eighteenth century BCE a time of troubles, lasting some two hundred years, began in Egypt. The Egyptian government, after its restoration by the Theban princes of the Middle Empire, was again in ruins. Semitic tribes from Asia had invaded the country, settling at first in the Delta, then penetrating the Nile Valley in ever-growing numbers. Barbarian intruders, the Hyksos, progressively wrested the royal prerogatives from the hands of the Egyptians. Two barbarian dynasties, the fifteenth and the sixteenth (ca. 1730–1530 BCE), reigned successively in Lower Egypt, while an indigenous Seventeenth Dynasty (ca. 1650–1552 BCE) ruled over Thebes. The Egyptian historian Manetho, who wrote in Greek at the beginning of the third century BCE, called them "shepherds" or "shepherd-kings"; he committed a misnomer, due to a flawed interpretation of the Greek term employed for the Egyptian expression *heqau-khasut*, signifying, rather vaguely, "princes from foreign lands." ·

The Hyksos did not have a good reputation among the Egyptians, whose national traditions depicted them as plunderers of cities and temples, cruel and impious barbarians faithful only to their god Seth, that veritable incarnation of evil in the Osiris legend, in which he symbolizes the harmful dry red earth, as opposed to the black soil of the Nile Valley. The desert, especially the eastern desert, was held responsible for all sorts of calamities that had befallen the Egyptians. For Manetho, the invasion of the Hyksos was an inexplicable "blow from heaven." But the bad reputation unjustly conferred on Seth, as well as on the Hyksos, was merely a chauvinistic variation on the theme of the foreign invader. The "god of confusion," as his detractors called him, was in fact the dynastic divinity of the Nineteenth Dynasty, two eminent representatives of which bore the name Sethos, a derivative of Seth. As for the Hyksos, their reign was far from the disaster that Manetho describes. To the contrary, it seems to have been politically sound and culturally fruitful.

The Hyksos did not seek to impose a foreign form of government upon the Egyptians; they adopted the existing state structures, turning them to their own profit. The cult of Seth, with its sanctuary at Avaris, was enshrined as an official religion, outwardly respectful of Egyptian tradition. It was only later that Seth was assimilated to Baal-Reshef, before the Greeks identified him with the monstrous son of Gaia and Tartaros, Typhon, whom Zeus destroyed by his thunderbolt. During this period, Avaris became a relay station between the near eastern religions and Egypt, whose patrimony was thus enriched. But the Hyksos did not reject the national gods and retained the name of Re in their royal titulary lists. The loyalty of the population of Lower Egypt was surely facilitated by this policy, which could serve as a model for "intelligent" invaders.

The Hyksos made many important material contributions to the country they had conquered. They introduced the Egyptians to the use of bronze metallurgy in the making of armaments. They taught them improved military strategy and tactics, such as the establishment of a fluvial war fleet and, above all, the massive use of the horse and the battle chariot, a typical aspect of their "knightly" culture. The Pharaohs of the New Empire were greatly indebted to the Hyksos for the military supremacy they were soon to gain over their eastern adversaries, thanks to their charioteer corps equipped with modern arms.

The migrations mentioned in the Bible can be situated during this era of foreign domination of Egypt, an outward-looking epoch, in vivid contrast to the previous period of "splendid isolation." Groups of pre-Israelites, caught up in the flux of Semitic tribal displacements, went down from Canaan toward the southwest and settled on the edges of the eastern Delta in the steppe region near Pithom, known in Genesis as the "land of Goshen" (Gen. 46:28–34, 47:1–6). Several texts dating from the reign of Thutmosis III mention the ʿApiru, implying their presence in Egypt toward the middle of the fifteenth century BCE.

During the first half of the sixteenth century BCE the Hyksos were expelled by Ahmosis (ca. 1552–1526 BCE), founder of the Eighteenth Dynasty, and native Egyptian Pharaohs once more took over the reins of power, which they were to hold firmly for the next five hundred years. The reign of Ahmosis and that of his successor Amenhotep (Amenophis) I (1526–1506 BCE) inaugurated the strength of the New Empire, with Thebes as its prestigious political and religious center. Even today, the grandiose monuments of Luxor and Karnak attest to the splendor of that epoch, whose summit was attained in the fourteenth century under the reign of Amenhotep III (1390–1352 BCE). His successor Amenhotep IV, called Akhenaton (1352–1336 BCE), is universally renowned, thanks not only to the seductive beauty of Nefertiti, his charming consort, but also to his religious reforms, whose goal was to assign the role of supreme divinity to Aton, the solar disk, in lieu of the Theban Amon. The power of the throne was seriously weakened while he reigned, a fact that the fabled riches of his son Tutenkhamon (1336–1327 BCE) were not enough to conceal. Only under the reign of the usurper general Horemheb (1323–1295 BCE) was it shored up again.

Horemheb was succeeded by Rameses I (1295–1294 BCE), founder of the Nineteenth Dynasty. The two following sovereigns, Sethos I (1294–1279 BCE) the warrior king, and his son Rameses II (1279–1212 BCE) are particularly interesting for us in the perspective of this book, for the troubles of the Hebrews began during their reigns. The royal government had to cope with the expansionist tendencies of the Hittites, who were about to burst out of Asia Minor in an attempt to extend their domination to the Near East and threaten northern Syria. Sethos I fought against the Hittites, and Rameses II pursued the struggle. At Qadesh-on-the-Orontes, he waged one of the most famous battles in the history of the ancient Middle East, followed by an equally famous peace treaty he cosigned in 1258 with the Hittite sovereign Hattushili III. By an extraordinary piece of luck, the text of this important document has come down to us in two parallel versions, an Egyptian and an Akkadian. The lasting peace that ensued allowed the sovereign to devote himself to construction work in the Theban region and the Delta. At the end of Rameses II's reign, the situation deteriorated and his son Mineptah (1212–1202 BCE) had once more to face the Hittite threat and resist the invasion of the Libyan hordes.

No traces of these events found their way into the Bible, which does not once speak of the rivalry between Egypt and the Hittite Empire, nor of the power struggle between Egyptian royalty and the clergy of Amon. Any speculation concerning the relations between the Mosaic religion and the heresy of Akhenaton is perfectly gratuitous, although the "great hymn" of the "Beautiful child of Aton" may have indirectly inspired one of the Psalms (Ps. 104). In fact, the doctrine of Akhenaton is not more "monotheistic" than the theories of the Heliopolitan theologians from which it was derived. They all are rooted in the idea that the divine, unique in its principle, cannot be represented on earth. The divine essence is thus concentrated in the life-giving astral body, to the detriment of the traditional divinities, who were, insofar as they were simply idols, the multiple expressions of this unique principle. The "Atonian" movement was more a rebellion against the all-powerful clergy of Amon than a veritable religious revolution, as was the case for the concept of an invisible God, creator of the universe, unapproachable through iconic or animal mediation.

In contrast to the absence of references to political events, the Bible faithfully depicts many features of Egyptian social life under the New Empire, in language that can pass the acid test of historical and archaeological verification with a reasonable degree of probability.

The presence of Asiatic foreigners at the Egyptian royal court during the Eighteenth Dynasty is illustrated by a personage who represents the "prototype" of the biblical Joseph: Aper-El, recently identified as the vizier of Amenophis III. The Egyptian court was not systematically xenophobic, and immigrants or their Egyptian-born progeny could even become high-ranking officials, such as Grand Officers of the Crown. A Hebrew may very well have had a similar career in the service of a Hyksos king, an Egyptianized Semite like himself. We now discover that this was perfectly possible under a national sovereign of the Eighteenth Dynasty. And it was still possible under the Nineteenth Dynasty, as attested by the example of Ben-Azen, the Asian cupbearer to King Mineptah. What was true for Joseph was also true for Moses; one should not, however, attribute the construction of the pyramids to the former, nor lend credence to the Judeo-Egyptian author Artapanos, who attributed the invention of Egyptian zoolatry to the latter.

Aper-El and Ben-Azen clearly stand out as exceptional cases; the majority of the immigrants led less enviable lives. Drawn to Egypt by the riches to be obtained there, they could hardly have relished the prospect of having to add to those riches without sharing in them. The strong increase of population in the region of the eastern Delta soon transformed it into a sort of labor pool for large-scale earthworks and other construction projects. The troubles of the Hebrews as related in Exodus should be seen in the perspective of the administrative measures entailed by the gigantic undertakings of the Eighteenth Dynasty Pharaohs in the Delta, such as the construction of the temple of Seth at Avaris toward the end of the reign of Sethos I and the foundation of a new capital, Pi-Rameses, during the first years of Rameses II. The Hebrews were obliged to participate in the realization of these projects by preparing mortar and making bricks; these labors did not exonerate them from working in the fields, where their lives were made "bitter with hard service" (Ex. 1:14). During this period one hears of "dusty ones" (*'Apiru*—Hebrews, or other enslaved semi-nomads—employed as haulers of stone for a temple (Leyden Papyrus 348). Yet others were to be found near the royal harem in the Faiyum.

In order to have the upper hand over such great masses of undisciplined laborers drawn from marginal groups, the Pharaonic government most certainly had recourse to rigorous means of constraint. Population control, and especially birth control, could very well have been applied to those liable to forced labor, who feared it as a mortal threat to their newborn children. Chapter 2 of Exodus relates how an Egyptian princess saved the life of a Hebrew child by sheltering him from the ill-treatments inflicted upon his people. This same child later rose up in revolt against the inhuman exactions of an overseer (Ex. 2:11–12). Egyptian documents from Deir el-Medineh today confirm the strict measures of worker control practiced at the time. Brick quotas, the use of straw, and leaves of absence were all prescribed and monitored. And this was daily life in Egypt during the thirteenth century BCE.

One can see how fragile are the links between Egyptological data and the biblical account of the Hebrews' sojourn. The former can verify the general social and economic background of the latter, but cannot corroborate the details of the biblical record concerning the actions of the biblical characters and the prodigious circumstances surrounding them. The Bible contains elements of a historical and geographical setting into which the sojourn of the Hebrews can be fitted; the literary amplifications inherent in the biblical text are due to ulterior orientations, unrelated to this setting. Egyptology can guarantee the historicity of the sojourn of the Hebrews and throw some light on the conditions obtaining at the time. It cannot afford us direct confirmation of the biblical account.

In this respect, it can prove instructive to compare the New Egyptian Empire with the contemporaneous Mycenaean world. The latter's historical image vis-à-vis the mythical one furnished by the Iliad and the Odyssey has its parallel in the Egyptological data vis-à-vis the biblical writings concerning Egypt. From the viewpoint of social verisimilitude, the biblical account of Egypt is more faithful to historical Egypt than the Homeric poems are to Mycenaean civilization. Homeric society was not that of Mycenaean Greece, as reflected in the recently deciphered Linear B tablets; it was that of the "dark ages" into which the Greek world was plunged after the downfall of the Mycenaean palaces in the thirteenth century BCE. In its political aspect, however, Homer's depiction of the Trojan War contains many allusions to the great upheavals that took place at the close of the Mycenaean palace era. Archaeology mirrors this divergence. The celebrated German amateur archaeologist Heinrich Schliemann, persevering in his obstinate quest for the ruins of Troy, finally succeeded. But at the end of the last century, when the very serious "Egypt Exploration Fund" began its excavations in the eastern Delta in the hope of finding a trace of the Hebrews, its efforts were foredoomed to failure. The bricks the Hebrews had fashioned for the Pharaohs of the Eighteenth Dynasty did not bear their signatures.

MOSES AND THE PHARAOH

The first fifteen chapters of Exodus describe in minute detail the departure of the Hebrews from the "house of bondage." There we learn how a Hebrew child, miraculously rescued from the waters of the Nile and reared by Pharaoh's daughter, was chosen to free his people from the state of slavery the Egyptians had imposed upon them, and how he accomplished this mission. On several points the biblical account can be made to correspond to historical facts, provided we render the flowery literary language a bit more down-to-earth.

Thus, the famous "plagues," described in chapters 7 through 12 of Exodus and which, during the yearly Passover seder, evoke the flight from Egypt, may be interpreted as natural phenomena proper to the Middle East, or even specifically Egyptian. Some of them can be explained by the capricious behavior of the Nile at the time of its yearly flooding. This is the case for the "blood" (Heb. *dam*, Ex. 7:14–25), due to the peculiar red color of the silt carried downstream from the river's sources, construed by the Egyptians as a bad omen; the "frogs" (*tzefarde'a*, Ex. 7:26–8:11); "lice" (*kinnim*, Ex. 8:12–15); "vermin" (*'arov*, probably flies or horseflies, rather than "beasts," Ex. 8:16–28), omnipresent in the Egyptian landscape; murrain, a cattle disease (*dever*, Ex. 9:1–7), frequently occurring at low-water time; and doubtless also for the "boils" (*shehin*, Ex. 9:8–12). "Hailstorms" (barad, Ex. 9:13–35) are rather astonishing for Egypt, but they have been known to occur in Syria and Palestine. Swarms of "locusts" (*'arbeh*, Ex. 10:1–20) regularly appear throughout the Orient. In the account of the battle of Qadesh, the Hittite invaders of the Syro-Palestinian region are compared to an army of locusts. The "darkness" (*hoshekh*, Ex. 10:21–29) that fell over the land of Egypt could well be due to the khamsin, a hot, sand-bearing wind of the Middle East, comparable to the African sirocco or the European *foehn*. As for the "death of the firstborn" (*makat bekhorot*, Ex. 11 and 12:29–42), beginning with that of the Pharaoh's son, this event may actually have occurred at the Court, then purposely inflated to national dimensions. We shall return to this point a bit later. The fact that the plagues appear again in Psalms 78 and 105 changes nothing in this respect.

Historians are far from unanimous concerning the date of the Exodus. By and large, two opposing hypotheses hold sway, a "high" hypothesis and a "low" one. According to the former, the departure from Egypt occurred in the middle of the fifteenth century, or even as early as the sixteenth century BCE; the latter puts it in the thirteenth century.

One variant of the "high" hypothesis would place the Exodus under the reign of Thutmosis III (1479–1425 BCE). The reasoning is based on calculations combining various data concerning the length of the stay in Egypt with two biblical references: an indication in 1 Kings (6:1), which dates the construction of the Temple of Solomon 480 years after the departure from Egypt, and a passage from Judges (11:26) establishing a time gap of 300 years between the war against Sihon the Amorite, king of Heshbon, and the period of Jephthah, one of the Judges of Israel. But the date of ca. 1448, obtained from these calculations, is very uncertain, since their constituent elements belong to texts written at different times, whose viewpoints vary widely; the length of time the Hebrews spent in Egypt itself differs in each account.

In order to rescue the "high" hypothesis, scholars had recourse to archaeology. Basing their reasoning on an analysis of excavations in Jericho and other sites mentioned in the biblical account of the conquest of Canaan under Joshua, some archaeologists may have drawn the conclusion that the Exodus must have occurred about 1470. This date, curiously enough, coincides with prior archaeological datings of the great volcanic explosion at Thera (Santorin), which left its violent mark on Crete and may possibly have reached Egypt. However, an enormous effort of imagination is required to place the cinders of the Thera volcano in the "soot of the furnace" (Heb. *piah kibeshan*; *aithale kamnias* in the Septuagint) that Moses strew "like dust" (*leavak*; *koniortos*) over all of Egypt, provoking boils in men and in beasts (the sixth plague). The archaeological findings in Canaanite territory are open to various interpretations, and the "high" hypothesis based on them is no more conclusive than are speculations drawn from biblical chronology.

In another variant of this hypothesis, the Exodus coincided with the expulsion of the Hyksos. This sets the date back by one century, to ca. 1550 BCE under the reign of Ahmosis, founder of the Eighteenth Dynasty. According to this variant, the biblical account is an amalgam of two different memory traces: an exodus-expulsion of the Hebrews, who had entered Egypt with the Hyksos and were driven out of the country with them; and the recollection of a flight, under the guidance of Moses. This idea of a double exodus stems from a very free interpretation of the Bible and is hardly tenable. It is worthy of attention, however, since it recalls a "shameful" version of the departure from

Egypt, which, in various accounts of the "Story of the Impure," was widely diffused in antiquity. This matter will be discussed again later.

We shall adhere to the "low" hypothesis, which places the departure from Egypt in the thirteenth century BCE, under the reign of Rameses II. It is preferable to the "high" hypothesis, in that it exploits the only chronological indication furnished by a very ancient element of the biblical account, which converges with historically controllable data, namely the participation under duress of the Hebrews in the construction of the "store-cities, Pithom and Raamses" (Ex. 1:11). This is an unmistakable reference to the new capital of Rameses II, Pi-Rameses. The Exodus would thus have taken place under the long reign of this king (1279–1212 BCE), the "new king . . . who knew not Joseph" (Ex. 1:8), the most famous of the Pharaohs, the very symbol of ancient Egypt, on a par with the pyramids or the Sphinx. Leading the Hebrews out of the clutches of so great a ruler was not the least of Moses' accomplishments. When did this departure occur?

Our answer is based on three elements: an Egyptian document and, to aid us in interpreting it, two points of reference, afforded by archaeology and the biblical tradition. The document is the famous stele of Mineptah (Merneptah), son of Rameses II, known as the "stele of Israel." Our first reference is provided by archaeological findings concerning the fall of Jericho, an event the Bible places after the death of Moses, and which supposedly occurred before the middle of the thirteenth century BCE; the second, biblical reference is, of course, the crossing of the desert, which took forty years, according to Jewish tradition. Let us try to combine these three data, beginning with the stele of Mineptah.

> The princes have prostrated themselves, saying "peace."
> Among the Nine Bows [the Nations] none raises his head.
> Devastated is Tehenu [Libya], pacified is Hatti.
> Plundered is the Canaan with every evil.
> Carried off is Ashkelon; seized upon is Gezer.
> Yanoam is made as that which does not exist.
> Israel is laid waste, his seed is not.
> Widowed is Hurru [Palestine] before Egypt.
> All the nations are reunited in peace.
> (K. A. KITCHEN, RAMESSIDE INSCRIPTIONS, OXFORD, 1964–84, 4, 17–19)

The inscription was discovered in 1895, in the funerary temple of Mineptah in western Thebes; since Israel does not figure prominently in the text, the term "stele of Israel" is a misnomer. The body of the text celebrates the victories of the Pharaoh over the Libyans; a brief epilogue sums up the submission of diverse Asiatic peoples, with Israel listed second from last, before the Hurrians. In the history of the Jewish people, however, the stele is of paramount importance, since it contains the first mention of Israel that has come down to us in an official document. In the eyes of some scholars, it could even be considered as Israel's "birth certificate." In our task of dating the Exodus, it can be of great aid.

The stele dates from 1207 BCE, the fifth year of the reign of Mineptah. If it bears any relation to the Exodus—notwithstanding the recent hypotheses of F. J. Yurco—this would mean that, by 1207, Moses and his people had already crossed the desert and joined forces with other groups of Hebrews, who had not known servitude in Egypt. But the "promised land" had not yet been conquered: in the text, the word "Israel" is actually preceded by a determinative designating a people and not a country. "Israel" would here refer to a people of wanderers, not to a community settled in the land of Canaan. The departure from Egypt would have been relatively recent; archaeological considerations and biblical tradition lead us to place it toward the beginning of the thirteenth century. If we take the Bible literally (forty years before the middle of the thirteenth century), the Exodus would have occurred in 1290, under Sethos I. But the great works of construction, evoked at the beginning of the Book of Exodus, had hardly begun at that time. Only under Rameses II were they were in full swing: the mention of his new capital, Pi-Rameses, clearly designates this Pharaoh. The date of the Exodus must therefore be adjusted forward to the first years of the reign of Rameses II, which began in 1279 BCE.

From this date onward, the story of Moses can be reconstructed within a satisfactory historical framework. He was taken in by Pharaoh's daughter, who reared him as an adopted son. His name, which stems from the Egyptian *mes, mesu*, "child," can possibly express this relation (the popular etymology "he who was drawn from the water" does not conform to the Hebrew syntax of Exodus 2:10, "Because I drew him out of the water," suggesting the drawer rather than the drawn). Adoption was a common practice in Pharaonic Egypt. A hieratic papyrus, No. 1946-96 of the Ashmolean Museum in Oxford, tells of an Egyptian lady, sole heiress to her deceased husband's fortune, who freed and immediately adopted three slaves born in the conjugal dwelling, in turn willing them her property (*adoptio mortis causa*, in Roman legal terminology). Here is a striking analogy to the story of Moses, himself a "slave" adopted by a lady of high rank. The princess was one day to be rewarded for this action and become a "daughter of the Lord," Bat-Yah, assimilated in the rabbinical tradition to Bitya, one of Pharaoh's daughters mentioned in Chronicles (1 Chron. 4:18). Moreover, although she was a firstborn child, her life was spared during the tenth plague, for the same reason.

In the Acts of the Apostles (7:22) we find the echo of another tradition, according to which Moses was instructed in "all the Egyptian wisdom," which rendered him "all-powerful in word and in deed." This does not necessarily imply that he was reared in the royal court like a prince. But he may have been a "child of the *kap*," that is, he could have been educated in the manner of foreign princes taken in charge by the Pharaoh. This was, most likely, the manner in which he acquired the knowledge necessary to serve in the royal administration. The role of Moses as an official in the service of the Pharaoh is in any case more plausible than the fiction of a "Moses prince of Egypt," rival of Rameses, as Cecil B. de Mille portrayed him in his famous film "The Ten Commandments."

Colossal statue of Rameses II   *Temple of Luxor.*

His youthful, formative years may have coincided with the reign of Horemheb, at the very end of the fourteenth century BCE. He "went out unto his brethren" (Ex. 2:11) under the reign of Sethos I, at the start of the thirteenth century, when the monumental construction projects in the eastern Delta began to take shape. The putting to death of a sadistic overseer, the flight to the land of Midian, the marriage to Zipporah, the episode of the burning bush, the revelation of the Name, and the return to Egypt bring us to a new reign. While Moses was taking his father-in-law Jethro's flocks out to pasture in the land of Midian (today Elath), "the king of Egypt died" (Ex. 2:23). His successor, whom we take to be Rameses II, had good reasons for preventing 'Apiru laborers from retiring to the desert. He had just overcome a dangerous band of pirates, had twice led his armies out against the Syrians, and was preparing to confront the Hittite king. This was not a time to allow Hebrews to flee the country: they would only swell the ranks of the Shosu, whose ceaseless incursions into Canaan were already hampering the movements of the Egyptian army. Amonherkhepshef, son of the king, was charged with rolling them back across the Negev to the borders of the Dead Sea. Under these circumstances, and notwithstanding the miracles which accompanied them, the arguments of Moses and Aaron carried little weight.

It was only when the Palace was stricken by a severe bereavement that the Pharaoh felt it necessary to yield ground. Egyptology tends to confirm the authenticity of the event. Rameses II, traditionally the father of some one hundred "royal offspring," had serious family problems. He himself had buried several of his princely heirs. His son Mineptah, officially designated as crown prince during his father's lifetime, was thirteenth in order of succession. The conflicts that broke out during the following generation illustrate only too well the growing uneasiness these deaths caused throughout his reign. In some ways the "death of the firstborn" represents an actual situation. Was Amonherkhepshef the king's son mentioned in Exodus 12:29? In 1272, the seventh year of the reign, he was fighting alongside his father. The next year the Egyptians were mobilized for a fresh Syrian campaign. From the ninth year onward—1270 BCE according to the chronology adopted by Egyptologists—the road lay open before the Hebrews. When all is said and done, the date of 1270 appears to be the best possible hypothesis for their departure from the land of Egypt.

THE DESERT ROAD

The migration across the desert under Moses' leadership after the deliverance of his people from bondage in Egypt, and the conquest of the Promised Land by Joshua, left their mark in Jewish memory; the historical verisimilitude of these recollections is indubitable, but their outlines are indistinct. The biblical text brushes a large fresco of the Hebrews' progress. Its most important stages are the miracle of the sea, which meant the definitive breaking away from Egypt, and the revelation of God (theophany) in the Sinai, where new fundamental experiences occurred: the giving of the Torah and the establishment of the Mosaic Covenant. Their importance is self-evident, but a convincing reconstruction can only be approximated, since the biblical story is not self-consistent, nor is it always readily compatible with geographical reality.

In our effort to follow the trail of Moses and his people through the desert, we must choose one among several possible reconstitutions of their journey, corresponding to the various traditions juxtaposed in the Book of Exodus. The oldest texts suggest a route along the edge of the "sea of Rushes" (14:9, 30), the "desert of Shur" (15:22), "Marah" (15:23) and "Refidim" (17:1), leading finally to the "desert of Sinai" (19:1). Historical geographers have not been able to identify any of these sites.

This uncertainty applies as well to a second itinerary, more precise in appearance: "Rameses," "Succoth" (12:37), "Etham" (13:20), "Pi-Hahiroth," between Migdol and the sea, over against "Baalzephon" (14:2). These detailed descriptions do not make the second itinerary preferable to the first. No one has been able to pinpoint the sites of Succoth and Etham. Pi-Hahiroth could well be the deformed name of one of the temples of Hathor and refer to a sanctuary dedicated to that goddess, east of the Gulf of Suez. The mention of Baalzephon ("Baal of the north") is disquieting, as it refers to a Phoenician sanctuary between the sea and Lake Sirbonis, along the imperial road following the Mediterranean from Pelusium to Gaza. The Hebrews were strongly advised not to take this "route of the Philistines" (Ex. 3:17), the main highway for the Pharaoh's armies on their way to Syria and Palestine. It would require a singular lack of prudence to try to flee along the line of fortresses which marked its path, referred to in Exodus by the mention of a tower or a fort ("Migdol"). These names may have been introduced *a posteriori* into the biblical account, in an attempt to fix the unfolding story in the readers' minds by giving it a more authentically Egyptian resonance. In any case, the route that leads Moses through the solitudes of the Isthmus to the Red Sea seems preferable.

The first remarkable episode in the crossing of the desert took place along this route: the miracle of the sea. There are several stages in the traditional rendering, recorded in chapter 14 of Exodus. The simplest and oldest scenario shows the armies of the Pharaoh in hot pursuit of the fleeing Hebrews, who had already reached the sea. The Lord protected his own: a pillar of cloud separated them from their pursuers; at nightfall, a strong wind caused the sea to go back; panic overcame the Egyptians, who rushed toward the ebbing sea and were engulfed by its waters. These events seem to depict, rather than a victory, a fatal accident that befell an army ill-prepared for maritime maneuvres.

The scenario was perfected over time. Strong winds roll back the waters of the "sea of Rushes" (or "of Reeds") far enough to each side to allow free passage for the fleeing Hebrews through the walls of water that close down afterwards around the chariots of the Pharaoh, inflicting great losses. This time, the Egyptian army is not annihilated at the shoreline, but in the midst of the sea. The victory of the Lord is reminiscent of the separation of the waters and the continents on the third day of creation (Gen. 1:9–10).

The battle waged against the fleeing Hebrews by the Pharaoh's charioteers has not been recorded in historical documents. We must content ourselves with the last of the four scenes engraved on the south wall of the "Court of the Cachette" in the temple of Amon in Karnak. They had been attributed to Rameses II; J. F. Yurco recently considered them an illustration of the victories, enumerated on his triumphal stele, of the Pharaoh's son Mineptah over his Canaanite foes. This last scene, unfortunately bereft of its inscriptions, is purported to represent the "annihilation" of Israel in Canaan. One may well ask how a crushing defeat ending in a rout could have been transmuted, some dozens of years later, into a victory for the Pharaoh depicted in the official imagery.

The fact is that, for the armies of the Pharaoh, this episode was a simple skirmish with a band of forced laborers who had managed to flee, an incident of negligible importance. For the Hebrews, on the contrary, it was a major event in which the Divine Hand had manifested itself, permitting them to escape from servitude and become a free nation. This was the veritable birth of Israel. Its remembrance is engraved forever in its profession of faith (Deut. 26:7–8).

The following episode in the desert march, just as weighty as the first, was the encounter between Moses and the Lord on Mount Sinai. Here again, history and tradition meet on uncertain ground. Among the various hypotheses, the best attempt at localization is the classical theory according to which Mount Sinai, the Horeb of Deuteronomy, lies in the southern part of the Sinai peninsula, in the region of Jabal Musa, guarded today by the monks of the Saint Catherine monastery.

It was there that the events described in chapters 19 to 34 of the Book of Exodus took place. The interpretation of this text is not easy; at best, we can only achieve an approximate reconstitution of its elaboration. The Lord first appears before Moses in the storm, and reveals the Decalogue to him. Moses ascends the mountain and receives the Tablets of the Law, engraved by the hand of God. The giving of the Torah, then, is the purpose of the revelation. The people, who stood apart from this meeting, are called upon to be faithful. Before the word itself had even been uttered, the Covenant had already been concluded. The scene was greatly amplified in successive revisions, assuming its definitive form with the merging of the episodes of the Golden Calf, Aaron and the seventy-two elders, the forty days Moses passed on the mountaintop, and the transmission of the Laws received there.

We shall not here venture even the slightest glimmer of a commentary on the Tablets of the Law, seen in the double perspective of the history of law and the history of religion. However, two points must be stressed. For the legal historian, according to the once widely-favored theory of Albrecht Alt, the Decalogue represents a very early example of apodictic style, in which normative formulations are couched in the imperative mode: for example, "Thou shalt have no other gods before Me"; "Thou shalt not make unto thee a graven image." This form is opposed to the casuistic style, dominant in oriental legal systems, including ulterior biblical legislation, which employs the formula: "if so-and-so does this or that, he will undergo such-and-such consequences."

As for the history of religion, one must stress the exceptional character of these two commandments. In the polytheistic context of the ancient Near East, the injunction to adore one God exclusively and to ban all images from his cult (Ex. 20:3, 4) was totally unprecedented. Throughout oriental and classical antiquity, the divine image was an essential factor in religious life. It constituted the irreplaceable core of an indispensable mediation between the gods and humans, the sole means of communication with the divinity, the only way of rendering his presence accessible to the faithful. Moses challenged the prime tenet of ancient faith by promulgating an aniconic religion, rejecting the very idea of idols and images serving as mediators between mankind and the divine, and by denying all validity to the principles of such mediation. This was a clean break with the past.

The first stage in the Egyptian adventure of the Hebrews ends here. We shall not follow them to the walls of Jericho nor in their conquest of the land "flowing with milk and honey," where the survivors of a refugee band were to be transformed into a well-articulated society, who would forge their new country into a state. Six centuries later, some of their progeny were again to be found on the banks of the Nile.

CHAPTER 2

The Stronghold
of Elephantine

A JUDEAN COLONY IN EGYPT

Between the end of the seventh century BCE and the beginning of the sixth, a new Jewish community arose in Egypt, during the troubled times that marked the end of the Israelite monarchy founded by Saul (1020), David (1000–970), and Solomon (970–931) some four centuries earlier. To bring these events into perspective, a brief glance backward may be useful.

Upon the death of Solomon, a political crisis ensued, which was soon to bring about the disruption of the kingdom, splitting it into two parts. The tribes of Judah and Benjamin, which had remained faithful to Rehoboam, the son of Solomon, formed the realm of Judah, whose capital was Jerusalem. To its north, the ten other tribes established the realm of Israel, or Ephraim, with Samaria as capital. In 722 the Assyrian king Shalmaneser V ("Enemesar," 727–722) and his son Sargon II (721–705) destroyed the northern kingdom. The realm of Israel was absorbed into the Assyrian Empire as one of its provinces. This disaster was the occasion of the mysterious disappearance of the ten tribes, whose destiny has been the object of fervent research, and whose trace appears from time to time in the most unlikely places, such as the Andean Cordillera. The search is still proceeding and, doubtless, will yet afford us new surprises.

The name of Samaria was soon extended to the whole of the northern province, whose remaining survivors, the Samaritans, were to have a singular destiny. Jewish tradition, as it is recorded in the Second Book of Kings (2 Kings 17:24–41), considers them the descendants of Assyrian colonists implanted in the country by Sargon II, and subsequently adopting Judaism. They themselves, to the contrary, claimed to be authentic "Israelites," the posterity of Jacob-Israel. Since they had no other prophet but Moses, and the Pentateuch was their unique Holy Book, they might appear as the true guardians of the ancient monotheistic belief. In fact, they were a Jewish sect whose members continued to observe the essential rites of Judaism, but held divergent views concerning the localization of the sanctuary in which the Eternal had ordained that the Hebrews offer Him their sacrifices: for the Samaritans, this sacred site was not Jerusalem but Mount Gerizim, overlooking

Nablus. Like the Jews, they have been subject to persecution throughout recorded history; their community has managed to survive, but only a few hundred are alive today.

One century after Assyria had destroyed Israel, Assyria was destroyed in turn. Having acquired a well-earned reputation for violence and brutality, it broke up under the pressure of the peoples it had brought under its heel. In 612, Nineveh, the capital, fell to an alliance of Medes and Chaldeans of Babylon. Over the ruins of that erstwhile empire, Babylon managed to reestablish its hegemony for a fleeting moment, soon giving way to the empire of Cyrus the Persian (539). The peak of this neo-Babylonian—or Chaldean—restoration was the reign of Nebuchadnezzar II, the biblical Nebuchadnezzar (605–562). In March of the year 597 he besieged Jerusalem. The capital of the southern kingdom held out ten years more under Zedekiah. But when the latter rebelled, Nebuchadnezzar let his troops march back to Jerusalem to quell the revolt.

In July and August of 587 the Temple was destroyed, and the Jews were deported into captivity in Babylon. They were to be freed a half-century later by Cyrus, whose gesture earned him the glorious title of Messiah, exceptionally attributed to a foreign sovereign (Isaiah 45:1). The return from exile was accomplished under the guidance of prestigious leaders such as Zerubbabel, Nehemiah, and Ezra. The Temple was rebuilt, and, with its autonomy guaranteed by the Persian sovereigns under whose protection it was placed, became the center around which a new Jewish entity was organized, an entity whose content was much more national and religious than political. For centuries to come, Jewish identity, now embodied in the concept not of a state but of a people and a religion indissolubly bound to one another, was to bear the mark of the specific structure in which it was reestablished when the Jews returned from captivity in Babylon.

The new Jewish presence in Egypt is to be studied in the light of this series of events, of paramount importance for the history of the Jewish people. The period concerned covers that of the last Egyptian Pharaohs (the Saitic dynasty) and then the era of Persian domination after the conquest of Egypt by Cambyses in 525 BCE. In the fifth century BCE, a military colony consisting of Aramean and Judean contingents was established on the island of Elephantine (Yeb, from the Egyptian 'iebew, "elephant place") near Syene (today Aswan). Elephantine was a fortress as well as a customs post, a veritable checkpoint for travelers, strategically situated at the first Nile cataract, gateway to Nubia. The soldiers who guarded the frontier have left us much written evidence of their presence, in the form of numerous documents in Aramaic, known as the "Elephantine archives." Some time later, the Greek documents from this same island of Elephantine, which rank among the oldest Greek papyri discovered in Egypt, were to provide us a description of daily life among the first Greco-Macedonian colonists, after Alexander's conquest of the country in 332–331 BCE.

The Aramaic documents concerning the Jews date mostly from the fifth century BCE, but the arrival of Jewish soldiers in Egypt certainly preceded the conquest of the country by the Persians. The problem is to determine how much earlier they had come. Several solutions have been suggested. A distinguished expert, B. Porten, placed their arrival in the middle of the seventh century, at the period when Manasseh, the king of Judah (697–642), might possibly have furnished troops to his Egyptian ally in the struggle against Assyrian domination. Other scholars date the wave of Jewish immigration to the reign of Josiah (640–609), the promoter of important religious reforms (622) tending to eliminate the syncretistic tendencies that had spread under Manasseh: rather than renounce their practices, some of those who were opposed to the reforms may have chosen to leave their country. Subsequently, the fall of Judah in 587 could have encouraged a flow of Jewish soldiers into Egypt. One should keep in mind the troubles that ensued when Gedaliah, appointed by Nebuchadnezzar as governor of the remaining territories surrounding Jerusalem, was put to death, and the Judean officers responsible for his assassination fled to Egypt, taking with them the prophet Jeremiah.

It is tempting to compare the evidence concerning the Jewish troops in Egypt with what we know of other foreign mercenaries in the service of the last Pharaohs. On one of the two temples of Abu-Simbel, hewn in stone on the shore of the Nile some 150 kilometers south of Aswan, graffiti by Greek, Carian, and Phoenician auxiliaries have come down to us. These soldiers had participated in the expedition against Nubia in 593 undertaken by Psammetichus II (595–589 BCE). No Aramaic inscription has been discovered there, but two Greek inscriptions, known as the "minutes," deserve more than a cursory glance, since they may put us on the trail of the Jews. Here are the texts as published by the French scholars André Bernand and Olivier Masson.

> When King Psammetichus came to Elephantine, this has been written by those who navigated with Psammetichos son of Theokles; they went beyond Kerkis, as far as the river allowed: Potasimto was in command of the foreigners [the "foreign legion"] and Amasis of the Egyptians. Those who wrote us [i.e. these words] were Arkhon son of Amoibikhos, and Pelekos son of Eudamos. (REVUE DES ÉTUDES GRECQUES 70 [1957], 1 : PP. 3–10)

> I, Anaxanor of Ialysos . . . when King Psammetichus launched his columns, for the first time, seconded by Amasis. (REVUE DES ÉTUDES GRECQUES 70 [1957], 2 : PP. 10–15)

Here we come upon Greek mercenaries in Egypt at the beginning of the sixth century BCE, at the very moment when Solon was writing laws for the city of Athens. Arkhon, son of Amoibikhos, and Pelekos, "The Hatchet," a nickname the son of Eudamos employs as a name, are Rhodians, as the Rhodian dialect of the inscriptions attests. Other graffiti mention one Python, also a son of Amoibikhos, probably the brother of Arkhon. Anaxanor, who came from Ialysos, to the northeast of Rhodes, also belongs to this group. None of these soldiers state their rank; they may have been officers commanding those expert sling-shooters celebrated in the *Anabasis* of Xenophon, where they are described as being able to launch their missiles twice as far as the Persians.

Among the soldiers of Psammetichus, a particularly interesting case is the officer who bears the same name (Psammetichos in Greek) but whose father is Theokles, a Greek.

Colossal statues before the great rock temple of Rameses II at Abu-Simbel   *A first encounter between Jews and Greeks?*

The latter appears to be one of the many Greek mercenaries who, from the seventh century BCE onwards, settled on the banks of the Nile. As a token of his devotion, he gave his Egyptian-born son the name of the ruling monarch. The boy had a brilliant military career. In the first inscription, he seems to have been the commander-in-chief of an army composed of Egyptians and foreign mercenaries. His name does not appear in the second inscription, where only the king and the Egyptian general Amasis are mentioned; the latter is described elsewhere as "the king's delegate, fighting for his master in foreign lands." Should one conclude that Amasis was second only to the sovereign as commander of the expedition, whereas our Psammetichos and Potasimto, mentioned afterwards, commanded lesser groups of soldiers? Actually, the king had remained in Elephantine, after having "launched his expedition," and Amasis is named last in the first inscription, as the leader of the Egyptians. Psammetichos son of Theokles, at the head of the list, seems to have played a major role. If he was not the leader of the expedition, he would have ranked at least as chief officer of fluvial navigation, in an army composed of Egyptians under the command of Amasis, and foreign elements under the command of Potasimto.

These foreign elements, or "foreign legion," as the French editors would have it, are designated by the word *alloglossoi:* "those who speak other languages." Herodotus (2,

154) applies the same term to the Ionian and Carian mercenaries, settled on the seashore by Psammetichus I and subsequently transplanted to Memphis by King Amasis (not to be confounded with our general!). Other languages, and not "another language" (*het-eroglossoi* would have been the term employed in that case): the "foreign legion" was multilingual. The mercenaries were to be distinguished by the languages they spoke, and not by their geographical origin. What were these languages? Greek dialects, surely, since the "signatories" at Abu-Simbel were Ionian and Dorian. Some were in Carian also, that little-known tongue spoken throughout a large region in Southwest Asia Minor, which furnished mercenaries for Saitic and Persian Egypt and, rapidly Hellenized after Alexander's victorious campaign, kept furnishing immigrants to Ptolemaic Egypt; among them figure well-known personages, such as Apollonios the dioiketes, the powerful Minister of Finance under King Ptolemy II Philadelphus, and Zenon son of Agreophon of Kaunos, the manager of his estate in the Faiyum. Lastly, the Phoenician tongue also figures on our list, in some Semitic graffiti. A good number of mercenaries in the army of Psammetichus can thus be identified.

And the Jews? As there are no Aramaic texts available, we must turn, by anticipation, to an important document in Judeo-Alexandrian literature from the Ptolemaic period. The author of the *Letter of Aristeas to Philocrates*, to whom we shall often refer, speaks of Jewish captives deported to Egypt by Ptolemy I, among whom he had chosen the finest, to be armed and sent off to garrison duty. He mentions what appeared to him to have been a precedent: "Once before," he notes (§13), "many had come after the Persian"—he is alluding to the conquest of Egypt by Cambyses—"and, before these, others yet sent as auxiliaries to fight with Psammetichos against the King of Ethiopia."

Who was this Psammetichos? Modern scholars waver between two kings: Psammetichus I and Psammetichus II. Why not Psammetichos son of Theokles, the Greco-Egyptian general in the service of King Psammetichus II during the Nubian campaign in 593 BCE? The king had, in fact, remained at his headquarters in Elephantine. If he had indeed left his army under the command of Psammetichos son of Theokles, and not Amasis, we may possibly have identified another component of the "foreign legion" under Potasimto's command: Judean soldiers sent to Egypt by one of the last kings of Judah. No mention was made of Potasimto, their immediate superior; only Psammetichos, their commander-in-chief, was named. Even if he were merely a naval expert, the Judean auxiliaries from Elephantine would have been rather well-placed to participate in an expeditionary force sailing under his orders, as part of an army composed both of Egyptians and *alloglossoi*. These soldiers would have passed on to other Jewish mercenaries the remembrance of their commander and his royal name, preserving it and eventually transmitting it to the unknown sources from which the author of the *Letter of Aristeas* obtained his information.

Should we retain this hypothesis, the beginnings of the Judean colony in Elephantine should be placed at the end of the seventh century BCE, perhaps during Josiah's time or, better yet, during the reign of his successor Jehoiakim (609–598 BCE), who chose to ignore the preachings of Jeremiah and remain faithful to Pharaoh Necho II, to whom he owed his kingship. Certain place-names in the Book of Jeremiah support this conclusion, as they indicate Jewish settlements in Egypt: Migdol, in the Delta; Daphne, once a Greek mercenary camp; Memphis, the capital; lastly, Patros, "the Southern country," with Elephantine as its center. Jews, then, were already stationed in Egypt at the arrival of the prophet.

The hypothesis of Jewish participation in the Nubian campaign of Psammetichus II postulates one of the very first encounters between Jews and Greeks. Had they been able to speak a common tongue, what subjects could possibly have served as common ground for discussion between the Pharaoh's Jewish mercenaries and their Ionian or Dorian fellow-soldiers? Homer and Moses? Most unlikely—certainly the colossi of the Abu-Simbel temple and the pretty Nubian girls were more agreeable topics, and held promise of livelier conversations. The great encounter was yet to come, that historic meeting which would reveal the existence of the Jewish people to the Greeks and sweep the Jews irresistibly into the orbit of Greek culture.

MIBTAHIAH AND HER HUSBANDS: A FAMILY OF NOTE DURING THE REIGN OF ARTAXERXES I

Various aspects of life in the Jewish colony have been brought to light by the Elephantine documents. The soldiers served both as frontier guards and as a regional police force to assure law and order. The garrison was divided into "companies" or "banners" (degel), the equivalent of the "thousands" of the old Israelite armies and, later on, of the Greek armies. The companies, in turn, were subdivided into "centuries," and these into "decuries." Each company was placed under the orders of a commander, whose name it bore. Those that are at present known to us are all of Iranian or Mesopotamian origin. As the same names were carried over two or three generations, the office would seem to be hereditary, unless one subscribes to the thesis of nominal permanence, regardless of the change of the titulary occupant. The entire garrison was placed under the orders of a commander-in-chief (rab hayla) whose headquarters were in Syene; his title corresponded to that of a Greek phrourarchos, commander of a garrison.

The soldiers lived with their families. Under the Persian administration, some of them had obtained plots of land as a reward for their service. The Achaemenids thus paved the way for the cleruchic system—concession of a parcel of land in return for military service—the Ptolemaic rulers were to establish after Alexander conquered the country. The soldiers had regular pay and special allowances for each family member and for themselves. They formed a veritable microsociety, whose specificity was guaranteed by the government in conformity with the principles of Persian imperial policy. Their religious life was centered on the temple of their national Deity, YHW: the Divine Name appears here in shortened form. As we shall see, things did not always go smoothly for the mercenaries in their dealings with their Egyptian neighbors, adorers of Khnum, the ram-god, master of the Nile's seasonal variations and the originator of all living creatures, whose sanctuary was also to be found on the same island. Their family lives and customs, unique in Jewish history of that epoch, were mirrored in their legal documents. Those that we possess pose fascinating problems regarding the nature of the social and legal rules and regulations prevalent in the Jewish community of Elephantine.

A dozen papyri acquaint us with Mahseiah son of Yedaniah and his family, Jewish notables, who made their appearance in 471 BCE, under the reign of Xerxes. Mahseiah had two sons and a daughter. One son was called Yedaniah, after his grandfather, the other Gamariah. Yedaniah had a son named for his grandfather Mahseiah, and Gamariah had three daughters and a son. This latter, like his uncle and his grandfather, was called Yedaniah; one day he would become the head of the Jewish community in Elephantine. We are evidently dealing with influential people, worthy representatives of their coreligionists.

This set of documents is centered around the personage of Mibtahiah ("The Lord is my assurance"), the youngest of Mahseiah's children. She was born about 480 BCE. When she was twenty, her father gave her a fine dowry and married her off to a Jew from Elephantine, Yezaniah son of Uriah. Unfortunately, the marriage contract has not been preserved, but two deeds of donation and conveyance, to be dated November 11, 460 (or December 1, 459), record Mahseiah's gifts to the new household. They comprise a gift of land to his daughter and a transfer of building rights to his son-in-law, to which a good number of restrictions and conditions were attached. Let us first read the donative act.

Elephantine *Fragment of the "Nile Mosaic" (Palestrina, National Museum).*

On the twenty-first of Kislev, that is the first day of Mesore, year 6 of King Artaxerxes, Mahseiah son of Yedaniah, a Jew, hereditary property holder in Elephantine the Fortress of the detachment of Haumadata, said to lady Mibtahiah, his daughter, saying: "I gave you in my lifetime and at my death one house on land of mine. Its measurements: length from bottom to top, thirteen cubits and one handbreadth; width from east to west, eleven cubits by the measuring rod. Its boundaries: above it the house of Dargamana son of Khvarshaina adjoins; below it is the house of Konaiah son of Zadak; east of it is the house of Yezan son of Uriah, your husband, and the house of Zekhariah son of Natan; west of it is the house of Espemet son of Peftuaneith, a boatman of the rough waters.

That house, land—I gave it to you in my lifetime and at my death. You have right to it from this day forever and your children after you. To whomever you wish you may give [it]. I have no other son or daughter, brother or sister, or woman or other man who has a right to that land except you and your children forever. Whoever shall bring suit or process against you, your son or daughter, or someone else of yours, regarding that land which I gave you, and shall complain against you [before] a prefect or judge, [he] shall give you and your children a sum of 10—ten—karsh by the royal standard, 2 silver quarters to the piece-of-ten. There shall neither be suit nor process. And the house is moreover your house and your children's after you. And they shall not be able to produce against you a new or old document in my name about that land to give [it] to another man. That document which they shall produce against you will be false. I did not write it and it shall not be accepted in suit while this document is in your hand.

And moreover I, Mahseiah, tomorrow or the next day, shall not reclaim [it] from you to give it to others. That land is yours. Build [on it] and give [it] to whomever you wish. If tomorrow or the next day I bring against you suit or process and say: "I did not give [it] to you," I shall give you silver, 10 karsh by the royal standard, 2 silver quarters to the ten-piece, without suit and without process, and the house is moreover your house. And should I go to law [take legal action], I shall not prevail while this document is in your hand.

Moreover, there is one document of withdrawal that Dargamana son of Khvarshaina, the Khwarezmian, wrote for me about that land when he brought suit about it before the judges and an oath to him was imposed upon me and I swore to him that it was mine, and he wrote a document of withdrawal and gave [it] to me. That document—I gave it to you. You hold it as heir. If tomorrow or the next day Dargamana or a son of his bring suit about that house, produce that document and in accordance with it bring a suit against him.

Attarshuri son of Nabuzeribni wrote this document in Syene the fortress at the instruction of Mahseiah. The witnesses herein: witness

Gamariah son of Mahseiah; witness Zekhariah son of Natan; witness
Hosea son of Pelaliah; witness Zekhariah son of Meshullam; witness
Maaziah son of Malkhiah; witness Shemaiah son of Yedaniah; witness
Yedaniah son of Mahseiah; witness Natan son of Ananiah; Zaccur son of
Zephanian; witness Hosea son of Deuiah/Reuiah; witness Mahsah son of
Isaiah; witness Hosea son of Igdal.

[Title on back:] Document of a house Mahseiah son of Yedaniah wrote
for Mibtah [Mibtahiah] daughter of Mahsah [Mahseiah]. (A. COWLEY,
ARAMAIC PAPYRI OF THE FIFTH CENTURY [OXFORD, 1923], NO. 8; B. PORTEN–A.
YARDENI, TEXTBOOK 2, B 2.3)

Mibtahiah appears to be the unique beneficiary. But we now learn that her husband
was also accorded certain rights. Mibtahiah's father, Mahseiah, was a colonist: a member of the elite group to whom tenures had been granted. Among the witnesses we find
the two brothers of Mibtahiah, Gamariah and Yedaniah, with his son Shemaiah, and
also Zekhariah son of Natan, who lives in the neighboring house. One can well understand all these precautions in the event of possible future disputes between relatives and
neighbors. Luckily, the husband of Mibtahiah is also her neighbor; since the terrain,
only some thirty square meters, was meager, the joining of the two lots would enhance
the couple's living space. The donation was completed by an act of transfer:

On the twenty-first of Kislev, that is the first day of Mesore, year 6 of
King Artaxerxes, Mahseiah son of Yedaniah, a Jew of Elephantine of the
detachment of Haumadata, said to Yezaniah son of Uriah in the same detachment, saying: There is land belonging to a house of mine, west of the
house of yours, which I gave to Mibtahiah my daughter, your wife, and I
wrote for her a document concerning it. The measurements of that house:
thirteen cubits and a handbreadth by eleven according to the measuring
rod. Now I, Mahseiah, said to you: Build up that plot, enrich it and dwell
herein with your wife. But that house—you do not have the right to sell it
or to give it affectionately to others except [to] your children by
Mibtahiah [who] have the right to it after you. If tomorrow or the next
day you build up that plot [and] then my daughter hates you and leaves
you, she does not have the right to take it and give it to others but it is
your children by Mibtahiah who have the right to it in exchange for the
work which you did. If she shall reclaim it from you, half the house shall
be hers to take; but the other half you have the right to in exchange for
the building [improvements] you have built into this house; and furthermore, of that half, it is your children by Mibtahiah who have the right to
it after you. If tomorrow or the next day I bring against you suit or process
and say: "I did not give you that land to build up and I did not write this
document for you," I shall give you silver, 10 karsh by the royal standard,
2 silver quarters to the ten-piece, without suit or process.

> Attarshuri son of Nabuzeribni wrote this document in Syene the
> fortress at the instruction of Mahseiah. The witnesses herein: witness
> Hosea son of Pelaliah; witness Zekhariah son of Natan; witness Gamariah
> son of Mahseiah; witness Zekhariah son of Meshullam; witness Maaziah
> son of Malkhiah; witness Shemaiah son of Yedaniah; witness Natan son of
> Ananiah; witness Zaccur son of Zephaniah; witness Hosea son of
> Deuiah/Reuiah; witness Mahsah son of Isaiah; witness Hosea son of Igdal."
> (COWLEY, NO. 9; PORTEN–YARDENI, TEXTBOOK 2, B 2.4)

This document, as well as the preceding one, had been drawn up by a notary of Syene whose father's name was Akkadian. The fact that Mesopotamian notaries worked on documents concerning Jews of Elephantine poses the problem of a possible influence of Babylonian law in the legal practice of the Jewish colony. Mahseiah granted to his son-in-law development rights over the land he had given his daughter. His son-in-law was also his comrade-in-arms, as both were serving under the orders of the same officer. Yezaniah may exploit the terrain as he sees fit, but he cannot transfer it to a third party. In case of divorce, he may keep half the house he may have built thereon, the other half remaining the property of Mibtahiah and the progeny of the couple. After their father's death, the children inherit his half of the house. Mibtahiah is subject to the same restrictions, limiting the rights of succession to their children as sole heirs. An important detail is to be stressed: Mibtahiah may initiate divorce proceedings. We shall return to this point.

All this display of generosity, tempered by so many safeguards, was not sufficient to assure the couple's happiness. The precautions taken by Mahseiah in favor of his future grandchildren proved to be useless. For a while Mahseiah and his daughter drop out of sight, and, when we come upon them again in November 446, Yezaniah is no longer there. Mibtahiah's husband seems to have died after some ten to twelve years of marriage, leaving her a childless widow. She may have recently remarried: we shall discuss this in a moment. In any case, Mibtahiah is the sole beneficiary of the legal act we shall now quote. Mahseiah had just been "confined to barracks" in the fortress, where his daughter devotedly tended to his needs. Mahseiah was not an ingrate: he offered Mibtahiah a second house, which he had bought from a neighbor, Meshullam son of Zaccur. Here is the deed of donation, dated November 17, 446 BCE.

> On the second of Kislev, that is the tenth day of the month of Mesore,
> year 19 of King Artaxerxes, Mahseiah son of Yedaniah, an Aramean of
> Syene of the detachment of Varyazata, said to Mibtahiah his daughter,
> saying: I gave you the house that Meshullam son of Zaccur son of Ater, an
> Aramean of Syene, gave me for its value and about which he wrote a doc-
> ument for me. And I gave it to Mibtahiah my daughter in exchange for her
> goods which she gave me. When I was garrisoned in the fortress, I consumed
> them but did not find silver or gold to repay you. Then, I gave you this

house in exchange for those goods of yours valued in silver at 5 karsh. And I gave you the old document that Meshullam wrote for me concerning it. I gave this house to you and withdrew from it. It is yours and your children's after you and you may give it to whomever you wish. I shall not be able—I or my children, or descendants who are mine, or another person—to bring against you suit or process regarding that house which I gave you and about which I wrote this document for you. Whoever shall institute against you suit or process—I, brother or sister, near or far, member of a detachment or member of a town—shall give you silver, 10 karsh, and in addition the house is yours. Moreover, another person shall not be able to produce against you a new or old document but only this document which I wrote and gave you. Whoever shall produce against you a document, I did not write it.

Moreover, behold these are the boundaries of that house: above it the house of Yaush son of Penuliah; below it is the temple of the God YHW; east of it is the house of Gaddul son of Osea and the street is between them; west of it is the house of Harudj son of Paltu, priest of the gods Hannu and 'Atti. I gave that house to you and withdrew from it. It is yours forever and give it to whomever you please.

Natan son of Ananiah wrote this document at the instruction of Mahseiah. And the witnesses herein: Mahseiah son of Y[edoniah] wrote with his own hands; Mithrasarah son of Mithrasarah; Vyzbl(w) son of 'trly, a Caspian; witness Barbari son of Dargi(ya), a Caspian of the place; Haggai son of Shemaiah; Zaccur son of Shillem.

[Title on back:] Document of a house which Mahseiah son of Yedaniah wrote for Miptahiah [Mibtahiah] his daughter. (COWLEY, NO. 13; PORTEN–YARDENI, TEXTBOOK 2, B 2.7)

As was the case with the first donation, this house was situated in the neighborhood of the temple of YHW. Mahseiah, a "Jew of Elephantine," has become an "Aramean of Syene": he had been transferred to an Aramaic regiment stationed at Syene. Among his neighbors we find a pagan priest, the servant of a divine couple, the Aramaic Hannu and 'Atti ('Atti could be identified with 'Anat). In the absence of a third sanctuary on the island, beside the temple of YHW, God of the Jews, and that of Khnum, Hannu and 'Atti must have had their temple at Syene. Here too, as in the preceding deeds, the mention of children is a reference to future events.

Mahseiah must have been impatient to become a grandfather, and one can well understand him. His daughter was still young, about thirty, and far from poor. Her doting father found her another husband. In the opinion of some scholars, Mahseiah had chosen Pia son of Pahi, an Egyptian architect assigned to royal construction projects. He was probably employed in the quarries at Syene, which furnished fine gray and pink granite to the entire country. This hypothesis was based on a document to be dated

Grant of the house *Aramaic papyrus from Elephantine, 446 BCE (B. Porten and A. Yardeni, Textbook 2, B 2.7).*

August 26, 440 BCE, that had heretofore been interpreted as a settlement following a divorce, this new marriage having been even more short-lived than the previous one. The text follows:

> On the fourteenth of Ab, that is the nineteenth day of Pahons [Pachon], year 25 of Artaxerxes, Pia son of Pahi, a builder of Syene the fortress, said to Mibtahiah daughter of Mahseiah son of Yedaniah, an Aramean of Syene of the detachment of Varyazata:
>
> About the suit which we undertook in Syene, a litigation about silver and grain and raiment and bronze and iron—all the goods and property— and the marriage document. Then, an oath was imposed upon you and you swore to me about them by Sati the goddess. And my heart was satisfied with that oath which you made to me about those goods and I withdrew from you this day and forever. I shall not be able to institute against you suit or process—neither you nor your son or daughter—regarding those goods about which you swore to me. If I institute against you suit or process, or a son of mine or a daughter of mine institutes against you a suit regarding that oath, I, Pia—or my children—shall give to Mibtahiah silver, 5 karsh by the king's standard, without suit or without process, and I am barred from every suit or process.
>
> Peteisi son of Nabunatan wrote this document in Syene the Fortress at the instruction of Pia son of Pahi. The witnesses herein: Naburai son of Nabunatan; Luhi son of Mannuki; Ausnahar son of Duma; Naburai son of Vishtana.
>
> [Title on back:] Document of withdrawal that Pia wrote for Miptahiah [Mibtahiah]. (COWLEY, NO. 14; PORTEN–YARDENI, TEXTBOOK 2, B 2.8)

Mibtahiah was evidently well able to protect her interests. She did not hesitate to bring her case before the local authorities and swear by the Egyptian goddess Sati, consort of Khnum the ram-god. Furniture, clothing, and precious metal, and not the land and houses of Mibtahiah, seem to be the objects of litigation. However, the hypothesis of an act of renunciation (withdrawal) following a divorce must probably be abandoned. If we accept Bezalel Porten's chronology, Mibtahiah, when she signed this document, had already been remarried for some time. Her dispute with Pia must have had other grounds, as Mibtahiah was then living with her second husband. She was married only twice, not three times. Like the candidate we have been obliged to eliminate for chronological reasons, this second husband, surprisingly, was also one of the king's architects, an Egyptian by the name of Eshor (Eskhor) son of Seiha. Their marriage act, dated mid-October 449 or 446, illustrates the lifestyle of a well-to-do household in the middle of the fifth century BCE:

> On the twenty-fifth of Tishri, that is the sixteenth of the month of Epeiph, year 16 [or 19] of King Artaxerxes. Eshor son of Seiha, a builder

of the king, said to Mahseiah, an Aramean of Syene of the detachment of Varyazata, saying:

I came to your house and asked you to give me your daughter Miptahiah [Mibtahiah] for wife. She is my wife and I am her husband from this day and forever. I gave you as bride-price for your daughter Miptahiah: silver, 5 shekels by the king's standard. It came unto you and your heart was satisfied. Your daughter Miptahiah brought me in her hand: silver money 1 karsh, 2 shekels by the royal standard, 2 silver quarters to the 10-piece. She brought into me in her hand: one new woolen garment, two-toned, 8 by 5 cubits, worth in silver 2 karsh, 8 shekels by the royal standard; 1 new shawl, 8 by 5 cubits, worth in silver 8 shekels by the royal standard; another woolen garment, finely woven, 6 by 4 cubits, worth in silver 7 shekels; 1 bronze mirror, worth in silver 1 shekel, 2 quarters; 1 bronze bowl, worth in silver 1 shekel, 2 quarters; 2 bronze cups, worth in silver 2 shekels; 1 bronze jug, worth in silver 2 quarters. All the silver and the value of the goods: in silver 6 karsh, 5 shekels, 20 hallurs, silver 2 quarters to the 10, by the royal standard. It came unto me and my heart was satisfied. 1 papyrus-reed bed on which are 4 stone inlays [?]; 1 tray of wicker; 2 ladles; 1 new palm-leaf box; 5 handfuls of castor oil; 1 pair of sandals.

Tomorrow or the next day, should Eshor die not having a child, male or female, by Miptahiah his wife, it is Miptahiah who has the right to the house of Eshor and his goods and his property and all that he has on the face of the whole earth. Tomorrow or [the next] day, should Miptahiah die not having a child, male or female, by Eshor her husband, it is Eshor who shall inherit from her her goods and her property. Tomorrow or the next day, should Miptahiah stand up in an assembly and say: "I hated Eshor my husband," silver of hatred is upon her head. She shall place upon the balance-scale and weigh out to Eshor silver, 6+1=7 shekels, 2 quarters, and all that she brought in her hand she shall take out, from straw to string, and go away wherever she desires, without suit or without process. Tomorrow or the next day, should Eshor stand up in an assembly and say: "I hate my wife Miptahiah," her bride-price will be forfeited and all that she brought in in her hand she shall take out, from straw to string, on one day in one stroke, and she shall go away wherever she desires, without suit or without process. And whoever shall stand up against Miptahiah to evict her from the house of Eshor and his goods and his property shall give her silver, 20 karsh, and execute for her the law of this document. And I shall not be able to say: "I have another wife besides Miptahiah and other children besides the children whom Miptahiah shall bear to me." If I say: "I have other children and wife besides Miptahiah and her children," I shall give to Miptahiah silver, 20 karsh by the royal standard. And I shall not be able to release my goods and my property from Miptahiah. And should I remove them from her [in accordance with this document], I shall give to Miptahiah silver, 20 karsh by the royal standard.

Natan son of Ananiah wrote this document at the instructions of Eshor. And the witnesses herein: Penuliah son of Yezaniah; [...]iah son of 'Uriah; Menahem son of Saccur; witness Re'ibel son on [...]. (COWLEY, NO. 15; PORTEN-YARDENI, TEXTBOOK 2, B 2.6)

This new husband was a curious sort of Egyptian. In the document translated above, he is called Eshor son of Seiha; his children sometimes called themselves "sons of Eshor" and sometimes "sons of Natan." Was Eshor the Egyptian taken into the Jewish community upon his marriage to Mibtahiah, and given a typically Hebrew name, Natan (short form of Yehonatan, Jonathan, "The Lord has given"), or was he given a double name at birth, as the son of Seiha the Egyptian and a Jewish mother? We do not know. But we do know that in Elephantine, the offspring of a mixed marriage, such as the second marriage of Mibtahiah, could be considered Jewish. Furthermore, onomastic evidence from our documents shows that the sons of Jewish fathers, with rare exceptions, bore Jewish names. The biblical principle of paternal filiation was here judiciously combined with that of maternal filiation, to the benefit of the community. This solution to the problem of mixed marriages was perhaps more efficient and surely less brutal than the contemporaneous laws of Ezra, ordering foreign wives to be driven from the community.

Mibtahiah was now to experience the tender pleasures of maternity: she bore two sons to Eshor, who were named for their maternal ancestors, Yedaniah and Mahseiah. When the father's untiring efforts to help his daughter through her matrimonial vicissitudes were at last rewarded, his joy must have been boundless.

Toward the year 420 BCE, Mibtahiah was again widowed. She was then some sixty years old. She did not remarry, and died five or six years later. There our story ends.

These joys and sorrows of a Jewish family in Achaemenid Egypt have taught us much about the microsociety of Elephantine. The attentive reader will have noted some particularities of social and family behavior. A striking feature is the rare degree of autonomy of Jewish women. Polygamy was admitted by biblical law, but, in Elephantine, restrictive clauses in marriage contracts rendered it impracticable. Women had patrimonial rights: we have seen how Mibtahiah was coproprietor of the household property and her husband's heiress. In fact, although the marriages were arranged by the father even for his divorced or widowed daughter, Mahseiah actually played the part of an affectionate parent, whose only concern was his daughter's welfare.

The principal distinguishing feature of the feminine condition in Elephantine was the woman's prerogative in matters of divorce. This proviso is in strict contradiction to the principle given in Deuteronomy (24:1–4), which governed Jewish divorce law throughout history and even today: the unilateral repudiation of the spouse by the husband by means of a letter of divorce. The singularity of Elephantine practice in this respect has provoked a good deal of discussion: was it due to Egyptian or Babylonian influence, or did it stem from ancient Hebrew legal practice, antedating Deuteronomy? In fact, even after that reform, a tendency to favor an egalitarian basis for divorce subsisted among the Jews. Within the Jewish community of Elephantine, this tendency became the rule. Several centuries later, a similar attitude was to prevail among Alexandrian Jewry. Partisans of marital equality would certainly approve the manner in which the Jews of Egypt treated the so-called "weaker sex."

"GOD OF HEAVEN" AND GOD OF THE FLOODS

The good relationship between the Jewish soldiers and the Egyptians of the island and the surrounding region should not lead one to imagine a sort of permanent idyll. The two communities were cramped together in a small space, and frictions were bound to arise. A permanent source of irritation was the basic incompatibility between the cult of YHW—"God of Heaven" according to the official denomination adopted by the Achaemenid chancellery and frequently employed in Elephantine documents—and the worship of Khnum, the ram-god, lord of the Nile floods, whose temple was located close to the Jewish sanctuary.

The existence of a Jewish temple in Elephantine in the fifth century BCE strikes us today as an anomaly, which historians have termed "predeuteronomic" or "paradeuteronomic," since it appears as an infringement of the Deuteronomic principle of the unity of worship. The temple at Elephantine was founded either before the reforms of Josiah (622 BCE), which proclaimed this principle, or afterwards, in reaction to it. The choice depends on the date we accept for its inauguration: either the reign of Manasseh in the middle of the seventh century BCE, or a period comprising the reign of Jehoiakim (609–598 BCE) and the fall of the kingdom of Judah (587 BCE); we have already encountered these problems of dating in the previous chapter. It was not a house of prayer, like the future synagogues in the Land of Israel and the Diaspora, but a genuine temple with its complement of priests to whom the tithe was paid, and where worship took place according to the biblical precepts, with burnt offerings, oblations, and incense, as was the practice in Jerusalem. This, then, was one of the "high places" condemned by the Deuteronomic reform, which ordained their elimination.

From the time of the exile until the reconstruction of the Temple in Jerusalem after the return of the Jews from Babylon, between 587 and 515 BCE, the sanctuary at Elephantine was the only place in the world where Jewish sacrificial worship was practiced. In a manner of speaking, Elephantine temporarily replaced Jerusalem. After the inauguration of the Second Temple in 515, there was no longer any justification for its continued existence, from the viewpoint of post-exilic Jewish authorities. And this was not the sole example of "deviationism" among the Jews of Elephantine.

Indeed, the members of the colony practiced a brand of Judaism differing in many respects from the principles introduced by Josiah's reforms, and adopted, after the return from captivity, by the builders of the new Jewish entity. Doubtless they observed the Sabbath, following the time-honored prescriptions of the Torah (Ex. 20:8, 23:12). From a simple ostracon, bearing the text of a letter written by a man to his wife, we learn that on the Sabbath, Jews abstained from crossing the Nile on boats and engaging in the transport of merchandise (ostracon Clermont-Ganneau No. 152). Now we can rest easy—but not for too long: other testimony concerning the religious customs of Elephantine Jews is rather disturbing.

Thus we learn (Cowley, No. 44, prior to 419 BCE?) that a Jew, involved in litigation on the subject of a she-ass, swore an oath "by the sanctuary and by 'Anat-Yaho." We have already seen how Lady Mibtahiah swore an oath by the Egyptian goddess Sati. Whereas she was merely accomplishing a formality for the Egyptian authorities in a dispute between herself and an Egyptian, this other quarrel concerning two members of the colony was apparently the sequel to a previous judgment by a Jewish tribunal. The invocation of a feminine divinity, along with that of the sanctuary, can hardly pass unnoticed.

We are even more perplexed when we come across a lengthy text concerning the poll tax for the upkeep of the Elephantine temple (Cowley, No. 22, beginning of 419 BCE?). It contains a detailed list of the sums collected and their distribution: 12 karsh 6 shekels for YHW, God of the Jews; 12 karsh for 'Anat-Bet'el; 7 karsh for 'Ashim-Bet'el. The latter two names are those of the consort and the son of Bet'el, supreme deity of the Arameans of Syene. Did the Jews of Elephantine pay these sums to their Syenese neighbors for the worship of these two divinities? Or did the Jewish God in Elephantine also have a divine consort, sometimes referred to in our documents as 'Anat-Yaho and sometimes as 'Anat-Bet'el? Furthermore, was this divine pair endowed with a son, 'Ashim-Bet'el, to constitute a triad?

In this perspective, it is difficult to ignore the language employed by the Judean emigrants to Egypt in response to the diatribes of Jeremiah: "We will certainly perform every word that is gone forth out of our mouth, to offer unto the queen of heaven, and to pour out drink-offerings unto her, as we have done, we and our fathers, our kings and our princes, in the cities of Judah, and in the streets of Jerusalem" (Jer. 44:17). The "Queen of Heaven" to whom they proclaim their attachment is none other, it would appear, than 'Anat-Yaho or 'Anat-Bet'el. From Jeremiah's time (about 580 BCE) onwards, the Jews of Egypt seem set on perpetuating doubtful forms of worship, which the reforms of Josiah had been unable to eradicate. Their archaic syncretism and their scandalous tolerance toward "other gods" were quite enough to arouse the prophet's righteous indignation.

In Jerusalem, Nehemiah, Ezra, and their followers, with the benevolent support of the Persian regime, had harnessed themselves to the task of reconstructing Judaism. They sought to establish contact with their Elephantine brethren, in order to lead them back to the straight and narrow path. The document, known as the "Passover papyrus," is our primary source of information concerning this endeavor. It consists of a letter,

The god Khnum, lord of the Nile's flooding *Temple of Esna.*

dated 419/418 BCE, addressed to Yedaniah, nephew of Lady Mibtahiah, and his colleagues of the Elephantine garrison, by one Hananiah, perhaps the brother of Nehemiah or one of his confidants. Its purpose was to bring about a reform of the religious calendar in Elephantine: the celebration of the Passover holidays and the Feast of Unleavened Bread was hereafter to take place from the fifteenth to the twenty-first of Nisan and no longer at the "time the sickle is first put to the standing corn" (Deut. 16:9), which varies with geography and agricultural conditions. The leaders of post-exilic Judaism, seeking to unify the communities of Jerusalem and Babylon under the authority of the high priest, wished to extend it to the Egyptian colony. This is to be considered either a preparatory or an executory measure, according to the date assigned to Ezra's mission, a matter on which historians differ (428 or 398 BCE).

Although it may have influenced ritual practice in the Elephantine sanctuary, this intervention did not call the temple's existence into question. Ten years later, a veritable upheaval occurred. The stirrings of Egyptian nationalism were to prove more efficacious in this regard than the harangues of Jeremiah and the efforts of the post-exilic Jewish renovators put together.

For the priests of Khnum the ram-god, the Jews who sacrificed lambs on the altar of their temple must surely have been perceived as committing deicide. For a long while they had unflinchingly tolerated their unpleasant neighbors, since the sovereign whom the Elephantine colonists faithfully served had certainly authorized the erection of the Jewish temple and was the guarantor of its inviolability. In the long run, a hostile reaction set in and violence broke out. Ever since 414/413 BCE, a simmering revolt of the Egyptians against their Persian conquerors had been gathering strength. In the springtime of 410 BCE, year fourteen of the reign of Darius II, several Egyptian regiments rebelled and, in the absence of Arshama (Arsames), the Persian satrap, rallied under the banner of Amyrtaeus, their chief. Several years later, he was to be proclaimed Pharaoh.

In the month of Tammuz of the same year—between mid-July and mid-August 410 BCE—a band of Egyptian rebels, with the support of Vidranga (Waidrang), the governor of Syene, vented their anger on the Jews by laying waste the sanctuary at Elephantine. The sack of the temple was followed by the pillage of Jewish dwellings. The leaders of the community appealed to a member of the satrap's staff (or perhaps to an influential coreligionist), demanding protection for their possessions and requesting the authorization to rebuild the temple. A rough draft of this request has been conserved in their archives.

> [Recto, Column 1:] Now we cried out in anguish. Detachments of the Egyptians rebelled. We did not leave our posts and nothing of damage was found against us. In the year 14 of King Darius, when our lord Arsames went to the king, the priests of Khnum the god did an evil act in Elephantine the Fortress in agreement with Vidranga who was chief here: they gave him silver and goods. There is part of the royal barley-house which is in Elephantine the Fortress; they demolished it and built a wall in the midst of the fortress of Elephantine.

[Column 2] And now, that wall stands built in the midst of the fortress. There is a well that was built within the fortress and [it] did not lack water to give the garrison drink so that whenever they were garrisoned there they could drink the water in that well. Those priests of Khnum stopped up that well. If inquiry be made of the judges, police and hearers who are appointed in the province of Tshetres, it would be known to our lord in accordance with this which we say. Moreover, we are not in question. . . .

(Verso) . . . Thus we are innocent. . . . Moreover, nothing reprehensible like that has been found against us. Moreover, the Egyptians did not allow us to bring a meal-offering there to YHW the God. . . , but they made a brazier to burn the beams. . . the fittings they took [and] made [them] their own. . . . And now, if it please our lord, may the wrong done to us be remembered, to us of the Jewish garrison!. . . If it please our lord, may an order be issued according to what we say! If it please our lord, may a [message] be sent, so that they protect the things which belong to us; that they rebuild our temple which they demolished. (COWLEY, NO. 27; PORTEN-YARDENI, TEXTBOOK 1, A 4.5)

The Jewish soldiers stressed their loyalty to the Achaemenid regime. They had remained at their posts, and they raised their voices in righteous protestation against Vidranga and his son, the leader of the army, who supported the rebels instead of protecting the loyal servants of the Great King. Their petition must have been received favorably, for the nationalist rebellion had since been quelled, Governor Vidranga made destitute, the vandals punished. Notwithstanding, three years after the sack of their sanctuary, the Elephantine Jews had still not been authorized to rebuild it.

In 407 BCE, on November 25, Yedaniah son of Gamariah and his colleagues tried another tack. They had already made an effort to influence the high priest in Jerusalem. This time, they attempted to exploit the conflicts opposing the high priest to the governor of Judah and the Samaritans, by writing to the sons of Sinoballit (Sanballat), the satrap of Samaria, and to Bagohi, civil governor of Judah. Two copies of this second letter have been preserved, a rough draft and a corrected version. Combining the two enables us to reconstitute the text.

To our lord Bagohi, governor of Judah, your servants Yedaniah and his colleagues the priests who are in Elephantine the Fortress. May the God of Heaven seek after the welfare of our lord abundantly and at all times, and grant you favor before King Darius and the princes a thousand times more than now, and give you long life, and may you be happy and strong at all times. Now, your servant Yedaniah and his colleagues say thus:

In the month of Tammuz, year 14 of King Darius, when Arsames had departed and gone to the king, the priests of Khnum the god who are in Elephantine the Fortress, in agreement with Vidranga who was chief here, said: "Let them remove from there the temple of YHW the God which is in Elephantine the Fortress." Then, that Vidranga, the wicked, sent a letter to Naphaina his son who was garrison commander in Syene the fortress, saying, "Let them demolish the temple of YHW the God which is in Elephantine the Fortress." Then, Naphaina led the Egyptians with the other troops. They came to the fortress of Elephantine with their weapons, broke into that temple, demolished it to the ground, and smashed the stone pillars that were there. Moreover, it happened that they demolished five stone gateways, built of hewn stone, which were in that temple. And their standing doors, and the bronze hinges of those doors, and the cedarwood roof—all of these which, with the rest of the fittings and other things which were there—all of these they burned with fire. But the gold and silver basins and other things which were in that temple—all of these they took and made their own.

And during the days of the kings of Egypt our fathers had built that temple in Elephantine the Fortress and when Cambyses entered Egypt he found that temple built. And they overthrew the temples of the gods of Egypt, all of them, but one did not damage anything in that temple. And when this had been done to us, we with our wives and our children were wearing sackcloth and fasting and praying to YHW the Lord of Heaven who let us gloat over that Vidranga. The dogs removed the fetter from his feet and all goods which he had acquired were lost. And all persons who sought evil for that temple, all of them were killed and we gazed upon them. Moreover, before this—at the time that this evil was done to us— we sent a letter to our lord, and to Yehohanan the high priest and his colleagues the priests who are in Jerusalem, and to Ostanes the brother of Anani and the nobles of Judah. They did not send us a single letter. Moreover, from the month of Tammuz, year 14 of King Darius, until this day we are wearing sackcloth and fasting; our wives are made as widows; we do not anoint ourselves with oil and do not drink wine. Moreover, from that time and until this day, year 17 of King Darius, they did not bring meal-offering, incense, or burnt-offerings in that temple.

Now, your servants Yedaniah and his colleagues and the priests of YHW, and the Jews, all of them colonists of Elephantine, say thus: If it please our lord, take thought of that temple to rebuild it since they do not let us rebuild it. Regard your obligees and your friends who are here in Egypt. Let a letter be sent from you to them about the temple of the God YHW to rebuild it in Elephantine the Fortress just as it was formerly built. And they will offer the meal-offering and the incense, and the sacrifice on the altar of YHW the God in your name and we shall pray for you at all times—we and our wives and our children and the Jews, all of them who are here. If you do thus until that temple be rebuilt, you will have merit before YHW the God of Heaven more than a person who offers him burnt-offerings and sacrifices worth one-thousand silver talents. Because of this we have sent you our instructions. Moreover, we sent in our name all these words in one letter to Delaiah and Shelemiah, sons of Sanballat, governor of Samaria. Moreover, Arsames did not know about what was done to us at all. On the twentieth of Marheshvan, year 17 of King Darius. (COWLEY, NOS. 30–31; PORTEN-YARDENI, TEXTBOOK 1, A 4.7–8)

This is an excellent summary of the situation as well as a most interesting description of ritual worship in Elephantine in the period following the dispatch of the "Passover papyrus." Their desire to rebuild the sanctuary put the Elephantine Jews in a delicate position in regard to the authorities in Jerusalem. For the high priest Yehohanan and his colleagues, the reconstruction of a diasporic temple was evidently unthinkable, as it was in absolute contradiction to the principle of unity of worship prescribed by the Deuteronomic code, the main pillar of post-exilic Judaism. For the Jewish leaders in Jerusalem, the sack of the Elephantine temple could be readily interpreted as a form of divine justice, a fit punishment for their dissident coreligionists. It was hardly surprising that the pressing letters from Elephantine went unanswered.

The Elephantine Jews were well aware of this and, in an attempt to circumvent Jerusalem by appealing to higher authority, sought to convince the real power behind Jerusalem, the dominant Persian regime, of the justice of their cause. The antiquity of the sanctuary, whose inauguration antedated Cambyses' conquest of Egypt, was a solid argument in its favor. Addressing the sons of Sanballat was also a clever ploy, as their father, a fierce adversary of Nehemiah, was on friendly terms with Bagohi. The latter, a wise politician and administrator, won the Samaritans over; together, they came to the aid of their coreligionists in Egypt. Bagohi decided to choose, among the various factions of the adorers of the "God of Heaven," the one most useful to the Great King, and to further its cause. His answer, countersigned by Delaiah, one of the sons of the Samarian satrap, in the form of a memorandum, was sent to Elephantine by messenger:

> Memorandum of what Bahogi and Delaiah said to me, saying: Memorandum. You may say in Egypt before Arsames about the Altar-house of the God of Heaven which in Elephantine the Fortress was formerly built before Cambyses [and] which that wicked Vadranga demolished in year 14 of King Darius: to rebuild it on its site as it was formerly and they shall offer the meal-offering and the incense upon that altar just as formerly was done. (COWLEY, NO. 32; PORTEN-YARDENI, TEXTBOOK 1, A 4.9)

The evocation of the sanctuary's antiquity had struck home. Yedaniah obtained satisfaction on all points but one: burnt-offerings were out of the question. The high priest of Jerusalem would henceforth have the unique privilege of presiding over this rite, and the ministers of the god Khnum were to be spared what they conceived as an offense. The satrap, Arshama, confirmed this decision, and the Jews of Elephantine were soon able to acknowledge receipt of an order he issued, clearly based on the terms set out above: the sanctuary was to be reestablished, but the God of the Jews was to receive only vegetable offerings and incense. The satrap pledged his goodwill and received a handsome gift in return.

> Your servants—one named Yedaniah son of Gamariah, one named Mauzi son of Natan, one named Shemaiah son of Haggai, one named Hosea son of Jathom, one named Hosea son of Nattum: all told five persons, Syenians who are hereditary property owners in Elephantine the Fortress—say thus: If our lord . . . and our Temple of YHW be rebuilt in Elephantine the Fortress as it was formerly built—and sheep, ox, and goat are not used there as burnt-offering but they offer there only incense [and] meal-offering—and should the lord make a statement about this, then we shall give to the house of our lord silver . . . and a thousand artabas of bar-ley. (COWLEY, NO. 33; PORTEN-YARDENI, TEXTBOOK 1, A 4.10)

Arshama returned to Egypt at the beginning of 406 BCE. The order authorizing the reconstruction of the Elephantine sanctuary must have been issued that same year, thus bringing to a close the episode of the sack of the temple and its sequels. One year later, Amyrtaeus, the ex-chief of the rebels, ascended the throne of Egypt, inaugurating the Twenty-eighth Dynasty, of which he is the sole representative. His reign lasted until the year 399 BCE, a period of six years. Originally restricted to the Delta, it was subsequently extended to the southern borders of the country. We possess a contract, drawn up in Elephantine in the fifth year of the reign of King Amyrtaeus, June 400 BCE (Cowley, No. 35; Porten-Yardeni, *Textbook 2*, B 4.6), thus confirming this extension but also raising a question. Were the Jews, after having faithfully served the Saitic and the Persian rulers, obliged to obey, even for a short period, the leader of a rebellion which, ten years earlier, had brought about the destruction of their temple?

Several months later, at the end of 399, Amyrtaeus was dethroned by Nepherites, founder of the Twenty-ninth Dynasty. For some sixty years, the Persian yoke no longer weighed upon Egypt. The last of the documents from the Elephantine archives, a letter by a Jew named Shawa son of Zekhariah to his friend Yislah in Memphis (Kraeling, No. 13; Porten-Yardeni, *Textbook 1*, A 3.9), dates from this period. Employing a polite but not overly monotheistic turn of phrase, the writer expresses the wish that "all the gods" (!) endow his correspondent "with abundant welfare for all time," and then informs him of Nepherites' accession to the throne. During his reign, we lose track of the Jewish colonists in Elephantine. The renewal of Egyptian nationalism proved fatal for them. The temple, which seems to have been rebuilt at some date between 406 and 401 BCE, was to be destroyed a very few years later, once and for all. There was no longer a Jewish colony in Elephantine.

As for Egypt, the country was not to maintain its newfound independence for more than half a century. In 343 Artaxerxes III reestablished Persian hegemony. A dozen years later, in 332/331 BCE, the Persians gave way before the army of Alexander, king of the Macedonians, conqueror and liberator. Egypt came under the Greco-Macedonian rule. The newcomers reduced the native element to a subordinate role, which was to last for a thousand years. After the death of Alexander, his generals seized the reins of power in all the conquered territories. One of them, Ptolemy son of Lagus, became the satrap (governor) of Egypt. During an ephemeral co-regency, the conqueror's posthumous son by his marriage with the Iranian princess Roxana formally shared the royal power with Alexander's dim-witted half-brother Philip Arrhidaeus. In 305 BCE, after their disappearance, Ptolemy assumed the royal title, as did the other successors (the *diadochoi*) of Alexander, perpetuating his domination by founding a dynasty that was to reign over the country for some three centuries, until the arrival of the Romans in 30 BCE. The birth of the Ptolemaic monarchy set the stage for the next phase in the history of the Jews in Egypt.

THE ZENITH:
PTOLEMAIC EGYPT

Alexandrian Judaism and Its Problems

ALEXANDER AND THE JEWS

The victorious campaigns of Alexander the Great (336–323 BCE) marked a turning point in the fortunes of Egyptian Judaism, and in the relations between the Jews and the Greeks. A new era in the history of the Mediterranean region began when Greek rationalism encountered Jewish spirituality. Alexander's conquests laid down the boundaries of a universal empire. Although it did not long outlast the conqueror's death, it was to serve as a model for the Romans, who gave us the legal and institutional foundations on which our modern states are built. Rome held political sway, leaving the task of spiritual guidance to others. We are in some measure the heirs of the defunct Roman Empire, but we are all the spiritual descendants of the Greeks and the Jews. On the twin pillars of the Logos and the Torah, Rome constructed the framework of Western civilization, which Christianity was to complete.

To be sure, it was not the first time the paths of the Jews and the Greeks had crossed. Ever since Mycaenean times, there had been contacts between the Greek and Syro-Palestinian worlds. One striking example, although probably of an indirect contact, was the adoption by the Greeks, in the earliest days of the city-state, of a script modeled on a Northern Semitic syllabary. This script appears indeed to have been transmitted to the Greeks through the agency of one or several non-Greek peoples. In the course of its transfer, the use of certain consonants (aleph, he, vav, yod) as *matres lectionis* for the transcription of vowel sounds was systematized. The Greeks indisputably deserve the credit for bringing the task to completion, which is not, of course, tantamount to calling them the "inventors" of vowels. To speak of a "Greek miracle" in this respect would be a gross exaggeration.

Other, more direct, although sporadic contacts may have occurred elsewhere. We have already seen how, in the days of Solon and Psammetichus II, Greek soldiers in the service of the Egyptian kings were sent to Nubia as members of a "foreign legion," in which Judean soldiers may well have served. We have no reason to question the assertions of the *Letter of Aristeas* concerning their participation in the Nubian campaign.

Nilotic landscape   *Upper Egypt.*

Encounters between Jews and Greeks are conceivable in such a context, but their importance seems to have been limited.

With the coming of Alexander, everything changed. The Greeks discovered the Jews and the Jews bettered their scanty knowledge of the Greeks. The immediate consequences of this mutual discovery were not of equal importance for both sides. For the Greeks, encountering Jews was an amusing surprise. On the periphery of the vast Persian empire, yet to be conquered, in the midst of a mountainous and rather unprepossessing region, a small nation had been found who, curiously enough, practiced monotheism as an everyday religion. Monotheism was not unknown to the Greeks. On this subject, one might even call to mind a sort of chronological coincidence concerning the Greeks and the Jews. Toward the middle of the sixth century BCE, during the period when the great prophet of the Exile known as the Deutero-Isaiah launched a challenge to the idols, proclaiming that there is no god but the God of Israel, Xenophanes of Colophon engaged in monotheistic meditations; Aristotle later referred to him as he who "scrutinizing the heavens proclaimed that God is one." However, for a Greek, monotheism can only be the subject of philosophical speculation and not of religious practice, polytheistic by definition. Given an entire people practicing monotheism, simple logic demands that they be a "people of philosophers." About 315–314 BCE, this very expression was employed by Theophrastus of Eresus, Aristotle's disciple and successor, in a text transmitted by the neo-Platonist Porphyry (third century CE) and quoted by Eusebius of Caesarea (265–340 CE)—this is the first time Jews or Judaism are mentioned in a Greek text:

> And indeed, says Theophrastus, the Syrians, of whom the Jews constitute a part, also now sacrifice live victims according to their old mode of sacrifice; if one ordered us to sacrifice in the same way we would have recoiled from the entire business. For they do not feast on the sacrifices, but burning them whole at night and pouring on them honey and wine, they quickly destroy the offering, in order that the all-seeing sun should not look on the terrible thing. And they do it fasting on the intervening days. During this entire period, being philosophers by birth, they converse with each other about the deity, and at nighttime they make observations of the stars, gazing at them and calling on God by prayer. They were the first to institute sacrifices both of other living beings and of themselves; yet they did it by compulsion and not from eagerness for it. (THEOPHRASTUS, ON THE PIETY, IN PORPHYRY, ON ABSTINENCE, QUOTED BY EUSEBIUS OF CAESAREA, PRAEPARATIO EVANGELICA, 9, 2)

We have no idea where Theophrastus (or Porphyry?) sought out the strange details that grace this passage. Actually, he was not as interested in the Jews, on whom he bestowed, following the above-mentioned logic, the flattering title of "born philosophers" (*philosophoi to genos ontes*), as by the problem of sacrifice. This text fit into current discussions among the Greeks, concerning animal sacrifice. If Theophrastus looked with "horror" (*deinon*) upon animal sacrifice as practiced by the Jews, it was because he considered it a degenerate form of vegetable offering, for him the original form of sacrifice. His final remark on animal and human offerings should be seen in this light. Perhaps this is how he interpreted the story of Cain and Abel, of which he may have heard. Cain, seeing his first, vegetable, offering rejected by the Lord, decided to sacrifice his brother, since he himself possessed no animals. Thus, the historical sequence—plants, human victims, animal victims—found its justification. The paradox of a "people of philosophers" practicing animal sacrifice in the form of a whole-burnt offering (Greek holocaust)—a practice which Theophrastus condemned—was an excellent weapon in the verbal battle he was waging. Thus, from the outset, the discovery of the Jews by the Greeks was immediately inserted into an ideological context concerning, first and foremost, the Greeks and their problems. The Jews and their "philosophy" interested the Greeks only insofar as they could serve to illustrate a discussion within this context.

The image of the Jew in Greek thought underwent a development whose stages can be rapidly outlined. After the discovery of a "people of philosophers," the next step was the realization that Jews were not alone in "philosophizing beyond the Hellenic reaches."

In this respect, the Brahmans of India were to be considered their spiritual cousins. A third stage designated a common ancestry for Jews and Brahmans: the Magi. With the establishment of this genealogy, situating the Jewish people as a branch of the main trunk of oriental wisdom, the Greeks had, for the time being, settled the "Jewish problem." But when the "philosophers" began to demand their recognition as "citizens," difficulties were to arise, modifying the Greek image of the Jew. From fanciful but, on the whole, favorable beginnings, it suffered a progressive deterioration; we shall return to this topic. For the moment, the Jews were far from being an object of passionate study for the Greeks, who had better things to do. The fabled riches of the Persian empire awaited them, since the great expanses of the East, at that time, were open to Greco-Macedonian penetration. A new world was being born, of which the Jews and their "philosophy" were but a part, and a negligible one at that.

For the Jews, on the contrary, the discovery of the Greeks was an overwhelming experience: it was a case of love at first sight—an unrequited affection, as is so often the case in unhappy love affairs. The Jews rapidly adopted Hellenism, which, at that period, was synonymous with culture. Alexander ushered in the birth of a Hellenized Judaism, destined to have its brief hour of glory in Egypt under the Ptolemaic dynasty, to be followed by dark days of misfortune, shared with the rest of the Jewish people under Roman rule, during the first two centuries of the Christian era.

The memory of this crucial moment in the history of Judaism survives in Josephus' *Jewish Antiquities*. The time is 332 BCE. Two years have gone by since Alexander set out to conquer the Persian empire. The official objectives of the campaign were vengeance for the humiliation suffered by the Greeks during the Persian wars, and the liberation of the Greeks of Asia Minor. In fact, more prosaic motivations were equally if not primarily involved. As the orator Isocrates put it, the Persians were rich but weak, the Greeks poor but valiant: what could be simpler than to try to seize the Great King's empire and the treasures stored in his palaces?

Alexander commanded a fine army, composed of Macedonians and levies of conscripts from neighboring regions and the Greek cities, some 32,000 foot soldiers and 5,000 horsemen in all. He had already been twice victorious over Darius: on the shores of the river Granicus in May 334 and at Issos (today Iskenderun) in Cilicia, in November 333. Between these battles, he had spent some months in the Phrygian city of Gordium where, with one stroke of his sword, he severed the famed "Gordian knot," a heavy-handed manner of appropriating the benefits of an oracle promising the mastery of Asia to the person who could untie the knot. He then marched southwards along the Syrian coast. Most of the Phoenician cities—Tripolis, Arados, Byblos, Sidon—offered no resistance. There was one exception: Tyre, an ancient metropolis situated on an island two kilometers off the coast, had barred Alexander from entering the temple of Melkart, who had been assimilated to Heracles, the presumed ancestor of Alexander himself. The conqueror decided to lay siege to the place, a siege that lasted from January to August 332. According to Josephus, it was during this period that he first came into contact with the Jews.

> Alexander . . . became master of Sidon and besieged Tyre; from there he
> dispatched a letter to the high priest of the Jews, requesting him to send
> him assistance and supply his army with provisions and give him the gifts
> they had formerly sent as tribute to Darius, thus choosing the friendship of
> the Macedonians, for, he said, they would not regret this course. But the
> high priest replied to the bearers of the letter that he had given his oath to
> Darius not to take up arms against him, and said that he would never vio-
> late this oath so long as Darius remained alive. When Alexander heard
> this, he was roused to anger, and while deciding not to leave Tyre, which
> was on the point of being taken, threatened that when he had brought it
> to terms he would march against the high priest of the Jews and through
> him teach all men what people it was to whom they must keep their oaths.
> (JOSEPHUS, JEWISH ANTIQUITIES, ED. R. MARCUS, 11, 317–19)

The high priest Jaddus (his name is mentioned in the following passage) was confronted
with a difficult problem, one that would recur time and again in the history of the Jewish
people: where do the limits of loyalty lie? On the one hand, he wished to remain faithful
to Darius. Was he not the legitimate descendant of Cyrus, the "Messiah" who had freed
the Jews from their Babylonian captivity, and of Artaxerxes, who had allowed them to
restore an autonomous national entity centered on the Temple of Jerusalem, and guaranteed their freedom of worship? But what price should be paid to preserve this loyalty?
Alexander was not to be trifled with. The Thebans, who thought they could resist him,
had been taught a bitter lesson: their city was razed and its inhabitants exterminated or
sold as slaves. Should loyalty to the Persian ruler be allowed to endanger the newly reconstructed Temple, the Holy City of Jerusalem and its inhabitants?

For an instant, the resistance of Tyre gave the Jews a brief respite. But their situation became critical with the fall of the Phoenician metropolis and the capture of Gaza,
the last coastal city to hold out against Alexander. Following the Theban example, the
two cities were destroyed and their population massacred or sold into slavery. Jerusalem
awaited its turn. Only divine providence could save it now.

> Alexander, after taking Gaza, was in haste to go up to the city of
> Jerusalem. When the high priest Jaddus heard this, he was in an agony of
> fear, not knowing how he could meet the Macedonians, whose king was
> angered by his former disobedience. He therefore ordered the people to
> make supplication, and, offering sacrifice to God together with them, be-
> sought Him to shield the nation and deliver them from the dangers that
> were hanging over them. But, when he had gone to sleep after the sacri-
> fice, God spoke oracularly to him in his sleep, telling him to take courage
> and adorn the city with wreaths and open the gates and go out to meet
> them, and that the people should be in white garments, and he himself
> with the priests in the robes prescribed by law, and that they should not
> look to suffer any harm, for God was watching over them. (JOSEPHUS,
> JEWISH ANTIQUITIES, 11, 326–28)

Jaddus, reassured, obeyed the orders he had received. He did what he had been instructed to do and confidently awaited the victor's arrival.

> When he learned that Alexander was not far from the city, he went out with the priests and the body of citizens, and, making the reception sacred in character and different from that of other nations, met him at a certain place called Saphein. This name, translated into the Greek tongue, means "Lookout." For, as it happened, Jerusalem and the Temple could be seen from there [Mount Scopus, Heb. *Har ha-tzofim*]. Now the Phoenicians and the Chaldaeans who followed along privately believed that the king in his anger would naturally permit them to plunder the city and put the high priest to a shameful death, but the reverse of this happened.
>
> For when Alexander while still far off saw the multitude in white garments, the priests at their head clothed in linen, and the high priest in a robe of hyacinth-blue and gold, wearing on his head the mitre with the golden plate on it on which was inscribed the Name of God, he approached alone and prostrated himself before the Name and first greeted the high priest. Then all the Jews together greeted Alexander with one voice and surrounded him. (JOSEPHUS, JEWISH ANTIQUITIES, 11, 329–32)

Were the splendid trappings of the priests and the Divine Name, which Alexander would in any case hardly have been able to decipher, enough to bring about this sudden and beneficent metamorphosis? Alexander's friends did not understand what was happening; they thought that their commander had lost his wits. But he himself then provided the explanation for his actions.

> It was he whom I saw in my sleep dressed as he is now, when I was at Dion, in Macedonia, and, as I was considering with myself how I might become master of Asia, he urged me not to hesitate but to cross over confidently, for he himself would lead my army and give over to me the empire of the Persians. Since, therefore, I have beheld no one else in such robes, and on seeing him now I am reminded of the vision and the exhortation, I believe that I have made this expedition under divine guidance and that I shall defeat Darius and destroy the power of the Persians and succeed in carrying out all the things which I have in mind. (JOSEPHUS, JEWISH ANTIQUITIES, 11, 334–36)

Thus, thanks to two premonitory dreams, Jerusalem was spared. Darius was still alive, but the high priest was no longer bound by his oath. Alexander went up to the Temple and, following the high priest's instructions, offered a sacrifice to the God of the Jews. The Book of Daniel was brought before him, with its prediction that a Greek would come to destroy the Persian empire (in fact, this book was written much later, about 164 BCE). The next day, before the people and at the high priest's demand, Alexander granted the Jews the freedom to live according to their ancestral laws and exempted

Alexander as Pharaoh before the god Amon *Bas-relief, Temple of Luxor.*

them from paying the customary tribute every seventh year. The privilege of living according to their ancestral laws was also extended to the Babylonian Jews and those of Media. Many Jews accepted Alexander's proposal to enlist in his army. A Jewish legend would have it that the male children born during the year following his visit were named Alexander, as a token of gratitude. Hereditary transmission from grandfather to grandson finally transformed it into a "Jewish" name, as it remains today.

Before examining the political import of this episode, let us dwell an instant on its historicity, which, to tell the truth, is highly suspect. This text of Josephus should be compared with the relation of another visit Alexander made to a famous temple: his pilgrimage to the sanctuary of Amon in the oasis of Siwah in Libya.

This pilgrimage took place during the first part of the year 331 BCE. Alexander had just seized Egypt. He had already chosen the site and approved the plans for a new city, the first of a long series to bear his name: Alexandria. He was to proclaim its foundation on his return from the sanctuary. The road to the sanctuary led through a waterless wasteland, where the south wind blew the sand over his footprints. Heaven sent him a teeming rain and two serpents—in other versions, two crows—to show him the way. Arrian of Nicomedia, the author of a very sober history of Alexander written during the period of the Antonines (second century CE), commenting upon his predecessors' hesitations, notes: "he was helped by a god, that I can affirm" (3, 3, 6).

When he came to the sanctuary, he was greeted by the priests and admitted into the "holy of holies" (cella): a royal privilege bestowed upon the new successor to the Pharaohs. Words were exchanged there between the king and the high priest of Amon (the "prophet"). In the absence of eyewitnesses, the exact tenor of their conversation is unverifiable. The same Arrian of Nicomedia, who, as we have just seen, firmly believed in divine intervention on Alexander's behalf, is judiciously silent on this point. He simply states that "after having heard what his heart desired," Alexander returned to Egypt (3, 4, 5). Diodorus of Sicily (first century BCE), who follows Cleitarchus of Alexandria (end of the fourth century BCE), is more specific:

> When Alexander was conducted by the priests into the temple and had regarded the god for a while, the one who held the position of prophet, an elderly man, came to him and said:
>
> "Rejoice, son; take this form of address as from the god also."
>
> He replied: "I accept, father; for the future I shall be called thy son. But tell me if thou givest me the rule of the whole earth."
>
> The priest now entered the sacred enclosure and as the bearers now lifted the god and were moved according to certain prescribed sounds of the voice, the prophet cried that of a certainty the god had granted him his request. (DIODORUS OF SICILY, LIBRARY OF HISTORY, ED. C. B. WELLES, *17, 51, 1–2*)

Alexander, enchanted by the oracle, showered Amon with gifts and headed back to Egypt. After organizing the country's administration, he promptly set off on his campaign of conquest. Flying from one victory to another, "Amon's son" carved out of the ruins of the Achaemenid dominions, the universal empire he had been promised. The high priest of Amon confirmed this promise by an oracular rite. The ceremony habitually took place outside of the holy walls, but Cleitarchus, blending two distinct rituals into one, wrongly situated it within the sanctuary. This need hardly concern us here, for the significance of the episode lies in the fact that it may well have served as a model for Josephus' description. In the Egyptian version, as well, the account is focused on the promise of universal hegemony. *Mutatis mutandis*, there is a striking similarity in the details of confirmation, in each case: the meeting with a high priest, the miraculous events preceding it, the visit to a renowned sanctuary, the rewards bestowed upon the Jews as upon the Egyptians. The reference to the Book of Daniel could quite possibly pinpoint the time and place in which Josephus' legend assumed a literary form: the latter half of the second century BCE, among the Hellenized Jewish readers of the "Tale of Alexander." Alexandria and its Jewish intelligentsia immediately come to mind.

This literary kinship and the borrowing it suggests do not lessen the significance of the scene described in the *Jewish Antiquities*. After all, we have no reason to assert flatly that Alexander never set foot in Jerusalem. He could very well have sent one of his officers in his stead; legend would have identified the proxy with the principal. Without leaving his headquarters, he could have acknowledged the surrender of Jerusalem, frightened into submission, as other cities of Syria and Phoenicia had been, by the fate of Tyre. But the crux of the matter is elsewhere; the episode necessitates a double interpretation, political and ideological.

From a political viewpoint, it teaches us that conquered Judea retained the status it had under the Persian kings: an ethnic and religious entity organized around the Temple and subject to priestly rule. The conquest, however, transformed its mode of application. The Jews of Jerusalem and Judea, like those of the eastern diaspora, were permitted to live according to the precepts of the Torah. But the Torah was no longer an "imperial law" for the Jews, as it had been in Ezra's day; it now was their "ancestral law," confirmed by the conqueror. Alexander granted the Greek cities of Asia freed from Persian domination the privilege of "living according to their ancestral laws" (*chresthai tois patroois nomois*). He did as much for the Jews. A similar formulation, in conformity with the same Greek tradition, is to be found in the "Seleucid Charter" of Jerusalem, that we know of through Josephus (*Jewish Antiquities* 12, 138–44). Josephus simply attributed this initiative to Alexander, anticipating by some 130 years the step actually taken by Antiochus III about 200 BCE, when he established the status of Jerusalem in the Seleucid empire.

On the ideological plane, Josephus' account of the episode of Alexander's visit to Jerusalem is to be interpreted as the expression of a political platform of cooperation and mutual understanding. A pagan sovereign, dispenser of privileges, agrees to respect and protect Jewish Law, receiving in exchange the dignified submission of his Jewish subjects and their loyal services as soldiers or government officials: an ideal definition of the relations between the Jews and the Hellenistic kings. The march of history was to fulfill this program only imperfectly, with several slips occurring along the way.

CAN ONE BE BOTH JEWISH AND GREEK?

The Jewish encounter with the Greeks produced a cultural shock of great proportions and incalculable consequences, which left its mark on Jewish daily life. In the following chapters, we shall endeavor to explore these various forms of acculturation and gauge their depth. As a general rule, one finds that adhesion to Greek cultural norms was fully compatible with fidelity to the principles of Judaism. In specific borderline cases, however, especially at the summit of the social pyramid, religious ties were occasionally strained beyond the breaking point. In the first century CE, Tiberius Julius Alexander, a scion of a noted Jewish family of Alexandria who made a brilliant career in the service of the Roman Empire, affords an example, which we shall examine in a later chapter. He had an illustrious predecessor in the third century BCE in the person of Dositheos son of Drimylos, an Alexandrian Jew who renounced his religion in order to attain the highest ranks in the Alexandrian royal court. It will prove interesting to compare the life of this courtier with that of an intellectual, the chronographer Demetrios, another Alexandrian Jew contemporary with the former but who, unlike him, remained faithful to the religion of his ancestors; his effort to conciliate his Judaism with Greek rationalism stands out in contrast to Dositheos' apostasy, thus bringing into sharp focus the question, of paramount importance for Jews in Hellenistic Alexandria: how to be both Jewish and Greek?

The Third Book of Maccabees, with which we shall be dealing later, begins with an account of a conspiracy against Ptolemy IV Philopator on the eve of the battle of Raphia (modern Rafah), in 217 BCE. One Theodotos, a disgruntled general, had enlisted the services of some trusted soldiers in an attempt to assassinate the king. The plot was foiled at the very last minute by a certain Dositheos son of Drimylos, "born a Jew but who had renounced his ancestral faith." Just before the arrival of the treacherous general and his henchmen, Dositheos spirited the monarch away from his tent, substituting a lesser mortal to be killed in the sovereign's stead.

Modern critics have considered this passage to be of doubtful authenticity; for them, the personage described in the Third Book of Maccabees was a fictitious one, modeled on the Book of Esther, in which Mordecai, with the help of Esther, saves the life of Ahasuerus by denouncing a plot to assassinate him. Dositheos would thus be a figment of the author's imagination; the name itself had been borrowed from a Jewish general who had served under Ptolemy VI Philometor. At the time of the battle of Raphia, there would have been no dignitary named Dositheos in Egyptian court circles.

A half-dozen Greek papyri and a demotic document invalidate this belief. Modern criticism was in error. A Dositheos son of Drimylos well and truly existed. He had climbed to the topmost ranks in the Ptolemaic court under Ptolemy III Euergetes I, the father of Philopator. Dositheos is rather a common name for an Egyptian Jew; Drimylos is much rarer. The concurrence of names and dates, as well as the course of his career, pleads in favor of the identification of this personage with that of the Third Book of Maccabees.

Our first piece of evidence is a letter from the dossier called the "Zenon Archive," the papers of a Greek from Caria (Asia Minor) who managed the estate of a fellow countryman, Apollonios, royal minister under Ptolemy II Philadelphus and Ptolemy III Euergetes. The document is to be dated March 240 BCE.

> Philon to Zenon greeting. If you yourself and those whom you wish to be so are in good health, it would be well. I too am keeping well. Please make a serious effort to settle the matter about which my brother Ptolemaios has sailed up to see you, in order that he may return to me quickly and that I shall not be prevented from sailing up if I need to; for I must be off from here shortly. I wrote to you once before about Hermokrates, as I had heard that you were exerting yourself to help him, and had myself informed him of this, and I really think that he will be set free in a few days. Several other people put themselves to trouble on his behalf, but the most effective was Kaphisophon son of Philippos the physician. The written report of the inquiry, which acquits him of all charges, is already in the hands of Dositheos the hypomnematographos in order that the king may read it before letting him be released, as this is the regular procedure. For the rest be prepared to receive a visit shortly. And of things at home, even if it troubles you to keep watch on my place.
> To Zenon, Philadelphia. (PAPYRUS MICHIGAN ZENON 55; CPJUD. I 127A)

Hermokrates had run into trouble and been imprisoned. He had himself advised Zenon of his plight in a separate letter. Zenon, who had spent several years in Alexandria in the service of Apollonios, had kept up his relations with influential people in the capital and could thus be of use in the present case. The affair was serious, probably involving embezzlement. The case had been brought before the royal court, and a decision had been taken in favor of the accused. Hermokrates certainly had personal contacts in high circles, since several influential persons had already intervened in his behalf during the inquiry (*anakrisis*). The "chief prosecutor" had done his job and passed the dossier on to Dositheos the *hypomnematographos* (the "grand archivist," literally: "memorandum-writer"), one of the two secretaries of the king, the other being the "grand chancellor." Dositheos had the file in his possession and was preparing to bring it before the king. The object of all these interventions was not to obtain clemency from the monarch but to hasten the dossier along, in its long journey from desk to official desk, Dositheos' being the last lap before it reached the king, whose approval was necessary for the release of the prisoner.

In his role of royal secretary, Dositheos appears again in another document, doubtless from the same period. This time, an inheritance was the subject of dispute:

> To King Ptolemy from Diodoros, greeting. I am being wronged by Damasippa who lives in Oxyrhyncha in the division of Polemon. I had obtained an order from Dositheos concerning the possessions of Diogenes

son of Rhodokles, a relative of mine, since his belongings descended to me according to the law; and he had a *thesmophorion* of Demeter in Dikaiou Kome, and likewise another in Oxyrhyncha. But Damasippa, who claims to be a relative [of Diogenes, has requested] a division of the effects connected with the inheritance, while I was in Alexandria, [and has acquired possession of the shrine] in Dikaiou Kome.

[Endorsed] "Diodoros against Damasippa about an inheritance." (PAPYRUS ENTEUXEIS 19; CPJUD. I 127B)

Although the last part of the papyrus is badly preserved, its import is clear. Diodoros claims to have inherited from Diogenes, a relative, two *thesmophoria*, shrines of Demeter (these must have been private sanctuaries, since they are part of a succession). A woman named Damasippa, claiming to be also a relative of Diogenes, had taken advantage of the absence of the rightful heir to usurp a part of his inheritance. He promptly lodged a complaint. What is especially interesting here is the fact that the legal successor could

The port of Alexandria *Painting from Gragnano (after J. Kolendo; Naples, National Museum).*

only obtain his due by a decree (*prostagma*) issued by the royal chancellery. This was the case, not because an intestate succession was involved, but because it included places of worship which, although private property, fell under the control of the state. The decree had been issued by Dositheos, so well known in Alexandria that to mention his title would have been superfluous. There can be no doubt that we are dealing here with the all-powerful royal secretary, the hypomnematographos Dositheos son of Drimylos.

He turns up again in company of King Ptolemy III, during a visit to the Faiyum. Preparations were being made to receive the sovereign and his suite with the proper pomp. One Herakleides had written to the banker Kleitarchos:

> Herakleides to Kleitarchos, greeting. Please send 5 fatted geese for Dositheos' visit with the king.
> [Verso:] Year 23, Phamenoth 6. Herakleides about contributions to be sent. To Kleitarchos. (PAPYRUS GRADENWITZ 2; CPJUD. I 127C)

The date corresponds to April 21, 224 BCE. Here again, Dositheos appears as a famous figure, so well known that it would have been superfluous to specify his rank. His presence at the king's side was enough to identify him as the *hypomnematographos* of Zenon's letter. It was not at all impossible for him to have also been a ship owner. This is suggested by a document from the time of Ptolemy III, which should be added to the dossier that Alexander Fuks had once assembled. We are dealing with certificates issued for river transport toward Alexandria.

> Klearchos, supercargo and guard, which we discharged at the Sarapeum in Rhakotis. Berenike's barge, carrying capacity 200, Herakleides master on board of Dositheos and Dionysios, carrying capacity 200, Achileus pilot on board. Discharge at the garden of Simaristos. (PAPYRUS RYLANDS IV 576)

The word here translated as "barge" is *phaselion,* a diminutive of *phaselos,* a kind of bean (fesole), a term employed by Horace and Catullus in this sense. The Berenike of our papyrus was at first identified as Queen Berenice, daughter of Magas and spouse of King Ptolemy III. During this period, members of the royal family frequently owned riverboats. However, one must remember that the queen's ships were always designated by the queen's title, *basilissa,* without mention of any name. A more likely candidate would be one of the ladies of the royal court: during the last third of the third century BCE, there were a half-dozen priestesses (*kanephoroi*) of Arsinoe Philadelphus who bore the name Berenike. One should likewise search among the courtiers to find the owners of the second ship, a kerkyroskaphe (from *kerkyros,* light boat, and *skaphos,* "hull of a ship"), which probably sailed under the orders of the same "master on board." Dionysios might have been the father of the Alexandrian bearing this same name, who appears in the year 188/187 BCE on a proxeny list discovered at Delphi. This is, of course, pure hypothesis, but Dositheos the secretary to the king is a much more serious candidate for the part-ownership of the barge.

The appearance of priestesses in the royal cult brings us to the final stages and the crowning achievement of Dositheos' career: in the twenty-fifth year of the reign of Ptolemy III Euergetes I, 223/222 BCE, Dositheos became an eponymous priest of the cult of Alexander and the deified Ptolemies. Today we possess three documents attesting this promotion, two Greek and one demotic. The first of these is the beginning of a lease of land registered in January–February 222 BCE in a village of the Oxyrhynchite nome.

> In the twenty-fifth year of the reign of Ptolemy son of Ptolemy and Arsinoe the gods Adelphoi, when Dositheos son of Drimylos was priest of Alexander and the gods Adelphoi and the gods Euergetai, the kanephoros of Arsinoe Philadelphus being Berenike daughter of Pythangelos, in the month Gorpiaios, at Tholthis in the Oxyrhynchite nome. (*Hibeh Papyrus I 90; CPJud. I 127e*)

Was the priestess Berenike the owner of the bean-barge mentioned above? Perhaps, but this is secondary. What counts is what we have learned about Dositheos son of Drimylos, eponymous priest.

The office of eponymous priest was one of the highest honors attainable in the service of the king. It was established about the year 290 BCE by Ptolemy I Soter, in honor of Alexander the Great. The first upon whom it was conferred was the king's own brother, Menelaus son of Lagus. The cult of Alexander was soon to be enlarged to include that of the deified Ptolemaic couples. To begin, there were the "Brother-and-Sister gods" (*Adelphoi*, Ptolemy II, and Arsinoe II, his sister and spouse) and the "Benefactor gods" (*Euergetai*, Ptolemy III, and Berenice II); Ptolemy IV Philopator established the precedence of the first royal couple, the "Savior gods" (*Soteres*). The list grew with the subsequent addition of the "Father-loving gods" (*Philopatores*, Ptolemy IV, and Arsinoe III), the "Manifest gods" (*Epiphaneis*, Ptolemy V, and Cleopatra I, daughter of Antiochus III), and the "Mother-loving gods" (*Philometores*, Ptolemy VI, and Cleopatra II). After the death of Arsinoe Philadelphus, sister and spouse of Ptolemy II, in July 270 BCE, a new priestess, *kanephoros* ("she who bears the basket"), was designated and regularly mentioned in dating formulae, along with the priest. About 211/210 BCE a second priestess was adjoined, the *athlophoros* ("she who carries the prize") of Berenice Euergetis, in honor of Queen Berenice II. This latter office was instituted by the son of Berenice, Ptolemy IV, perhaps in expiation of her assassination, carried out at his instigation.

The Ptolemaic eponymous priesthood was a purely Greek office; no Egyptian name figures among the priests and priestesses who succeeded one another in Alexandria. However, a Hellenized Jew who, in the course of his career, had risen in the ranks of the king's service could perfectly well aspire to this privilege. As far as the Greeks were concerned, there was no problem, no obligation to be converted; the very idea of conversion to paganism is anachronistic in the context of the third century BCE. From the

Jewish point of view there is, on the contrary, a total incompatibility between fidelity to Judaism and the holding of priestly office in a non-Jewish religion. Consequently, for the author of the Third Book of Maccabees, Dositheos, a "Jew by birth" (*to genos Ioudaios*), was a renegade: "he has changed his religion and renounced the faith of his fathers" (*ton patrion dogmaton apellotriomenos*).

If we grant that all the texts quoted above deal with the same person, then the work of the late lamented Israeli scholar Alexander Fuks can help us to retrace the steps of his career. Born somewhere between 270 and 265 BCE, Dositheos rose rapidly in the hierarchy of the royal court, where, by 240 at the latest, he acceded to the office of hypomnematographos, "Grand Archivist to the King," under Ptolemy III Euergetes I. In the spring of 224 he was still a member of the royal entourage and toured the Faiyum with the king. Along with other courtiers, he was also engaged in river transportation. One year later, in 233/232, he was promoted to the highest Alexandrian dignity, the eponymous priesthood of Alexander and the deified Ptolemies. After the death of Ptolemy III at the end of 222, he served his son and successor, Ptolemy IV Philopator, whose life he saved during the battle of Raphia in June 217. We do not know how his own life ended.

A splendid career. But the author of the Third Book of Maccabees, a fervent Jew, was not especially proud of his compatriot. In his view, renegades deserved nothing but death. He made mention of Dositheos, since he was exploiting a literary source which referred to him. The plot against the life of Ptolemy Philopator has every aspect of a historical fact. Polybius (5, 81) knew of it but attributed its authorship to an Aetolian from the Seleucid camp, while our author leaves us with the impression that it was an internal conspiracy. Did Polybius use less reliable source material than the author of the Third Book of Maccabees? Let us simply state that the episode of the death plot and the role of Dositheos lend this work an element of historical authenticity. In due time, we shall bring this up again.

Our anonymous author, who frowned upon the career of Dositheos, would surely have approved the efforts of another Alexandrian, the chronographer Demetrios, representative of a totally different Judeo-Alexandrian lifestyle: culturally Greek but Jewish at heart. It was not an easy task in the third century BCE.

To our knowledge, Demetrios was the first Jewish historian to write in Greek. He lived during the reign of Ptolemy IV Philopator (222–205 BCE). The latter part of the third century brought hard times to the Jews. The Third Book of Maccabees places the first conflict between the royal government and the Jewish community in Philopator's reign; only by a last-minute miracle was the community saved from extermination. Was Demetrios one of those who were spared? It is hard to say, not only because of doubts concerning the historicity and the dating of this event, but also because we know practically nothing of the man himself. All we know is that he wrote a work *On the Kings of Judea*, an eye-catching title, perhaps contrived to justify the placing of a history of the Jewish people on the bookshelves next to the works (lost to posterity) containing the history of the Hellenistic monarchs. In fact, the six fragments that have come down to us seem to foreshadow Josephus' *Jewish Antiquities*, employing the method the celebrated historian was to adopt three centuries later.

These fragments of biblical history, "translated and improved" by Demetrios the Alexandrian, are quite strange. Demetrios is reputed to have been the first Jewish author to engage in historical criticism. All well and good. But there is more to the picture: the idea that the credibility of a people's history could best be guaranteed by its antiquity was very much in the air in those days. The very credibility of Jewish history, as recorded in the biblical writings, was thus in question. Demetrios had become involved in the contest of "intellectuals" playing the game of "the older the better." To win the race, it was obviously necessary to know one's starting point. And here other difficulties arose.

If one started counting from the First Olympiad (776 BCE), one would soon be beaten by the Orientals, whose pyramids and holy books are so ancient that they correspond to the Greek mythological epoch, before the beginning of history proper. Some Greeks rose to the challenge and tried to raise the stakes by rationalizing mythology, in an effort to construct a scientific pre-history for their culture, which would place it at least on an equal footing with oriental antiquity. In the third century BCE, the anonymous author of the Parian Chronicle managed, by dint of acrobatic calculations, to place the reign of Cecrops, first—and legendary—king of Athens, in the sixteenth century BCE. A wasted effort. The Egyptian priests had no trouble proving that their history was older than that of the Greeks. If necessary, they would not balk at considering Homer or Thales as profoundly indebted to the wise men of Egypt. Berossus, a Babylonian who wrote in Greek, followed in their footsteps: since the antediluvian Oannes, half-man, half-fish, a Babylonian like the author, had instructed mankind in the arts and sciences, there was nothing left for the Greeks to invent.

As this game was obviously over before it could begin, the Greeks renounced competing on these terms. The superiority of their culture was not to be sought in its antiquity. They relegated the uncertainties of a too-distant past to the unverifiable domain of myth. "I write what appears to me to be true," declares Hecataeus of Miletus, around 500 BCE, adding, "the fables the Greeks bandy about among themselves are nothing but idle fancies." Much later, Josephus, that fervent admirer of the Torah, would invoke the frivolous diversity of the Greeks concerning their proper origins, as opposed to the implacable unicity of Jewish tradition. For this reason, and because of its great antiquity, he preferred Jewish history to Greek.

Josephus followed along the route that his Alexandrian predecessor had marked out three centuries earlier. Demetrios, whose mind was Greek but whose heart had remained faithful to the Jewish religion, was faced with a dilemma. Unlike his Greek intellectual guides, he was not free to detach the smallest parcel of Jewish history from its parent body. There is nothing "holy" in Greek history, nothing remotely comparable to the sacred history of the Jews, under whose crushing weight Demetrios was obliged to labor.

As an Alexandrian scholar and man of letters, he should have consigned a large part of this history to some mythological closet. As a Jew, he had to accept it in its entirety: there is no place for mythology in the Torah!

This, then, was his dilemma: how could a Jew be modern while remaining true to his origins? Could he integrate inherited traditional values into the culture that has formed his thinking, a culture that derides them as mythological and puerile? Demetrios was to find a solution in the works of Eratosthenes of Cyrene, head librarian of the Alexandrian Library under Ptolemy III, and guardian of the king's son, the future Philopator. This scholar, who knew that the world was round and had measured the length of the terrestrial circumference, was the inventor of mathematical chronology; his writings in this field had brought a measure of order into Greek historiography. Demetrios was obviously his disciple, had studied his works and adopted his methods.

With immense courage, Demetrios undertook the impossible task of recounting the sacred history of the Jews as if it were a true story. Assuredly, his was not the first attempt to rationalize the history of Israel: the author of the unit formed by Chronicles and the Books of Ezra and Nehemiah had already taken a few steps in this direction. Demetrios, however, carried this tendency to its very limits, guided by what he took to be the ultimate in scientific perfection: the language of numbers. This is his interpretation of the passage in Genesis (29:31–30:24), which treats the posterity of Jacob.

> Demetrios says that Jacob was seventy-five [read: seventy-seven?] years old when he fled to Haran in Mesopotamia. He was sent by his parents because of the hidden resentment Esau had for his brother (this because his father had bestowed the blessing upon him thinking he was Esau) and so that he might obtain a wife while there. Thus Jacob set out for Haran in Mesopotamia, leaving behind his father Isaac who was 137 years old, whereas he himself was seventy-seven years old.
>
> Thus, after he had spent seven years there, he married Leia [Leah] and Rachel, the two daughters of Laban, his maternal uncle. At that time he was eighty-four years old. Now in the next seven years twelve children were born to him: in the eighth year and tenth month, Rubi [Reuben]; and in the ninth year and eighth month Simeon; and in the tenth year and sixth month Levi; in the eleventh year and fourth month Juda [Judah]. Now because Rachel was not bearing children, she became jealous of her sister and made her own handmaid Zelpha [Zilpah] lie with Jacob. This was at the time that Balla [Bilhah] also became pregnant with Nephtali [Naphtali], that is, in the eleventh year and fifth month, and in the twelfth year and second month she gave birth to a son whom Leia named Gad. And in the same year and twelfth month by the same woman he fathered another son, Aser [Asher], who was also named by Leia.
>
> And Leia, in return for the fruit of the mandrakes that Roubel [Reuben] brought unto Rachel, once again became pregnant at the same time as her

handmaid Zelpha, that is, in the twelfth year and third month; and, in the
same year and twelfth month she gave birth to a son and gave him the
name Issakhar. And once more Leia, in the thirteenth year and the tenth
month, gave birth to another son whose name was Zabulon [Zebulun]; and
in the fourteenth year and eighth month the same Leia gave birth to a
son by the name of Dan. At the same time that Rachel became pregnant,
Leia also gave birth to a daughter Deina [Dinah]. And in the fourteenth
year and eighth month Rachel gave birth to a son who was named Joseph.
Thus it is seen how in the seven years spent with Laban twelve children
were born. (Eusebius, Praeparatio Evangelica, 9:21, 1–6)

Demetrios follows the biblical text of the Septuagint: this was seemingly the first time
the Alexandrian version of the Torah, then only a half-century old, was exploited by an
author writing in Greek. The spelling of proper names is that of the Septuagint: Leia for
Leah, Zelpha for Zilpah, Balla for Bilhah, etc. Some obvious alterations due to faulty
transmission of the text may easily be rectified: Zilpah is Leah's maidservant and not
Rachel's; Dan is the son of Bilhah and not of Leah. But a minute scrutiny of the biblical text, in Hebrew or in Greek, would not reveal the slightest trace of the profusion of
dates and figures that fill his narrative. Modern scholars sometimes amuse themselves by
checking out their internal logic, correcting them if necessary. The entire work bears
this stamp. How could Moses have espoused Zipporah over a gap of three generations?
How many years elapsed from the time of Adam to the entry of Joseph's kin into Egypt?
From the flood to Jacob's arrival in Egypt? From Abraham to Jacob? The numerical an-
swers to these questions aroused emotional responses in Demetrios' breast. To the contrary, the sacrifice of Isaac or Jacob's struggle with God leaves him cold; he relates these
events in an appallingly arid manner. The rape of Dinah and its subsequent revenge, that
typically Mediterranean drama which, when we read it today, can still make the hair on
our necks stand on end, is reduced, in Demetrios' rendering, to a matter of figures: Dinah
was sixteen years and four months old when she was ravished by Shechem.

Frankly speaking, the "royal history" of the Jewish people, as recounted by Demetrios,
is a royal bore. He puts us to sleep with his dates and figures. He probably thought them
necessary if he were to be taken seriously. Who, one might well ask, would dare put
into question the authenticity of a historical account couched in the bloodless language
of a statistical report, that supreme form of the academic discourse?

Were he alive today, Demetrios would be able to set up a computerized data bank of
biblical history. His efforts to use reputedly modern methods would certainly have earned
him substantial academic support. Did he enjoy a similar success in Alexandria—for example, membership in the Alexandrian Museum and the personal congratulations of
King Philopator, miraculously reconciled with the Jews, as we shall see, after the miracle at the hippodrome? History is silent on this point.

As a representative of Alexandrian erudition, Demetrios has his place in Greek literature; as a chronographer, he belongs to the Jewish tradition. Although he hardly

could have imagined it, he might well be a pretender to the title of founder or, at least, precursor of traditional Jewish chronology. Three centuries later, the Seder Olam Rabbah, the basis for all subsequent rabbinical computations, was to adopt this very same method. Insofar as the Greek reader was concerned, Demetrios had labored in vain. His scientific interpretation of the Torah interested the Greeks as little as did the Torah itself; in this respect his exploit was completely illusory, a perfect example of one of those "intermediary expectations" (as Yosef Yerushalmi put it) Jews periodically place in the societies and the cultures that have welcomed them, and to which they have adhered, throughout the long trek of their history.

A Love Story

The career of Dositheos son of Drimylos embodied a radical choice: that of a Jew who renounced Judaism in order to become completely Greek, whereas Demetrios attempted to create a kind of Judeo-Hellenistic alloy, through an intellectual effort of a high order. A third configuration, the opposite of the first, may well be imagined: the accession of a pagan to Judaism. The story of a well-known and likable couple, Joseph and Asenath, offers a moving illustration of the latter case. Like Demetrios' work, this story is part of the larger body of Judeo-Alexandrian literature, Greek in language and cultural background, but Jewish in content and moral purpose. We shall not here attempt a detailed analysis of this literary corpus, but merely sketch its outlines, in order to place the novel in its proper perspective.

Judeo-Alexandrian literature began with an astonishing masterpiece: the translation of the Torah into Greek, followed by the Prophets and the Writings, the whole of which has come down to us under the name of the Septuagint. Above and beyond its religious and philological importance, the work raises many subtle questions for the historian, concerning the motives for its creation, and the real place of the Greek Torah in the institutional context of the Ptolemaic monarchy. We shall devote a chapter of the present volume to these problems.

Two works stem directly from the Greek version of the Torah. The first, known as the *Letter of Aristeas to Philocrates*, is a fictional account of the translation. Its author was a Jew for whom, in the words of Victor Tcherikover, "Judaism was nothing but Hellenism enriched by the idea of a unique God." He was a great admirer of the Torah in Greek, whose perfect conformity with the exigencies of Alexandrian philology lent it, in his eyes, a certain superiority to the Hebrew original. Much ink has been spilt over the question of the date when the Letter was completed. The proposed "window" begins with the reign of Ptolemy IV Philopator (222–205 BCE) and ends with that of Titus (79–81 CE). Scholars today seem to favor a period during the second part of the reign of Ptolemy VIII Euergetes II (ca. 146–116 BCE). Opinions also differ widely as to its original purpose. They range from that of an "editorial" advocating the propagation of the Septuagint (or of a revised version of the Septuagint)—a work intended to accredit the Torah in Greek in the eyes of the Jewish community in Alexandria—to that of a "diary of a trip to Jerusalem" by an Egyptian Jew.

For the author of the *Letter to Aristeas*, the initiative of this translation was to be credited to Ptolemy II, a thesis that, as we shall see, a comparison with the demotic Case Book tends to corroborate. The idea of a royal initiative for the Greek Torah had another noteworthy proponent in the philosopher Aristoboulos, whose *Explanations of the Mosaic Writ* was dedicated to Ptolemy VI Philometor. The monarch was then apparently the sole occupant of the throne, thus enabling us to place the work between 176 and 170 BCE. Curiously enough, in his enthusiasm for the Law of Moses, Aristoboulos did not hesitate to affirm that Pythagoras and Plato were already conversant with it; logically, this would imply the existence of a Greek translation, or a least a partial one, prior to the Septuagint. Modern critics tend to raise an eyebrow at this piece of news, which they attribute to the ambition of the Jewish establishment in Alexandria to place a Jewish source at the fountainhead of Greek literature. A papyrus from Oxyrhynchos (XLI 2944) should lead us to temper this hypercritical point of view. It does not, of course, confirm the chimerical idea of Plato or Pythagoras as admiring readers of the Torah of Moses. It does at least suggest that some biblical themes—in the present case, the famous scene of the Judgment of Solomon, as recounted in the First Book of Kings (3:16–28)—were known to the Greeks prior to the death of Plato. Aristoboulos was not lying, he just exaggerated a bit.

Judeo-Alexandrian writers had also explored other paths. We have just seen a historian at work, in the person of Demetrios the chronographer. In the second century BCE, another Jewish author, who bore the Persian name of Artapanos, wrote a sort of historical novel in which Joseph and Moses appear as the "prime inventors," the instructors of the pagans in the arts of astronomy and agriculture, as well as in philosophy and religion. Moses, rather unexpectedly, here becomes the founder of Egyptian zoolatry. In the realm of poetry, Ezekiel (not to be confused with the prophet!) must be mentioned. Taking Aeschylus and Euripides as models, he cast the Exodus from Egypt in the mold of a Greek tragedy, which quite possibly may have been acted out before a Jewish audience in Alexandria—and elsewhere. Another poet, Philo (not to be confused with the philosopher!), sang the praises of the Sacred City of Jerusalem in archaic hexameters.

Judeo-Alexandrian philosophy reached its culminating point in the work of Philo, a sublime attempt to achieve a synthesis between Platonic idealism and biblical spirituality. We shall meet Philo later, in the role of a Jewish notable from Alexandria, at the head of a deputation to Rome. We shall also have occasion to examine a curious work already mentioned, the Third Book of Maccabees, a pathetic account of an incident presented by the author as the first serious conflict between the Jews and the Ptolemaic monarchy. One should not forget the Judeo-Egyptian elements in the third book of the Sibylline Oracles, whose oldest passages go back to the middle of the second century BCE. This book was to earn a lasting popularity, thanks to its happy mixture of Homeric form and Apocalyptic contents. We shall end our list (which might easily be lengthened) with the Wisdom of Solomon, set down in Egypt, presumably toward the end of the first century BCE, a splendid example of a particular sort of Jewish mysticism that had flowered among the Hellenized Jews of Alexandria, and certainly the finest gem in the crown of this literary corpus.

Some problems arise concerning these works. Generally speaking, should we class all of Judeo-Alexandrian writing under the traditional heading of "apologetic" or "missionary" literature, intended to justify Judaism and propagate its principles among pagan neighbors? This would amount to taking the whole for one of its parts. Certain works, specifically conceived for the non-Jewish reader, such as *Against Flaccus* or the *Embassy to Gaius*, were of unmistakably apologetic tenor, but the rest of Philo's writings, and all those written before him in Greek by Egyptian Jews could very well have been destined exclusively for the Jewish reading public.

Victor Tcherikover, in defending the latter thesis, took what may appear to be an extreme stance. But the problem is not an easy one. Did men like Demetrios the historian or Aristoboulos the philosopher primarily address a Greek public, in an attempt to counter the myth of the "people of philosophers"? Or did they wish to reassure their Hellenized Jewish compatriots of the superiority of their own tradition to the wisdom of the Greeks? In recounting the history of the Greek translation of the Torah, why did its Jewish author resort to the transparent fiction of one Greek (Aristeas) addressing another (Philocrates)? Was it to reach a pagan readership, or to convince fellow Jews that the prestige of the Torah was so great that the Greeks themselves could not help but admire it? Before speaking of "double talk," one must attempt to answer these probably insoluble questions.

We can be certain of one thing (and this tends to reinforce Tcherikover's thesis): the signal lack of interest on the part of the Greek and pagan literati for Judeo-Alexandrian writings. This is manifest for the Torah, first of all, which was available in Greek as early as the second quarter of the third century BCE. The Ptolemaic administration was aware of the Torah as a legal document, regulating the Jewish "civic law," but it made practically no impression on Greek literature as such. The "biblical echoes" in authors such as Callimachus or Theocritus are purely imaginary. It is not easy to prove that Ocellus Lucanus, a second-century BCE Pythagorician, read Genesis in Greek. One must wait for the first century CE before coming upon the first uncontested reference to the Bible in Greek in a non-Christian Greek text: an allusion to Genesis in the treatise *On the Sublime*, attributed to the neoplatonic writer Longinus. In its turn, rabbinical Judaism was not very appreciative of these Jewish books in Greek, beginning with the Septuagint, which had, in the meantime, become the Bible of the Christians. Judeo-Hellenistic literature fell almost into oblivion.

Among the books that survived, the story of Joseph and Asenath is a very special case. Its anonymous author was most probably a Hellenized Jew, a fervent reader of the Septuagint. Marc Philonenko, to whom we owe the most recent French edition of the work, notes that it can be classed with equal ease either in the pseudepigraphical literature of the Old Testament or in a body of Greek novels. This scholar describes it as a "mystical novel written in Greek, during the Roman period, by a Jew of Egyptian origin." An earlier date has also been envisaged: if we place it, not at the beginning of the Roman Empire, but at the end of the second century BCE, we could then attribute the authorship of the oldest Greek novel—the first novel in Western literature—to an Egyptian Jew.

In ancient and in medieval times, it was exceedingly popular, appearing under various titles, the prettiest (and the most complete) of which is "Life and confession of Asenath daughter of Pentephres, priest of Heliopolis, and how Joseph the admirably handsome took her for wife…" There are two variants of the original Greek text, a long and a short one. It has been translated into Latin (abridged medieval version), Syriac (sixth century), Armenian (similar to the Greek text, but longer; some forty-odd manuscripts, from the thirteenth to the nineteenth centuries), Slavonic (fifteenth century), Romanian, Neo-Hellenic, Anglo-Saxon, Ethiopian, and Arabic (the latter two versions are no longer available).

The story has its origin in two brief passages from Genesis. The first (Gen. 41:45) informs us that Pharaoh had offered Joseph a wife: Asenath daughter of Poti-phera (Pentephres in the novel), priest of On (the Egyptian name of Heliopolis). In Genesis 41:50–52, we learn that two sons, Manasseh and Ephraim, were born of this marriage. But how could the handsome Joseph marry a pagan woman? For the biblical Joseph, the question was meaningless. Since he lived before the Torah had been given to the Jews, neither the warning in Exodus (34:16) nor the prohibition in Deuteronomy (7:3–4) could possibly have concerned him. Moreover, neither proscription applied directly to Egyptian women. The biblical Joseph was even less worried about the laws broadening the hostile attitude toward intermarriage that Ezra, in a far-distant future, was to promulgate (Nehemiah 10:31).

This was not at all the case for our fictional Joseph, who had been transported into the universe of Hellenized Judaism, the world of the author and the readers of his novel. Marc Philonenko remarks that "the problem can only arise within the framework of Judaism and is really important only for the Jewish diaspora of Egypt." One can readily subscribe to his conclusion. To see why, let us examine the book.

During the first of the seven plentiful years, Joseph had been sent by Pharaoh to gather up all the wheat in the country. On his route lay Heliopolis, the "City of the Sun," birthplace of the doctrines that underlay the heresy of Akhenaton (Amenophis IV) in the fourteenth century BCE. The Greeks had a high opinion of the science and the wisdom of the priests at Heliopolis, so "well-versed in celestial lore." The story leads us to the home of one of these priests, Pentephres, father of the eighteen-year old Asenath. The author stresses the girl's non-Egyptian features, reminiscent of Hebrew canons of beauty. All the well-born Egyptian youths, including the son of Pharaoh, aspired to wed her.

Et les autres xij chaumbres estoient a
vij vierges qui seruoient asseneth et
estoient tres belles. et lome nauoit o
ques parle a elles ne enfant masle⸱⸱⸱
En la chaumbre asseneth estoient iij
fenestres. la premiere tres grant par
tieners orient. La seconde deuers midi
et la tierce uers aquilon. et en celle chā
bre estoit vn lit dore couuert de draps
de pourpre tissus a or et a iacinctes
et la dormoit asseneth seule. ne on
ques lome nauoit sis sus ce lit⸱ Et
entour celle maison auoit vn grāt
estre clos de tres hault mur. Et en cel
estre auoit iiij portes de fer. et a chas
cune porte gardez auoit xviij hōmes
tres fors et iennes et bien armez⸱ et
en la dextre partie de cel estre estoit vne
fontaine viue⸱ Et apres la fontaine
vne citerne qui receuoit liaue et ar
rousoit tous les arbres qui estoient
plantez en lestre qui estoient biaus
et portans fruit. Et asseneth estoit
grant cōme sarre⸱ graceuse cōme
rebecque⸱ et bele cōme rachel⸱

Dieu enuoia vn message a
putiphar que il vouloit aler
en sa maison⸱ et il en ot grāt
ioie⸱ et dist a sa fille ioseph fort
de dieu doit venir a ci te vn
cil tonent ahm pour feme⸱ et
elle en ot despit et dist⸱ Je ne
vueil pas estre feme dun chetif
mais de fil de roy⸱ Et sicomme ils par
loient vn message vint qui dist⸱ vez
ci ioseph⸱ et asseneth sen fui en sa
tour haulte⸱ Et ioseph vint seant
en vn char qui fu a pharaon et estoit
dore et le trainoient iiij cheuaux tot
blans cōme noif en farine et en her
nois dorez⸱ Et ioseph estoit vestu du
ne cote blanche tres resplendissant
et vn mantel de pourpre tissus dor
et auoit vne couronne doree sus son
chief⸱ et en celle couronne estoient
douze tres fines pierres esleues⸱ et
sus ces pierres auoit xij estoilles dor
Et tenoit en sa main verge royal a
nam doune tres plain de fruit⸱ et pu
tiphar et sa feme vindrent alencōtre

Ci deuise lystoire cōment ioseph reprist
asseneth mourir les ydoles⸱ Et cō
ment il parla ali apres son pere⸱ et
cōment elle voult baisier ioseph p̄
le cōmandement de son pere⸱ et ioseph
le refusa⸱

et la couurirent⸱ Et entra ioseph en les
tre et les huis furent clous⸱ Et quāt
asseneth le vit de sa tour si fu trop
esmerueillee de la parolle que elle a
uoit dite de lui⸱ Et dist vez ci le soleil
qui est venu du ciel a nous en son

Joseph and Asenath *Vincent de Beauvais, Miroir Historial, 13th century* CE *(Paris, National Library).*

But Asenath disdained their courtship. She had little choice in the matter, as she lived a cloistered life, locked in a tower surrounded by a great courtyard, next to her father's house. She could not have actually seen many young men, other than the eight sentinels who guarded the four gates of the house, and passersby, whom she glimpsed from the window of one of her rooms. Asenath lived in a ten-room apartment on the highest floor of her tower. In the first, three-windowed room were the gold and silver idols to whom she made sacrifices, pious pagan that she was. The second room contained her wardrobe; the third, her treasures. The seven remaining rooms housed her seven serving-women, virgins as beautiful as stars, all born the same night as their mistress.

Joseph arrives, amid great pomp. The parents of Asenath seize the opportunity to marry off their daughter to this handsome young man who had obtained the King's trust. Joseph would make an ideal match, and the fact that he was Jewish did not seem to matter to them. Asenath was not of this opinion, however. If she had been obliged to choose among her official suitors, she would have preferred the son of Pharaoh, and spoke of the "shepherd's son from Canaan" with disdain. But when, from one of her windows, she laid eyes upon Joseph in his fine raiment, seated on a chariot drawn by four white horses, she abruptly changed her mind. It was a case of love at first sight; she was filled with remorse at having heretofore disdained this young lord. Thenceforth she had but one desire: to be his servant forever.

Her parent's joy can well be imagined. But it was to be short-lived. Pentephres invites Asenath to greet his guest. Joseph politely greets the daughter of his host. He would like to have her as his "sister"; marrying a heathen was, for him, out of the question. What an insult and what a deception for poor Asenath! In utter distress, she ran back up to her rooms. But she would not give up Joseph. She preferred to renounce her idolatry. Too late, at least for the moment, for Joseph had already taken his leave. He was to return in a week's time, an interminable period of agony for the young girl, who wept, clothed herself in black, and covered her head with ashes. She flung her rich vestments out the window, and her idols followed, shattered into a thousand fragments.

Asenath recovered on the eighth day, stretched out her hands to the east, looked up at heaven, and confessed her sins to God in a moving prayer. And lo, a miracle occurred. The morning star rose in the east, the heavens opened and a young man clothed in light descended, a young man resembling Joseph, but more luminous: he was the commander of the army of the Lord. He told Asenath to bathe her face and to put on a spotless dress. She returned before him, a bright sash girding her loins and her head covered with a veil. The angel instructs her to remove the veil. The Lord has hearkened unto her prayer. Henceforth Asenath will be "renewed," she will eat the bread of life, she will drink the cup of immortality and will be anointed with the unction of incorruptibility. She shall no longer be called Asenath, but "City of Refuge." The angel will tell all to Joseph, whom she will espouse. Asenath may already dress herself in her wedding garment. A honeycomb appears; the angel gives a morsel to Asenath that she may eat. Out of the honeycomb comes a swarm of bees, surrounding Asenath. The angel kills off the bees who wanted to sting the girl, then resuscitates them. He then has the honeycomb consumed by fire. At Asenath's request, he blesses the seven serving girls, before disappearing.

A servant comes to announce the arrival of Joseph, who has returned. Asenath goes into her room to clothe herself in her most beautiful garments. Joseph enters the house of Pentephres. Asenath comes to bathe his feet. Her father doubtless wished to celebrate the marriage as soon as possible. But Joseph, loyal minister to His Majesty, insisted on obtaining her hand from the king himself. The next day, they both appear before the Pharaoh, who gives them his benediction and orders the marriage to take place. Mazal tov! Congratulations! Joseph and Asenath lived happily ever after and their union was blessed by two children who would, one day, represent the "house of Joseph" among the heads of the twelve tribes of Israel.

Joseph's spouse was thus converted or, more properly, "initiated" into Judaism under mysterious and romantic circumstances. The Alexandrian Jewish readers of Joseph and Asenath did not think of Asenath as an Egyptian girl, as modern commentators would have us believe. The author had taken great pains to remind us that Asenath did not resemble Egyptian girls. The honeycomb associated with her conversion could certainly be attributed to the Egyptian goddess Neith; it could also, and more reasonably, be interpreted as a reference to the Greek religion, in which honey is often symbolically associated with rites of birth and death. Does Asenath not reawaken to a new life through her conversion to Judaism? But, even more than the symbolism of the story, social considerations offer a key for the interpretation of the book.

A mixed marriage between a Jew and an Egyptian woman was, of course, not totally unthinkable, but very difficult to imagine in view of the documentary evidence now available. Marriages between "Hellenes"—under which heading the Jews fell—and native Egyptians were a very rare occurrence in Hellenistic Egypt. Not that they were forbidden by law, as was marriage with foreigners in Athens at the epoch of the orators (fourth century BCE), but because a kind of "cultural agamy" rendered them impracticable. Actual practice was a far cry from the intermixing of populations that the erstwhile partisans of an integrated Greco-Egyptian civilization had been wont to imagine.

Exceptionally, in certain circles and at certain times, the barriers were lifted. At Pathyris, in Upper Egypt, during the second century BCE, Greek soldiers and the higher strata of the local population lived in close contact. A new sort of military organization drew equally upon Hellenes and the Egyptian elite. An excellent example is furnished by the family of Dryton son of Pamphilos, of Cretan origin and citizen of Ptolemais. Indigenous notables, officers and high priests, espoused the daughters of "Cretan" and "Cyrenean" settlers in Egypt. One could conceive of a Jew marrying the daughter of an Egyptian priest. The novel of Joseph and Asenath, however, does not have Pathyris for background. The problem the Jews of Egypt had to solve was not the avoidance—or the acceptance—of family alliances with Egyptian notables; they had to find a way to reconcile their friendship with their fellow Greeks and their desire to preserve their proper identity, which mixed marriages could jeopardize.

The question was a very serious one, to which no clear answer seems yet to have been given, either in practice or in theory. To say the least, one has that feeling on comparing Philo's vigor in defending the prohibition of mixed marriages (*On the Special Laws*, 3, 29) with his apology for matrimonial ecumenism, which he simultaneously recommends (3, 25). The author of Joseph and Asenath set forth a simple and optimistic solution: the son of the Jew marries the daughter of the Greek, but she first espouses the ancestral faith of her husband. It was only in the second century BCE, after the process of conversion to Judaism had been "invented," that this solution could become common practice. Beneath its fictional surface, was the novel not a kind of celebration of the much-desired wedding between Judaism and Greek culture?

Rabbinical Judaism was to give its own answer to the question. It can be found in the thirty-eighth chapter of the Pirke de-Rabbi Eliezer (Extracts from R. Eliezer), a Midrashic work, probably written during the eighth century CE, but placed under the authority of a famous tanna (sage of the Mishnah) of the second generation (ca. 80–110 CE), Eliezer ben Hyrcanus: Asenath was not the daughter of a heathen priest, but the child of Jacob's daughter Dinah, who had been raped by Shechem son of Hamor the Hivite. The Bible recounts only how Simeon and Levi revenged their dishonored sister (Gen. 34:25–29). The Midrash prolongs the biblical account: Dinah, pregnant by Shechem, gave birth to a baby girl that an eagle (or the archangel Michael) immediately transported to Egypt and deposited on the Heliopolitan altar. The priest Poti-phera, the Pentephres of the novel, and his wife took in the child and reared it as their own daughter. We know the rest.

In that version, Joseph and Asenath conform to the principles of rabbinical Judaism: one cannot convert to the Mosaic faith for the love of a man or a woman! In some older Midrashim, more inclined to proselytism, Asenath is still the natural daughter of Poti-phera. But in the version attributed to R. Eliezer, Joseph marries his own niece, Jacob's granddaughter, the fruit of rape but Jewish nonetheless because she was born of a Jewish mother. Before he was massacred by Dinah's brothers, Shechem had been circumcised, along with his father and all the male members of his tribe: he could thus pass for a Jewish father. But what counted for the compiler of the Pirke de-Rabbi Eliezer was, evidently, the Jewishness of the mother. Between Alexandria and the Midrash, the Mishnah had instituted the strict rule of maternal filiation. Gone forever were the days of love matches with converted heathens; gone too, the marriage between Judaism and Hellenism. Times had changed. The Alexandrian solution had been censored.

CHAPTER 4 ✑

A New Diaspora

AMONG THE "HELLENES"

The co-existence of Jews and Greeks was a complex phenomenon. The "parallel lives" of Dositheos son of Drymilos and Demetrios the chronographer afforded us a glimpse into its manifestations among the higher reaches of Alexandrian society: the "intellectuals" and the entourage of the king. The love story between Joseph and Asenath offered a further illustration in a fictional transposition centered on the difficult problem of mixed marriages. Thanks to the documentary evidence of the papyri and inscriptions, we can now examine the various aspects of this phenomenon in the daily life of Ptolemaic society.

The Macedonian conquest opened the floodgates of a new Jewish immigration to Egypt. According to Josephus, and to older accounts he ascribes to Hecataeus of Abdera, Jewish and Samaritan soldiers served in the ranks of Alexander's armies, in Babylon as well as Egypt. In the third century BCE, there were no barriers at all between Egypt and Palestine; the latter was an integral part of the Ptolemaic Empire from 302 to 198, thus greatly facilitating Jewish immigration to Alexandria and towns of the chora, the "countryside."

What were their numbers? The figures quoted in the *Letter of Aristeas* (§ 13) are subject to caution: 100,000 Jewish prisoners deported to Egypt, among whom Ptolemy I chose 30,000 elite troops to settle in his kingdom. As a fraction of the total population of Palestine, which was, doubtless, no greater than that of the State of Israel today, this figure seems exaggerated. Philo also exaggerated, and in greater measure, when he spoke of one million Jews in Alexandria by the first century CE (*Against Flaccus*, 43). This would represent about two-thirds of all Greek-speaking settlers in Egypt, of whom only a small fraction were Jews. For this reason, we prefer the recent assessment of Diana Delia: about 180,000 Jews, roughly a third of the 500,000–600,000 inhabitants of Alexandria.

Josephus' figures (*The Jewish War*, 2, 385) appear more credible than those of Philo: he estimated the entire population of Roman Egypt at 7.5 million inhabitants, a number that took into account only the chora, and not the city of Alexandria. Adding half a million more for the capital, we get a grand total of approximately 8 million people, 6.5 million of whom were native Egyptians and 1.5 million were Greek-speaking immigrants. The Jews could have represented about 4 percent of the total, somewhat more than 300,000 persons, over half of whom lived in Alexandria. This proportion represents three times the Jewish percentage of the total population of France today and is remarkably close to the percentage of Jews in the United States.

The former, Aramaic-speaking diaspora had not entirely disappeared. Nothing more had ever been heard from the Elephantine colony since the beginning of the fourth century BCE; the Jewish garrison must have been replaced by other, non-Jewish elements. But the descendants of Yedaniah son of Gamariah and his fellow soldiers might well have prospered in the land of Egypt up to and beyond the Macedonian conquest, "recycling" themselves as civilians if necessary. Toward the turn of the fourth/third century, in an Egypt that Alexander had just conquered, a Jewish merchant, 'Abihi, and his partner Jonathan were running a flourishing business. An Aramaic papyrus containing one of 'Abihi's memorandums has come down to us; goods and payments appear alternately, and not in parallel columns, as they would in modern accounting. We shall leave the study of comparative bookkeeping methods to the specialists, and devote our attention to the list of clients and their names. Here are some extracts of the register:

RECTO, COL. 1

[In flagon(s) of] fours/fourths in our presence:

Khelal [?]: 1 ka at 1 shekel, 2 quarters; 1 shekel remains [to be paid].

Nikias/Nikaios: 6 logs at 3 q[uarters]; 1 m[aah and a] h[alf] remain [to be paid].

[Entry] Nikias/Nikaios: 6 logs at 3 q[uarters]; 1 q[uarter] remains [to be paid].

Apollonios [son of] Jason: 1 ka [and a] h[alf] at 2 sh[ekels], 1 q[uarter].

Y[o]naya: 4 logs at 2 q[uarters].

Y[o]naya: 1 [+] 1 [= 2] logs at 1 q[uarter].

[Entry] Nikias/Nikaios: 6 logs at 3 q[uarters].

I: 2 logs.

Natan [son of] Nadb[a]i: 1 log at 1 m[aah and a] h[alf].

Y[o]naya: 3 logs at 1 q[uarter], 1 m[aah and a] h[alf].

[Entry] Nikias/Nikaios: 6 logs at 3 q[uarters].

Y[o]naya: 1 + [x] logs.

COL. 2

Nabis: 6 logs at 3 q[uarters].

Y[o]naya: 4 logs at 2 q[uarters].

[Entry] Nikias/Nikaios: 6 logs at 3 q[uarters] ; 2 q[uarters] remain [to be paid].

Yehudah: 2 logs at 1 q[uarter] [corrected from 2 q(uarters)].

[Entry] Nikias/Nikaios: 1 log [at] 1 m[aah and a] h[alf].

Y[o]naya: 2 logs at 1 q[uarter].

Y[o]naya: 1 ka [and a] h[alf] at [1 +] 1 [= 2] [she(ekels)], 1 q[uarter].

In flagon[s] of fives/fifths:

Isidoros [?]: 2 logs at 1 q[uarter].

Pyrrhos/Poros: 1 ka at 1 sh[ekel], 2 q[uarters].

Herakleides: half [a ka] at 3 q[uarters].

Lysimachos: 7 logs at 3 q[uarters], 1 m[aah and a] h[alf].

Kestos/Kostas [?] : 6 logs at 3 q[uarters].

PN: 5 logs at 2 q[uarters], 1 m[aah and a] h[alf] [corrected from 4 logs at 2 q(uarters)].

Abieti [son of] Netina: 2 q[uarters].

COL. 3.

Abieti [son of] Netina: 3 q[uarters] [whole line erased].

Isidoros: 4 logs at 2 q[uarters].

Y[o]naya: 6 logs at 3 q[uarters].

Bacchios: 9 logs 1 sh[ekel], 1 m[aah and a] h[alf].

Y[o]naya: 2 logs at 1 q[uarter].

Yehudah: 5 logs at 2 q[uarters] 1 m[aah and a] h[alf].

[corrected from 3 logs at 1 q[uarter], 1 m[aah and a h(alf)].

Y[o]naya: 3 logs at 1 q[uarter] 1 m[aah and a] h[alf].

Rehabel: 1 log at 1 m[aah and a] h[alf].

'Abdi [son of] PN: 4 log[s] at 2 q[uarters].

VERSO, COL. 7

Account of the grain which I wrote [and] gave to 'Ab[i]hi:

Shelamzi[o]n from the aftergrowth of Zebadiah, wheat: 1 s[eah] 1 q[uarter].

Shabbetit daughter of [G]abri, wheat: 1 s[eah] 8 q[abs and a] h[alf].

Arsinoe daughter of Y[o]hanan, wheat, 22 a[rtabes].

[Entry] Arsinoe, barley: 15 [+] 1 [= 16] a[rtabes], [2 +] 4 [= 6] q[abs].

PN daughter of wheat . . . mine: 19.

From Y[o]hanan [son of] Y[o]ezer: 3 flagons; [from Yohanan the priest:] 1 flagon.

[vacat]

From Shabbetai [son of] Yashib: 2 flagons; from Natn[a]i: 1 flagon.

From Haggai [son of] Diaphoros/Dipyros: 2 flagons.

Tasa daughter of Hanniah son of Kese: 3 a[rtabes] superior [wheat]." (Cowley, No. 81; Porten-Yardeni, Textbook 3, C 3.28)

Let us set aside logs and flagons to glance at the names. What a mixture of Jewish, Greek and Egyptian! Jewish names predominate: 'Abdi, the hypocoristic (diminutive) form of 'Abadiah ("Servant of the Lord"); 'Abih(a)i ("My Father lives"); Haggai ("Born on a holiday"); Natan, Netina, and Natnai, short forms of Yehonatan ("God-given"); Nadbai, short form for Nadabiah ("Devoted to the Lord"); Shabbetai and Shabbetit ("Born on a Sabbath day"); Shim'on, hypocoristic form of Shama'iah ("The Lord has heard"); Yashib ("May God bring back!"); Yehudah ("Praise to the Lord"), or Judah, the name of the fourth son of Jacob; Yohanan ("The Lord has favored"), John in English; Yonaia ("The Ionian" or "The Greek"), an ethnic appellation employed as a proper name in Aramaic; Shelamzion ("Peace of Zion," Selampsious or Selampsione in its Greek variants); Zebadiah ("The Lord has gratified").

Several Greek names appear: Apollonios ("From Apollo") and his father Jason (phonetic equivalent of Joshua); Bacchios ("From Bacchus"); Diaphoros ("The Distinguished"); Isidoros ("Gift of Isis"); Kestos (certainly not "Kostas," in common use today, but impossible to account for during the period in question); Lysimachos ("Who causes the combat to cease"); Nikias ("The Victorious"); Poros ("The Passenger") or Pyrrhos ("The Redhead"); Herakleides ("Descendant of Heracles"), as well as Nabis, the name of a renowned Spartan king, and Arsinoe, that of famous queens. Few Egyptian names are listed; we may note in passing the feminine name of Tasa ("The Guardian") rendered in Greek as Tase, Tases, Tasis (Thasis), and Thaseus. Rehabel ("El has set free") could be either Jewish or Phoenician.

Some cases call for closer scrutiny. That of Yohanan, a Jew who named his daughter Arsinoe in honor of the queen, is quite simple. But did the Jew Hanniah son of Kese give the Egyptian name of Tasa to his daughter because she was born to his Egyptian wife? This "abnormal filiation," to use a term familiar to papyrologists, would indicate a mixed marriage. In Elephantine, as we have seen, mixed marriages endangered neither the religious integrity nor the demographic equilibrium of the Jewish community. The novel of Joseph and Asenath highlights the problem of the mixed marriage, as one aspect of the general problem of Judeo-Greek relations in Hellenistic times. Since the Greek sources from that period are silent concerning marriage between Jews and native Egyptians, the case of Hanniah father of Tasa and his supposedly Egyptian wife would represent a very interesting exception in this regard.

The next case of "abnormal filiation" is also rather strange. Did Diaphoros, a Greek, marry a Jewess and give his son the Jewish name of Haggai? Or are we dealing here with a Jew bearing a Greek name (a sign of early Hellenization), perhaps one of Alexander's soldiers, who had settled in Egypt and, upon the birth of his son, reverted to traditional onomastic practice?

The last person to be mentioned here is Apollonios son of Jason. He might have been simply a Greek, with a Greek name and a Greek patronymic. But if we assume that he was Jewish, his case would represent a very rapid progress of the Hellenizing trends in Jewish onomastics: Jason, a Jew who was one of the first to Hellenize his Hebrew name Yehoshua (Joshua), did not hesitate to give his son a purely Greek name referring to a heathen divinity. We shall soon meet a group of Jews who bore names derived from Apollo. Apollonios son of Jason may have been one of them.

The checkered character of Egyptian society in the wake of the Macedonian conquest is mirrored in the register of 'Abihi. While 'Abihi was busying himself with his accounting, or some years before, a marriage took place in Elephantine between Herakleides, a Greek of Temnos, and Demetria, a young girl from the island of Cos. The witnesses to the ceremony came from Temnos and Cos, of course, but there were also witnesses from Cyrene and from far-distant Sicily (Elephantine Papyrus 1; July-August 310 BCE). Among the Greek-speaking immigrants, a process of intermixing had begun: far from blending into a "mixed" Greco-Egyptian civilization, Ptolemaic society was rapidly becoming polarized in an antagonistic opposition of the conquering Greek speakers to the conquered Egyptians. The great majority of Jews found themselves on the conquerors' side of the fence.

One of the first symptoms of this new cultural allegiance was the replacement of Aramaic by Greek, as the daily language of the Jews. Aramaic did not disappear completely from Egypt but, in the few known cases of its use, Jews were no longer necessarily implicated. Thus, a batch of Aramaic ostraca from Hermopolis published in 1966 does not refer to Jewish immigrants, but to colonists of Syrian or Mesopotamian origin. From Ptolemaic times until the Early Roman Empire, we have only three or four Aramaic texts dealing with Jews and Judaism in Egypt. They do not weigh heavily in the balance, compared to the 500 or so Greek documents related to the Jewish diaspora. This quantitative disproportion is, perhaps, not too meaningful. One should not forget that most of the latter documents bear upon dealings between Jews and Greek officials. Private letters by Jews in Greek are most rare; it is conceivable that Aramaic was still in use here and there, if not in the documents that have come down to us. Even if this were true, it would not invalidate the undeniable triumph of Greek.

The rapidity and the thoroughness of the transformation are attested by the inscriptions of the Alexandrian cemeteries at Chatby and El-Ibrahimiya, on the coast, east of the ancient promontory of Lochias, near the Jewish quarter. They date from the reigns of Ptolemy I Soter and his son Ptolemy II Philadelphus, in the first part of the third century BCE. These military cemeteries were not an exclusively Jewish burial place; they contained the remains of Athenians (such as a certain Archestratos), Achaeans, Arcadians, Thessalians, Megarians, and Cretans, one and all mercenaries in the service of the Ptolemies. One of the earliest tombs has been dubbed "the tomb of the soldiers"; save one, the names graven on the tombstones are those of Galatian mercenaries.

The Jewish inscriptions of Greco-Roman Egypt, first collected by J. B. Frey in the second volume of his *Corpus Inscriptionum Judaicarum* (CIJ II), are now available in an excellent English edition due to William Horbury and David Noy; here and later, we shall refer to both collections. The first inscription to be cited (CIJ II, No. 1424; Horbury-Noy, No. 3) is couched in Aramaic; it bears the name of "Akabiah son of Elioenai." Akabiah is a theophoric (God-bearing) name, from the root *'qb*, "to keep," "to grasp," "to retain" (as in Yaakov, Jacob): "the Lord has kept." The patronymic, Elioenai, literally "Toward the Lord my eyes do turn," is a name that often occurs in the Bible and other Jewish texts. Akabiah son of Elioenai, perhaps a man of priestly descent, must have been a brand-new immigrant, still faithful to the onomastic customs of his ancestors.

On the second epitaph, also in Aramaic (CIJ II, No. 1425; Horbury-Noy, No. 4), the beginning of a date can be distinguished: "the tenth day" (month and year unknown), and the beginning of a name, of which only four letters subsist: aleph, pe, lamed, vav, leaving us to choose between Apollo(nios) and Apollo(doros) or Apollo(dotos). Greek papyri from Egypt mention several Jews named Apollonios. One appears in a loan contract from Krokodilopolis in 182 BCE (we shall soon make this person's acquaintance) and another, also called Jonathas, is mentioned in the will of a Cyrenean, Philon son of Herakleides, likewise drawn up in Krokodilopolis in 238/237 BCE. Two Ptolemaic tax-farmers, Apollonios son of Dositheos, in Edfu (CPJud. I 70–72; 114), and Ap(ollonios?) son of Sollaios or Salamis (CPJud. I 67 and 68), might be regarded as Jews. A certain Apollonios son of Philippos, indubitably Jewish (*Ioudaios*), is to be found in a recently (1991) published lease contract concluded in Samaria (Faiyum) in 232 BCE (*Corpus Papyrorum Raineri* XVIII, 7). We may add to our list the name of Apollonios (transcribed *'plnys*, without vav) son of Jason in the Aramaic accounts of 'Abihi quoted above, assuming that he was a Jew, and not one of the Greek clients of 'Abihi. The Acts of the Apostles (18:24–28) mention a certain Apollos (a diminutive of Apollonios), a converted Alexandrian Jew who had made some trouble for Paul of Tarsus. Our epitaph, contemporary with 'Abihi's register, completes our miniature roster of Egyptian Jews with names derived from a famous heathen deity. Apollo(doros) and Apollo(dotos) are not to be excluded, if we consider these compound names as illustrative of a tendency to give an authentically Greek cast to the Hebrew "God-given," Yehonatan, Natanael or Matatyahu, rendered elsewhere by Theodotos, Theodoros, or Dositheos.

A third and last inscription, quite legible, bears traces of Aramaic letters (*dmtr* = Demetrios?) and numerals (CIJ II, No. 1426; Horbury-Noy, No. 5). The inscriptions on all the other Jewish tombs are written in Greek. We find one Iosepos, deceased at the age of thirty-four (CIJ II, No. 1427; Horbury-Noy, No. 1); one Philon, son of a man with the equine name of Hipp(olytos), Hipp(ostratos) or Hipp(odamos), deceased at

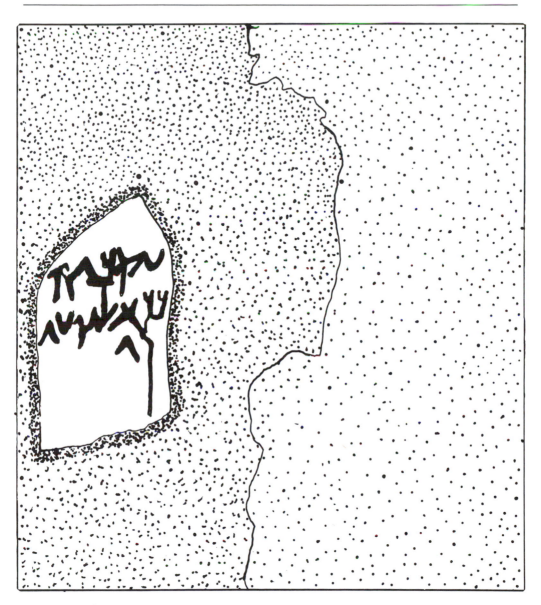

Akabiah son of Elioenai *Jewish tomb from the Alexandrian cemetery of El-Ibrahimiya, 3rd century* BCE *(Alexandria, Greco-Roman Museum).*

the age of fifty (CIJ II, No. 1428; Horbury-Noy, No. 2); one Psyllas, of whom we know nothing (CIJ II, No. 1431; Horbury-Noy, No. 8); and two women: Simotera daughter of Heliodoros, a Jewish woman of Sidon (CIJ II, No. 1430; Horbury-Noy, No. 7), and a certain Ioanna Euphrosyne (CIJ II, No. 1429; Horbury-Noy, No. 6). This latter is a interesting case of double name, presenting perhaps an clumsy attempt of onomastic doubling: the Grecianized Hebrew name Yohanna, a feminine form of the widespread Y(eh)ohanan ("The Lord has favored"), is accompanied by what intended to be its semantic equivalent in Greek, Euphrosyne ("Mirth" or "Joy," "The Merry" or "The Joyful"). As Horbury and Noy remark, the biblical association of *euphrosyne* with redemption could support the possibility of an intentional correspondence between Greek "Joy" and the Hebrew name suggesting the thought of divine "Grace"; their conclusion is however that "probably this double name is one of the majority which have no inner link of meaning."

These documents are typical examples of the prevailing onomastic tendencies among the Jews of Egypt. Hebrew names were retained, but in a Hellenized form: Abramis instead of Abraham, Josepos instead of Yoseph, Iakoubis or Iakoubos instead of Yaakov. These alternate with Greek names, some of which, as Ptolemaios or Arsinoe, expressed devotion to the royal family. Jews had no qualms about giving their offspring the name of a heathen hero or god, such as Herakleides (Heracles) or Demetrios (Demeter). Others found ways to compromise by means of semantic equivalence or phonetic assimilation, turning Itzhak ("He laughs") into Gelasios ("The Laugher"), and Yehoshua into Jason. Greek influence is manifest everywhere.

The adoption by the Jews of the Greek language and culture was a symptom of their absorption into the society of the conquerors. The Jews in Egypt belonged to the community of the dominant group of Greek-speaking immigrants, the "Hellenes." This sense of unity was not a Hellenistic invention. Scattered as they were over vast expanses of territory divided into many regions with innumerable cities, the Greeks, from their very beginnings, considered themselves members of one ethnic, cultural and religious whole. And the great intermixing that took place in Alexander's armies strengthened these ties. A new closeness became manifest with the emergence of a "common language" (*koine dialexis*, or simply koine) derived from Attic Ionian. Henceforth, throughout the monarchies born of Alexander's conquests, from the cataracts of the Nile to Macedonia and from Syria to Libya, whatever the origin of the speaker, he spoke the same language.

We have just mentioned the earliest Greek document from Egypt, preserved in a papyrus from Elephantine: the marriage contract of a young man of Temnos and a young girl from Cos, drawn up in 310 BCE. Thirteen years had barely elapsed since the death of the conqueror, yet one could search this document in vain for the slightest trace of the Aeolic dialect spoken in Temnos, a Greek city in Asia Minor, or the Doric dialect spoken on the island of Cos. It was couched entirely in koine. The dialects had begun to disappear, and would henceforth only subsist in vestigial form (Tsakonian, in the

Peloponnese, even in our day), and in poetical convention. Everywhere else, from great literature to the humble document, the triumph of the common language was complete.

Mastery of the Greek tongue and adherence to Greek culture were, however, insufficient in themselves to qualify a person as a "Hellene." Some Egyptians, especially those who wished to make their career in the Ptolemaic administration, took the trouble to learn Greek. To no avail. They remained Egyptians, natives of such-and-such a village, simple subjects of the Ptolemies. On the contrary, the Hellenes regarded themselves as "citizens." As such, they enjoyed the privileges of the dominant minority, with a civic or a quasi-civic status. This point is of prime importance in our present perspective.

The Hellenistic monarchy did not replace the Greek city, but was superimposed on it. Political power was vested in the king, but the city subsisted as an actual or ideal framework, without which no Greek could lead a full life. Within the boundaries of their kingdoms, the rulers respected and protected the traditional notion of citizenship; thus, the three Greek cities of Alexandria, Naucratis, and Ptolemais, in Egypt, housed citizens in the ancient Greek sense of the term. Nevertheless, a great many Greek-speaking immigrants lived in the countryside or, more precisely, in the great provincial townships. Despite their urban aspect and their names, which often contained the term *polis*, the towns did not possess the legal status of a polis, the traditional Greek city-state. The desire of their Greek inhabitants to be "citizens" could, however, be fulfilled within the institutional framework provided by the cultural unity of the Greek universe in the Hellenistic period.

The Greek concept of citizenship was flexible enough to include Greek immigrants living outside the Greek city. In order to retain his status of "citizen," an immigrant settled in the Egyptian chora had only to prove his "foreign," non-Egyptian origin: one's place of birth was an essential element of one's identity. Even after several generations had gone by, the descendants of the Athenian or Cretan immigrants to Egypt were still "Athenians" or "Cretans" by hereditary right, transmitted from father to son. They were "Hellenes," the equals of the citizens of Alexandria or Ptolemais.

The status of Hellene applied not only to those who had immigrated from an authentic city or federation of cities, like Athens or Crete, but also to a great mass of individuals from the northern and northwestern regions of the Greek-speaking world, whose social organization was foreign to that of the city-state. These included regions once considered barbaric, now Hellenized and integrated into the Greek cultural sphere, such as Thrace and, of course, Macedonia, home of the royal family and many of the Ptolemaic elite. In Ptolemaic Egypt, the Macedonians and Thracians were "Hellenes," like their Thessalian, Magnetian, Beotian, or Acarnanian counterparts. And one should not forget the Aetolians, whom Thucydides suspected of eating their meat raw like veritable savages, and whose idiom—a Greek dialect!—he dubbed "absolutely unintelligible." The qualification of "Hellene" was extended to the peoples of Asiatic and Semitic origin from the countries conquered by Alexander, as long as they could speak Greek and were willing servants of the royal dynasty.

In this manner, the Hellenistic monarchy promoted the cultural unity of the Greeks to the level of an institution, generously extending its meaning to heretofore unknown dimensions. Freed of its ancient limits that, during the classical era, had subordinated individual liberties to the interests of the civic body, the community of Hellenes suscitated new solidarities, born of neighborliness and comradeship-in-arms, which were superimposed upon the particularisms of the antique national traditions. Everyone was free to practice the worship and follow the customs of his ancestors. A Hellene's origin could not be a cause for discrimination.

This state of affairs suited the Jews perfectly. A Jew who had become a citizen of a Greek city in the classical sense of the term—a doubtful hypothesis for the epoch but one that could later apply to some rare cases under the Roman domination—would be obliged to perform certain civic and religious duties, entailing serious risks. In Sparta, he would have been obliged to share the not-very-kosher *syssitia*—the daily fare of the Lacedemonian warriors—with his "peers"; in Athens, he could not reasonably refuse to celebrate the rites of the goddess Athena. For a good Israelite, these were not particularly commendable practices. On the contrary, a Jew belonging to the Hellenic community in Ptolemaic Egypt would not have been confronted with a similar problem. Without relinquishing his Jewish faith, he could be Greek in language, culture, and social status. If his Greek neighbor could worship Sarapis, the Alexandrian divinity *par excellence*, why should he himself be prevented from attending the synagogue and praising his own invisible, "anonymous" God in his prayers? Just as his neighbor was an *Athenaios* (Athenian) or a *Makedon* (Macedonian), he was a *Ioudaios* (Jew), a label that immediately established his identity as a member of the Jewish people and set him apart from Egypt and the Egyptians by confirming his inclusion in the minority of conquering Greek speakers.

Some scholars imagined that the Jews in Egypt were divided into distinct autonomous bodies called *politeumata*. The term *politeuma*, as applied to the Jewish diaspora in Egypt, is attested only in a literary text dealing with Alexandrian Jews, the *Letter of Aristeas*, where it does not have a precise technical meaning. As for the chora, we have no direct evidence of the presence of a Jewish *politeuma*. The reference to *politikoi nomoi* ("civic laws") in the royal regulation presented by a Jewish litigant to the local court in Krokodilopolis is not, as we shall see, sufficient proof of the existence of a Jewish *politeuma* in this town. The same applies to the poetical use of the terms *politai*, "fellow citizens" (CIJ I, No. 1489; Horbury-Noy, No. 114), *polis*, "city," and *politarches*, "ruler of a city" (CPJud. III App. I, 1530 A; Horbury-Noy, No. 39), in the epigraphical material from Tell el-Yehoudieh. The idea that the measure of autonomy enjoyed by such purely imaginary *politeumata* "could easily stand comparison with that accorded to Greek cities at the time" (H. Hagermann) is totally unwarranted.

If the Jews in Ptolemaic Egypt enjoyed a kind of "civic status," it was not because they were organized in "civic communities"; the deciding factor was their inclusion in the community of Hellenes, a "civic body," as opposed to the native population. These considerations help us to understand the astonishing rapidity and the amplitude of Hellenization among the Jews in Egypt. Aside from the immediate attraction of Greek culture, the possibility of inclusion within the dominant and privileged group, without prejudice to the practice of a particular religion, presented considerable advantages.

SOLDIERS OF THE PTOLEMIES

Since the days of the Elephantine garrison, the military life had always drawn the Jews to Egypt. Formerly the faithful servants of the last Pharaohs and the Persian sovereigns, they now rallied under the banner of the Ptolemies. As we already know, Ptolemy I, following in the footsteps of his Saitic and Persian predecessors, brought a number of Jews to the country, among whom he chose the bravest to be trained as soldiers. There were no lack of opportunities: each of the three Syrian wars of 320, 312 and 302 BCE brought about forced (by capture) or voluntary immigration. Hecataeus of Abdera, quoted by Josephus (*Against Apion* 1, 186) tells how, once Ptolemy I had gained mastery over Syria after the battle of Gaza (312 BCE), "many of the inhabitants, having learned of his kindliness and humanity, desired to accompany him to Egypt and to associate themselves with his realm."

We shall presently learn of the establishment of a Jewish military colony in the "land of Onias" near Leontopolis, in the second century BCE. But well before this, as early as the third century BCE (Hibeh Papyrus I 96; CPJud. I 18; 260 BCE), Jewish soldiers had obtained grants of land on the outskirts of several towns and villages in the Faiyum: Krokodilopolis, the capital, Kerkeosiris, Samaria-Kerkesephis, Apias, Trikomia, Hephaistias. Yet others obtained similar plots closer to the Nile, in the Herakleopolite nome. As we shall shortly discover, there were also Jewish soldiers in Upper Egypt.

Our documents reveal the existence of Jewish cleruchs, soldiers to whom the king had granted *kleroi*, plots of land to be tilled, as a reward for their military service. By stretching things a bit, we could compare the cleruch to the medieval vassal, except that the land the former received did not endow him with the slightest personal power. In this respect, one could speak of "fiefs without seigniory," as Claire Préaux cleverly put it. The area of the plots varied between 20 and 100 arouras (5 1/2 and 28 hectares: 1 aroura = 2756 square meters). The size of a cleruch's plot determined his social standing: in Ptolemaic Egypt a "hecatontarouros" (a cleruch with 100 arouras of land) was well worth a "pentacosiomedimnos" (a citizen of the first qualified voting class with an income equal to or greater than 500 bushels of grain) in the Athens of Solon. Jews were eligible for grants of *kleroi* in all categories, on an equal footing with other Greek-speaking immigrants, whatever their origin. In a document we shall soon discover, Jewish cleruchs with lots of 80 arouras appear as witnesses to a loan contract.

The rights and privileges conferred on the cleruchs by the monarchy evolved in favor of the recipients. The initially precarious and revocable grants of tenure gradually became private property, freely transferable and inheritable. The rights of the native Egyptian peasant evolved in the opposite direction: although he, too, tilled land granted by the king, he himself was simply a tenant farmer. The "royal peasant" (*basilikos georgos*) was obliged to cultivate the "royal land" (*basilike ge*), roughly half of all the arable land in the country. His rights, granted by royal prerogative, shrank progressively in number and in quality, contract giving way to constraint. The evolution of Ptolemaic society was dominated by two symmetrical and opposite factors: the growing fortune of the immigrant cleruch and the increasing misery of the native peasant. Jews as such were not singled out as objects of hostility by the rest of the population but, since they were part and parcel of the dominant Greek-speaking minority, they could sometimes appear hateful in native eyes. Seen in this light, the Egyptians were no more anti-Semitic than they were anti-Persian, anti-Greek or anti-Roman.

In the next chapter, we shall make the acquaintance of some Jewish settlers in the Faiyum during the second century BCE. Here are two documents, also from the Faiyum of the second century BCE, which throw some light on the social status of the Jewish colonists and their degree of absorption into the prevalent Greco-Macedonian society.

The first document is a list of plots of land distributed to the cleruchs. By their modest dimensions, they would seem to be abandoned land, partly barren (*eremos*), whose tilling had been forced upon neighboring cultivators. Out of some twenty beneficiaries, there are a half-dozen Jewish or seemingly Jewish names:

Theogenes son of Theogenes, 2 arouras.

Ezeikias son of Ezeikias, 1 aroura estimate at 2.

Eumachos son of Eumachos, 2 arouras, of which desolate land 1, corn-producing 1, estimate at. . . .

Philotas son of Philotas, [arouras?] 17, of which desolate land . . . , corn-producing . . . estimate at 1/2

Paraibates son of Paraibates, 2. . . .

Dositheos son of Kaimion, 2 arouras, of which desolate land 1, corn-producing 1, estimate at 2.

Zenon, 1 1/2 arouras, estimate at 3/4.

Theodosios son of Ammonios, 16 arouras of desolate land.

Numenios, hekatontarches [?] 4, of which 2 arouras are desolate land, 2 are corn-producing, estimate at 1/2.

Antipatros son of Dositheos, 4 arouras, estimate at 5/6.

Kar[...], son of Dositheos, 2 1/2 arouras, of which one is desolate land, 1 corn-producing, estimate at. . . .

Hermogenes son of Aristokles, 2 arouras, estimate at 1.

Polemon son of Ptolemaios, 1 aroura, estimate at 2/3.

[X. son of Y.], 2 arouras, estimate at 5/6.

[X. son of Y.], 2 arouras, estimate at 2/3.

Kalippos, 5 arouras, of which desolate land . . .

Theodosios son of Zoilos, 5 arouras of which desolate land 2, corn-producing land 3, estimate . . . [total of] dry land 25 arouras, of which desolate land 9, corn-producing land 16.

Diome[...], 4 arouras, of which desolate land 2, corn-producing land 2, estimate at 1/2. (TEBTUNIS PAPYRUS III 1019; CPJUD. I 29)

Second on the list is a Hellenized Hebrew name, Ezeikias (Ezekias: Hizekiah/Hizekyahu, "The Lord is my strength"). Curiously enough, it is also the name of his father. The Jewish practice that does not favor giving the father's name to the son was not yet customary (there are other examples). Dositheos son of Kaimion seems to be Jewish also. His patronymic, otherwise unknown, might be a Hellenized variant of Haim. The other cleruchs in the list who may have been Jewish are Theodosios son of Ammonios, Antipatros son of Dositheos, Kar[...] son of Dositheos, and Theodosios son of Zoilos. We are on unsure onomastic ground here.

Our second document, probably of military provenance, is more promising in this regard. It consists of a list of names and patronymics (some are repeated, for unknown reasons) to which the person's origin (*ethnikon*) is appended. The composite nature of the military unit (Jews and Macedonians) is evident:

. . . son of Hippodamos, a Jew,

. . . son of Hippodamos, a Jew,

. . . son of Straton, a Macedonian,

. . . son of Straton, a Macedonian,

. . . son of Ptolemaios, a Macedonian,

. . . son of Ptolemaios, a Macedonian,

. . . son of Ptolemaios, a Macedonian,

. . . son of Ptolemaios, a Macedonian,

. . . son of Sabbathaios, a Jew

followed by another Jew and five Macedonians, after which the list is continued in a second column:

Dorion son of Dorion, a Macedonian,

Sarapion son of Demetrios, a Macedonian,

Dositheos son of Artemidoros, a Jew,

Theodoros son of Theodoros, a Macedonian,

Neilos son of Apollonios, a Macedonian,

Ph[...] son of Dorion, a Macedonian,

Theodoros son of Theodoros. . . . (TEBTUNIS PAPYRUS III 1075; CPJUD. I 30)

Funerary stele of a Hellenistic mercenary *(Galatian?) 2nd century BCE (Istanbul, Museum of Archaeology)*.

Some of the persons designated as *Ioudaioi*, Jews, bore Jewish patronymics, such as Sabbathaios, or reputedly Jewish names, such as Dositheos; others, such as Artemidoros and Hippodamos, had purely Greek names. In the necropolis at Chatby we already came upon a man whose name could be reconstituted as Hippodamos; he was almost certainly a Jew. We do not know the origin of the last-mentioned on the list; he could be Jewish, although he bears his father's name, as did Ezeikias son of Ezeikias in the preceding document. Three lines above we find Theodoros son of Theodoros, who is Macedonian! Onomastic criteria are insufficient to classify a soldier as Jewish; a Theodoros or a Dositheos is not necessarily a Jew, nor is an Artemidoros necessarily a "heathen."

In certain cases, the Jewish soldiers of the Ptolemies had risen to positions of command. We shall soon meet a police officer, Ptolemaios son of Epikydes, who played an active role in the foundation of a synagogue in Athribis. In the following document, the name of a Jewish cavalry officer from Thebes appears on a papyrus written on the fourteenth of June 158 BCE, in modern reckoning. It concerns the sale of a house that was either confiscated or seized by the royal treasury as unowned or escheated property (without legal heirs):

> [The price of a house] put to sale in Diospolis Magna on the twenty-eighth of Choiak of the twenty-third year through Ptolemaios the superintendent of the revenues in the Thebaid and Theon the royal scribe in the presence of Dionysios himself and Harnouphis the topogrammateus, Imouthes the village scribe, Megisthenes the phrouarchos, Lichas the archiphylacite, Aristogenes one of the officers serving with Hippaios, Iasibis the epistates of a hipparchy, and many others, through Timarchos the herald of the soldiers, etc. (PAPYRUS HAUNIENSIS 11; CPJUD. I 27)

Iasibis is a Greek variant of the Hebrew name Yashib or Yashub, an abbreviated form of Eliyashib ("May God bring back!"), rendered in the Septuagint as Iasoub, Iasoubos, Iasseib, or Iasseb. A century earlier, another person bearing the same name (Yashub) was to be found among the clients of the Jewish merchant 'Abihi in the Aramaic papyrus quoted above. The rapid success of our Iasibis may have been due, in part, to the fact that the reigning king was the "philo-Semitic" Ptolemy VI. But any "Hellene," whatever his origin, was eligible for staff status under the reign of the Ptolemies. Had he lived a century earlier, Iasibis might have had a similar career.

Only his religion differentiated a Jewish soldier from a Macedonian, a Greek, or a soldier of any other non-Judean origin. The Jews, carrying out the policy of cooperation first formulated in the legend of the visit of Alexander to Jerusalem, were careful to demonstrate their fidelity to the Ptolemaic monarch. But nothing should lead us to believe, as some authors do, that they were more loyal or braver than the Thessalians, the Beotians or the Aetolians. Some Bulgarian scholars have attempted to endow their more-or-less mythical Thracian ancestors with the privileged status of "peasants of honor," somewhere between the native Egyptians and the conquering Greco-Macedonians. A closer scrutiny of the documents rapidly shatters this illusion. Nor is it more realistic to dream up an image of the Jewish colonist in Egypt as a model of devotion and courage. The sole factor distinguishing the Jew from others is his abiding attachment to the faith of his ancestors, the mark of his difference.

"GOD THE MOST HIGH" AND "SPLENDOR OF ISRAEL"

For a Jew, adherence to Greek culture did not inevitably lead to apostasy. The case of Dositheos son of Drymilos was rather exceptional. The great majority of Jews did not follow in the footsteps of Dositheos but, to paraphrase the author of the Third Book of Maccabees, "remained faithful to the religion of their fathers." Whatever the degree of the Jews' acculturation, there were never any signs of Judeo-pagan syncretism. The proof of this assertion can be found in what has come down to us of Jewish synagogue practice in Egypt.

In the absence of archaeological remains, Ptolemaic Egypt has left us much precious information concerning the synagogue, an institution that had appeared in the diaspora and would assume a central role after the Temple in Jerusalem was destroyed in 70 CE. Several inscriptions and papyri are at our disposal, such as dedications and bookkeeping documents; we also possess fragments of the Septuagint used in the synagogues and a description of the Great Synagogue in Alexandria bequeathed to us by the Talmud. All this evidence can help us broaden our knowledge of the origins and the functioning of the synagogue, in Egypt and elsewhere.

The two documents reproduced below are the oldest we have concerning synagogues in Egypt. Both date from the middle of the third century BCE. The first originated in Schedia, near Kafr ed-Dauwar, southeast of Alexandria. Schedia was an important customs post on the Nile; the Jewish settlement here may have had some relation to the river guard, which, according to Josephus (*Against Apion* 2, 64), had been entrusted to the Jews. The second inscription, bought from a dealer at Medinet el-Faiyum, comes from Krokodilopolis, capital of the Arsinoite nome. The two texts are practically identical:

> On behalf of King Ptolemy and Queen Berenice his sister and wife and their children, the Jews [dedicated] this house of prayer. (*CIJ II, No. 1440; HORBURY-NOY, No. 22*)

> On behalf of King Ptolemy, son of Ptolemy, and of Queen Berenice his wife and sister and their children, the Jews in Krokodilopolis [dedicated] this house of prayer. (*CPJUD. III, APPENDIX I, No. 1532A; HORBURY-NOY, No. 117*)

The Ptolemy here concerned is Ptolemy III Euergetes I (246–222 BCE). The queen is Berenice II daughter of Magas, king of Cyrene, and of Apama daughter of Antiochus I. She was not the sister of Ptolemy III, but his cousin, because Magas was the half-brother of Ptolemy II, father of Ptolemy III; both were children of the same mother: Berenice I, successively wife to Ptolemy I and Philip, the father of Magas. The word "sister" (adelphe) should not be taken literally; it is used here in an honorary manner, although royal marriages between authentic brothers and sisters were assuredly not a rarity during Hellenistic times. The mention of children (the elder child was the future Ptolemy IV Philopator, who was to reign from 222 to 205 BCE) indicates a date between 245 and 222, since the royal marriage took place in 246.

The coincidence of dates and contents in these two dedications is significant. It shows that, by the middle of the third century BCE, Jewish life in Egypt by no means longer confined to Alexandria and its suburbs. There was also an important Jewish settlement in the Arsinoite nome, today the Faiyum. "The Jews of Krokodilopolis" formed a group in the capital of the nome (called Ptolemais Euergetis from 116 BCE until Byzantine times, when its name became Arsinoiton polis; the modern appellation of "Arsinoe" is only attested in a few isolated cases). It was this group who founded the synagogue and was the collective author of the dedication, an act presupposing a common effort and a good measure of internal solidarity. Furthermore, placing the synagogue under the patronage of the royal family could well be taken as a pledge of loyalty. The king, for his part, manifested his goodwill by according his authorization for its erection. We shall soon learn that the monarchy could go a step further, by granting the right of asylum to a synagogue, as it had for heathen temples.

Despite its name, the "City of Crocodiles" (Krokodilon polis) was not a city (*polis*) in the traditional sense, but rather a large township. It was a pole of attraction for the cleruchs, who promptly rented out to Egyptian peasants the plots of land they had received from the king, themselves preferring the pleasures of urban life. The Jews followed the example of their Greek comrades-in-arms, disdaining the delights of the countryside for a more "civilized" existence, a practice tending to accentuate the widening gap between the inhabitants of rural Egypt and the Greek-speaking townspeople.

Our synagogue was certainly not the only one in Krokodilopolis. There is no reason to identify it with either of the two synagogues mentioned in a bill for water supply (London Papyrus III 1177; CPJud. II 432), dated just before the revolt of 115–117 CE. But it very well may have been the one mentioned in a papyrus from the end of the second century BCE (Tebtunis Papyrus I 86; CPJud. I 134), where it is listed among other property situated in the eastern suburbs of the city. If this were the case, we should be able to pinpoint its location at the city limits, near the so-called "canal of Argaitis."

It appears that the synagogue had a garden, which had been rented out to an Egyptian who planted it with beds of flowers and vegetables. The terms employed have led to its interpretation as a "sacred garden." The terrain adjoining a synagogue could well be termed "sacred," by assimilation to similar usage for land belonging to heathen temples. The building itself could then be called a "sacred place," *hagios topos*, or even a "temple," *hieron*—a classical example of semantic displacement. What actually seems to be sacred in this document is not so much the garden itself (we would then have *hiera paradeisos*, a feminine adjective for a masculine noun), but the ground. In Ptolemaic Egypt, *hiera ge*, "sacred earth," was a well-known technical term for one category of landed property. At the edge of the city, several plots of ground had this legal status. One of them belonged to the synagogue, another to a certain Hermione daughter of Apollonides. Legal terminology should not be confused with sacredness!

It was not by accident that this synagogue was located in a suburb of Krokodilopolis. Other sources show that synagogues were often located at the edges of a city. One might think the Jews of Egypt wished to distance themselves from their "idolatrous" neighbors. Notwithstanding, in the purely Jewish regions of Judea, where no pagans dwelt, synagogues were frequently to be found next to the city walls (Gamla) or a fortress (Masada and Herodium). This marginality would seem to have other, deeper causes, originating in the striving for purity inherent in Judaism itself. In one variant, which

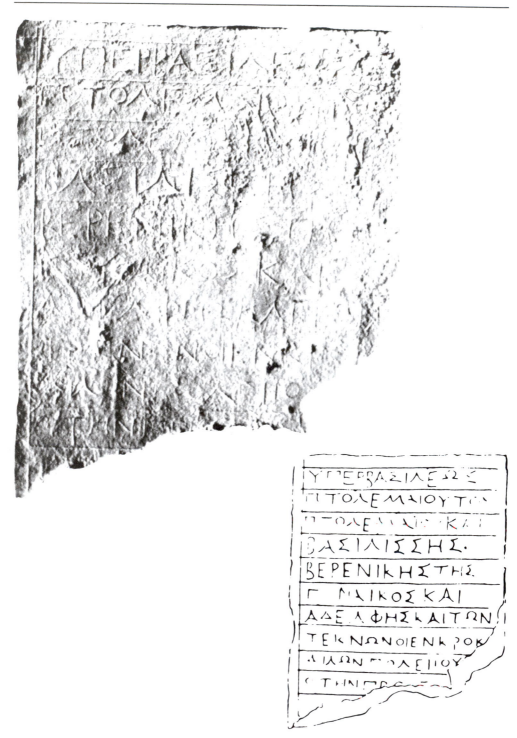

Dedication of the synagogue of Krokodilopolis in the Faiyum
(Alexandria, Greco-Roman Museum).

facilitated the ritual bath, the synagogue was placed on the seashore. This was the case for Delos. It was also the case for Alexandria.

There was a Jewish quarter in Alexandria, called the "Delta"—the fourth letter of the Greek alphabet. In the first century CE, it was situated on the coast northeast of the city, at some distance from the ports. There are some clues suggestive of another Jewish settlement to the northwest, near the western harbor (Eunostos), later the site of the Church of Saint-Theonas. But Jewish tombs dating from the third century BCE in the cemetery of Ibrahimiya, to the east of Alexandria, confirm the existence of a north-eastern Jewish quarter since the very beginnings of the Ptolemaic period. Although the enemies of the Jews, such as Apion, could mock their seeming banishment to the poor suburbs, the Jews might well retort that its seaside location, and its proximity to the royal palace, rendered the Delta quarter both agreeable and respectable (Josephus, *Against Apion* 2, 33–37). It is tempting to take it as the location of the great synagogue of Alexandria.

The Delta quarter, it is true, was not a ghetto. Jews also lived elsewhere in Alexandria; the philosopher Philo informs us that there were several synagogues in all the sectors of the city (*Embassy to Gaius*, 132). We have already encountered the synagogue of Schedia, to the southeast of Alexandria. During the reign of Cleopatra VII, the exis-tence of another synagogue in the southwestern suburb of Gabbary is attested (CIJ II, No. 1432; Horbury-Noy, No. 13). But the largest and most renowned of all, as Philo remarks, was built right in the heart of the Delta quarter. Its description by Rabbi Judah ben Ilai, dating from the Antonine epoch, has been preserved in the Talmud.

> It has been taught, R. Judah said: Whoever has never seen the double colonnade [*diple stoa*, i.e., the basilica-synagogue] of Alexandria in Egypt has never seen Israel's glory in his entire life. It was like a large basilica, with one colonnade within the other.
>
> It sometimes held twice as many people as those who went forth from Egypt.
>
> There were seventy golden thrones set up there, adorned with precious stones and pearls, one for each of the seventy elders, each one worth twenty-five talents of gold, with a wooden platform in the middle.
>
> The minister of the synagogue stood on it. When someone stood up for reading, the officer in charge waved the scarf, so the people could respond "Amen." For each and every blessing he waved the scarf and they re-sponded "Amen".
>
> They did not sit in a jumble, but each craft sat by itself, so that when a traveler came, he could join his fellow craftsmen, and on that basis his livelihood was provided. (*Jerusalem Talmud, Sukkah 5:1, 55a–b*)

The terminology employed in this text calls for a few comments. In Hebrew, the term for synagogue is *bet ha-knesset*, "the house of the assembly." In the inscriptions and pa-

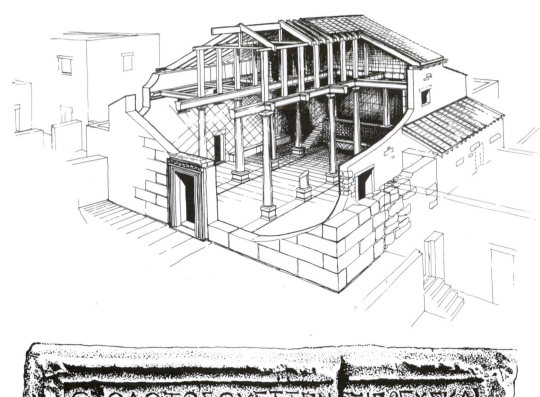

(Top) **Drawing of the synagogue of Gush-Halav, in Upper Galilee** (restoration); (bottom) **Inscription of Theodotos** *1st century* CE. *Limestone slab, found in 1913 or 1914 in Jerusalem, which reads, "Theodotos son of Vettenos, priest and officer in charge of the synagogue, son of an officer in charge of the synagogue, grandson of an officer in charge of the synagogue, built the synagogue for the reading of the Law and the teaching of the Commandments, and the guest house and the rooms and the water supplies as an inn for those who come from abroad; which synagogue his fathers had founded, and the Elders, and Simonides."*

pyri found in Egypt, the term employed (with one rather obscure exception) was *proseuche*, "house of prayer." The same term was used for the synagogue in Delos. One of the two above-mentioned synagogues in Krokodilopolis was called *eucheion*, a synonym of *proseuche*, in order to distinguish it from its neighbor, patronized by Theban Jews who had settled in Krokodilopolis.

The word *synagoge*, "congregation," was reserved for a meeting or for the community itself. Thus, in a papyrus from the end of the first century BCE (Rylands Papyrus IV 590; CPJud. I 138), we are told of a meeting (*synagoge*) of a Jewish association in a house of prayer (*proseuche*). A document dating from Diocletian's reign relates how a Jewish woman and her two (or three) children, who had been enslaved, were redeemed by the Jewish community of Oxyrhynchos, *synagoge ton Ioudaion*, represented by its leaders (Oxyrhynchos Papyrus IX 1205; CPJud. III 473, 291 CE). In the Septuagint, *synagoge* is employed to translate the Hebrew terms designating a congregation (*kahal, 'edah*). Conversely, Theodotos son of Vettenos, in his famous dedication of a synagogue in Jerusalem (first century CE), uses the term synagogue for the building itself. It would appear that, in their lexical choice, the Jews of the Egyptian diaspora wished deliberately to underscore the sacred character of their place of congregation, which the word synagogue was incapable of expressing.

The preference of R. Judah for the terms *stoa* (portico) and *basilike* (basilica), rather than *proseuche* or *eucheion*, may easily be explained by his profound admiration for Greek and Roman architecture. It surely does not mean—as Peter M. Fraser, in his monumental work on Ptolemaic Alexandria (1972), would have us believe—that the building was a kind of souk, or marketplace, rather than a synagogue in the proper meaning of the term.

The use of optical signals during the reading of the Torah suggests a building of truly vast dimensions. But it may also have been a ritual, perhaps transmitted and preserved in the liturgy of the orthodox Christian Church in our day, in which the deacon waves his *horarion* (a cloth) during the rite, in a manner reminiscent of ancient Jewish synagogue practice. In our talmudic description we rediscover the figure of one million Jews dear to Philo, since the post-Exodus desert census put the total number of Hebrews, excluding the Levites, at 604,550 souls, corresponding to the biblical 600 "thousands" of Israelites (Ex. 12:37; Num. 1:46).

The seventy golden thrones of the Talmud of Jerusalem are another stereotype. In the Talmud of Babylon, these became the seventy-one thrones, corresponding to the number of members of the Jewish Sanhedrin, a correspondence that has led some scholars into the error of believing that there was a Sanhedrin in Alexandria, cast in the mold of its supposed counterpart in Jerusalem. On the contrary, the existence of two officers—the beadle (*hazzan ha-knesset*) and the caretaker (*ha-memuneh*)—has been confirmed by papyrological evidence. The text we have quoted also attests the customary hospitality extended to strangers, a tradition that the Christian hospices (*xenodocheia*) of Byzantine Egypt were to adopt and perpetuate.

The dedications cited at the beginning of this chapter show that the synagogues at Schedia and Krokodilopolis were founded by the local Jewish communities. Other similar cases may be adduced. In the latter part of the reign of Ptolemy VIII Euergetes II (145–116 BCE), thus two synagogues were founded in Xenephyris, near Damanhur, and in Nitriai (modern Wadi Natrun or, more probably, el-Barnugi) in the Western Delta (CIJ II, Nos. 1441–1442; Horbury-Noy, Nos. 24–25). Other synagogues were founded by individuals, either personally or in affiliation with a group; families occasionally furnished the necessary equipment for a house of prayer. These cases are illustrated by two inscriptions from Athribis (today Tell Atrib, near Benha) in the Delta, dating from the second or the first century BCE.

> On behalf of King Ptolemy and Queen Cleopatra, Ptolemaios son of Epikydes, chief of police, and the Jews in Athribis [dedicated] the proseuche to God the Most High. *(CIJ II, Nos. 1443; HORBURY-NOY, No. 27)*

> On behalf of King Ptolemy and Queen Cleopatra and their children, Hermias and his wife Philotera and their children [gave] this place for sitting for the proseuche. *(CIJ II, Nos. 1444; HORBURY-NOY, No. 28)*

The first text is particularly interesting, since it acquaints us with a local *euergetes* (benefactor), an officer of police (*epistates ton phylakiton*) who had associated himself with the Jewish community of Athribis for the erection of a synagogue. As it was rather improbable that a non-Jew would take such an initiative, and even more so that his offer would gain the approval of the community, we may draw the almost certain conclusion that the person concerned was a Jew. His official rank should not be a cause for astonishment. We have already encountered a Jewish cavalry officer and should recall that the military profession was open to all those who spoke Greek and belonged to the dominant group of "Hellenes."

Another point worthy of attention is to be found in the second text: the object of the dedication was not the synagogue itself, but the hall (*exedra*) where the congregation gathered. The Greek wording "for the proseuche" is not to be taken too literally. The *exedra* had been offered to the community, which is not to be identified with a building. A new wing, with one open side, provided with seating, had been added to the very edifice the *epistates* Ptolemaios had sponsored, in association with the Jews of Athribis. The inscription thus attests a stage in the building's history.

The most important point, however, is the invocation, in the first text, of "God the Most High." In the most ancient synagogue dedications, there was no mention of the divinity to whose worship a house of prayer was consecrated. The mention of the king (*hyper basileos*) or the royal family signifies that the buildings were erected under royal auspices or, if one prefers, in the honor of the reigning sovereign, and not, as some commentators have imprudently written, that the buildings were "dedicated" to the sovereigns themselves. Jews, in their prayers, could ask their God to grant long life to King Ptolemy, just as they are free today to pray for the health of the President of the United

States, be he a Democrat or a Republican. But it would be erroneous to believe that the Ptolemies were an object of veneration in the *proseuchai*. To all evidence, the prayers were addressed uniquely to the God of Israel.

His ineffable Name (*Shem ha-meforash*; *anephoneton onoma*, as Origen has it; *ineffabile nomen* for Jerome) was the stumbling block. YHWH, the Hebrew Tetragrammaton, was illegible for Greeks. Kyrios ("Lord"), Greek equivalent of the Hebrew Adonai—the traditional Hebrew substitute (*kere*) for the Tetragrammaton—would have been too obscure for a casual non-Jewish passerby. He would have been sorely puzzled by this anonymous divinity, whose sanctuaries had been erected under the auspices and the implicit or explicit protection of the Ptolemies themselves. The problem was solved by choosing, among the numerous divine names, the one most likely to kindle a religious sentiment in the breast of a Greek: *El-Elyon*, "God the Most High" (Gen. 14:18–20; Deut. 32:8), *Theos hypsistos* in Greek. *Hypsistos*, a superlative without a positive, is evocative of the supreme deity; Sophocles had applied this term to Zeus. Throughout the ancient world, it soon acquired a Jewish coloration. A word of caution, however: it could well appear in a non-Jewish context, since every human group was entitled to its own supreme god! Conversely, the God of the Jews could also be a "great God" (*theos megalos*), a God "who grants prayers" (*epekoos*), a highly valued virtue among divinities in Hellenistic days (CIJ II, No. 1432; Horbury-Noy, No. 13).

The existence of a liturgy in synagogue practice, prior to the fall of the Temple, has not been clearly established. A recent survey (by Lee I. Levine) has produced no proof of the existence of prayer as it is practiced today. Even in Jerusalem itself, Theodotos' inscription does not mention prayer as one of the habitual activities of the synagogue. The proximity of the Temple cannot explain this silence. Since in the eyes of the faithful the uniqueness of the Temple was sacred, geographical distance could in no manner justify the practice of "parallel" worship. Leontopolis was an exception, due to very particular historical circumstances and which had another context: the sanctuary in Leontopolis was not a house of prayer but a veritable temple. One may draw the conclusion, then, that the principal form of synagogue worship, in Egypt as in Judea, was the reading of the Torah, not prayer in the proper sense of the term, but nonetheless a form of veneration. The talmudic text quoted above, describing the reading of the Torah by the faithful in the Great Synagogue of Alexandria, is to be taken seriously in this respect. It concurs with the inscription of Theodotos, with Philo, Josephus, and also with the Gospels (Luke 4:16–22; Acts of the Apostles 13:13–16).

We do not know when the custom of the regular reading of the Torah in the synagogue was institutionalized. The Ptolemaic papyri containing the oldest fragments of the scrolls of the Septuagint suggest that this practice was more ancient than is generally admitted. In the Cairo scroll of Deuteronomy (Papyrus Fouad 266), dating from the first century BCE, a division of the text points to the current, and probably even more ancient, practice of a triennial reading cycle. The scroll is a copy of the Torah that probably belonged to a synagogue in the Faiyum, where it was employed for public readings. The presence of priests (*kohanim*) authorizes us to believe that the "benediction of the kohanim" (*birkat kohanim*) was practiced, a rite whose antiquity is now attested by amulets discovered in 1979 in the Valley of Hinnom to the southwest of Jerusalem. They date from the seventh century BCE and contain the oldest fragments of Scripture (Num. 6:24–26) in our possession today.

Some *proseuchai* seem to have had annexes: the inscription of Nitriai, cited above, mentions a house of prayer and its "appurtenances" (*ta synkyronta*). They may have been rooms for the study of the Torah. Philo, in speaking of a synagogue, employs the word *didaskaleion*, "school." We have seen how, in Athribis, a Jewish family had made a gift of a meeting hall (*exedra*) to the *proseuche*. There were also rooms for visitors, as shown, for Jerusalem, by Theodotos' inscription, and for Alexandria, by the Talmud. In Xenephyris, in the Delta, the pylon (gateway) of the synagogue was the object of a dedication. This supposes an enclosed space with a massive portal, as in Egyptian temples. In some cases, if not systematically, the *proseuche* was a monumental structure. In Egypt, most of the synagogues must have resembled those discovered in Judea and on the Golan, rather than the one in Delos, which was little more than a remodeled villa. The erection of such buildings would have necessitated the services of an architect, such as Alypos, who "made" (*epoiei* or *epoiesen*) the Gabbary synagogue during the reign of Cleopatra VII.

Direct testimony for Egypt is lacking but we presume that, as in other countries, each *proseuche* had its ritual bath (*mikveh*). In Judea, the mikveh was next to the synagogue building; in Delos, it was inside it. Running water was necessary; it was usually piped in from an aqueduct or, more rarely, drawn from a nearby spring, as in Delos. In Krokodilopolis, the synagogue was conveniently placed next to a canal, which could be used to fill the mikveh. We have seen that two synagogues in this town later became clients of a water-distributing service. Their bills were particularly high, amounting to twice as much as the prices paid by public baths and four times the price of certain fountains. Some scholars concluded that the Jews had been overcharged, but this is a shaky hypothesis. Since the fall of the Temple, there had been a tax levied on the Jews, *Ioudaikon telesma* (we shall return to this point), but if the synagogues had a high water bill, it was because they used more than an average amount of water.

The administration of a synagogue entailed the appointment of a specialized staff, headed by a chief: *rosh ha-knesset* in Hebrew, *prostates* in Greek. This temporary office was sometimes held jointly, as attested by the two *prostatai*, Theodoros and Achillios, whose names appear as a dating element on the dedication of the Xenephyris synagogue. As strange at it may seem, a statue (of which only the pedestal has survived) was erected in Alexandria in honor of Artemon son of Nikon, former *prostates*, head of a synagogue (but which?) in the eleventh year of an unidentifiable reign (CIJ II, No. 1447; Horbury-Noy, No. 20). This is the sole instance, among all the Greek documents from Egypt, where the word synagogue could possibly refer to a building. Another interpretation, according to which Artemon, a "Judaizer," would have made a donation to a non-Jewish association (Horbury-Noy), could also be envisaged.

In Krokodilopolis, in the Faiyum, the community had designated one of the "magistrates," *archontes*, to take care of the water bill we spoke of above. Jewish *archontes* in Herakleopolis appear in a recently published papyrus from the second century BCE (Munich Papyrus III 49); they are probably the heads of the local synagogue. In the Great synagogue in Alexandria, mention was made of a *hazzan*, whose Greek equivalent is *nakoros* (*neokoros*), a term attested twice in papyrological documents, once in 218 (Papyrus Enteuxeis 30; CPJud. I 129), and again in 114 or 78 BCE (PSI XVII Congr. 22). His duties in the synagogues of the Hellenistic-Roman period were those of the modern *shamash*, beadle, or verger, rather than that of a cantor, the modern *hazzan*; according to the Tosefta, he was charged only with blowing the trumpet to announce the beginning of the Sabbath. The latter papyrus also mentions a *nakorikon*, a term that seems to designate the sums contributed by the community for the beadle's salary. Community financing of synagogue services was probably a common practice throughout Egypt.

In addition to the reading of the Torah, the synagogue occasionally opened its doors to other activities, poorly defined in our sources. In the first century BCE, an association (*synodos*), whose purpose is hard to determine because of the fragmentary state of the papyrus in which it is mentioned (Rylands Papyrus IV 530; CPJud. I 138), held its meetings (*synogogai*) in a house of prayer (*proseuche*). Are we dealing with a sort of "burial society"? Associations of this sort are known to have existed among the Greeks in Egypt, from the third century BCE onward (Papyri Enteuxeis 20–21). An ostracon from Edfu (Apollinopolis Magna), also from the first century BCE, bears witness to the existence of a Jewish "club," whose membership included a "wise man" (*sophos*, the Greek equivalent of a *hakham*). The club sponsored a series of banquets, among which the Passover Seder may have figured. Although our document does not specify this point, the synagogue would have been an appropriate venue for this sort of gathering.

We close this chapter with one other function of the synagogues: the right of asylum. The king, if he wished, could confer upon pagan temples the privilege of sheltering refugees. In a similar manner, synagogues could become the recipients of this privilege, enabling them to grant asylum to all those who sought protection from injustice of any sort. A bilingual Greco-Latin inscription attests the granting of such a privilege to a synagogue in Egypt.

> [Greek text:] On the orders of the queen and king, in place of the previous plaque about the dedication of the proseuche let what is written below be engraved. King Ptolemy Euergetes [proclaimed] the proseuche inviolate.
>
> [Latin text:] The queen and king gave the order. (*CIJ II*, No. 1449; HORBURY-NOY, No. 125)

The Ptolemy Euergetes who granted the right of asylum to this synagogue may have been Ptolemy III Euergetes I (246–222 BCE), under whom the earliest synagogue dedications are to be found. A more likely candidate is Ptolemy VIII Euergetes II (164–146 and 145–116 BCE), under whose reign the synagogues of Xenephyris and Nitriai in the Delta were established. The Delta seems to have been the point of origin of the alabaster stele bearing the inscription; the eventful character of his reign could also lend credence to this hypothesis.

As for the queen and king who had renewed the privilege cited in the lower part of the inscription, written in Latin, a majority of modern commentators, following Theodor Mommsen, opted for Zenobia, queen of Palmyra, and her son Vaballathus. This would place the inscription as late as 269–271 CE. Another choice, which now appears preferable thanks to Jean Bingen, is that of the last Cleopatra and one of her co-regents, her brother Ptolemy XIV, or (rather) Ptolemy XV, Caesarion, the son she had borne to Julius Caesar. This would bring the date back some three centuries, to the period between 47 and 31 BCE, the stele taking its place among the numerous examples of the privilege of asylum, liberally bestowed upon various places of worship in Egypt by the last of the Ptolemies. The use of Latin could be explained by the presence of Roman troops, on the eve of the Roman conquest of Egypt.

CHAPTER 5

A Law for
the Jews of Egypt

THE GREEK TORAH AND THE DEMOTIC CASE BOOK

At the end of the fourth century BCE, the Jews who returned to Egypt in the wake of the Macedonian conquest took with them their most treasured possession: the Law, the Torah of Moses in the form that Ezra had established a century earlier. We can lend credence to the words of Hecataeus of Abdera, when, in a "revised version" elaborated in Judeo-Egyptian circles and quoted by Josephus, he relates the arrival in Egypt of a Jewish "high priest," accompanied by several of his followers; this was soon after the battle of Gaza (312 BCE). He had taken care to bring along a scroll of the Torah for public reading.

> Of a different nature is the evidence of Hecataeus of Abdera, at once a philosopher and a highly competent man of affairs, who rose to fame under King Alexander and was afterwards associated with Ptolemy, son of Lagus. He makes no mere passing allusion to us, but wrote a book entirely about the Jews, from which I propose briefly to touch on some passages. . . .
>
> Hecataeus relates that after the battle of Gaza Ptolemy became master of Syria, and that many of the inhabitants, hearing of his kindliness and humanity, desired to accompany him to Egypt and to associate themselves with his realm. Among these, he says, was Ezekias, a chief priest of the Jews, a man of about 66 years of age, highly esteemed by his countrymen, intellectual, and moreover an able speaker and unsurpassed as a man of business. Yet, he adds, the total number of Jewish priests who receive a tithe of the revenue and administer public affairs is about fifteen hundred. Reverting to Ezekias, he says: This man, after obtaining this honor and having been closely in touch with us, assembled some of his friends and read to them the whole scroll, in which was written the story of their settlement and the constitution of the state. (PSEUDO-HECATAEUS, AFTER JOSEPHUS, AGAINST APION 1, 183–89)

Toward 300 BCE, the arrival in Alexandria of a Jewish priest, bearing a scroll of the Torah, was a perfectly conceivable event. However, the word *archiereus,* "high priest," should not be taken too literally. The term commonly designated a member of the sacerdotal aristocracy and not the high priest in office. Our Ezekias may have been the grandson of the homonymous governor (*pehah*) of Achaemenid Judea, whose name can be found on some of the silver coins of the fourth century BCE discovered in Bet-Tzur and Tel-Yammeh, in Israel. It was customary at the time to read the Torah aloud on Sabbath days or holidays. Ezekias read from the Hebrew text, but the problem of a Greek translation was soon to arise. This poses the delicate question of the origins and the purpose of the Septuagint, the Greek version of the Scriptures set down in Alexandria.

Who had decided to translate the Torah into Greek, and why was the decision taken? Two opposing doctrines are currently professed. Elias Bickerman was among the proponents of a royal initiative. This thesis is founded on a Jewish legend, later adopted by the Christians, first attested in the *Letter of Aristeas to Philocrates* and by the philosopher Aristoboulos (both already mentioned in previous chapters), who attributed the initiative of the translation to King Ptolemy II Philadelphus. For the circumstance, they coupled him, rather awkwardly, with the Athenian statesman, Demetrius of Phalerum, counselor to Ptolemy I Soter. During the reign of Soter, Demetrius had been unwise enough to favor the succession of the king's eldest son in preference to Philadelphus; when the former was pushed aside and the latter mounted the throne, the Athenian fell into disgrace. Although the new ruler condemned the man, nothing could stop him from adopting his ideas. In our day, similar displacements frequently occur. How many reforms have been proposed by a government, and enthusiastically adopted by its former opponents, once they are voted into office? The writings of Clement of Alexandria testify to this ambiguity: he followed a tradition which hesitated between Ptolemy I and Ptolemy II Philadelphus. As we shall see, the historical context appears to favor the son, rather than the father.

A second opinion, defended notably by Paul Kahle and, more recently, by Arnaldo Momigliano, replaces the translation of the Torah in the perspective of synagogue practice. The Jewish immigrants had adopted the Greek language so rapidly and so completely that they no longer understood Hebrew and were in dire need of a version of the Scriptures they could understand. Just as an Aramaic translation, the Targum, accompanied the reading of the Torah in Jerusalem and in Judea, a Greek translation was used in Alexandria and throughout Egypt. The future Septuagint was, at first, a kind of Greek Targum. Several translations, offering greater or lesser degrees of variation, were currently employed. Toward the end of the second century BCE, a decision was made to provide a unified text to supplant all these variants. According to Kahle, it was this revised version, later to become the official text of the Christian Church, that the *Letter of Aristeas* was supposed to promote.

Let us hear, firstly, the testimony of the *Letter.* The king had allotted a sizable sum of money to Demetrius of Phalerum, now the chief librarian of the Alexandrian Library, to enable him to assemble all the important works of universal literature. The librarian had heard about the laws of the Jews, which surely were worthy of transcription and a place in the royal library. "What are you waiting for to do it, since you have the wherewithal?," asks Ptolemy. "But they have to be translated," replies the librarian, and acquaints his sovereign with the particularities of the Hebrew language and its script, stressing the obstacles to be overcome before a reader could gain access to the texts.

No matter! The king decided that a letter was to be sent to the high priest in Jerusalem and ordered the librarian to prepare a report on the project. Eleazar, the high priest in office, was cooperative, and forthwith dispatched seventy-two translators to Alexandria, so that each of the twelve traditional tribes was represented by six persons. He chose the most competent scholars, both highly expert in Hebrew letters and steeped in Greek culture. Upon their arrival in Alexandria, a great banquet was offered them, "in conformity with their customs" (a kosher meal?); by royal decree, the feast was prolonged for an entire week. The king bombarded his guests with questions, receiving in return a string of edifying counsels amounting to a veritable treatise on the difficult business of kingship (*peri basileias*). Now, the real work could begin.

> Demetrius, who had come to meet the translators, led them across the pier which was seven stadia long that led to the Island of Pharus, passed over the bridge, moved to the north, assembled them in a place that had been prepared for them near the beach, a magnificent dwelling surrounded by silence, and invited them to proceed with the work of translation, all the wherewithal being supplied. They set to work and agreed on each point by mutual discussion and confrontation. From the resulting text, Demetrius had a copy made up in due form. Until the ninth hour they held session, after which they were free to tend to their corporeal needs, and all that was necessary for this was provided for them. Moreover, each day, all the morsels that had been prepared for the king, Dorotheos [the courtier who had the translators in his charge] had them prepared for them also, for the king had so ordained.
>
> At the break of day, they came to the court every day, and when they had greeted the king, they retired to their individual dwelling. After having washed their hands in the sea, according to the custom of all Jews, they set themselves to the task of reading and translating each passage. Every day, they gathered in the place that was so agreeable by its tranquillity and its light, and they carried out the work prescribed for them. Now, it came about that the work of translation was done in seventy-two days, as though such a thing had been due to a premeditated decision.
>
> When the work was done, Demetrius assembled the community of the Jews on the spot where the work of translation had been accomplished, and he had it read to the entire congregation, in the presence of the translators who, moreover, were acclaimed by the people with enthusiasm,

for their considerable contribution to such a good work. They gave Demetrius a similar ovation and asked him to send their leaders a copy of the entire Law. After the reading of the scrolls the priests, standing, the elders of the translators and the delegates of the community (*politeuma*), as well as the leaders of the people, made this declaration: "Now that the translation has been so well done, with piety and with rigorous exactitude, it is well that this work stay as it is, without the slightest alteration." At these words, there was a general acclamation; then they asked them to pronounce an anathema, according to their custom, against anyone who altered the letter of the text, either by prolonging it or by changing it in any manner whatsoever, or else by cutting out a part of it: an excellent measure to keep it forever immutable. (LETTER OF ARISTEAS TO PHILOCRATES, *301–11*)

The king was delighted. Suddenly imbued with a boundless admiration for the ancient biblical legislator, he exclaimed with astonishment: "How could such a masterpiece possibly fail to attract the attention of our poets and historians?" The sovereign's enthusiasm was shared by his faithful subjects, the Jews of Egypt. They were to celebrate the occasion by an annual feast on the island of Pharus, a custom still practiced during Philo's time, in the first century CE. A Christian legend soon took shape, perpetuating its remembrance from one century to the next, amplifying its supernatural content until, by the fourth century CE, Epiphanes of Salamis proposed a curious scenario: the translators had been isolated by pairs, in thirty-six separate little houses; by divine intervention, the thirty-six completed versions were completely concordant, down to the least iota! Jerome, a great translator in his own right, considering these excesses unworthy of serious attention, raised his voice in protest. The final arbitration was to come from the rabbis. The prevailing opinion among the sages of the Talmud, favorable to the new Greek version of the Bible by Aquilas the Proselyte, a disciple of Rabbi Akiba, was hostile to the Septuagint, which had, meanwhile, become the Bible of the Christians. In their eyes, the day the Torah was translated into Greek in Alexandria was an unlucky one, as ill-fated as the day the Israelites had fashioned the Golden Calf.

The subsequent history of the Alexandrian translation throws little light on its origins. Are we then condemned to choose between the thesis of a royal commission for the Library of Alexandria, and the thesis of a Greek Targum designed uniquely to fulfill the needs of the Jewish diaspora in Egypt? This would amount to placing oneself needlessly on the horns of a dilemma. The mere fact that the Jewish subjects of King Ptolemy no longer understood the language in which their national Law was couched was not sufficient cause for the ruler to be afflicted with *agrypnia*, that noble anxiety which robs overscrupulous monarchs of their well-deserved slumber. Nonetheless, Ptolemy's curiosity concerning the literature of foreign peoples is in perfect harmony with the overall project of assembling all the world's masterpieces in the Great Library in Alexandria.

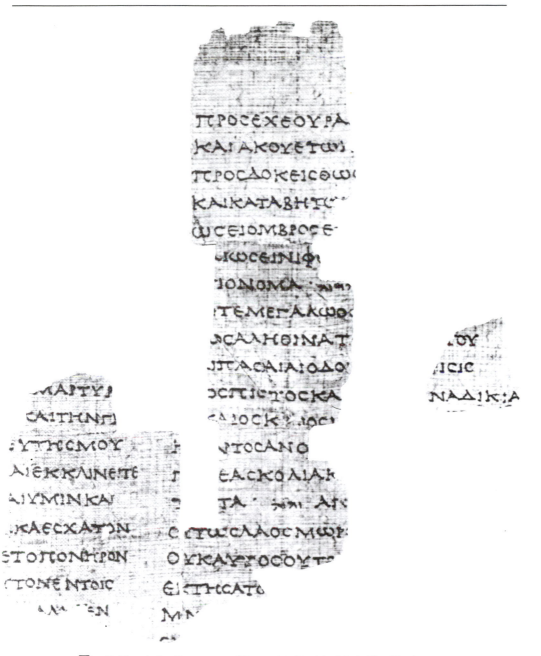

The Bible of the Septuagint (Deut. 31:28–30; 32:1–7) *Fuad Papyrus No. 266, 1st century* BCE *(Cairo; deposited in the French Institute of Eastern Archaeology).*

Above and beyond the "cultural politics" of the Ptolemies, other, more practical motives could have been at work, deepening and strengthening the king's interest. The Jews accounted for a considerable percentage of the Ptolemaic kingdom's population, in Egypt as well as in Judea, which was an integral part of the realm throughout the third century BCE. Although they belonged to the reigning minority, the Jews were set apart by their religious practices, which referred to a Law reputedly of divine inspiration. Guaranteeing the respect of this Law could only prove advantageous to the regime. But, for the effective application of the Law, the royal judges and officials, throughout the land, needed full access to the texts. In other words, a Greek translation was necessary; the practical concerns of the monarchy were convergent with the religious needs of the Jews of Egypt.

In this respect, it is highly instructive to compare the Greek Torah with what we know of the Ptolemaic regime's attitude toward the national traditions of the native Egyptian population. We shall then be able to place the undertaking described in the *Letter of Aristeas* in its proper perspective, within the framework of actual legal practice in Ptolemaic Egypt, at the beginning of the third century BCE. To gain some historical perspective, let us first make a brief trip backwards in time.

Alone among their middle eastern neighbors, the ancient Egyptians did not seem to have found it necessary to possess a corpus of written law. Nothing in hieroglyphic documents bears any resemblance to the great Sumerian and Akkadian legislative monuments in cuneiform: the Code of Hammurabi, the Laws of Eshnunna, the Hittite Laws, the Assyrian Laws, etc. The legislative efforts of the Egyptian sovereigns begin to appear clearly in our sources only at the end of the New Empire, the Saitic restoration and rule of the Persians. The most noteworthy was the codification attributed to Darius I, the second Persian ruler of Egypt. Seen in the light of papyrological texts from Ptolemaic and Roman times, the testimony of Diodorus of Sicily (I, 95) becomes meaningful.

The first document we should evoke here is an Egyptian papyrus at the Bibliothèque Nationale in Paris. On one side, it bears a text known as the "Demotic Chronicle"; on the other, whose state renders its decipherment difficult and uncertain, we can make out an account of the codifying process. We learn that, in the third year of his reign (519 BCE), Darius ordered the satrap of Egypt to name a commission of "wise men" chosen among the ranks of Egyptian warriors, priests, and scribes, to "set down in writing the Egyptian law that obtained up to the forty-fourth year of the reign of Amasis." Amasis, the next-to-the-last king of Egypt before the Persian conquest, had reigned for exactly forty-four years (570–526 BCE). Since we may safely ignore the ephemeral reign of his successor, Psammetichus III (526–525 BCE), who lost Egypt to Cambyses, the object of Darius' initiative was nothing less than the codification of all of Egyptian law prior to the conquest. After sixteen years of labor, the commission accomplished its task. According to our document, a great compendium was elaborated in two official copies, an "Assyrian" copy, in Aramaic, the official tongue of the Achaemenid chancellery, and an "epistolary" copy, in demotic Egyptian.

Did the work of Darius survive the Macedonian conquest of Egypt? In order to answer this question, we shall have recourse to a second document, already famous: a lengthy Egyptian papyrus from the Ptolemaic era, found during the excavations of 1938–39, but published only in 1975 under the misleading title of "The Demotic Legal Code of Hermopolis West." The term is inexact, both in the Roman meaning—a collection of imperial laws, such as the Theodosian Code and the Code of Justinian—and in the modern meaning of a collection of legal rules in a given domain, such as the French Civil Code. In fact, the text is a collection of practical prescriptions devised to assist native judges and notaries in their daily routine, by furnishing models for the redaction of acts and sentences, and suggestions for the solution of difficult cases. It should not be compared to the work of Justinian, nor to that of Napoleon I.

Should we drop the idea of a code and speak of a "commentary"? This approach does not solve the problem, as it postulates the previous existence of a text forming the object of this commentary, a legislative monument of which we possess no direct evidence. In lieu of a false code, we would now have an imaginary code, the existence of which is merely hypothetical. Should we follow the reasoning of P. W. Pestman, of Leyden, who speaks of a "manual," a term that seems to fit our document better than "code" or "commentary," if taken in its practical meaning ("handbook") rather than its didactic meaning ("schoolbook")? If we search for the author of such a "manual," complications would ensue. The fact that, over a long period of time, several copies of the book were available, leads us to believe that it was not simply a private compilation of arbitrary character, but an authorized manual. The authority in question might have been that of King Bocchoris, the "father of our manual" (as Pestman suggests). Yet, a manual whose validity is based on the authority of a sovereign to impose its use upon judges and notaries is no longer a manual, but a statute! We have come full circle, back to the "code."

One can begin to measure the inadequacy of using Roman or modern notions ("code," "statute," "commentary," "manual") to define the nature of the demotic compendium. Perhaps we can find a way out of our dilemma by examining the actual conditions in which it was elaborated: the work was carried out by a body of Egyptian priests, working in the singular atmosphere of the "Houses of Life" attached to their temples, producing and copying religious, scientific or juridical material for the Egyptian clergy and their clientele. Our compendium falls into the class of "sacred books," *djemaneter* in Egyptian. Rather than a "code" or a "manual," it should be termed "The Priestly Case Book." The "commentator" was not a single individual but a series of successive generations of Egyptian priests, zealous guardians of the national law. Theirs was a pragmatic approach, with special attention to borderline cases, where practical incertitudes could cause conflicts. They were more concerned with particular situations than desirous of establishing general norms. Concerning marriages, for example, they paid little attention to the "normal" case in which a written deed engaging the husband to support his wife was given directly to the latter, but concentrated on the exceptional situation in which the deed was presented to the father of the bride. Since the manner of handling normal cases was obvious, the treatment of dubious cases had to be specified in detail.

Have we discovered the key to the problem of the codification of Egyptian law attributed to Darius? Its purpose may well have been the coordination of the customary rules that the priests—who were members of the royal commission—had noted down in their "sacred books." The goal was only partially attained. The priests, guardians of the Case Book, perpetuated its contents, although local variants might differ from one religious center to another. The Hermopolis text is not, in fact, the sole testimony to their activity in this domain. Shortly after the publication of this document, the Italian scholar Edda Bresciani edited, in 1981, other fragments of the compendium, which had been discovered in Tebtunis, in the courtyard of the temple of Sobek (Suchos), the crocodile god. Ten years later, in 1991, other fragments came to light, among the Carlsberg papyri deposited in the Carsten-Niebuhr Institute of the University of Copenhagen. They are supposedly of Memphite origin and date from ca. 100–50 BCE. And the list is not closed.

We can now come to the heart of the matter. In 1978, the British scholar John Rea published a papyrus from Oxyrhynchos (XLVI 3285), which established the fact that, probably under the reign of Ptolemy II Philadelphus, the demotic Case Book had been translated into Greek. The translation is preserved in a copy effectuated during the Antonine period, in the second century CE. This does not, of course, furnish the proof that it was still of practical use to the provincial authorities of Roman Egypt. It simply proves that it was of ideological interest for the Egyptians, desirous of conserving their national patrimony. The Oxyrhynchos papyrus corresponds only partially to the Hermopolis text, with so many differences of detail that it cannot be considered a Greek version of this document. The translation was based on another variant of the compendium, not to be found among those we have evoked above. It seems to have been the "official version" of the compendium, accepted. if not commissioned, by the Ptolemaic monarchy.

We must firmly stress the parallel between the two "holy books" translated into Greek under the first Ptolemies: the Egyptian priestly Case Book and the Torah of Moses. There is no written account of the translation of the compendium, not even a legendary one, such as we possess for the Septuagint. Egyptians well-versed in Greek were not rare in Alexandria, and it would be easy to imagine a group of translators working under the direction of a Hellenized Egyptian scholar such as Manetho, who, at the beginning of the third century BCE, wrote a history of his country in Greek. What is lacking is an Egyptian Aristeas, to transmit the glory of the exploit to future generations. We cannot know whether the fruit of their labors shared a bookshelf in the Alexandrian Library with the Greek text of the Torah of Moses. From the viewpoint of legal history, the two translations do have much in common, since they belong to the same Ptolemaic judiciary system as it was functioning in the third century BCE.

THE LAW OF MOSES AND THE JUSTICE OF THE KING

Ptolemaic Egypt offers the legal historian a particularly interesting example of plurality of laws. The local law of the indigenous Egyptian population was still in force after the conquests; we have treated the manner and means of its survival in the preceding section. The immigrants had imported their own juridical traditions: the Greek *nomoi*. In the cities—Alexandria, Naucratis, Ptolemais—these were couched in the traditional form of written legislation, often influenced by the reigning monarch. In the chora, they took the form of a substantially homogeneous customary law. The diversity proper to the legal systems of ancient Greece was gradually eliminated, a process that had already begun in the fourth century BCE, when the growing influence of Athens tended to dominate intercity commerce. In the great "melting pot" of Alexander's army, the differences in the legal traditions of the soldiers' original "homelands" had been reduced to such a point that a "common law" of the Greeks prevailed in the Hellenistic world. Drawing a parallel between law and language, scholars have coined the notion of a "legal koine", to define this phenomenon.

Over and against the Greek and Egyptian *nomoi*, the will of the Ptolemaic sovereign was expressed in royal regulations (*diagrammata*) and ordinances (*prostagmata*). The scope of royal law was theoretically unlimited but was, in practice, restricted to questions concerning the administration of the economy and the interests of the royal treasury. How did the Torah of Moses fit into this picture?

Despite the contrary opinion previously professed by some scholars, we are certain today that the Ptolemies did not strive to unify the legal rules throughout the kingdom. As the names of Solon, Lycurgus, Zaleucus, and Charondas may serve to testify, the idea of a vast codification, covering an entire state, was certainly not foreign to Greek tradition. And, as we have seen, it concurred with that of the Achaemenids. The Ptolemies, however, preferred another solution to the problems created by the existence of legal rules of unequal weight and of various provenance. They did not work on the substance of the law itself but operated by the formal bias of the administration of justice. The originator of this ingenious judiciary system was Ptolemy II Philadelphus.

Thanks to research by the late lamented Hans Julius Wolff, the system is now well known. The king reserved the right of intervention in any and all litigations, either directly (Dositheos son of Drimylos treated such a case, as we have seen) or indirectly, through the *chrematistai*, royal judges, itinerant at first, afterwards assigned to each nome as permanent judicial authorities. The kingdom was blanketed by a double network of jurisdictions, each authorized to treat the cases falling within its specific nationally determined competence: for cases involving Greek-speaking immigrants, in the cities and in the chora, the dicasteries, local law-courts; for those involving the indigenous population, the courts of *laokritai* ("people's judges"), staffed by Egyptian priests. In the application of the law, priority lay with royal legislation. But the king, well aware of the limits of his regulations and ordinances, decided that, in the absence of a clear royal regulation, the judges of the dicastery (local law-court) should resort to "civic laws," *politikoi nomoi*. If these were insufficient to guide them to a decision, then each judge would have to "follow the dictates of his conscience," as we say today, in accordance with the "most equitable view" (*gnome dikaiotate*). In a similar fashion, the *laokritai* were to apply Egyptian law, the "law of the land," *nomoi tes choras*.

A lawsuit involving Jewish litigants, which took place in the Faiyum in 226 BCE, affords us our first glimpse of this hierarchy of judiciary rules. One Dositheos, an Egyptian Jew, had sued Herakleia daughter of Diosdotos, also a Jewess. The case was to be judged in the dicastery of Krokodilopolis. All the judges were Greek. The lady in question was accompanied by her legal guardian, an Athenian born in Egypt. One might note, in passing, the atmosphere of friendly understanding between Jews and Greeks. The case itself was not of great moment. Dositheos had accused Herakleia of insulting him in public and ripping his coat, causing him 200 drachmas' worth of damages. At the last minute, however, he lost his nerve and failed to appear before the court. Herakleia did not desist but, taking up her proper defense, produced, *inter alia,* an extract of a royal regulation, a *diagramma*, probably a fragment of an "organic law" that served as a guide for the rendering of justice in the framework of the judicial system created by Ptolemy II Philadelphus. In the minutes of the proceedings, the *diagramma* is literally quoted:

> And whereas the code of regulations [diagramma] which was handed in by Herakleia among the justificatory documents directs us to give judgments in a . . . manner on all points that any person knows or shows us to have been dealt with in the regulations of king Ptolemy [diagrammata], in accordance with the regulations; and on all points not dealt with in the regulations, but in the civic laws [politikoi nomoi], in accordance with these laws; and on all other points to follow the most equitable view [gnome dikaiotate]; but when both parties have been summoned before the court and one of them is unwilling to put in a written statement or plead his case or acknowledge defeat [?] . . . he shall be judged guilty of injustice; we have dismissed the case. (*PAPYRUS PETRIE III 21G* + *PAPYRUS GUROB 2; CPJUD. I 19*)

Dositheos lost his case by nonappearance. But we have learned two interesting things: first, that there was a hierarchical order for rules of law applicable to litigations in the dicasteries; second, that the dicasteries were widely competent. They were not simply courts "for Greeks" but were authorized to deal with plaintiffs identifying themselves, linguistically or culturally, as Hellenes. Any Hellene could require the judges of the dicasteries to try him according to "civic laws." As a Hellene, a Jew could invoke the royal diagramma bearing this authorization. There was obviously a close link between royal justice and the laws applicable to Jews. What exactly was this link?

To answer this question, we must thoroughly understand all the terms of the regulation. In the present state of our knowledge, we may not be able to offer an irrefutable

Ptolemy II Philadelphus and his sister-wife Arsinoe II *The Gonzaga Cameo, 3rd Century* BCE *(Hermitage, St. Petersburg).*

interpretation. The *diagrammata*, expression of the king's will, create no major difficulties. Neither does the "most equitable view," *gnome dikaiotate*, a well-known traditional Greek notion concerning the problem of gaps in the law. Our papyrus converges with the testimony of Demosthenes and some epigraphic documents, confirming the Panhellenic character of the principle.

The term "civic laws," *nomoi politikoi*, is more obscure. According to Hans Julius Wolff, it designated the "national laws" of the litigants. If these latter were of common origin, citizens of the same city or their descendants or, as in the present case, members of the same ethnic community, Wolff believed that the king, in the absence of the appropriate royal legislation, had authorized the judges to apply the laws of their home-land. A curious problem arises here, since one never hears of an Athenian law, for example, being applied to plaintiffs of Athenian origin. For when they immigrated to Egypt, the Greek-speaking colonists had not imported their ancestral law, with the unique exception of the Jews, who had imported theirs! But, whatever the degree of solicitude King Ptolemy may have entertained for the Mosaic Law, royal regulations were not conceived for the sole use of the Jewish population.

H. J. Wolff's hypothesis should accordingly be interpreted with a grain of salt: the regulation should be taken more as an intention than a reality. When the Alexandrian lawmakers were pondering the clauses of the *diagrammata*, they may well have envisaged the possibility of applying the litigants' national law as a subsidiary law, to fill the gaps of the royal legislation. But that project was not carried out. In actual practice, the term "civic laws" came to designate the laws of the Greek-speaking immigrants; they were "civic," since they were applicable to the Hellenes, "citizens" as opposed to the village world of the native population. In other words, the term became synonymous with Greek "common law," the legal koine.

The intentions of the legislator had, nonetheless, highly important practical consequences. Whatever be the proper meaning of the term *politikoi nomoi*, whether the "civic laws" stemmed from the litigants' national legislation (as the legislators had intended) or from the documents actually employed in practice (everyday reality), the legal traditions of the Greek-speaking population became the official legal corpus for the dicasteries, liable to judiciary sanction. Egyptian law, for its part, termed *nomoi tes choras*, the local law, became the legal corpus for the courts of the *laokritai*. The two groups of *nomoi*, corresponding to the two groups of the population, had been raised to the status of "laws of the court," *leges fori*, for their respective tribunals. Greek versions facilitated the enforcement of legal dispositions not originally formulated in Greek.

A comparison of the Septuagint with the Greek translation of the Egyptian Case Book leads us to the conclusion that the Greek Torah obtained its official consecration by its insertion into the Ptolemaic judiciary system. When the Persian king Artaxerxes entrusted Ezra and Nehemiah with the mission of reconstituting a Jewish entity in Achaemenid Judea, the Torah of Ezra, confirmed as a royal law for the Jews of the realm, was centered on the Temple, rebuilt after the return from captivity in Babylon. Two centuries later, when the Seleucid ruler Antiochus III chose to reconfirm the privileges of the Temple and the Jewish people, he resorted to the typically Hellenistic form of a "charter," which conferred upon the inhabitants of Jerusalem the same right as that enjoyed by the citizens of the Greek city: to "live according to their ancestral laws." A Jewish legend, we have seen, attributed the authorship of this privilege to Alexander himself.

In Egypt, the confirmation of the Jewish Law could not refer to the Temple, nor take the form of a "charter," but could be achieved on the basis of judicial sanction, within the framework of a system established to protect the laws and customs of the kingdom's inhabitants, priority being given to the king's interests. The Torah, once it was translated into Greek, could become a *nomos politikos*, a "civic law," guaranteed by Ptolemaic justice. In the lawsuit brought against her by the Jew Dositheos, Herakleia the Jewess invoked, in her defense, the regulation authorizing the application of "civic laws." Had she been counseled by an expert, she might have even invoked the authority of Exodus (21:18ff.) concerning assault and battery. As it turned out, the nonappearance of her adversary led only to the application of the clause condemning default.

We shall now cite a second papyrus, containing the complaint of a woman married to a Jew. Her woes are worthy of our compassion, and the information her testimony affords brings grist to our mill. She had addressed her case (May 11, 218 BCE) to the king:

> To King Ptolemy greeting from Helladote, daughter of Philonides.
>
> I am being wronged by Jonathas, the Jew. . . . He has agreed by a written contract [in accordance with the civic] law of the Jews to hold me [as wife]. Now he wants to renounce [and claims for] 100 drachmas, and also the house: he does not give me my due, and shuts me out of my house . . . and absolutely wrongs me in every respect.
>
> I beg you therefore, my king, to order Diophanes, the strategus, to write to . . . the epistates of Samareia not to let [me be wronged, but] to send Jonathas to Diophanes in order [that he may inquire into the case]. For by this means [I shall no longer be wronged, but having sought your protection, I shall obtain justice].
>
> Farewell.
>
> [Verso:] Year 4, Dios 3, Phamenoth 27.
>
> Helladote daughter of Philonides concerning dowry and. . . ." (*Papyrus Enteuxeis 23; CPJud. I 128*)

Helladote, to judge from her name and patronymic, seems to be Greek. Since she had become the spouse of a Jew "according to the civic law of the Jews," she must have been integrated into the community of her husband. The late Edoardo Volterra suggested that this document may have been a reference to the traditional formula for a Jewish marriage contracted "according to the law of Moses and Israel" (*kedat Moshe veYisra'el*). Volterra's hypothesis could be reinforced by a variant of the formula in which "Israel" is replaced by "Jews" (*Yehudaei*)—an exact counterpart of the Greek *ton Ioudaion*, "of the Jews"; that variant, attested in documents found in the Dead Sea region as well as in Palestinian marriage and divorce acts from the Cairo Geniza, was quoted by the Talmud as having been current among Alexandrian Jews (Jerusalem Talmud, Ketubot 4:8; 29a). In any case, since the Ptolemaic judge would not have been able to understand the expression "Law of Moses," *nomos Moyseos*, Helladote preferred to invoke the authority of the Torah, the "civic law of the Jews" (although the marriage formula is not to be found in the biblical text). In Ptolemaic Egypt, this appears to have been the current appellation of the Greek Torah. The author of the Letter of Aristeas also called it "the Law of the Jews," *nomos ton Ioudaion* (§ 30).

As for Helladote's husband Jonathas, the situation is clear: his actions were obviously based on the Torah. He repudiated his spouse in the traditional manner sanctioned by Deuteronomy 24:1, the basis of Jewish divorce law. That ruling was in flagrant contradiction with current Greek matrimonial custom, which recognized the equality of husband and wife in divorce proceedings. The numerous marriage contracts preserved in the papyri we possess contain clauses providing for divorce with the torts attributed to one or the other spouse, and, later on, even by mutual consent. The husband promised formally not to repudiate, literally not to "throw out" (*me ekballein*) his wife. Now Helladote had well and truly been "thrown out." The incompatibility between Jewish law and Greek practice was precisely the cause of Helladote's outrage and the prime motive for her complaint.

Thanks to this misadventure, we have been able to learn a most important fact: Jewish Law, that is, the Greek Torah, had truly become a "civic law," *politikos nomos*, among other "civic laws" applicable to Greek-speaking immigrants. Henceforth, the Septuagint had its place among the other "civic laws" as the "civic law" for the Jews of Egypt. We have still to learn what use the Jews would make of their newfound liberty to live according to the Law of their forefathers.

"The Law of the Land Is Law"

We have reason to believe that, by and large, the Jews of Egypt observed the Judaic commandments. A papyrus from the "Zenon Archive" dating from the third century BCE attests the respect of the Sabbath: in a tally of brick deliveries, the number of bricks delivered on the seventh day of the month of Epeiph was replaced by the Greek word for Sabbath, *sabbata* (Papyrus Cairo Zenon IV 59762; CPJud. I 10). We find one of Zenon's employees taking Sabbath leave, undoubtedly with the consent of his employer. The man's name, as Octave Guéraud suggested and Victor Tcherikover specified, may even have been Sabbataios, "born on the Sabbath day." Symbolic in this instance, it was a commonplace name at that time. One wonders how the royal Jewish soldiers managed to reconcile the sabbatical pause with their military obligations. With some mutual concessions, a viable working agreement must have been possible.

In Jewish family life, several instances of conformity to traditional practice have been evoked. In Lady Helladote's complaint, the "Law of the Jews" seems to have served as the legal basis for her marriage as well as her divorce. But two hundred years later, a Jewish couple from Alexandria, in defiance of the biblical ruling, were to put an end to their union by mutual consent (Berlin Papyrus IV, 1102; CPJud. II, 144).

In this regard, these two methods of divorce corresponded to a duality both of views and of practices among the Jews of that period. One current subscribed to the unilateral repudiation of the wife by the husband, while the other recognized reciprocity in this domain. As we have seen, the latter practice, whereby the wife could initiate divorce proceedings, had already been that of the Jews in Elephantine. Greek influence obviously abetted the flourishing of the egalitarian tendency by affording it a favorable social climate. Spurred, doubtless, by a desire to accentuate the difference between Jews and non-Jews, rabbinical Judaism was to have the last word, eventually imposing unilateral repudiation as the sole accepted procedure. Egalitarian pressure persisted for a long while, however, as attested by clauses in marriage contracts enabling the wife to initiate divorce proceedings, with judiciary assistance.

This example demonstrates the flexible character of the "oral law," the halakhah, during the epoch of the Second Commonwealth, before its codification in the Mishnah, about 200 CE. The terrain of commercial transactions offers many instances of the incertitudes of Jewish law and the tensions arising from the antagonistic gravitational pulls of the Torah and the foreign environment. The prohibition of loans with interest will serve as touchstone.

The Torah sets down the rule three times: in Exodus (22:24), Leviticus (25:35–37) and Deuteronomy (23:20–21). The latter text proclaims the absolute prohibition of loans with interest among Jews: "Thou shalt not lend upon interest to thy brother: interest of money, interest of victuals, interest of anything that is lent upon interest. Unto a foreigner thou mayest lend upon interest; but unto thy brother thou shalt not lend upon interest; that the Lord thy God may bless thee in all that thou puttest thy hand unto, in the land whither thou goest in to possess it."

Upon the basis of the biblical texts, enriched by oral tradition, the rabbis had elaborated a most subtle doctrine that condemned not only interest itself, *ribbit*, but any form of enrichment resembling interest, "the dust of interest" (*avaq ribbit*). During the Ptolemaic epoch, the Jews of Egypt could not, of course, have known of the future talmudic formulation of rabbinical doctrine, but they were perfectly aware of the biblical interdiction, thrice repeated in the Torah.

Hellenistic practice did not require them to distance themselves from the straight and narrow path: the free loan was well established in Greek tradition. An ancient Greek usage, still attested in Ptolemaic Alexandria, was the *eranos*, or friendly loan, in which several friends "chipped in" to help out a comrade in difficulty. Other solutions were available, offering credit without charge. A loan placed within the contractual form of a deposit (*paratheke* or *parakatatheke*) was automatically exempted from interest. The only drawback was that the creditor was empowered to reclaim his "deposit" at will, as is the case in present-day banking practice, which, in this respect, harks back to Hellenistic days. The deed of loan could also contain a specific renunciation of interest, thus simplifying matters. For an observant Jew, wishing to conform at once to biblical injunctions and current usage, the situation was ideal.

So much for theory; let us try now to gain some insight into everyday practice, by examining two contracts from the second century BCE, involving Jews from the Faiyum. The first contract, drawn up toward the end of the reign of Ptolemy V Epiphanes, on the fourth of November 182 BCE, specified the conditions under which Apollonios son of Protogenes lent money to his friend Sostratos son of Neoptolemos. The creditor and the debtor were both Jewish.

In the twenty-fourth year of the reign of Ptolemy son of Ptolemy and Arsinoe, gods Philopatores, the priest of Alexander and the gods Adelphoi and the gods Euergetai and the gods Philopatores and the gods Epiphaneis, and the athlophoros of Berenice Euergetis, and the kanephoros of Arsinoe Philadelphus, and the priestess of Arsinoe Philopator being those officiating at Alexandria, on the twenty-eighth of the month of Dystros, being Thot twenty-eighth, in Krokodilopolis in the Arsinoite nome.

Apollonios son of Protogenes, Jew of the epigone, has lent to Sostratos son of Neoptolemos, Jew of the epigone, two talents three thousand drachmas of copper money without interest for one year from the date above written on the security of the house belonging to him and its court and all appurtenances situated at Apias in the division of Themistos, of which the measurements are, from south to north twenty cubits, from west to east twenty cubits, and the adjacent areas, on the south the house of Sopatra, on the north and east streets, on the west the house of Harpalos and Sostratos [belonging?] to them at the date above written.

Sostratos shall repay this loan to Apollonios within the year, and if he does not repay it as stated, Apollonios shall have the right to lay claim to the security in accordance with the regulation [diagramma]. Sostratos shall guarantee to Apollonios this security and shall produce it unencumbered, unpledged, not liable for another debt, and free from royalties. If he does not guarantee it or produce it as stated or if any risk occurs with regard to this security in whole or in part in any way, Sostratos shall repay this debt to Apollonios forthwith within the year; and if he does not repay it as stated, Sostratos shall forthwith forfeit to Apollonios the loan increased by one half and for the overtime interest at the rate of two drachmas per mina per month. This contract shall be valid everywhere.

[Second hand:] Through Boubakos also called Stheneus [the notary public].

[Third hand:] Apollonios, aged about 35, tall, fair, with rather bright blue eyes and protruding ears.

Sostratos, aged about 35, of middle height, fair, blue-eyed, with a scar over his right eyebrow. (TEBTUNIS PAPYRUS III 817; CPJUD. I 23)

These two Jews of "the epigone," born in Egypt, have pure Greek names. Had the document not specified that they were *Ioudaioi*, Jews, there would be no way of guessing this fact. However, dealing as it does with two Jews, the papyrus and especially its last lines suddenly take on new meaning. A "portrait" is sketched out: that of two Jews born in Egypt about the year 200 BCE, of the same age (35 years). These descriptive details provide a rare opportunity to learn something about the physical appearance of King Ptolemy's Jewish soldiers. But disappointment (or relief?) follows: nothing we find here, or in the other rare papyri we dispose of, can help us distinguish a Jew from a Greek. Much bad faith is needed to see in Apollonios' protruding ears a typically Jewish feature. And what is one to make of his bright blue eyes, more precisely "bluish" (*hypocharops* or *hypocharopos*, "slightly tinted with azure"), or the bluish (*epicharops*) eyes of his partner? In any case, this is what Jews from the Faiyum looked like, some 2200 years ago.

Now for the facts. The one-year loan of two and a half talents was granted without interest (*atoka*). Were Apollonios and Sostratos following the precepts of the Torah: "unto thy brother thou shalt lend without interest"? Apollonios did in fact take precautionary measures, by accepting the mortgage on his friend's house as a guarantee of the debt. There is nothing out of the ordinary here, but the following stipulation is disturbing, since it contains a penalty of 50 percent (*hemiolion*—"the loan increased by one half")—in case of nonreimbursement at the end of the one-year period, and the "overtime" interest rate is 2 drachmas per mina per month, amounting to a 24 percent yearly rate (1 mina = 100 drachmas). This was the official rate of interest, fixed by a regulation (*diagramma*) of Ptolemy II Philadelphus in the first half of the third century BCE. The biblical interdiction makes no distinction between capital interest and interest on arrears, and the rabbis condemned them both with equal severity. Bah! Apollonios need have no qualms of conscience, as the loan was nominally free of interest, provided Sostratos took care to reimburse his creditor on time.

But here is another contract, drawn up in Trikomia in the Faiyum, some years later (April 16, 174 BCE).

> In the seventh year of the reign of Ptolemy son of Ptolemy and Cleopatra, gods Epiphaneis, when Philostratos was priest of Alexander and the gods Soteres and the gods Adelphoi and the gods Euergetai and the gods Philopatores and the gods Epiphaneis and and the gods Philometores, Aspasia daughter of Chrysermos being athlophoros of Berenice Euergetis, Isidora daughter of Apollonios being kanephoros of Arsinoe Philadelphos, and Eirene daughter of Ptolemaios being priestess of Arsinoe Philopator, on the thirteenth of the month of Gorpiaios, being Phamenoth thirteenth, in Trikomia in the division of Themistos in the Arsinoite nome.
>
> Judas son of Josephos, Jew of the epigone, has lent to Agathokles son of Ptolemaios, Jew, of the detachment of Molossos, taktomisthos [paymaster], stationed in the Herakleopolite nome, two talents five hundred drachmas of copper money for twelve months from the date above written with interest at two drachmas per mina per month. This loan is the amount which Agathokles still owed to Judas out of five talents that he had received from Judas as an advance toward a retail trade business in partnership according to a written agreement, of which Ananias son of Jonathas, Jew of the epigone, is the guardian. Agathokles shall repay to Judas the aforesaid loan and the interest in the month of Mecheir of the eighth year [March–April 173 BCE]; but if he does not repay it as stated, he shall pay it increased by a half. This agreement is valid.

Witnesses: Deinias son of Aineas, Thraseas son of Sosibios, Thebon son of Phanokles, Samaelos son of Joannes, all four Jews of the epigone; Theodoros son of Theodoros, who is also known as Samaelos, Nikanor son of Jason, both Jews, 80-arouras holders, of the First Hipparchy settled by Dositheos.

[Second hand:] I, Agathokles, have received the two talents and the five hundred drachmas, the amount of the loan above written, and have deposited the agreement, which is valid, with Deinias as its keeper.
(TEBTUNIS PAPYRUS III 818; CPJUD. I 24)

We shall not bicker over the date of this interesting contract, but shall take note in passing that the anonymous stereotyped formula of the preceding document gives way here to a list of the eponymous priest and priestesses who were actually in office at the time. The papyrus records a transfer of credit ("novation") in which, with one exception, all the persons mentioned are Jews: the two associates, who are also the creditor and the debtor, all the witnesses, the "keeper" of the contract and most probably Dositheos, who is either one of the eponymous officers of the First Hipparchy or the officer charged with the distribution of land allotments among the cleruchs. A third hypothesis casts him as the Jewish general whom Josephus associated with the high priest Onias (*Against Apion* 2, 49). If this were so, the only non-Jew would be Molossos, the commanding officer of the infantry detachment to which Agathokles belonged.

Greek soldiers in Egypt *Fragment of the "Nile Mosaic" (Palestrina, National Museum).*

The ethnic designation of the others is clearly set down. Their names and patronymics are either Hellenized Jewish names (Ananias, Jason, Joannes, Jonathas, Josephos, Judas, Samaelos) or Greek names rendering theophoric Jewish names, particularly in favor among the Jews of Egypt (Dositheos, Theodoros). There are also some purely Greek names (Agathokles, Aineas, Deinias, Nikanor, Phanokles, Sosibios, Thebon or Theron, Thraseas). All these persons were either soldiers on active duty, provided with parcels of honorable proportions, or descendants of soldiers; the epigone ("the descendants") functioned as a sort of recruiting pool for the Ptolemaic army. The reigning sovereign was Ptolemy VI Philometor, the well-known "philo-Semite" who had promoted some Jews to important military posts, as was the case for Onias and Dositheos (it does not matter whether the latter was actually the one mentioned in our document). Indeed, it would be hard to imagine a more faithful image of the Jews in Egypt at the dawn of the second century BCE than the one provided by our document. Solidly settled in the country for several generations, deeply rooted in the Ptolemaic military, they were equally affirmative of their identity, confirmed by their distinctive national origin (*ethnikon*): they were *Ioudaioi*, Jews.

Let us return now to the law of interest on loans. At first glance, Judas and Agathokles, as well as their coreligionists who served as witnesses, would appear to be transgressors. The situation can easily be reconstructed. Our two friends were partners in a business whose nature was a bit obscure. The Greek words (*ergasia metabolike*) used to describe it can apply either to an exchange office or a retail business. The second hypothesis is more likely; one can readily imagine a sort of PX for the soldiers stationed in the Herakleopolite nome, the necessary funds being supplied by Judas, the "capitalist." It appears that, out of the 5 copper talents (30,000 drachmas) of initial capital, slightly less than 3 talents (17,500 drachmas) had actually been invested; Agathokles was thus obliged to return the remaining 12,500 drachmas to Judas. The latter was accredited with this sum, in the form of a one-year loan bearing a 24 percent interest rate, the legal norm. Business is business, not only between "brothers," but among partners.

Can we be sure that the biblical interdiction had been transgressed? To reply to this question, it will prove useful to consider our document in the perspective of the rabbinical discussions treating the basis of the prohibition, and their prolongations in Western Christianity.

Was not the law of *ribbit* formulated in a specific economic and historical context? At that remote epoch, were loans not essentially consumers' loans in an agricultural civilization? John Calvin held this opinion: he distinguishes money from capital, setting the consumers' loan, for which the prohibition would be justified, against the investors' loan, for which it would not. Within a Christian context, the Calvinistic position was defended by the great sixteenth-century French jurist Charles Dumoulin, who esteemed that the Holy Scriptures do not prohibit interest in general, but only the kind of interest that could do injury to charity and the love of one's neighbor. Closer to our time, a traditional Jewish commentator, Baruch Halevy Epstein, the author of a commentary on the Pentateuch entitled *Torah Temima* (2nd ed. Vilna, 1904), gave a similar verdict. During the remote epoch when agriculture was the principal activity and source of revenue for the Jews, interest would have been unthinkable; with the beginnings of commerce, interest could no longer be condemned out of hand.

The debate may well have had its roots in the Greco-Roman period. In Abraham Weingort's doctoral thesis on interest and credit in talmudic law (Paris 1979), in which one may find a more detailed discussion of the problem, the author admits to having been initially seduced by these rationalistic arguments, which contended that Moses would not have prohibited interest "had he known that it could be profitable." Further investigation led him to the conviction that the sages of the Talmud were already aware of this reasoning and had rejected it, maintaining the interdiction under all circumstances.

This controversy reveals the gap between theory and practice in the legal dealings of the Jews at the time of the Second Commonwealth. Our document could well mirror the opinion holding that necessary investment could legitimately produce interest. Since the question was still open to debate, our Jews were perhaps persuaded, in all good faith, of the legitimacy of their operation, which the Talmud was only to condemn some centuries hence. Evidence from the Faiyum of the second century BCE would thus attest practices which had indirectly inspired the partisans of interest on investment capital, precursors of Calvin and Dumoulin.

How, then, are we to interpret the terms of the first contract, recording a loan without interest? Can a loan granted "without interest," *atokon*, really be profitless for the lender? Many modern scholars answered in the affirmative, and constructed hypotheses concerning the "disinterestedness" of the Jews and its possible influence on their pagan neighbors. More recent research tends to picture them as the victims of an illusion.

The adjective *atokos*, "without interest," may, in certain cases, describe a truly free loan. But this is rarely so. In the majority of instances, an "interest-free" loan was in fact a loan with built-in interest: interest deducted in advance from the amount of the loan (I borrow 100 drachmas, I receive 50); or else incorporated into the loan, as an addition to the amount lent (I receive 100 drachmas, but I declare that I have received 150)—in both these cases the debtor has to reimburse more than he receives. Such "interest-free" loans may have conveniently camouflaged illegal profits, entailing usurious rates of interest. In lieu of interest, the debtor might offer the creditor the use of a field, a garden, a house (*antichresis*), of much greater value than a mere 24 percent per year. Another twist was the obligation to mortgage one's property as a guarantee, the creditor knowing full well, from the outset, that the debtor would be unable to repay the loan. This sort of operation, technically "free of interest," actually concealed an iron-bound buying-and-selling deal, enabling the creditor to acquire property or real estate at prices well below the market level. This, then, was how money was lent "without interest" in Hellenistic Egypt.

We have no serious reason to insinuate that Apollonios son of Protogenes wanted to "swindle" his "brother" Sostratos, lending him money for the sole purpose of buying his house at a bargain price one year later. During the second century BCE, houses were known to have changed hands at prices attaining four copper talents. The sum of two and a half talents agreed to by Sostratos may have been a perfectly just price for his house. Moreover, one cannot prove that this "interest-free" loan was actually intended to cover up an actual sale. After all, the loan may have really been free of interest, who knows?

What is paramount here is the fact that a careful examination of papyrological documents has enlarged our knowledge of the manner in which the Jews in Egypt went about their business dealings with regard to the injunctions of Jewish Law. Some light has also been cast on the mutual give-and-take of the confronting traditions. In the domain of credit and remuneration of debt, there was no Jewish influence on the Greeks, nor on the Egyptians. As we have seen, the Greeks had not waited to meet the Jews before establishing a system of free credit. By signing an "interest-free" loan contract—whose authentic character was purely hypothetical and also highly improbable—a Jew could not have exerted any influence on his Greek or Egyptian neighbor's comportment.

The converse would be closer to the truth. In the practice of law, the choice of language and of formulae is determinative. Language is the vehicle of law. Jews who drew up Greek contracts followed Greek law. We have certainly endeavored to place our documents within the pattern of the general evolution of Jewish doctrine concerning the bases of the provisions forbidding loans with interest between Jews. But everyday reality was probably more prosaic. Victor Tcherikover was certainly right in his observations concerning the comportment of the Jewish soldiers of the Faiyum: in a manner that modern orthodox Judaism might deem excessively liberal, they applied, by anticipation, the principle the famous Babylonian amora Mar Samuel was to enunciate in the third century CE, in his treatment of commercial transactions and fiscal obligations: *dina demalkhuta dina*, "the law of the land is law."

CHAPTER 6

A Jewish Temple
in Ptolemaic Egypt

THE ECHOES OF THE MACCABEAN CRISIS

Toward 200 BCE, when the Ptolemies lost their grip on Palestine, communications between the Egyptian Jews and their coreligionists in Jerusalem and in Judea were considerably impaired. Nevertheless, many links subsisted, and both sides exerted all their efforts to avoid a complete break. According to the author of the *Letter of Aristeas* (presumably written in the middle or near the end of the second century BCE), the seventy-two translators of the Torah came from Jerusalem, a choice that could be interpreted as a kind of homage to the national home of Judaism (today, we would speak of the "centrality of Israel"). To reassure his Judeo-Alexandrian readers, steeped in Greek culture, the writer informed them that the translators chosen by the high priest Eleazar were not only "past masters of Jewish letters," but were equally well-read in Greek literature (§ 121). The real or imaginary availability of this "brain-trust" would tend to confirm the advanced state of Hellenization of Judea, if not at the epoch of the translation (beginning of the third century BCE), then at least by the time the letter was written.

Both the Egypto-Syrian wars and the dynastic quarrels of the Ptolemies tended to strengthen the links between Judea and the Egyptian diaspora. While Judea, under the reign of Antiochus IV Epiphanes (175–163 BCE), was being racked by the struggles between "traditionalists" and "Hellenists," by the persecutions, and by the revolt of the Maccabees, the Jewish diaspora in Egypt had attained the apogee of its successful trajectory, under the reign of Ptolemy VI Philometor (185–145 BCE). The philosopher Aristoboulos, we may recall, dedicated his work on the Law of Moses to this king. In the letter quoted below (2 Macc. 1:10), Aristoboulos was addressed as the king's "private tutor" (*didaskalos*); as Victor Tcherikover suggested, he might actually have been the royal "counselor for Jewish affairs."

Josephus goes a step further in asserting that Ptolemy VI and Cleopatra II, his sister-wife, had "confided their kingdom to the Jews" (*Against Apion* 2, 49), which is tantamount to carrying the "philo-Semitism" of Philometor beyond the bounds of reason. But one can be sure that the king could by no means afford to neglect Jewish support in his prolonged struggle against the Seleucid Antiochus IV, who had twice invaded Egypt, from which he was reluctantly to withdraw only under strong Roman pressure. It also seems that a certain Ananias, a Jewish general, had saved the tiny kingdom of Alexander Jannaeus (103–76 BCE) from being swallowed whole by the Ptolemaic empire, by brandishing the threat that this annexation would immediately provoke the general hostility of the Egyptian Jews toward their sovereign, Cleopatra III (*Jewish Antiquities* 13, 354).

The Hasmoneans, for their part, were aware of the goodwill borne to them by most, but not all, Egyptian Jews. They sought to strengthen the ties between the two communities in many ways; for example, by inviting the Egyptian Jews to join them in the celebration of the newly established Feast of Hannukah, to commemorate the consecration of the Temple by Judas Maccabaeus in December 164 BCE. A twofold attempt was made to attain this goal, as attested by the preface to the Second Book of Maccabees, couched in the form of a letter from the Palestinian Jews to their Egyptian brethren:

> To their brothers, the Jews of Egypt, greeting! Their brothers, the Jews of Jerusalem and the land of Judea, wish them peace and prosperity! May the Lord shower you with His blessings and may He remember His Covenant with Abraham, Isaac, and Jacob, His faithful servants. May He confer on you all a heart to adore Him and to do His will generously and unstintingly. May He open your hearts to His Law and His precepts and may He cause peace to prevail. May He answer your prayers, reconcile Himself with you and not abandon you in times of need. This is the prayer that we address to Him, here and at this time. Under the reign of Demetrius, the year 169, we the Jews, we wrote to you: "In the distress and the crisis that fell upon us in those years, since Jason and his partisans defected from the Holy Land and from the kingdom, they went as far as to set fire to the great gate of the Temple and to shed innocent blood; then we prayed to the Lord, our prayers were granted, we offered a sacrifice and the finest flour, we lit the lamps and set out the breads." And now, we write you to ask you to celebrate the Feast of the Tabernacles of the month of Kislev in the year 188. (*2 MACC. 1:1–9*)

The Demetrius here alluded to is Demetrius II, the Seleucid king who reigned from 145 to 138, then from 129 to 125 BCE. The date of the first message cited in the letter, 169 of the Seleucid era, corresponds to 143/142 BCE. By the same reckoning, the date of the letter itself would be 124 BCE; "the Jews of Jerusalem and Judea" stand for the Jewish ruler and high priest, John Hyrcanus son of Simon the Hasmonean, the second son of Mattathias. The reference to the "Feast of Tabernacles" (Sukkot), which occurs during the month of Tishri (September-October), is either erroneous or should be interpreted as a transposition: the "month of Kislev" (November-December) proves that Hannukah, the Feast of the Consecration, was intended.

A second letter follows (2 Macc. 1:10–12:18); supposedly addressed by Judas Maccabaeus to the aforementioned Aristoboulos, the philosopher, it is in fact a forgery, whose unique purpose was to support the request formulated in the first letter. We know that the present form of the Second Book of Maccabees is an abridged version of a lengthier work, written in Greek by a Cyrenean Jew named Jason; this abridgment and the Greek translation, from the original Hebrew, of the First Book of Maccabees, if not actually elaborated in Alexandria, may both have been conceived with the Judeo-Egyptian reading public in mind.

In a like manner, the Book of Esther, in a Greek version due to a Palestinian Jew, was introduced into Egypt, probably in 78/77 BCE, during the reign of Ptolemy Auletes, the father of the seductive Cleopatra. It was accompanied by a letter requesting the Egyptian Jews to join their Palestinian brothers in the celebration of the Feast of Purim, commemorating the deliverance of the Persian Jews who had been saved from extermination by the charms of Queen Esther. Warnings against the dangers of excessive acculturation were issued; one example is the Greek translation that the grandson of Jesus ben Sira, a Palestinian Jew who had emigrated to Egypt, made of his grandfather's work, the apocryphal Wisdom of Jesus Ben Sira or Ecclesiasticus, prescribing traditional Jewish values as a shield against immoderate Hellenization. Fate sometimes plays strange tricks: some parts of the original Hebrew version, lost in the Middle Ages, turned up in the late nineteenth century in the Genizah of the Cairo synagogue, while others were discovered in the ruins of Masada, in 1964; but, as luck would have it, the Greek Siracides is the only complete version of this work that has come down to us intact.

This is the context of our next episode, set in Leontopolis, the "Land of Onias," where a new Jewish temple was to see the light of day in Egypt, during the sixties of the second century BCE, a crucial period for the Hellenized Orient. The victory of Aemilius Paullus over Perseus at Pydna, followed by the ultimatum delivered in the Alexandrian suburb of Eleusis to Antiochus IV by Popilius Laenas, the Roman envoy, had served notice to the easterners that their political destiny was henceforth in the hands of Rome. In Judea, the Maccabean crisis was to reveal that the historic encounter between the Jews and the Greeks, despite its immense cultural and political fruitfulness, also had its darker side. The world was to learn that the fundamental incompatibility between Judaism and Hellenism constituted a sort of time bomb, fated, sooner or later, to explode.

In Egypt, the invasion of the country by Antiochus IV Epiphanes in 168 and the revolt of Dionysios Petosarapis in 165 BCE had brought about a crisis; the economy was on the brink of ruin and a governmental reaction was inevitable. In the wake of the revolt, a great amount of farmland had been abandoned; there were few, or no volunteers, and the royal administration was obliged to resort to constraint. In August or September 165, a royal "Edict on Farming" was promulgated. Its tenor has only recently come to light in a papyrus from the Genoa collection, unfortunately in poor condition. Its stipulations were previously known through a circular that Herodes, the minister of finance (*dioiketes*), addressed in 164 to the local administrative agents, who had committed many errors while enforcing the provisions of the edict.

The circular sent out by Herodes was preceded by a letter addressed to one Onias (col. 1, lines 1–19), a person not precisely identified, but whose high rank in the Ptolemaic hierarchy is implicit in the particularly courteous tone of the message. It begins cordially with news about the good health of the entire royal family, a most unlikely subject to be broached to a subordinate officer. The letter is to be dated September 21, 164 BCE:

> Herodes to Onias greeting. King Ptolemy is well and King Ptolemy the brother and Queen Cleopatra the sister and their children, and their affairs also are as usual; if you also are in good health and all else is in order with you, it would be as we wish; we too are progressing well enough. The copy of the letter addressed to Dorion the hypodioiketes is subjoined. Understanding therefore that consideration for those engaged in sowing the seed is a common duty incumbent on all those interested in the administration, be good enough to use every effort and take every precaution both that none of those unable to work in the fields be impressed, and that none of those who are able be shielded on any pretext whatsoever; and further, that everything be performed in the manner laid down in the minute sent you by us. Take care of yourself to keep in good health. Farewell.
> Year 6, Mesore 24. (*PARIS PAPYRUS 63; CPJUD. I 132*)

The extremely polite and ceremonious tone of the letter confirms the high status of the addressee, although only three letters of his name remain: ONI. We may take it for granted that the missive was addressed "to Onias," Oni[ai]. Onias (the Hellenized form of Honio) was none other than the Judean high priest who had taken refuge in Egypt during the Maccabean crisis. Under the reign of Ptolemy VI Philometor, he was the moving spirit behind a singular enterprise, whose sequels were to last some two centuries, until the reign of Vespasian.

"AN ALTAR OF THE LORD IN THE MIDST OF THE LAND OF EGYPT"

The Oniads were the descendants of Zadok, high priest in the time of Solomon. They had occupied the office of high priest since Onias I, son of Jaddus, the high priest who had, according to legend, opened the gates of Jerusalem to the victorious Alexander on the eve of his conquest of Egypt and the Persian empire. They were to retain their hold on the high priesthood until the advent of Jason "the Hellenist," brother of Onias III. About 172 BCE, the latter, after having taken refuge in a pagan temple in Daphne, near Antioch, was assassinated by order of a fellow "Hellenist," Menelaus, Jason's successor. His son, Onias IV, who had fled to Egypt, was the Onias of our papyrus.

According to Josephus, Onias IV was still an infant when his father was killed, and it was only some ten years later, when Alkimus succeeded Menelaus to the priesthood, about 162, that he left for Egypt. However, the priestly chronicles Josephus consulted had been tampered with, in an attempt to legitimize the succession of high priests, and Josephus had been misled. In his *Jewish Antiquities*, Jason and Menelaus appear as brothers to Onias III; this is true for the former but not for the latter. Josephus had been duped by a corrupt tradition, falsely incorporating Menelaus into the Oniad lineage. The *curriculum vitae* of Onias IV had also been altered.

Our papyrus shows that the arrival of Onias IV in Egypt must have occurred well before 164 BCE, since by that date he was already a high dignitary in the Ptolemaic court. He had come to Egypt under the priesthood of Jason, or at the beginning of that of Menelaus; moreover, he could not have been a mere child, but must already have been old enough to rise rapidly in rank among the courtiers of Ptolemy VI. It would have been very reasonable for the partisans of the Oniads to send the young man off to Alexandria, in their desire to safeguard this latest scion of a distinguished priestly lineage, of which he was to be the last representative. Until the day when he would be able to return to Jerusalem, he was put into "high priestly reserve" in foreign territory, under the protection of Ptolemy VI. But that day never dawned.

If we follow this line of reasoning, we should credit Onias with the praiseworthy intention some modern scholars attributed to his father: the construction of a Jewish temple in Egypt, in response to the profanation of the Temple in Jerusalem. If it was erected prior to September 164, the date of our letter, we might be tempted to place its construction in the period from December 167 to December 164, during which the Temple of Jerusalem had been placed under the sign of the "abomination of desolation" (1 Macc. 1:54). This Greek equivalent of the expression *shikkutz shomem* ("the abomination that makes desolate") in the Book of Daniel (9:27; 11:31; 12:11) actually designated, as Elias Bickerman has convincingly demonstrated, the altar of the Syrian god Baal Shamem which, during those three years, overlooked that of the God of the Jews. In order to maintain the practice of sacrificial worship, which had been compromised by the profanation of the Temple in Jerusalem, Onias would thus have decided to transfer it to Egypt.

Josephus quotes an exchange of letters between the high priest and the royal couple. The subject under discussion was Onias' project for the erection of a temple in Leontopolis in the Heliopolite nome, dedicated to "God the Most High," an expression we have already encountered. In his first letter, Onias informed the sovereigns of his decision. He had found a fitting site and was strongly motivated. Official approval was still lacking but, in view of the services he had rendered the Ptolemies, he had good reason to believe he would obtain it. One should recall the context of rivalry between Ptolemy VI and "Ptolemy the brother," the future Ptolemy VIII Euergetes II, and the military prowess of our Onias, who may have been the Jewish general mentioned by Josephus.

Many and great are the services I have rendered you in the course of the war, with the help of God, when I was in Coele-Syria and Phoenicia, and when I came with the Jews to Leontopolis in the nome of Heliopolis and to other places where our nation is settled; and I found that most of them had temples [hiera], contrary to what is proper, and that for this reason they are ill-disposed toward one another, as is also the case with the Egyptians because of the multitude of their sanctuaries and their varying opinions about the forms of worship; and I have found a most suitable place in the fortress called after Bubastis-of-the-Fields, which abounds in various kinds of trees and is full of sacred animals.

Wherefore I beg you to permit me to cleanse this temple, which belongs to no one and is in ruins, and to build a temple to God the Most High in the likeness of that at Jerusalem and with the same dimensions, on behalf of you and your wife and children, in order that the Jewish inhabitants of Egypt may be able to come together there in mutual harmony and serve your interests. For this indeed is what the prophet Isaiah foretold: "There shall be an altar in Egypt to the Lord God," and many other such things prophesy concerning this place. (JEWISH ANTIQUITIES 13, 64–68, ED. R. MARCUS)

A curious idea indeed, this project of building a Jewish temple on the ruins of a stronghold once dedicated to the Egyptian goddess Bastet-the-Wild ("Bubastis-of-the-Fields"), in a spot teeming with sacred animals! The project of unification of worship, heretofore practiced in various houses of prayer scattered about the country, was not a very convincing one. The comparison with Egyptian temples was artificial, for the use of the term *hiera*, "temples, sanctuaries," for both synagogues and heathen temples, could not efface the real difference between them, as Onias should have been the first to know.

A prophecy of Isaiah offered him an ambiguous argument. The prophet had actually said (19:19): "In that day shall there be an altar to the Lord in the midst of the land of Egypt, and a pillar at the border thereof to the Lord." Modern authors had been wary of this passage, which they took for a gloss, inserted into the biblical text in order to legitimize *a posteriori*, the sanctuary of Leontopolis. But the presence of this very same passage in a manuscript from Qumran dispelled their hesitations. The fact remains that the first clause alone of the passage is applicable to Onias' project, as Leontopolis was really situated "in the midst of the land of Egypt." The second clause is applicable rather to the Jews of Elephantine, actually situated at the southern frontier. Strangely enough, the royal couple were aware of these subtleties. Here is their answer:

King Ptolemy and Queen Cleopatra to Onias, greeting. We have read your petition asking that it be permitted you to cleanse the ruined temple in Leontopolis in the nome of Heliopolis, called Bubastis-of-the-Fields. We wonder, therefore, whether it will be pleasing to God that a temple be

> built in a place so wild and full of sacred animals. But since you say that
> the prophet Isaiah foretold this long ago, we grant your request if this is to
> be in accordance with the Law, so that we may not seem to have sinned
> against God in any way. (JEWISH ANTIQUITIES 13, 70–71, ED. R. MARCUS)

King Ptolemy and his sister-wife were more scrupulous than the Jewish high priest.
But Onias was so persistent, and they so wished to please him, that they washed their
hands of the matter by acquiescing. Nonetheless, the sympathy Ptolemy VI felt for the
Jews in general is not sufficient reason for us to consider him a sort of proselyte for the
Jewish cause. Some modern scholars have questioned the authenticity of this correspondence, which they deemed a forgery designed either to discredit the project or, on
the contrary, to respond in advance to eventual criticism from Alexandrian Jewish circles hostile to Onias' enterprise. These suspicions cannot alter the actual course of history. The temple was actually built, obviously with the approval of the royal pair; its
location, indicated by Josephus, has been corroborated by epigraphical evidence.

Tell el-Yehoudieh, "the knoll of the Jews," near Shibin el-Qanatir, north of Heliopolis
(not to be confounded with the Leontopolis of the Leontopolite nome in the Delta, today Tell el-Moqdam) has been recognized as the site of ancient Leontopolis. One guarantee of its identity is its Arabic name; epigraphical evidence furnishes another, in the
mention of the "land of Onias," equivalent to the term employed by Josephus. The
Greek name of Leontopolis, "city of the lions," is quite fitting for a secularized sanctuary of Bastet (Bubastis), the smiling feline goddess, originally a lion-goddess, and who
had become a cat-goddess by the time of Onias. Many statuettes represent her in semi-
human shape; she occasionally had the aspect of a bejeweled queen, seated but with
muscles tensed, ready to spring.

What did the temple of Onias look like? We have little to go on, for, notwithstanding
the opinion British archaeologist W. M. Flinders Petrie once professed, no one has yet
been able to discover the slightest trace of it. The site of Tell el-Yehoudieh has been
explored several times but never thoroughly searched. We are obliged to fall back on
Josephus, despite all his contradictions. In his *Antiquities* (13, 73; 387–88), he speaks of
a building modeled on the Temple of Jerusalem, fulfilling Onias' desires, but of more
modest dimensions. In his *Jewish War*, he gives a finer and a more detailed description.
The latter seems to be an addendum to the former text, more exact, insofar as Josephus
would then have been able to consult official documents from the prefectoral chancery
in Alexandria.

> Induced by this statement, Ptolemy gave him [Onias] a tract, a hundred
> and eighty furlongs distant from Memphis, in the so-called nome of
> Heliopolis. Here Onias erected a fortress and built his temple (which was
> not like that in Jerusalem, but resembled a tower) of huge stones and sixty
> cubits in altitude. The altar, however, he designed on the model of that in
> the home country, and adorned the building with similar offerings, the

fashion of the lampstand excepted; for, instead of making a stand, he had a lamp wrought of gold which shed a brilliant light and was suspended by a golden chain. The sacred precincts were wholly surrounded by a wall of baked brick, the doorways being of stone. The king, moreover, assigned him an extensive territory as a source of revenue, to yield both abundance for the priests and large provision for the service of God. (THE JEWISH WAR 7, 426–30, ED. H. ST. J. THACKERAY)

The tower (*pyrgos*) was a typical feature of the Egyptian landscape. It was either square or cylindrical; it could serve as a dwelling, as the main building of an agricultural domain, or yet again as a suburban home. The tower of Onias was some thirty meters (sixty Greek cubits) high and could very well have been the central building of a settlement whose purpose was both religious and military. In any event, like its predecessor in Elephantine, it was a temple, with its priests and its Levites and its sacrificial worship.

Strangely enough, the rabbis knew of its existence but did not condemn it. They compared sacrifices offered or vows taken in the sanctuary of Onias with similar acts in the Temple of Jerusalem, and pursued their discussions concerning their relative value. Priests who officiated in Leontopolis could not officiate in Jerusalem; they were comparable to the priests of the "high places," the targets of Josiah's reforms (2 Kings, 23:9). The Egyptian sanctuary, then, was not deemed "schismatic" by the sages of the Talmud, since it was founded by a legitimate high priest. The opinion of the sages can help us to clarify that of the late Arnaldo Momigliano: to consider that the temple of Leontopolis "was meant to rival Jerusalem" is certainly somewhat exaggerated. Actually, since its foundation was associated with the formation of a military colony under the commandment of Onias, the new temple was simply intended to serve the religious needs of the Jewish soldiers in the "land of Onias." Philo of Alexandria made no mention of it.

One detail of Josephus' description deserves our attention: he speaks of a golden lamp, instead of the chandelier. Once again, we are referred to Isaiah:

> Moreover the light of the moon shall be as the light of the sun,
> And the light of the sun shall be sevenfold, as the light of the seven days,
> In the day that the Lord bindeth up the bruise of His people,
> And healeth the stroke of their wound.
>
> (ISAIAH 30:26)

To interpret this prophecy, the Targum had recourse to a calculation: seven times seven times seven or, if one prefers, seven jubilees, making 343 years during which a symbolic sun would shine upon the chosen people, resettled by the Lord after the exile. Onias may have adopted a similar interpretation and replaced the menorah by a lamp symbolizing the sun. Josephus, in turn, came upon this figure in his sources but, ignoring its mystical meaning, interpreted it as the length of time the temple of Onias would endure: "From the construction of the temple," he wrote (*The Jewish War* 7, 436), "to its closing, 343 years had elapsed."

Taken at its face value, this figure is unacceptable. Founded in the middle of the second century BCE, the temple of Onias was closed in 73/74 CE. That makes more than two centuries, but hardly 343 years. One may well hesitate before assigning an exact date to its foundation; we have admitted the possibility of it being before 164 BCE. In any event, it must be situated within the context of the Maccabean crisis. The date of its closure can be pinpointed with precision, by aligning the testimony of Josephus with the chronology of the prefects of Egypt.

Josephus tells us that, after the fall of Masada (*The Jewish War* 7, 420–36), some fighters, having escaped from the disaster and taken refuge in Egypt, had attempted to foment a revolutionary movement within the ranks of their fellows. The prefect of Egypt, Tiberius Julius Lupus, brought news of this to the ears of Vespasian, who ordered the demolition of the temple in Leontopolis: in Roman eyes, that vestige of the bygone glory of the Oniads was a dangerous symbol of the independence of the Jewish people. Lupus and his successor, Valerius Paulinus, contented themselves with stopping the services and closing the sanctuary. Lupus was in charge from 71 until 73 CE; Paulinus succeeded him at the end of 73 or the beginning of 74. At that time the sanctuary was shut down permanently.

Images of the "Land of Onias"

From the tombstones of the Jewish cemetery at Tell el-Yehoudieh, the modern name of Leontopolis, we can learn something about the daily lives of those who lived in the "land of Onias." The epitaphs form a homogeneous group, unique among the Jewish inscriptions of Egypt. By scholarly consensus they date from the reign of Augustus; they would thus refer to the survivors of Onias' garrison, born on the eve of the Roman conquest of Egypt in 30 BCE, and the representatives of the generation following the conquest. Certain epitaphs, however, may be more ancient.

Whatever their date, these texts throw considerable light on Jewish life in Egypt toward the end of the first century BCE. Looking beyond the stereotypes of funeral poetry, one may find some clues to prevailing mental attitudes, family relationships, and religious feeling. Their testimony should not be neglected, although any conclusions drawn from them should not be applied indiscriminately to the entire Jewish diaspora in Egypt. Among the eighty-odd inscriptions in the lot, we have chosen four metrical epitaphs. The most touching and the most complete refer to women. The first concerns a young mother, who died in childbirth:

> This is the grave of Arsinoe, wayfarer. Stand by and weep for her, unfortunate in all things, whose lot was hard and terrible. For I was bereaved of my mother when I was a little girl; and when the flower of youth made

me ready for a bridegroom, my father joined me in marriage with Phabeis, and Fate led me to the end of my life in the travail of my first-born child. I had a small span of years, but great grace bloomed upon the beauty of my spirit. This grave hides in its bosom my chastely nurtured body, but my soul has flown to the holy ones. A lament for Arsinoe.

In the twenty-fifth year, Mechir 2 [28 January 5 BCE?]. (CIJ II, No. 1510; HORBURY-NOY, NO. 33)

The wording is banal. One must search attentively to discover, behind the Greek stereotypes, some specific Jewish elements. Greek epigrams habitually exhort the reader to shed tears over the departed. Nonetheless, the frequency and the insistence of these injunctions in the epitaphs of Tell el-Yehoudieh is most striking. Was this a consequence of the Jewish practice of lamentation? To describe the first child of the deceased, we find the Greek word *prototokos* (instead of *protogonos*) "born the first," a term relatively rare in pagan funerary texts but which appears several times in the Septuagint. Did familiarity with the latter exert an influence on the author of the epitaph? Fate (Moira) is a Greek term. The imperishable beauty of the soul as opposed to the ephemeral beauty of the body is a universal consolatory theme, no more pagan than Jewish or Christian. The soul, detached from the body "raised in purity" (*agnotraphes*, a new word), takes its flight to meet the "holy ones," *hosioi*: once again, a term frequently to be found in the Septuagint and on Jewish epitaphs.

Another Arsinoe, who died at the age of twenty, has left us a remembrance in the form of a dialogue in elegant Doric:

> The stele bears witness.
> "Who are you that lie in the dark tomb? Tell me your country and your father."
> "Arsinoe, daughter of Aline and Theodosios. The famous land of Onias reared me."
> "How old were you when you slipped down into the shadowy region of Lethe?"
> "At twenty I went to the mournful place of the dead."
> "Were you married?"
> "I was."
> "Did you leave him a child?"
> "Childless I went to the house of Hades."
> "May the earth, the guardian of the dead, be light on you."
> "And for you, stranger, may she bear fruitful crops."
> In the sixteenth year, Payni 21 [15 June 14 BCE?]. (CIJ II, No. 1530; HORBURY-NOY, NO. 38)

In her posthumous dialogue, this second Arsinoe insists upon the ties that united her to her native "land of Onias." Her name, and those of her loved ones, are relatively neuter, but Theodosios has a Jewish connotation, as do all "God-given" names. "Lethe," the river of oblivion, is no more surprising in a Jewish epitaph than "Hades," the kingdom of the departed, a term found in the Septuagint and in Judeo-Alexandrian literature. It was employed by the very pious author of the Third Book of Maccabees to describe his coreligionists, threatened by death. The "mournful place of the dead" (*goeros choros nekuon*) is evocative of the biblical Sheol: "The shades tremble beneath the waters—The nether-world is naked before Him" (Job 26:5–6). The two concepts, Hades and Sheol, evolved in parallel, the darkness from which there is no return to the light giving way to a place of penitence and the expiation of earthly sins.

Arsinoe regretted having died childless (*ateknos*). Although this sentiment may not be specifically Jewish, there was nothing to stop her surviving relatives from attributing it to the deceased. The bereaved family, in its desire to commemorate the departed one in polished verse, had had recourse to a poet more attentive to stylistic effects than to strict Jewish orthodoxy (providing we can define "Jewish orthodoxy" in that period). But this in itself is not cause enough to brand the inscription "pagan," an expression of "heretic Judaism," as Arnaldo Momigliano did.

And here is Rachelis, dead at the age of thirty:

> Fellow townsmen and strangers, all weep for Rachelis, chaste, friend to all, about thirty years old. Do not weep vainly for me. If it was decreed that I should live but a short time, yet I await a good hope of mercy. And Agathokles, about 38 years old. (*CIJ II*, No. 1513; HORBURY-NOY, No. 36)

The adjective *pasiphile* ("friend of all") is frequently found in the Tell el-Yehoudieh inscriptions. E. Bernand notes that it could "be indicative of the sentiments which inspired the members of that Jewish community." Another commentator has stressed the contradiction between the exhortation to lament, couched in traditional terms, and the uselessness of mourning: "Without a doubt, something had to be said that had not yet been expressed in verse. Had Rachel not become a Christian?" If the inscription really dated from the epoch of the Early Roman Empire, as some scholars suppose, this unproven hypothesis would not be totally absurd, even though, during that period, a Judeo-Christian would have been more likely to appear in Alexandria than in Leontopolis. Agathokles, with whom she shared her hope of eternal life, was a close relative, probably the husband of the deceased, who had died later and whose remains were interred in their common tomb. His name was then added, in the free space on the last line of the tombstone.

To close this chapter, let us read the epitaph of Horaia and her family:

> This is the tomb of Horaia, wayfarer. Shed a tear! Daughter of [...]laos, she was unfortunate in all things, and fulfilled three decades of years. Three of us are here, husband, daughter, and I whom they have burned [inflamed with grief?]. [My husband died] on the third, then on the fifth my daughter Eirene, to whom marriage was not granted, and I then with no place or joy was laid here after them under the earth on the seventh of

Epitaph of Arsinoe, a young Jewish woman who died at the age of twenty   *Cemetery of Tell el-Yehudieh (Leontopolis) (Alexandria, Greco-Roman Museum).*

Choiak. But stranger, you have clearly learned all there is to know from us; tell all men of the swiftness of death.

In the tenth year, Choiak 7 [3 December, 20 BCE?]. *(CIJ II, NO. 1509; HORBURY-NOY, NO. 32)*

An entire family reposed here: a woman, her daughter, and her husband; they had all died during the same week, at two-day intervals. Horaia, "the Beauteous," was a rare enough name in Egypt; she was the last to pass away, after her daughter Eirene and her husband. Is the verb *pyroo*, "to burn," used rhetorically to describe her distress, or is it to be taken literally? Was she "consumed by grief" or had her remains been incinerated? Scholars hesitate. The term in question appears in two other epitaphs from the same site; in one, the "burned" parents are called upon to weep over their daughter, deceased in her tenth year. Some authors take this to signify a veritable incineration, an infringement of the traditional Jewish rejection of cremation, except in exceptional cases such as victims of the plague.

Horaia and her family may well have succumbed to a contagious disease, since they had died at such close intervals. But the words "laid . . . under the earth" (*etethen hypo gen*) imply a burial and not an incineration. Likewise, in the epitaph quoted above, the injunction to shed tears was addressed not only to close relatives, but to passersby and to "brothers." It concerned the living, among whom the close relatives were to be found. They were "burning with sorrow." This must also have been the case for Horaia. At all events, one should not extrapolate from her epitaph and those of other Jews "burned" in the necropolis of Tell el-Yehoudieh, to further the idea of a "heretic" brand of Judaism, tending to abandon interment in favor of incineration.

CHAPTER 7 ❧

At the Wellsprings
of Pagan Anti-Semitism

MODERN FANTASIES AND ANCIENT MYTHS

The well-known fantasy of the Jew as merchant and usurer has left its mark on modern historiography by shaping, retrospectively, our image of Jews and Judaism in the
Greco-Roman period, especially in Egypt. In 1936, Jean-Baptiste Frey, the Superior of
the French Seminary in Rome, author of the corpus of Jewish inscriptions to which we
have often referred, declared that "the Western diaspora was born of the business spirit."
In the fifth century BCE, the Jews of Syene and Elephantine were "in a manner of speaking, the bankers of Egypt," according to the Irish scholar J. P. Mahaffy. It goes without
saying that there was not the slightest trace of a Jewish bank in Elephantine at that
time; as we have seen, the Jews of Elephantine were mercenaries. L. Jullien, the author
of a book on the Alexandrian Jews of antiquity, edited in Alexandria in 1944, asserts
that "the Jews of Judea brought with them [to Egypt] that keen sense of commerce that
is one of the features of their race."

The detractors of the banker-Jew point their finger at a real-life character: Alexander,
the brother of Philo the philosopher, a very rich Alexandrian Jew who handled enormous sums of money, "the Rothschild of Antiquity," in the words of Ulrich Wilcken,
one of the founders of papyrology. A clumsy comparison, for it could apply only to
Alexander's wealth and not to his occupations: he was the inspector-in-chief of customs (alabarch) and not a banker, even if he did occasionally lend sums of money, for
instance to his eternally indebted friend, Agrippa I King of Judea. Unlike the
Rothschilds, he never founded a dynasty of bankers and community leaders.

In Alexandria there were also lesser Jewish "capitalists," the *poristai* mentioned by
Philo in his description of the massacre that took place in 38 CE, under Caligula: having lost their deposits, they were obliged to cease their activities, as was the case for the
farmers, the boatmen, the merchants, the artisans (*Against Flaccus*, 57). We are obviously dealing with what we today would call a socio-professional category, one among
others. The range of Jewish occupations, as Philo's testimony shows, did not differ from
that of the non-Jewish inhabitants of the city. The entire population of Alexandria,

Jews and non-Jews included, could easily be differentiated along those lines; had statistics been available, they would in all likelihood have corroborated this statement. In the rest of the country, there were Jewish officials, Jewish salaried workers, artisans, and agricultural workers. In Ptolemaic Egypt, there was no specifically "Jewish" vocation. Arnaldo Momigliano was perfectly right when he asserted that the Hellenistic Jews "were active in too many different branches to render themselves antipathetic in any particular one of them" (Cérisy Symposium, 1975).

The notion of a "Mr. Average-Jew" is equally misleading, because of its excessive generality. In a state founded on military conquest, the conquerors were, first and foremost, soldiers. The Jews were members of Greek society, a military society by definition. Despite some remarkable exceptions such as Pasis-the-Jew, Zenon's right-hand man in Philadelphia, whom we have already met, or Sabbathaios and his son Dosas, potters in the Faiyum who shared the workshop of the Egyptian Petesouchos and his two sons (Berlin Papyrus VI 1282; CPJud. I 46) in the second or the first century BCE, the typical Egyptian Jew at that time was a soldier in the service of the king.

This brings us to another facet of the problem: ancient myths. As a military representative of an oppressive foreign power—Persian or Greek, it mattered little—the Jew could appear detestable in Egyptian eyes. At the same time, his "separatism" could easily arouse the reprobation of his Greek comrade-in-arms, whose lifestyle he shared but whose table he shunned. Among the Egyptians and the Greeks, negative reactions toward the Jews made their appearance; the image of the Jew in ancient literature was to be profoundly altered.

Somewhere around 300 BCE, a peculiar image of the Jews had made its way into Greek thinking: we have already described the fantasy picturing the Jews as a people of "born philosophers." That image subsequently evolved in two completely opposite directions. On the one hand, during the Hellenistic epoch, Jews and Judaism were still looked upon with favor, a trend that was prolonged under the Roman Empire. As late as 280 CE, the rhetor Menander of Laodicea (focal point of a recent debate on the effects of Caracalla's edict of 212 CE generalizing Roman citizenship) recommended the assemblies of Jews in Syria-Palestine as an inspirational theme for speeches in the "demonstrative genre." Menander considered the well-attended Jewish festivals just as worthy of notice as Olympia, for its games, or Delphi, whose fame—for a Greek, of course—was due to its position at the center of the world.

On the other hand, a second and more ominous current appeared, malevolent, critical, and threatening to the Jews. At the root of this negative image lay an Egyptian motif picturing the Jews as undesirable intruders who had left the land of Egypt in an inglorious manner, having been stigmatized as sick in their persons, and then driven out of the country. The Jews were described as lepers and the carriers of other pestilential afflictions, seemingly a racist opinion, inasmuch as racism condemns others as victims of a supposedly irreversible physical inferiority, and leprosy was then an incurable disease. This brand of discourse was very popular among Greek or Greco-Egyptian authors and continued to flourish in Rome. Josephus, in his *Against Apion*, had selected a few choice items of gossip, the better to oppose and denounce them. We shall borrow a sample, attributed to Lysimachos, the author of a work on Egypt (*Aegyptiaca*), probably set down in the first century BCE, which contains a chapter hostile to the Jews.

> I will next introduce Lysimachos. He brings up the same theme as the writers just mentioned [i.e., Manetho and Chaeremon], the mendacious story of the lepers and cripples, but surpasses both in the incredibility of his fictions, obviously composed with bitter animus. His account is this:
>
> "In the reign of Bocchoris, king of Egypt, the Jewish people, who were afflicted with leprosy, scurvy, and other maladies, took refuge in the temples and lived a mendicant existence. The victims of disease being very numerous, a dearth ensued throughout Egypt. King Bocchoris thereupon sent to consult the oracle of Ammon about the failure of the crops. The god told him to purge the temples of impure and impious persons, to drive them out of these sanctuaries into the wilderness, to drown those afflicted with leprosy and scurvy, as the sun was indignant that such persons should live, and to purify the temples; then the land would yield her increase.
>
> "On receiving these oracular instructions, Bocchoris summoned the priests and servitors at the altars, and ordered them to draw up a list of the unclean persons and to deliver them into military charge to be conducted into the wilderness, and to pack the lepers into sheets of lead and sink them in the sea. The lepers and victims of scurvy having been drowned, the others were collected and exposed in the desert to perish. There they assembled and deliberated on their situation. At nightfall they lit up a bonfire and torches, and mounted guard, and on the following night kept a fast and implored the gods to save them.
>
> "On the next day a certain Moses advised them to take their courage in their hands and make a straight track until they reached inhabited country, instructing them to show goodwill to no man, to offer not the best but the worst advice, and to overthrow any temples and altars of the gods that they found. The rest assenting, they proceeded to put these decisions into practice. They traversed the desert, and after great hardships reached inhabited country: there they maltreated the population, and plundered and set fire to the temples, until they came to the country now called Judea, where they built a city in which they settled. This town was called Hierosyla [sacrilege] because of their sacrilegious propensities. At a later date, when they had risen to power, they altered the name, to avoid the disgraceful imputation, and called the city Hierosolyma and themselves Hierosolymites." (LYSIMACHOS, IN JOSEPHUS, AGAINST APION 1, 304–11; ED. H. ST. J. THACKERAY)

For the Jews of Egypt, this heap of malicious lies could not go unchallenged. The rejoinder has come down to us thanks to Alexander Polyhistor, a Greek writer from Miletus who, in the first century BCE, gathered fragments of a large number of Jewish-Hellenistic authors; many of them survived in the *Praeparatio Evangelica* of Eusebius of Caesarea: Christian writers used Jewish texts as weapons for the defense of Christianity. The fragment that concerns us here was signed by Artapanos, the Judeo-Egyptian author of a work entitled *On the Jews* or *Ioudaika*, a kind of popular novel in a historical setting, written toward the middle or the latter half of the second century BCE.

It begins with Abraham and Joseph, presented as the founders of Egyptian civilization. The former taught astrology to the Pharaoh. The latter had not been sold by his brothers but had come to Egypt as a voluntary immigrant, with the help of his Arab neighbors: the Arabian kings, descendants of Ishmael, the great-uncle of Joseph (by coming to the aid of their cousins, they were simply fulfilling their family obligations). Having been charged by the Pharaoh with the administration of the country, Joseph quickly set it in order. Artapanos informs us that, before his coming, the Egyptians tilled their land "without rules," and consequently the poorer farmers were oppressed by the more powerful. To set things right, Joseph shared out the land, delineating property limits by the placing of markers, and introduced surveying methods. The Egyptians were extremely pleased with his innovations. We have already learned how he married Asenath, the daughter of a priest of Heliopolis. The couple became the proud parents of fine children. When Joseph's brothers and his father Jacob rejoined him in Egypt they came, not as poor farmers in search of the wheat lacking in Canaan, but as the bearers of great riches.

Here we have a Joseph who knew how to organize the realm of the Pharaohs in the Greek manner: land-sharing, ordering of the political arena, promulgation of measures tending to assure social justice. His work was furthered by Moses, the adopted son of Princess Merris (how the author came up this name remains a mystery). Artapanos identified Moses with Musaeus (Mousaios), a mythical pre-Homeric poet who becomes, in this version, the teacher of the bard Orpheus. Moses was not only Orpheus' teacher (we shall return to this point in the following chapter) but also a great creative genius, the veritable founder of the Egyptian state. He invented ships, derricks to move the huge stones used in their monumental constructions, the arms the Egyptians needed, the hydraulic apparatus without which their agriculture could not function, their war machines, and even their philosophy. It was he who divided the realm into thirty-six nomes and placed them under the tutelage of thirty-six different gods. He instructed the priests in sacred literature and brought the disorganized masses under the thumb of the clergy.

Of course, all these blessings soon earned him the boundless admiration and the gratitude of the priests. According to Artapanos, his unmitigated success also awoke the jealousy of the reigning Pharaoh, Chenephres. Moses had two narrow escapes from the mortal snares the envious sovereign laid in his path. After the death of Chenephres, the Lord ordered Moses to leave the land and to lead his people to their "ancient homeland." He had to overcome the resistance of the new Pharaoh. Artapanos' version of the Exodus, which follows, is diametrically opposed to the accounts of the Egyptian authors who wrote in Greek.

The flight itself was preceded by a series of wonders resembling those of the biblical account, but with some impressive variants. Thus it came about that Pharaoh, having desired to learn the Divine Name, had Moses whisper it into his ear, whereupon he fell into a dead faint, from which Moses resuscitated him, in the manner in which Elijah resuscitated the son of the widow (1 Kings 17:17–24). The rod with which Moses struck the Nile did not change its waters into blood but swelled them to such a degree that they submerged all of Egypt. Artapanos notes that "it was from that time that the flooding of the Nile began." The king, harried by the calamities that had befallen his country, finally allowed the Jews to leave. On the third day, they came to the Red Sea. Artapanos continues:

> Now the Memphians claim that Moses, being familiar with the countryside, watched for the ebb tide, then led the multitudes through the dry part of the sea. The Heliopolitans, on the other hand, claim that the king rushed down on them with full force, carrying with him all the sacred animals because the Jews were crossing the sea, having taken the possessions of the Egyptians. The divine voice came to Moses instructing him to strike the sea with his rod and divide it. When Moses heard this, he touched the water lightly with his rod and the stream divided, and the multitude passed through the dry channel. When the Egyptians went in together in hot pursuit, he says that a fire blazed in front of them, and the sea again flooded their path. All the Egyptians were consumed by the fire and the flood. After the Jews had escaped the danger, they spent forty years in the desert. (EUSEBIUS, PRAEPARATIO EVANGELICA, 9, 27, 35–37)

In his description of the passage through the Red Sea, Artapanos used a device familiar to the historians of his time: the alternative explanation, offering the reader the choice between a rational and a magic interpretation. Both stem from Egyptian sources, thus increasing the credibility of his account. At any rate, there is no longer any reference to contagious diseases or the expulsion of undesirable elements. A great benefactor of Egypt took his departure after having remodeled the country, now the pride of its inhabitants. Artapanos killed two birds with one stone, refuting the anti-Jewish fabrications and simultaneously attributing the invention of Egyptian civilization to Joseph and Moses, thus establishing the chronological precedence of Judaism to Hellenism, with Egypt in the role of intermediary.

Can this polemical exchange be of aid to us in our effort to seize the underlying historical reality? Artapanos substituted the Jewish version of the Exodus for the Story of the Impure, based on Pharaonic sources. The French Egyptologist Jean Yoyotte pointed out that a good part of the Egyptian image of the Jews, coherent enough in its own fashion, was linked to the priestly view of foreign enemies in general and the Persian empire in particular. Can we attribute it to a specific historical event, to wit, the conquest of Egypt by Cambyses in 525 BCE? Jean Yoyotte believes we can.

He bases his hypothesis on the idea that the Persians had chosen, from among the ranks of their armies, "the Judean soldiery," and had assigned them the task of carrying out a plan designed to demoralize the conquered Egyptians, by destroying their most treasured possessions: their gods and their temples. "To shatter the hopes the Egyptians placed in their gods, their sacred animals and their temples," he writes, "the Persians must have discovered among the Jewish contingent, soldiers determined to carry out this task—and when it came down to it, the Jews were probably the toughest ones."

In Egypt, at the time of the Persian conquest, pagan anti-Semitism would thus have first seen the light of day as a reaction of the Egyptians to the depredations of Jewish soldiers, whose intransigence was abetted by the hostility of the prophets of Israel to the "house of bondage." This is an attractive hypothesis, insofar as it brings to the fore the irrationality of the phenomenon: in the first recorded case of anti-Semitism, the chosen targets would have been Jewish soldiers in the service of the Persians, Aryans *par excellence*! But the available historical data do not lend credence to this idea.

In the first part of this book, we have seen how the proximity of Jewish worshipers to the Egyptian adorers of Khnum the ram-god led to a violent dispute, which took place on the island of Elephantine at the end of the fifth century BCE. A temple had effectively been put to sack. But it was the temple of the Jewish God that had been laid to waste, and not that of Khnum! In their petition to obtain the authorization to reconstruct their pillaged sanctuary, the Jews of Elephantine, it is true, invoked the destruction of Egyptian temples at the time of the Persian conquest. But nothing proves that they had had a hand in the matter. On the contrary, had they been involved, their calling those events to mind would have amounted to a tacit legitimation of the destruction of the Jewish temple, in retaliation for previous destructions imputable to the Jews. Yedaniah and his colleagues would not have been so clumsy in their dealings.

Egyptian myths inspired the Greeks, who had their own brand of anti-Jewish mythology, which flourished in Hellenistic times and under the Roman Empire as well. Implanted in Rome, it was nourished by certain authors, such as Tacitus and Juvenal, who seasoned it with a literary flavor. In the words of Josephus, these were "fables they tell about the Jews." One of the most tenacious was the fable of the ritual murder, every seven years—or every year—of a previously fattened foreigner, whose entrails were then eaten by the Jews. This fantasy was to make a new appearance in the commentaries on the Jewish revolt in the second century CE, and we shall have occasion to return to it.

Two more serious accusations lie hidden behind these fabrications. Above all, the Greeks reproached the Jews with their "separatism," their "unsociability" (*amixia*). Hecataeus of Abdera had already asserted that Moses had "introduced an unsocial and intolerant mode of life." His complaint was taken up and amplified by other authors. In addition, the Jews were accused of "atheism" (*atheotes*), because of their refusal to accept the gods of other peoples. Their manifestations of religious discipline—the

Sabbath pause, circumcision, dietary prescriptions—were interpreted as deviations, in flagrant contradiction with the social legacy of the Greek city. The Jews pretended to share the benefits of the Greek system of values but rejected a great portion of it as irreconcilable with their religious principles. In other words, they desired to be both "citizens" and "different."

The fantastic embroidery of the Egyptians on the theme of the foreigner driven from the land, and the depictions, by the Greeks, of the Jew as cannibal, were ideological expressions of real social and political conflicts. The Egyptians had as little sympathy for the Jewish soldier under the orders of a foreign king as the Greeks had for the "separatist," "atheistic" Jew, easily transformed in their imagination into an inhospitable, man-eating Cyclops. Did these anti-Jewish words produce anti-Jewish acts?

The sack of the Jewish temple at Elephantine comes to mind once more. However, to label it an "explosion of anti-Semitism" would be an overstatement as well as an anachronism. It was simply a local incident, rather to be ascribed to Egyptian nationalistic feelings than to a specifically anti-Jewish brand of hatred. Outright violence against the Jews in Egypt was to erupt only much later, under Roman rule, after the aggravation of the tension between Rome and Alexandria, for which the Jews were to pay. In the last part of this book, we shall examine this in detail. What concerns us now is to ascertain whether such acts had taken place in Ptolemaic Egypt. To this end, we shall turn to a literary work by a Judeo-Alexandrian author, giving an account of what he believed to be the first confrontation between Jews and Greeks under the Ptolemies.

THE MIRACLE AT THE HIPPODROME

The situation of the Jews could not fail to be affected by the crisis that came upon the Hellenistic world toward the end of the third century BCE. The Ptolemies were to lose their hegemony over Judea. Antiochus III, the victorious Seleucid sovereign, at first sought to assure himself of the loyalty of his Jewish subjects. Toward 200 BCE, he issued a charter that confirmed their religious and national autonomy. But some thirty years later, the revolt of the Maccabees brought the Jews squarely up against the Seleucid regime. In Egypt, a lesser conflict arose between the Jewish community and the Ptolemaic rulers. It was not as grave as the Judean crisis, but it was serious enough to have left its mark in Jewish memory. Traces of this struggle can be found in a historico-moralistic novel, known as the Third Book of Maccabees, which has been conserved in some manuscripts of the Septuagint.

Its author, whose name we do not know, was an Alexandrian Jew. His prose style is hardly a model of clarity and simplicity. The definitive redaction of the work dates either from the end of the Ptolemaic epoch, or the beginning of the Roman domination. The data establishing this "window" are the following: on the one hand, the work is prior to the fall of the Second Temple (70 CE); on the other hand, in evoking the miraculous survival of the three friends of Daniel in the fiery furnace, the author borrowed an expression from the amplified Greek version of the Book of Daniel, dating from the first century BCE. But the story it relates is older.

We should not be misled by the title. The only common ground it shares with the Maccabean revolt is the theme of narrow escape from mortal danger, through the intervention of divine providence. In the words of an early twentieth-century author, L. E. Tony André, "Tradition having later generalized the name of the Maccabees, all those who struggled for national independence, or whose attachment to the faith of their fathers had exposed to persecution, were called by this name." In our case, the story was set in the Egypt of Ptolemy IV Philopator (222–205 BCE); as we shall soon see, this dating is problematic. The author tells how a plot to exterminate Egyptian Jewry was foiled.

In the last quarter of the third century BCE, the Seleucid ruler Antiochus III embarked upon the conquest of Palestine; Ptolemy IV warded off the attack: the "Fourth Syrian War" had broken out. On June 23, 217 BCE, Ptolemy won a brilliant victory near Raphia, at the extreme southern border of Palestine, near the Egyptian frontier. Following close on the heels of his defeated adversary, he reconquered his former dominion, where he was joyously acclaimed by a population who preferred the trusteeship of the Ptolemies to domination by the Seleucids. The author depicts the victorious Ptolemy, on his triumphant march on Jerusalem.

Filled with admiration by the splendor of the Temple, Philopator expressed the desire to visit all of it, including the Holy of Holies, whose access was exclusively limited to the yearly visit by the high priest. Faced with this sacrilegious project, the faithful began to weep and proclaim their disapproval loudly. The king was deaf to their supplications. The high priest Simeon (Simeon II son of Onias II, the high priest at that time; for certain authors, he was none other than the celebrated sage Simon the Just) implored divine mercy to spare the Temple from profanation. His prayers were answered. Suddenly stricken with paralysis, the impious king collapsed to the ground before the gate of the Temple. But this was not the sole miracle to occur, as we shall now discover.

On his return to Egypt, Philopator decided to take his revenge on the Jews. He promulgated a decree that he ordered to be engraved on a pillar near the tower of his palace. No Jew of Alexandria was to enter a synagogue without offering a sacrifice to the pagan god Dionysus; a census was to be taken of all the Alexandrian Jews, in order to deprive them of their legal status, and in addition they were to be branded by a red-hot iron with the sign of ivy, the emblem of Dionysus; however, those who voluntarily embraced the worship of that god were to be spared and, in reward, be granted Alexandrian citizenship.

Some complied, but the great majority refused. Irritated by their refusal, the king extended the anti-Jewish measures to the entire diaspora of Egypt. He had the support of some of his subjects, who had already accused the Jews of religious particularism. An order (*prostagma*) was issued to the local authorities in which, after giving a laudative summary of events following his campaign against Antiochus (a fine opportunity to contrast his elevated behavior with the perfidy of the Jews), Philopator decreed that all the Jews of Egypt were to be conveyed to Alexandria, there to suffer the supreme punishment, as well befits traitors. The rebellious Jews were declared guilty of fomenting a plot against the throne. Once they had been punished, the king hoped that the realm would again enjoy peace and prosperity. Whoever dared to hide a Jew, young or old, even babes and sucklings, was to be put to death, he and all his family. All houses in which a hidden Jew was discovered were to be set afire. On the other hand, any person who denounced the guilty parties would receive a reward of two thousand drachmas from the royal treasury, as well as other benefits: the honors of Dionysus or, if the informer was a slave, his liberty.

> In every place that this decree reached, a feast was set up for the heathen at public expense with exultation and gladness, for the hatred that had long grown entrenched in their hearts was now given free expression. But for the Jews there was unceasing grief and lamentations and tearful cries; their hearts were altogether inflamed with groaning, as they bewailed the unforeseen destruction that had suddenly been decreed against them. What province or city, what inhabited place at all, or what byways were not filled with lamentations and groans for them? For with such cruel and pitiless spirit were they sent away, one and all, by the respective generals that their inordinate suffering made even some of their enemies, perceiving the common pity before their eyes, reflect on the uncertain revolutions of life and weep at their utterly miserable expulsion.
>
> For there was carried away a multitude of old men covered with hoary hair, forcing the sluggishness of their limbs, which were stooped with age, to a quick pace because of the shameless and violent driving. Young women who had but lately entered their bridal chamber for sharing wedded life, uttering cries of lamentation instead of joy, their myrrh-drenched locks sullied with dust, were driven on unveiled, and with one accord chanted a dirge instead of a marriage hymn, as if mangled by heathen whelps. In prisoners' bonds and exposed to view, they were forcibly dragged to the embarkation aboard ship. Their husbands too, in the flower of their youth, wore halters about their necks instead of garlands, and instead of feasting and youthful ease they spent the remaining days of their nuptials in dirges, seeing Hades at their very feet. They were embarked in the manner of wild beasts, driven under the constraint of iron bonds; some were riveted to the rowers' benches by their necks, others were made fast by the feet with unbreakable fetters. Their light was cut off by thick planks above, so that, their eyes being kept in darkness altogether, they might throughout the voyage receive the treatment due traitors. (3 MACC. 4:1–10; ED. M. HADAS)

All the prisoners were then transported to Schedia (where, as we have noted, one of the earliest consecrations of a synagogue had taken place), some miles from

Alexandria. They were crowded into the hippodrome, near the Canopus Gate, to the east of the Jewish quarter, where they were exposed to the view of anyone entering or leaving the city. Their Alexandrian coreligionists were forced to rejoin them, by order of the king. The name of each and every one was then to be registered: a difficult task, since they were so numerous. The process dragged on for days, from sunrise to sunset. Meanwhile, the king basked in contentment at the thought that the traitors would soon receive their just deserts. However, after forty days of labor (how the prisoners managed to survive is not known), the recording process came to a halt, for lack of papyrus and calami. This was due to the invincible providence of Heaven, which had come to succor the Jews, and allow the author to extol the numerical strength of the Jewish population in Egypt. Incidentally we learn that, luckily, all had not been arrested and conveyed to Alexandria, so great were their numbers.

Abandoning the register, the captors set to work in earnest. The king called upon a man named Hermon, in charge of the war elephants. Five hundred elephants were to be worked up to a pitch of frenzy by inhaling immense clouds of incense and drinking great quantities of strong wine. Maddened by this brew, they were to be loosed upon the prisoners in the hippodrome. This was the punishment of the "plotters": they were to be trampled to death by a troop of enraged elephants! But the Lord, in His merciful providence, had not forgotten His faithful. When Hermon came to the king to announce that all was ready for the execution, he found his master plunged into a deep sleep. One day's reprieve for the Jews! The next day, their torturers went back to work. A fresh miracle occurred, affording a new reprieve: the king had completely forgotten the orders he had issued! When he had recovered from his amnesia, Philopator reconfirmed them, vowing to pursue his goal by invading Judea, slaying its inhabitants, and burning the Temple of Jerusalem.

At sunrise, the next day, the streets leading to the hippodrome were filled with great crowds of people. Everybody wanted to enjoy the show. The elephants, inebriated with great quantities of spiced wine, launched themselves with fury upon the captives. Behind the elephants, urging them on, the king's soldiers followed *en masse*. Upon seeing the dust kicked up by the herd and hearing the formidable noise they made, the Jews believed their last hour had come. They began to weep, to lament, to embrace one another; mothers held their infants tightly against their bodies, parents hugged their children. In the midst of the crowd, an aged man called Eleazar, of priestly lineage, arose and prayed to the Lord, recalling the past perils from which the Jews had been saved. Just as he was about to end his prayer, the king appeared before his victims. Amongst the Jews, a great cry broke forth and rose to heaven. The Lord had heard them. One more miracle was to occur, the last one, the decisive one.

> Then, the greatly glorious, almighty, and true God, making His countenance manifest, opened the gates of heaven, from which two glorified angels of terrible aspect descended, visible to all except the Jews, and they

confronted the force of their adversaries, and filled them with confusion and terror, and bound them with immovable fetters. And a great horror seized the body of the king also, and oblivion covered his vehement insolence. And the beasts turned back on the armed hosts that followed them, and began to tread them down and destroy them. The king's wrath was turned to pity and tears for the things he had previously devised. For when he heard the outcry and saw them all prostrate to meet their death, he wept, and angrily threatened his friends, saying: "You usurp the kingly power, and you surpass the tyrants in cruelty; you are even endeavoring to deprive me, your benefactor, of my rule and even of my life, secretly contriving, as you do, measures disadvantageous to my kingship. Who has driven from their homes those who faithfully kept our country's strongholds, and foolishly gathered them, every one, here? Who has so unlawfully overwhelmed with indignities those who from the beginning have been more conspicuous than all peoples in their goodwill toward us, and who have frequently encountered mankind's worst dangers on our behalf? Loosen their unjust bonds, loosen them utterly; send them back to their own in peace, when you have begged their forgiveness for what has already been done. Set free the children of the Almighty and heavenly living God, who from the days of our ancestors until now has conferred upon our estate unimpaired stability and glory."

These things the king said; the Jews were set free in an instant, and praised the Holy God their Savior, having but just escaped death. (3 MACC. 6:18–29)

All's well that ends well. The Jews of Egypt had been saved from extermination. King Philopator, having repented, called for his dioiketes and ordered him to furnish the wherewithal for a great seven-day feast. Around the joyous banquet table, the king and his courtiers were reunited with the Jews; yesterday hangmen and victims, today newly reconciled friends. There had never been a "Jewish plot"! The only plotters were the king's own courtiers who had overstepped the limits of their authority and had almost rendered him, the king, responsible for the massacre of his most faithful servants. After the festivities, these latter were sent back to their homes, where their sovereign had thoughtfully authorized them to celebrate their miraculous salvation by an annual holiday.

Philopator then addressed a new circular letter to the local governors, recommending the Jews to their care and spelling out a "revised version" of recent events in which all the blame fell upon the royal counselors. The king himself was guiltless. "With the goodwill he bears to all men," he had pardoned the innocent Jews. Their confiscated goods were to be returned. We do not learn whether nor how the king's evil counselors had been punished. But Philopator, endorsing the argument that anyone capable of betraying his God might also betray his sovereign, granted the Jews the right to take revenge upon the renegades. The apostates' throats were cut. The list of corpses comprises those of the soldiers who had been trampled to death by the elephants. Although their lives had been included in the bill for the spectacle, no one has ever mentioned them since; they were doubtless indigenous Egyptians, conscripted into the Ptolemaic army for the battle of Raphia.

Josephus also had heard the story of the miracle at the hippodrome; in his account of the episode, he did not place it under the reign of Ptolemy IV Philopator, but some half-century later, during that of Ptolemy VIII Euergetes II, known as "the Big-Bellied," Physkon in Greek (145–116 BCE). Comparing the two versions is instructive:

> Ptolemy Philometor and his consort Cleopatra [Cleopatra II, sister and wife of Ptolemy VI, then of Ptolemy VIII] entrusted the whole of their realm to Jews, and placed their entire army under the command of Jewish generals, Onias and Dositheos. Apion ridicules their names, when he ought rather to admire their achievements, and, instead of abusing them, to thank them for saving Alexandria, of which he claims to be a citizen. For, when the Alexandrians were at war with Queen Cleopatra and in imminent danger of annihilation, it was they who negotiated terms and rid them of the horrors of civil war. "But," says Apion, "Onias subsequently advanced at the head of a large army against the city, when Thermus, the Roman ambassador, was actually on the spot." He was right and perfectly justified in so acting, I venture to say.
>
> For, on the death of his brother Ptolemy Philometor, Ptolemy surnamed Physkon [Ptolemy VIII Euergetes II] left Cyrene with the intention of dethroning Cleopatra and the deceased king's sons, and iniquitously usurping the crown himself. That was why, on Cleopatra's behalf, Onias took up arms against him, refusing to abandon at a crisis his allegiance to the throne. Moreover, the justice of his action was signally attested by God. For Ptolemy Physkon, though (not) daring to face the army of Onias, had arrested all the Jews in the city with their wives and children, and exposed them, naked and in chains, to be trampled to death by elephants, the beasts being actually made drunk for the purpose. However, the outcome was the reverse of the intentions. The elephants, without touching the Jews at their feet, rushed at Physkon's friends, and killed a large number of them. Afterwards Ptolemy saw a terrible apparition, which forbade him to injure these people. With his favorite concubine (some call her Ithaca, others Eirene) adding her entreaty to him not to perpetrate such an enormity, he gave way and repented of his past actions and further designs. That is the origin of the well-known feast the Jews of Alexandria keep, with good reason, on this day, because of the deliverance so manifestly vouchsafed to them by God. (JOSEPHUS, AGAINST APION 2, 49–55; ED. H. ST. J. THACKERAY)

The concision of Josephus' account lends it a credibility hardly to be accorded to the romantic pathos of the Third Book of Maccabees, and his dating, too, has an authentic ring to it.

The first years of the reign of Ptolemy VIII were marked by the struggle for power between him and his sister Cleopatra II. The Alexandrian Jews, as well as Onias and his army, had sided with the queen. But Physkon triumphed. Since Onias had already led his troops out of the city, others were to pay the ransom of "treason" (whereas the author of the Third Book of Maccabees maintained that all the Jews of Egypt were involved in the hippodrome affair, Josephus limited it to those of Alexandria). A kind of *coup de théâtre* then occurred: the king and his sister were reconciled, and so completely that they became husband and wife (Cleopatra had formerly been the wife of her brother Ptolemy VI Philometor). At the very last moment, the king decided not to take revenge upon the Jews, who had had the courage to side with the queen against him. On the occasion of the royal marriage, the former adversaries of Physkon were granted an amnesty. Their unexpected salvation eventually was transformed by legend into a manifestation of divine providence.

Victor Tcherikover preferred Josephus' version. Other interpretations, obviously, are possible. Later dates have been proposed: 88 BCE, during the hostilities that pitted Ptolemy IX Soter II Lathyros allied to Cleopatra III against Ptolemy X Alexander I, or under the reign of Caligula in 38 CE. For centuries, scholars have held lengthy debates on the historicity of the miracle at the hippodrome. The fictional trappings of the Third Book of Maccabees have been carefully examined and compared with historical data from other sources, in order to determine the degree of truth to be imputed to its contents.

As early as the sixteenth century, the Genevan philologist and theologian Isaac Casaubon (1559–1614) pointed out the similarities between that work and the writings of Polybius. They may have had a common source in Ptolemy of Megalopolis, the author of an anecdotic account of the reign of Ptolemy IV. But the two writers may have used different sources for their material; this seems to be the case for the initial episode concerning the plot against Philopator's life. Moreover, the anonymous author of our novel turns out to have been more of a poet than an historian: M. Z. Kopidakis, in an interesting thesis, has shown that he was greatly influenced by Aeschylus, the most "religious" of the Greek tragic playwrights.

Several features of the tale are reminiscent of other Judeo-Hellenistic literary works: the Book of Esther, the Book of Judith, the *Letter of Aristeas to Philocrates*, the Second Book of Maccabees. The reference to a feast, appearing both in Third Book Maccabees and Josephus, tends to support the hypothesis of an explanatory myth, conceived to justify the celebration of an anniversary. But, simply to account for a Jewish holiday, was it really necessary to bring in five hundred elephants and to cast king Philopator in the rather inglorious role of Israel's persecutor?

Decidedly, this moving story raises more problems than it solves. All the efforts of

War elephant from India   *Terra cotta, 3rd or 2nd century* BCE *(Paris, Louvre).*

historical criticism notwithstanding, one can not flatly rule out the possibility of the event having occurred during the reign of Ptolemy IV. The portrayal of this king as a cruel, spiteful monarch, but also a great builder and lover of architecture, corresponds with the data to be gleaned elsewhere. Dositheos son of Drimylos, mentioned at the very beginning of the novel, had long been considered by modern scholars to be a fictional character, until the papyri finally restored him to his rightful place in history. The inscription on the stele in Pithom, erected by the Egyptian clergy in honor of Philopator, recounts how the king, during his sojourn in Syria after the victory of Raphia, "went into the temples that were there." This tends to lend credence to the historicity of his attempt to make his way into the Temple of Jerusalem. Despite the apparent sobriety of Josephus' version, it is not more solidly grounded in fact than that of the author of the Third Book of Maccabees. To cite one weak point in his version, was not the intervention of the king's concubine simply borrowed from the Book of Esther?

One could go on and on. We shall limit our examination to three particularly meaningful points: the "Dionysianism" of Philopator, the elephants, and the census of the Jews.

Dionysiac ideology was all that the Ptolemaic rulers had to offer in the way of a political platform. The Ptolemies had seized upon the myth of the deified Alexander, the "New Dionysus," which they appropriated to further their own political ends. The Dionysiac associations played the role of devoted servants of the monarchy. The episode of the Roman embassy to Alexandria, where Ptolemy VIII "Physkon" and Scipio Aemilianus found themselves face-to-face, gives some measure of the distance between the Dionysiac ideal of the Ptolemies and the rigor of Roman mentality, steeped as it was in stoicism.

Ptolemy IV was a particularly fervent zealot of Dionysus. A most interesting proof of his proselytism is offered by a royal decree, conserved in a papyrus (Berlin Papyrus VI 1211; C. Ord. Ptol. 29). It is hard to ascertain the exact object of the decree. The late Belgian scholar, Marie-Thérèse Lenger, in her *Corpus des Ordonnances des Ptolémées* (Brussels, 1964), summarized the questions it raises. Did its author intend to convene a synod in Alexandria, in which priests charged with the initiation of neophytes into the Dionysiac mysteries were to compare their various theological traditions and unify their doctrines? Did he attempt to promulgate the official worship of the god, perhaps going as far as to establish it as the religion of the state? Did he wish to compile a register of the members of private, secret sects consecrated to these mysteries, which were scattered throughout the country? Was he trying to gather information with a view to new fiscal measures?

These questions cannot readily be answered. We can only be sure that the author of the decree was greatly interested by the cult of Dionysus and took ample measures to further it. For a long while, both the author and the date of the decree were uncertain. Thanks to the British papyrologist E. G. Turner, we do know today that its author was Ptolemy IV Philopator and its date was prior to 215/214 BCE. This dating is in perfect accord with the account given in the Third Book of Maccabees of the decisions taken after the battle of Raphia, in 217 or 216 BCE.

Now for the elephants. Those veritable battle tanks of the Hellenistic armies often turned the tables of victory in combat. Polybius confirms the use of war elephants in the battle of Raphia. It seems that Philopator's elephants, less well-trained than those of Antiochus, had caused much damage among the Egyptian troops themselves. One cannot help thinking of the poor soldiers who were trampled to death in the Alexandrian hippodrome.

The figure of five hundred is not simply a figment of the imagination. According to Strabo, it was the exact number of elephants that Seleucus I had at his disposition at the very end of the fourth century BCE. They had been offered him by an Indian king. One should not take this number literally, however. Like our "thousands of times," the Indians used it as a synonym for "a great number." Pliny the Elder (*Natural History*, 6,

85) relates that, during Emperor Claudius' reign, the envoys from Ceylon declared that their island contained five hundred cities (*oppida*), an expression meaning only that they had numerous towns. This Indian reference suggests the idea that Philopator, who had only African elephants, seized Indian elephants of the vanquished Antiochus as booty of war. The ancients held the Asian elephant to be superior in strength and combativeness to his African counterpart; not only in size and weight, but also, and above all, because the Asian elephants were traditionally better trained and more efficiently disciplined. This is no proof that Philopator sent his animals out against the Jews, but the fearsome presence of the pachyderms in Alexandria fits the context of his epoch better than it does that of the struggles between Ptolemy VIII and his sister. In Hellenistic iconography, one might add, the elephant was associated with the Dionysiac ceremonials.

Our third and last point: the census. In Roman Egypt, from the reign of Augustus onward, a census of the population was habitually taken every fourteen years, by means of a "house-by-house register" (*kat' oikian apographai*). This system had its antecedents in the sporadic monitoring operations implemented by the Ptolemaic rulers, especially in periods of war. A demotic ostracon found in Karnak informs us that a general census of land had been taken under Ptolemy II Philadelphus, in 258/257 BCE, in connection with the expenses of the Second Syrian War.

It is highly probable that the Fourth Syrian War, which concerns us here, had occasioned similar measures, for both persons and goods. The levying of an army for Raphia entailed a general tax increase for the entire population. Egyptian warriors played a major role in winning the war, which was followed by a series of uprisings among the indigenous population, sparked by the unbearable tax burden placed upon them. Ten years after Raphia, the Thebaid was to secede from Egypt and install a government of "national" (in fact, Nubian) Pharaohs: Hurganophor or Haronnophris (206/205–201/200) and Ankhonnophris or Khaonnophris (201/200–187/186), names scholars had previously read as "Harmakhis" and "Ankhmakhis." The Ptolemaic rulers were obliged to come to terms with the native resistance, conceding to the rebels a measure of religious and political rights. This "Egyptianization" of the royal government was accompanied by an implacable tightening of the fiscal noose, which it tended to camouflage.

In this context, census taking would have not been an unusual measure. And it would have proved especially disagreeable to Jews, traditionally allergic to any kind of numbering process. In Jewish tradition, census taking has always been fraught with danger. In cases of absolute necessity, offerings were prescribed to avoid the plagues it could bring about (Ex. 30:12). When Satan induced King David to count the people of Israel, they paid a high price in the loss of 70,000 souls by the hand of the Lord (2 Samuel 24; 1 Chron. 21). The Lord does not wish his people to be counted. Had he not promised (Gen. 22:17, 32:13) that they would be as innumerable as "the stars of the heaven, and as the sand which is upon the seashore"? For the Jews, the taking or even the planning of a census was perceived as a mortal danger.

Mortal danger, last-minute salvation—it seems that a conflict between the Jews of Egypt and the Ptolemaic regime took place under Ptolemy Philopator, at the end of the third century BCE. How did things come to this pass? One should discard, as totally anachronistic, the idea of a forced conversion of the Jews to the worship of Dionysus. Ptolemy IV and his sister-wife Arsinoe III were not Ferdinand and Isabel of Castile. One would rather opt for another solution: Philopator had decided to treat the Jews as a Dionysiac sect, to whose members the rulings set out in his decree were applicable. The stubborn resistance of the Jews almost succeeded in bringing about a tragedy, which was averted in the nick of time. Legendary embroidery accounted for all the fanciful dressing, and the author of the novel drew the theological lessons necessary for the moral edification of his coreligionists.

How could the king and his entourage have assimilated Judaism with Dionysiac worship? Philosophical reflection is of little help here; from a philosophical point of view, Judaism and Dionysiac religion represent two diametrically opposed visions of man's place in the universe, vis-à-vis the divine, as well as vis-à-vis the rest of creation. The king and his counselors were not encumbered with theological subtleties; they were exclusively concerned with the outward aspects of the ambiguous links between Jewish religious practice and the Dionysiac cult.

In synagogue practice, the mystery surrounding the worship of an invisible God could have appeared "Dionysiac" enough to the Greeks. On a higher level, certain tendencies of Judeo-Alexandrian literature may have left a similar impression. The Judeo-Alexandrian authors were wont to stress the common points between the Jews and the Orphics, a mystical sect with manifold ties to Dionysiac rites. The philosopher Aristoboulos, commentator of the Torah and Ptolemy VI Philometor's "counselor for Jewish affairs," embellished his writings with Orphic verses illustrating the uniqueness of the divine, a theme common to Jewish and Orphic thinking. Soon afterwards, as we have seen, Artapanos transformed Musaeus (Mousaios), Orpheus' son, into his teacher, whom he identified with Moses. As much as to call the Orphics the disciples of the Jews! If one concedes this, only one more step is needed to confuse Dionysus with the God of the Jews. The Jews themselves helped to further the confusion.

The Greeks were not the only ones to make assimilations of this sort. The first mention of Jews in Rome, in 139 BCE, was also placed under the sign of confusion: the Jewish God had been assimilated with Dionysus, the Roman Bacchus, represented by Sabazius, a Phrygian divinity. Valerius Maximus, a contemporary of Tiberius, tells how the praetor Gnaeus Cornelius Hispalus had accused certain Jews of trying to corrupt Roman morals by preaching the cult of "Jupiter Sabazius," and had sent them packing back to where they had come from. The cult had been identified with that of the "God of armies," Lord Sabaoth, either by Valerius Maximus' source (the historian who had taken note of this event) or by the praetor Hispalus himself. The date coincides with that of the mission Simon the Hasmonean had dispatched to draw up a friendship treaty with the Romans. The authorities seem to have reacted to an attempt by some members of the deputation to spread religious propaganda. Thus, a half-century after the "conspiracy of the Bacchanals" had been suppressed in 186 BCE by a celebrated senatus-consultum, the God of Israel, whom the Romans took for a sort of Semitic Bacchus, was declared *persona non grata* in Rome. Plutarch (*Convivial Questions*, 6) and Tacitus (*Histories*, 5, 5) inform us that the muddle persisted as late as the second century CE.

King Philopator may have been the first to promote the confusion. Was he following the advice of some courtier, perhaps the renegade Dositheos son of Drimylos who had saved his life at Raphia? Were this true, Dositheos would have been a precursor of Menelaus, the Hellenized high priest who was to urge King Antiochus IV Epiphanes to prohibit the Jews from practicing their religion in Judea. Since the Jews had been classed as members of a Dionysian sect, they were subject to the decreed measures of control, and their leaders were to present their "sacred books" to the Alexandrian authorities. The Jews raised their voices in protest. As was the custom in Alexandria, they took to the streets. To disperse the crowds of demonstrators, the king may have ordered out his elephants, just as present-day authorities order out police brigades with tear gas grenades. Before it was too late, however, Ptolemy realized his mistake and managed to avoid the spilling of blood. But the remembrance of the incident was perpetuated in legendary form.

Were one to accept this reconstruction, it would follow that the episode of the hippodrome was due to the political clumsiness of those at the helm, and is not to be construed as an overtly anti-Jewish act on the part of the Ptolemaic monarchy. The Jews certainly lost many of their illusions at this time, and their loyalty to the Ptolemies must have been sorely tried. Within the limits imposed by their faithfulness to the laws of their forebears, they had been prepared to serve their king with all the devotion of which they were capable, according to the program outlined during Alexander's visit to Jerusalem. By rewarding their subjects' loyalty with measures of harassment that, moreover, they perceived as a mortal danger, the royal regime was to prove itself guilty at once of ingratitude and outrageous behavior. The Jews were deeply upset, and the remembrance of their disappointment was embodied in the Third Book of Maccabees.

Philopator's error does not, of course, exclude the possibility of another conflict a half-century later, between the Jews and Ptolemy VIII. Placing the "miracle at the hippodrome" in its proper historical perspective does not entail the obligation to choose between Philopator and his grandson Physkon. In order to relate the events that had taken place under the latter's reign, Josephus (or his informant) could have made use of a scenario that had already been composed to describe the dramatic events in the Alexandria of Ptolemy IV. A fine story is well worth telling a second time, even if chronology has to take a thrashing!

In the light of these accounts, it is impossible to impute to either of our two monarchs the inglorious title of "inventor of pagan anti-Semitism in Ptolemaic Egypt". In both cases, political motives were paramount: neither Ptolemy IV Philopator nor the

Ptolemy IV Philopator   *(Paris, National Library, Cabinet of Medals.)*

"pot-bellied" Ptolemy VIII gave vent to scornful or hateful feelings, without which the word "anti-Semitism" is meaningless. Nevertheless, something important had happened: the Jews of Egypt had discovered that life in the service of a Ptolemaic king was not always a bed of roses.

"THEY LOATHE THE JEWS"

We have just examined some Greco-Egyptian and Judeo-Alexandrian writings, which must now be confronted with the testimony of contemporary documents. Does the everyday life of the period furnish evidence of enough hostility toward the Jews to justify the literary amplifications on both sides?

Choosing the proper sources is not an easy task. How are we to isolate the necessary material? How are we to select, from the thousands of ancient documents, mainly Greek papyri from Egypt, those which enable us to test the hypothesis of a pagan anti-Judaism? The testimony here could very well be equivocal, vitiating the conclusions we might draw from it. Take this private letter of Theban origin, for example, written in Greek on papyrus, which may be paleographically dated to the second century BCE. Menon, an Egyptian Greek, was telling his brother Hermokrates about a mare and a Jew whose identity is undisclosed:

> Menon to his brother Hermokrates, greeting. I hope you are well. I am, and so are Aphrodisia and our daughter, and the slave-girl and her daughter. You wrote to say that you had bought [sent?] the mare, and it would be delivered [handed over?] by a Jew whose name I do not know. I am writing to say that he did not give me the mare, nor the carriage which went with it.
>
> I should be obliged if you would buy two staters of purple dye for me and two for Aphrodisia.
>
> To Hermokrates. (U. WILCKEN, CHRESTOMATHIE, NO. 57; CPJUD. I 135)

What is this all about? The writer begins with a message he had received from his correspondent, employing a verb of which only a part is legible, due to the bad state of the papyrus: the ending of the perfect infinitive active, -kenai. Restoring [egora]kenai, "having bought," gives one possible reading: "You wrote me you had bought a mare; know that the Jew who should have delivered it has not done so." A crooked dealer had not kept his word. Ulrich Wilcken seized upon this reading and proceeded to denounce a lying Jewish horse dealer ("ein betrügerischer jüdischer Pferdehändler"), the type of individual whose behavior was sufficient to arouse and nourish popular anti-Judaic feelings. The authors of an abominable collection of anti-Jewish texts from Greek and Roman antiquity, edited in Hamburg in 1943, Eugen Fischer and Gerhard Kittel, were jubilant. They classed our Jewish horse dealer under the heading "crooks and guttersnipes" ("Spitzbuben"), in their sympathetic catalogue.

Not so fast, retort the advocates of a less malevolent interpretation: the proper reconstitution of the verb is not [egora]kenai, "having bought," but [apestal]kenai, "having sent." The crooked dealer disappears, to be replaced by an honest and, above all, obliging gentleman: a Jew who was willing to convey a horse and carriage to the writer of the letter. They had not yet come, simply because the benevolent agent had not yet been able to take care of the matter. Just give him a little time to attend to it! And let's not speak of a crooked deal, nor of anti-Semitism! On the contrary, solidarity and friendship reigned supreme between Jews and Greeks in the second century BCE Thebaid. Everything depends on one-half of a verb.

There are more explicit papyrological documents. Another private letter, subsequent to the one we have just examined, is now at the French Institute of Oriental Archaeology in Cairo; it was published in 1957 by Alexander Fuks in the first volume of the *Corpus Papyrorum Judaicarum*. Luckily, Fischer and Kittel could not have known of it.

> Herakles to the manager Ptolemaios many greetings and good wishes of good health. I have asked Iap[...] in Memphis, about the priest of Tebtunis, to write a letter for him, in order that I may know how things

stand. I ask you to take care that he does not fall into a trap and take him by the hand; when he will have need of anything, do for him as you do for Artemidoros and, in particular, give me the pleasure of finding the same lodgings for the priest: you know that they loathe the Jews. Greet [...]ibas, Epimenes and Tryphonas, . . . and take care of yourself. (*PAPYRUS IFAO INV. 104; CPJUD. I 141*)

Here we have it. This message leaves little room for doubt: taken literally, it would clearly confirm the fact that there were anti-Semites in Memphis, the religious capital of ancient Egypt and one of the oldest Greek settlements in the country. In the words of Roger Rémondon, who has reread and commented upon this text, these people had a "violent physical hatred" for the Jews. Jews "fill them with loathing"; or, if one prefers: "they vomit the Jews," *bdelyssontai Ioudaious*. The Greek verb employed here has semantic connotations linking it to medical literature and to stage comedy; taken figuratively, it expresses disgust and contempt so intense as to be barely controllable. Seen in this light, the letter would furnish decisive evidence of an authentically popular brand of anti-Semitism in first-century BCE Egypt. The intellectual anti-Judaism of the well-read Alexandrian Greeks and Egyptians had its counterpart in the chora, whose inhabitants were imbued with a "scornful hatred" of the Jews.

We should, nonetheless, proceed carefully in our judgments. We do not know the identity of the persons named in the text. Tryphonas, a common name among the Jews at that period, could indicate a Jewish milieu. Who was "the priest of Tebtunis," whose name was not even mentioned? The context excludes the idea of a heathen priest. He was most certainly a Jewish priest, a *kohen*, a term the Greeks rendered by *hiereus*; he had come from Tebtunis in the Faiyum and had to stop over at Memphis, where he would need lodgings for a short stay. Was his final destination the temple of Leontopolis, northeast of Memphis? The key character in the interpretation of this letter, however, is Herakles, its author. We know nothing of his official functions nor of his social status, but his background and mindset are easily discernible.

Although his name was borrowed from pagan heroic mythology, this man was a Hellenized Jew, a reader of the Septuagint. The verb he used to designate the feelings of the people of Memphis toward the Jews, *bdelyssomai*, "to feel a loathing; to make loathsome or abominable," is hardly ever found in Greek papyri, but it occurs some fifty times in the text of the Greek Bible, and the corresponding noun, *bdelygma*, "abomination," appears 120 times. We have already come across the term "abomination of desolation" apropos of the Maccabean crisis. The first occurrence is to be found in Genesis (43:32), in reference to the Egyptians, who "might not eat bread with the Hebrews; for that is an abomination (*bdelygma*) unto the Egyptians." Herakles may have had this verse in mind, or perhaps the beginning of the Book of Exodus (1:12), relating how the Egyptians "were adread" (*ebdelyssonto*) "because of the children of Israel."

In other words, the person who wrote this letter was employing a kind of coded language, the language of Jewish readers of the Alexandrian Bible, with its own particular

"The Anti-Semites of Memphis" *Private letter. Papyrus, 1st century* BCE *(Cairo, French Institute of Eastern Archaeology).*

expressions, as familiar to the addressee as they were to the writer himself. The gist of the message was filtered through a perfectly transparent metaphor: Herakles reminded his correspondent that he must beware of the Memphians who "were not exactly fond of them," to substitute one metaphor for another. To believe the Memphians were literally seized with the desire to vomit would amount to miscalculating the distance between metaphor and reality. And who could guarantee that only "the Anti-Semites of Memphis" (the title of Rémondon's study) were seized by nausea at the sight of a Jew? How could one be certain that the Gauls or the Iberians were immune to similar aversions?

To return to our Egyptian concerns, a document such as the one we have just examined furnishes convincing proof of the reality of popular hostility toward Jews in the Ptolemaic kingdom. This letter in itself does not provide sufficient justification for the omnipresence of a "violent physical hatred," but one certainly cannot deny the existence of pagan anti-Judaism in late Ptolemaic Egypt. We have not yet come to the stage of the "teaching of contempt," which was to become the hallmark of Christian anti-Semitism. But it is enough to exempt the primitive Christian Church from the odious privilege of having "invented" anti-Semitism.

All in all, the Jews in Egypt had not fared too badly under the Ptolemies. A few dark clouds had appeared on the horizon, but not enough to alter the generally sunny and peaceful atmosphere of the period. Changes were in the making now: the conquering Romans were soon to reduce the Ptolemaic monarchy to the rank of a province of their empire.

THE TWILIGHT:
EGYPT IN THE
ROMAN EMPIRE

The "Jewish Question" in Alexandria

THE DECLINE

When, in the month of August of the year 30 BCE, Octavianus, the future Emperor Augustus, conquered Egypt, the history of the Jewish diaspora entered into a new phase, a period of decline. It was to end with the total disappearance of Hellenized Jewry, following the rebellion of 115–117 CE. In this process, political considerations played a predominant role. The Hellenistic monarchy and the Roman Empire had fundamentally different policies concerning the legal status of the Jewish population.

Under the Ptolemies, the Jews had been part of the community of "Hellenes," the dominant group of Greek-speaking conquerors. When the Romans, in their turn, conquered Egypt, the situation was altered from top to bottom. There was no room within the limits of Roman law for the community of Hellenes, a cultural rather than a national concept. It was made up of differentiated elements, each with its own particular identity, and the sum of these elements could not be recognized as a single "nation" or "people." Conversely, the links that bound the Hellenes to their original motherlands were not solid enough to justify individual citizenship. In Roman eyes, the descendants of Athenian immigrants from the era of the first Ptolemies could not pretend to be citizens of Athens, nor could the descendants of Samian immigrants claim to be citizens of Samos, nor could those of the Corinthians be citizens of Corinth. The mass of individuals who called themselves "Greek" and considered themselves to be citizens were neither a "city" nor a "nation"; as a group, they were too heterogeneous, and their constituent parts were unclassifiable. They were doomed to disappear. The coming of the Romans sounded the death knell of the "Hellenes." Under Roman rule, they were literally pulverized. Provincial society was totally restructured. For the Jews of Egypt, it was a veritable disaster.

In matters of personal status, the Romans were inflexible. One was either a citizen or one was not. The Greek citizens of Alexandria had nothing to fear; their rights were guaranteed. Such was also the case for the two other Greek cities, Naucratis and Ptolemais and, from 130 CE on, for Antinoopolis, founded by Hadrian on the spot where

Augustus as sovereign of Egypt *(Cairo, Egyptian Museum.)*

the handsome young Antinous, his favorite, had drowned in the Nile. But the Greeks of the chora, provincials who were not citizens of a Greek city of Egypt, were relegated to the rank of "Egyptians," on the same level as the natives. A vast "third estate" was thus created, comprising the posterity of the Hellenes as well as the entire indigenous population.

This juridically inevitable situation was embarrassing for the Roman conquerors, who depended upon Greek elements to staff the local administration. They had to find a way to "save" those Greeks whose citizenship had become too vague to be taken seriously. They hit upon a means to circumvent the obstacle: fiscality came to the aid of legality. All Egyptian males from fourteen to sixty-two years of age were subjected to a personal tax (*capitatio, laographia*); the descendants of the Hellenes obtained a special reduced rate, a privilege based on a triple criterion: urban residence, the possession of landed property, and Greek education. The Greeks of Egypt, natural partners of the Romans in the business of running the country, were incorporated into orders of provincial notables (in the Roman sense of the term *ordo*).

For the Jews, the restructuring of provincial society entailed a sudden and deplorable deterioration of their status. The descendants of the soldiers we encountered in the preceding chapters of this book were not included in the new orders of notables. The selection process had left the Jews on the sidelines. Not a single Jewish name can be found among the numerous documents dealing with the processing of qualification (*epikrisis*) for the fourteen-year old sons of notables, to warrant their eligibility for the reduced tax rate. It is hard to determine the exact reasons for their elimination, which may in some measure have been due to the Jews themselves, allergic as they were to all census-taking procedures; we have dealt at length with the account, in the Third Book of Maccabees, of Ptolemy Philopator's initiative, and the horror it raised among the Jews. The fact remains that, under Augustus, the Jews were suddenly wrenched from their erstwhile condition as an integral part of the Greek-speaking minority. They had been "Hellenes"; now, they had suddenly become "Egyptians."

Things were not much better in Alexandria. Although the Jews were the social equals of the Greeks, they were not Alexandrian citizens, save in very few instances. We shall shortly examine the case of a Jew whose father had been a citizen of Alexandria before the Roman conquest, but had not been able to transmit his citizenship to his son. His was an exceptional case, as rare as was the promotion of an Alexandrian Jew to the rank of a Roman citizen. Only one family of rich notables is known to have achieved this status: the alabarch Alexander and his sons, the objects of imperial favor, probably that of Augustus himself.

Some scholars believe that the Jews of Alexandria had their own communal organization, the Jewish *politeuma*, under the autonomous leadership of a council of elders, which, under the reign of Augustus, had replaced the "chief of the people" (ethnarch) mentioned by Strabo. But, whatever the hopes and demands of the Jews, the strictures of Roman law would prevent a body of this sort from assuming a status comparable in any measure to that of the Alexandrian Greeks. The Jews obtained some privileges of a religious nature, such as exemption from appearing in court on the Sabbath, the right to receive a pecuniary indemnity instead of a measure of oil during public distributions, the right to consider the theft of their sacred books a grave crime (sacrilege), punishable as such, or the substitution of the stick for the whip in cases of corporal punishment. Apart from these meager concessions, their disgrace was complete, in Alexandria and throughout the land.

Under the reign of Augustus, toward 5/4 BCE, an Alexandrian Jew addressed a petition to the prefect of Egypt, Gaius Turranius, affording us a moving illustration of this state of affairs. We possess a rough draft of the document, signed by one Helenos son of Tryphon (Berlin Papyrus IV 1140; CPJud. II 151). In introducing himself to the "most powerful governor," he started off by calling himself an "Alexandrian" (*Alexandreus*) but, thinking better of it, crossed out the word and replaced it by a longer expression: "one of the Jews from Alexandria" (*Ioudaios ton apo Alexandreias*). Alexandria was certainly his "own homeland" (*idia patris*), but he was not a citizen. He decided against trying to pass himself off as such, since this would be considered an egregious offense.

His father, however, seems to have been an "Alexandrian" (*Alexandreus*). Strictly speaking, he possessed Alexandrian citizenship. Helenos himself was born around 67 or 66 BCE, under the reign of Ptolemy XII Auletes, the father of the beautiful Cleopatra. As he specifically stated (we shall return to this point presently), he was over sixty years old at the time of his petition. We do not know why he had not inherited his father's citizenship. Perhaps the mother of Helenos was not the daughter of a citizen. Like Athenian law at the time of Pericles, Alexandrian law apparently required both maternal and paternal ancestry for the establishment of citizenship. Or had his father acquired citizenship after Helenos' birth, under the reign of Cleopatra VII, possibly as a reward for services rendered to Julius Caesar or Mark Antony? We do not know. In any case, he had not bequeathed it to his son.

The rest of the draft is not very legible, but the words that can be made out—"gymnasium," "ephebate," "poll tax"—give us a good idea of its contents. Helenos had been wronged and was complaining: Alexandrian citizenship had been denied him, and he was obliged to pay the poll tax. But the arguments he invoked were not very convincing: his domicile (he had always lived here); the Greek education (*paideia*) that his father, within the measure of his means, had given him; lastly, the fact that, under the government of the "first prefects," he had never been questioned by the authorities. Since Gaius Turranius (7–4 BCE) was the fifth Roman prefect of Egypt, Helenos had for some years enjoyed a status now being contested by the provincial administration. He must have been denounced, or simply discovered during a routine check.

Neither his place of residence, his Greek *paideia*, nor the lengthy period during which he had enjoyed the rights of citizenship were weighty enough considerations. He lacked a legal basis to justify his status. He was an Alexandrian Jew, but it was out of the question for him to be recognized as a genuine "Alexandrian." Probably counseled by the scribe that had helped him prepare his petition, and who was abreast of the current legal dispositions, Helenos was doubtless well aware of the weakness of his case. His arguments were not likely to convince the governor, and he fell back on his last line of defense, a far cry from his lofty civic ambitions: he had passed the age limit and no longer had to pay the poll tax. This was equivalent to a confession of disillusionment: real citizens, Roman or Greek, never paid the personal tax.

Although he was an Alexandrian Jew, Helenos could not feel at home in his native city. And if he left it for a provincial town, he would not even be looked upon as a Greek. Like his coreligionists who dwelt in the chora, he was nothing more than an "Egyptian"—a humiliating situation, which illustrates the state of disgrace into which the Jews had fallen under the Roman domination of Egypt. The ancient Judeo-pagan quarrels were to flare up again, feeding the fires of conflict. In incisive words, Josephus paints a picture of the tense atmosphere that reigned in Alexandria immediately after the Roman conquest.

> At Alexandria there had been incessant strife between the native inhabitants and the Jewish settlers since the time when Alexander, having received from the Jews very active support against the Egyptians, granted them, as a reward for their assistance, permission to reside in the city on terms of equality [ex isomoirias] with the Greeks. This privilege was confirmed by his successors, who, moreover, assigned them a quarter of their own, in order that, through mixing less with aliens, they might be free to observe their rules more strictly; and they were also permitted to take the title of Macedonians. Again, when the Romans took possession of Egypt, neither the first Caesar [Augustus] nor any of his successors would consent to any diminution of the honors conferred on the Jews, since the time of Alexander. They were, however, continually coming into collision with the Greeks, and the numerous punishments inflicted daily on the rioters of both parties by the authorities only served to embitter the quarrel.
> (JOSEPHUS, THE JEWISH WAR 2, 437–89; ED. H. ST. J. THACKERAY)

This situation was doomed to lead to an explosion at the very first opportunity. And the opportunity was to appear under the governorship of A. Avilius Flaccus, prefect of Egypt between 32 and 38 CE, during the reigns of Tiberius (14–37 CE) and of Caligula (37–41 CE). The philosopher Philo of Alexandria has given an account of events, which can be rounded out by the testimony of the papyri.

THE VILE DEEDS OF FLACCUS THE PREFECT

At the beginning of the year 32 CE, the Roman emperor Tiberius appointed his friend and "companion" Aulus Avilius Flaccus to be governor of Egypt. Upon his arrival in Alexandria, Flaccus instituted a series of reforms, winning him the praise of Philo but provoking a hostile reaction on the part of the Alexandrian nationalists. Philo extolled the virtues of Flaccus, whom he found "sagacious and assiduous, quick to think out and execute his plans, very ready at speaking, and at understanding what was left unspoken better even than that what was said" (*Against Flaccus*, 2).

The reason for this exaggerated praise was that Philo's book *Against Flaccus* was intended to serve as a manual of moral edification for the prefect's successor. The philosopher wished to illustrate the manner in which a gifted and zealous administrator could end up in disgrace by misusing his power and overstepping the limits of the moral rules a decent governor should obey. Rather than giving an objective account of the man, he painted a portrait of Flaccus as an ideal governor, whose conduct was modeled on that of a virtuous Hellenistic monarch. Objectively speaking, unlike so many of his colleagues who were incorrigible amateurs, Flaccus was evidently quite serious and well-intentioned at the beginning of his term of office. His desire to "acquaint himself thoroughly with Egyptian affairs" should be to his credit.

By way of contrast, Flaccus' adversaries are presented in an exaggeratedly negative fashion. Three Alexandrians are singled out as targets: Isidoros the gymnasiarch, an Alexandrian notable (literally "head of a gymnasium"), his friend Lampon the clerk, and their companion, Dionysios. Isidoros, who is described as a "vulgar" person (*ochlikos*), a "demagogue" (*demokopos*), a "troublemaker and enemy of peace and quiet," a member of shady associations and the king of drunkards, is certainly not a very recommendable character. Neither is his friend Lampon, depicted as an unscrupulous and venal clerk who had sent many people to their death; the Alexandrians had given him the inglorious title of "pen killer" (*kalamosphaktes*). The third man, Dionysios son of Theon, fared no better; the three were lumped together as the incarnation of urban violence. Philo's patriotism was outraged: "the reputation of the city is besmirched" by their doings; the trio's satiric tirades against Flaccus are "disconcerting in their stupidity." We shall soon compare Philo's judgment of Isidoros and his friends with that of an Alexandrian tradition, both anti-Jewish and anti-Roman; needless to say, it is the exact opposite of the portrait Philo painted.

Philo approved the actions of Flaccus, who obliged Isidoros to flee Alexandria. But the governor was soon to regret his decision. On March 16 of the year 37, Tiberius died. Two days later, his great-nephew Gaius Caligula, son of Germanicus Caesar and Agrippina the Elder, was proclaimed emperor. Flaccus was opposed to this succession and had thrown his weight behind another candidate, Tiberius Gemellus, Caligula's cousin. He was now in danger of losing the governorship of Egypt, a charge he very much wanted to retain. The person who was to replace him had already been designated: the praetorian prefect, Q. Naevius Cordus Sutorius Macro, another favorite of Tiberius and a friend of Flaccus, to whom Caligula was morally indebted, as we shall soon see. But Macro was driven to suicide, and never embarked for Egypt.

Flaccus was thus granted a reprieve, until a worthy successor could be found for this important office. He could count on a year, more or less. Now he had to consolidate his position by contracting alliances. His former enemies, the Alexandrian nationalists, might prove useful in his predicament. During Flaccus' lame-duck governorship, a strange encounter took place at the Sarapeum of Alexandria. A papyrus from Oxyrhynchos, a fragment of the s.-c. *Acts of the Alexandrian Martyrs*, describes the scene:

> Flaccus went then to the Sarapeum, after giving orders that the business be carried out secretly. Isidoros also went up to the Sarapeum with Aphrodisia and Dionysios, and entering the sanctuary, Isidoros and Dionysios made a reverence to the god. Just then the old man threw himself down, and bending his knee [before Sarapis] and being close to Dionysios, he said: "Dionysios, my lord, behold me an old man in front of Sarapis. Do not try to struggle against Flaccus, but sit down in council with the elders. . . . Change your mind, Dionysios, my son."
>
> Dionysios replied: "You counsel well; but surely you do not want me to refuse Flaccus again. If I am to meet him by the new moon I shall go, and willingly."
>
> Flaccus came up, and seeing Isidoros, he said : "Well, the affair is all arranged. Who of you is ready to conclude?"
>
> The minister of worship said: "I beseech you, Lord Sarapis, to do no harm to Isidoros and Dionysios. I swear to you. . . ."
>
> Dionysios said: "Let us count out five talents all in gold, as we propose, in the middle of the sanctuary. Isidoros will do his best to protect his affairs." (OXYRHYNCHOS PAPYRUS VIII 1089; CPJUD. II 154)

Despite the fictional quality of this account, it has a historical bent: in the political context at the beginning of Caligula's reign, an intrigue between the disgraced governor and the Alexandrian nationalists would have been quite plausible. Flaccus was attempting to patch up his quarrel with the demagogues he had so vigorously opposed when Tiberius was still alive. Isidoros, who had been obliged to go into exile, had now returned. The meeting was placed under the aegis of the god Sarapis.

The divine protector of the Alexandrians was actually an early product of religious syncretism. The Polish scholar Anna Swiderek, in an attractive hypothesis, attributes his invention to the Hellenomemphites, Greeks who had already settled in Memphis and come into contact with Egyptian traditions even before the Macedonian conquest. Many Egyptian temples were consecrated to Sarapis, whose Alexandrian sanctuary, situated in the Rhakotis district, formerly an Egyptian village, was particularly well-known. Its construction dates from the middle of the third century BCE, and it remained in use some seven centuries, until 391 CE, when it was shut down by order of the Christian emperor Theodosius I. It housed a magnificent statue of the god, attributed by a Greek tradition to the sculptor Bryaxis, one of the decorators of the Halicarnassus Mausoleum. In their struggle against the Empire, which they carried right into the Roman capital, the Alexandrians benefited by the protection of this divinity, of whose intercessions the reader will soon discover a most striking manifestation.

Sarapis   *Roman epoch (Alexandria, Greco-Roman Museum).*

At the meeting between Flaccus and the "extremists," a moderate faction was represented by "the old man," and also the clergy, of whom the "minister of worship" was doubtless the spokesman. The presence of Aphrodisia, about whom we know nothing, lent a note of feminine charm to the proceedings. Several political tendencies, then, participated in the negotiation. The tidy sum of five gold talents was at stake, a token of the accord between Flaccus and his former opponents. These five talents have raised many questions. A possible explanation is that they were a "temple deposit" (*depositio in aede*), a common practice in antiquity, in which the temples played the role of our modern safe-deposit boxes by offering adequate protection to precious objects. Aware of the danger threatening him, Flaccus placed a part of his immense fortune under the protection of Sarapis, authorized his partners to invest it, and allowed them to keep the interest, hoping to recover the principal, once the storm was over. Misplaced confidence, as we shall see.

To protect his rearguard, Flaccus decided to stir up the glowing embers of the Judeo-pagan quarrel. A pretext was soon found. The king of Judea, Agrippa I, on his way from Rome to his kingdom, which Caligula had recently enlarged, stopped off at Alexandria. Agrippa wished to pay a visit to Philo's brother, the alabarch Alexander, from whom he often borrowed money to cope with his endless financial problems. This time he took pains to erase his erstwhile image of a perpetual scrounger and threw a great party. His ostentation was most displeasing to the Greeks of Alexandria, who put on a parody of the royal visit in which the role of the king was played by a simpleton, one Carabas, possibly the ancestor of a personage in the Puss-in-Boots fable, and which also recalls a similar scene from the Gospels.

Far from siding with the king, who was a friend and an ally of the Emperor, Flaccus fanned the flames by proposing the erection of statues of Caligula in the city's synagogues. The Jews immediately shut down their houses of prayer. Flaccus issued an edict proclaiming all Jews "foreigners" in Alexandria. The city was no longer their "own homeland," their *idia*; they could now be displaced at will. The vulnerability of the Jews' position after the Roman conquest is all too evident. The conflict was to attain the proportions of a veritable pogrom. For Flaccus, this was a way of sealing his bargain with the Alexandrian nationalists. Let Philo speak:

> The city has five quarters named after the first letters of the alphabet.
> Two of these are called Jewish because most of the Jews inhabit them,
> though in the rest also there are a few Jews scattered about. So then what
> did they do? From the four letters they ejected the Jews and drove them to
> herd in a very small part of one. The Jews were so numerous that they
> poured out over beaches, dunghills, and tombs, robbed of all their belong-
> ings. Their enemies overran the houses now left empty and turned to pil-
> laging them, distributing the contents like spoils of war, and as no one
> prevented them they broke open the workshops of the Jews which had

been closed as a sign of mourning for Drusilla, carried out all the articles they found, which were very numerous, and bore them through the middle of the marketplace, dealing with other people's property as freely as if it were their own. *(PHILO, AGAINST FLACCUS, 55–56; ED. F. H. COLSON)*

Philo held Flaccus responsible for handing the Jews of Alexandria over to the tender mercies of the enraged mob. A reference to the period of mourning for Drusilla, the favorite sister of Caligula, helps us pinpoint the date: August of the year 38. In a single day, all the Jews of the city had been thrown out of their homes and despoiled of all their possessions. But the worst was yet to come: Philo describes the sufferings of his people as "so excessive that anyone who spoke of them as undergoing wanton violence or outrage would be using words not properly applicable"; he thinks he "would be at a loss for adequate terms to express the magnitude of cruelty." Philo continues:

> Multitudes of others also were laid low and destroyed with manifold forms of maltreatment, put in practice to serve their bitter cruelty by those whom savagery had maddened and transformed into the nature of wild beasts; for any Jews who showed themselves anywhere, they stoned or knocked about with clubs, aiming their blows at first against the less vital parts for fear that a speedier death might give a speedier release from the consciousness of their anguish. Some, made rampant by the immunity and licence that accompanied these sufferings, discarded the slower weapons and took the most effective of all, fire and iron, and slew many with the sword, while not a few they destroyed with fire. Indeed, whole families, husbands with their wives, infant children with their parents, were burnt in the heart of the city by these supremely ruthless men who showed no pity for old age nor youth, nor the innocent years of childhood. And when they lacked wood for fire they would collect brushwood and dispatch them with smoke rather than fire, thus contriving a more pitiable and lingering death for the miserable victims whose bodies lay promiscuously half-burnt, a painful and most heart-rendering spectacle. *(PHILO, AGAINST FLACCUS, 66–68)*

This is not an objective account; it certainly contains some exaggerations, as did Philo's portraits of Isidoros the gymnasiarch and his companions. Philo was presenting the Jewish point of view and, in common with all ancient writers, had recourse to stereotyped expressions. In an attempt to convey the full measure of the sufferings inflicted on his fellow Jews, he compared their fate with that of the vanquished in battle. The victor's attitude toward the conquered foe, implacable by definition, seemed "extremely kind" compared to the ferocity of the Jews' persecutors toward their victims. A willful exaggeration, granted. But would it be wise to consider all the elements of the scene depicted by Philo as fictional?

The Jews that were burnt, for example: were their persecutors attempting to stigmatize a crime imputed to their victims? Death at the stake was rare in antiquity. In the

Near East, it was reserved as punishment for some particularly offensive sexual crimes and for false accusation. Under biblical law, the daughter of a priest, "if she profane herself by playing the harlot . . . shall be burnt with fire" (Lev. 21:9). In the Roman Empire, arsonists were executed by cremation, the punishment symbolically reproducing the crime ("mirroring punishment," as legal historians call it). This calls to mind the Christians transformed into living torches by Nero, who had accused them of trying to set Rome afire; Henryk Sienkiewicz, the Polish Nobel prize-winner, has reconstituted the horrible spectacle in his novel *Quo Vadis*. Little by little, the practice of burning offenders was extended to all sorts of political crimes. The Alexandrians, as we shall learn, accused the Jews of sowing the seeds of disorder and fomenting plots to destabilize the Empire. In his *Histories* (5, 5), Tacitus took this reproach quite seriously and went even further, accusing the Jews of harboring a hatred for the rest of mankind, a hatred so intense that, although they themselves were much inclined to debauchery, they avoided all intercourse with foreign women. Since, in the eyes of their detractors, the Jews were the declared enemies of the human race, they might well be prevented from executing their sinister projects by being condemned to perish in flames. But Jews were capable of taking violent revenge: twenty-eight years later, it would be their turn to threaten the Greeks with fire. For the moment, let us hark back to Flaccus' time and listen yet again to the words of Philo:

> Many also while still alive they drew with one of the feet tied at the ankle and meanwhile leaped upon them and pounded them to pieces. And when by the cruel death thus devised, their life ended, the rage of their enemies did not end, but continued all the same. They inflicted worse outrages on the bodies, dragging them through almost every lane of the city until the corpses, their skin, flesh, and muscles shattered by the unevenness and roughness of the ground, and all the parts which united to make the organism disservered and dispersed in different directions, were wasted to nothing. (PHILO, AGAINST FLACCUS, 70–71)

Neither women nor notables were spared. The men, in chains and their hands tied behind their backs, were marched to the marketplace, where they were undressed and whipped like vulgar criminals. As for the women, systematic raids were organized. Some problems arose in this regard:

> Then, if they were recognized to be of another origin, since many were arrested as Jewesses without any careful investigation of the truth, they were released. But if they were found to be of our nation then these onlookers at a show turned into despotic tyrants and gave orders to fetch swine's flesh and give it to the women. Then all the women who in fear of punishment tasted the meat were dismissed and did not have to bear any further dire maltreatment. But the more resolute were delivered to the tormentors to suffer desperate ill-usage. (PHILO, AGAINST FLACCUS, 96).

The torture undergone by the Jewish women of Alexandria calls to mind the martyrdom of the elderly Eleazar, and of the seven brothers and their mother, related in the Second Book of Maccabees: all preferred to die rather than to touch swine's flesh. This literary kinship does not mean that Philo's account is to be taken as a case of pure borrowing. The pagans were aware of the Jews' abstention from eating pork, in conformity with the biblical commandment (Lev. 11:7–8), a practice they found absurd. At the time of the Jewish mission to Caligula in Rome, the mere mention of this prohibition was enough to induce uncontrollable laughter among the Emperor's courtiers. Others wondered whether the Jews venerated the pig, a rumor echoed by Plutarch: according to this fantasy, they abstained from eating the flesh of this animal, who had taught them "sowing and plowing."

The Alexandrian pogroms provided an excellent opportunity to put these hypotheses to the test. It is particularly interesting to note that there was no distinctive outward sign that which could differentiate an Alexandrian Jewess from a non-Jewess. The ordeal of swine's flesh could turn the trick. For the men, identification was less difficult, thanks to circumcision; Tacitus, quoted above, termed it "a distinctive sign instituted by the Jews so that they could recognize one another." In addition to the Jews, only Egyptian priests, circumcised according to an ancient custom antedating the covenant with Abraham, ran the risk of being summarily massacred if they happened to be in the wrong neighborhood.

For Flaccus himself, all this cruelty was of no avail. In October 38, during a banquet, he was arrested by a centurion sent from Rome by the emperor, who had a good memory and, in spite of all the efforts of the governor, had never forgiven him for having belonged to the wrong political clan. After having solemnly pledged to plead the governor's cause, Isidoros and his gang then betrayed him. He was exiled to the island of Andros where, some months later, he was assassinated by Caligula's henchmen.

What an ignominious end for a gifted prefect! Philo attributed his fate to divine providence, and described his last days in all-too-lavish detail: his isolation, his remorse and its handmaiden, insomnia, his despair, the hatred of the relentless emperor. His possessions were seized but were not sold off at auction, because of their exceptional quality. Philo observed that "wealth was not with him, as it is with some rich men, inert matter, but everything had been carefully selected for its elaborate workmanship, his cups, clothes, coverlets, utensils, and all the other ornaments of the house, all were of the choicest material"; it would have been a shame to scatter such a fine collection to the four winds. The whole lot was confiscated on the spot. No one ever found out what became of the five talents.

The destitution of Flaccus did not settle the Judeo-pagan dispute. Both the Jews and the Greeks continued to plead their respective causes before the emperor. A Greek delegation, composed of "elders" (gerontes), left for Rome just after the advent of Caligula, soon to be followed by another, whose members included Isidoros and Apion, the man that Josephus (in Against Apion) had singled out for attack. Toward the end of 39, a Jewish embassy under the leadership of Philo the philosopher was to confront these

Greeks in Rome. In his *Embassy to Gaius*, Philo has left us an excellent description of their misadventures: fifteen months of waiting for Gaius Caligula to deign to receive the Jews, an ordeal made even more unbearable by the emperor's progressive madness. In his folly, he had ordered an enormous gilded statue of himself to be placed in the Temple of Jerusalem, to punish the Jews of Jamnia (Yavneh), who had dared destroy an altar of the imperial cult, set up in that city by its Greek minority. A disaster was averted *in extremis*, thanks to the sagacity of Publius Petronius, the Roman governor of the province of Syria, and the intercession of King Agrippa I, a personal friend of Caligula.

At long last, a hearing took place in the gardens of Maecenas (*Embassy to Gaius*, 349–67). The least one could say of this welcome was that it lacked warmth. The Jews respectfully greeted the "August Emperor." Gritting his teeth, the latter responded with a sneer: "So you are the god haters, the people who do not believe that I am a god. Why, the rest of the world acknowledges me as a god, yet you refuse to pronounce the title!"

The Jews' "atheism" was well known to the world of antiquity, and Gaius could hardly have ignored it. It is less certain that he uttered the ineffable Divine Name, as Philo asserts, perhaps to emphasize the abject blasphemy of the mad emperor. The Jews proclaimed their loyalty, insisting that their sacrifices were intended to insure the emperor's health, safety, and victories. Caligula was not to be duped: "Granted," said he, "that this is true and that you have offered sacrifices. But it was to another God, even if it was on my behalf. What is the good of that? You have not sacrificed to me." The rest of the interview bordered on the farcical; it was impossible to pursue a serious discussion of the Jews' political claims and their legal foundations. Caligula finally calmed down. "He became gentler and merely said: 'I think that these men are not so much criminals as lunatics in not believing that I have been given a divine nature.' With that he left us and told us to go away too."

Philo returned to Alexandria, while some members of the Jewish delegation remained in Rome. On January 24, 41 CE, Gaius Caligula was assassinated, and the Roman Senate proclaimed the reestablishment of the Republic. But the army intervened and offered the imperial throne to Caligula's uncle Claudius. The new emperor would now have to arbitrate the growing disputes between Jews and Greeks, which continued to flare up in Alexandria and would soon spread to Rome.

JEWS, ALEXANDRIANS, AND CLAUDIUS THE EMPEROR

For some two months now, deputations had been arriving in Rome to congratulate Claudius, the new Emperor. The Alexandrians had joined the movement: Greek and Jewish missions had already come, and their conflictual presence was the occasion for a curious lawsuit the new Emperor was called upon to judge. Toward the end of April 41 CE, the Greeks of Alexandria had summoned the Jews to court, in order to teach the Romans how to govern their worldwide Empire. We are already acquainted with the litigants: on the accuser's bench, a member of the Greek delegation from Alexandria, the gymnasiarch Isidoros son of Dionysios; the accused: Agrippa I, King of Judea.

This case has not aroused the interest of many scholars. Legal historians tend to balk at these semidocumentary, semiliterary fragments of papyri known as "Acts of Alexandrians"—*Acta Alexandrinorum*, our unique source of information concerning it. Formally, we have to deal with the official minutes of the Alexandrian embassies to Rome, imperial visits to Alexandria, and trials over which the Emperor presided. These supposedly word-for-word accounts have, in fact, been charged with literary embellishments to a degree we cannot precisely ascertain, making it difficult to sift out fact from fiction. A first authentic rendering of a delegation or of a trial was used as a theme upon which more or less fanciful variations could be embroidered. By the early third century CE a compilation had been made, consisting of one or more central cores of historical reality enveloped in a literary casing, the whole forming a sort of fictional chronicle. Since they were dedicated to the glory of the Alexandrians who had dared fearlessly to confront imperial Rome at the cost of their lives, these texts were also currently called "Acts of Pagan Martyrs of Alexandria."

Several factors appear to guarantee the historicity of Isidoros' trial: the convergence of the litigants' portraits with other accounts, particularly those of Philo of Alexandria; the plausibility of the scenes described; the legal logic of the proceedings. The fact that the trial has left no traces in what we possess of classical literature is not a strong enough argument to put its historical existence into question; other, more important events, such as the birth of Jesus of Nazareth or Caracalla's generalization of Roman citizenship, have not been directly recorded in the works of classical authors that have come down to us. This omission may perhaps be justified by certain very particular circumstances of the case. We shall therefore take the calculated risk of reading the papyrological file on the trial of Isidoros as an historical document.

The dossier is composed of five fragments of papyri, published between 1895 and 1974, relating events that took place in the first century CE. All in all, there are eight columns of text in varied states of preservation, which may be regrouped to match the four stages of the trial. In this manner, Isidoros' lawsuit can be presented as a four-act play; a letter addressed by Emperor Claudius to the Alexandrians, several months after the trial, will serve as epilogue.

Philo of Alexandria left us vivid images of Isidoros and his companion in misfortune, Lampon the clerk. To call them unflattering is to put the case mildly. One should keep in mind, however, that Philo the Jew was stigmatizing those he held responsible for the pogrom of the summer of the year 38, of which his coreligionists were victims. In Philo's eyes, Isidoros was nothing but a "terrorist chief" (*stasiarches*). His portraits are certainly tendentious, but the philosopher's posthumous prestige encourages scholars today to speak of Isidoros and his companions as "fanatical nationalists," "anti-Semitic leaders," and even "political gangsters."

Quite a different set of images emerge from fragments of papyri that have at long last come to light. They depict Isidoros as a respectable politician, an Alexandrian patriot, a fluent orator, and a courageous champion of the Roman Empire, whose welfare he defended with all his might; Lampon, his devoted companion, had steadfastly stood by him throughout an arduous trial and bravely followed him to his death. If, in lieu of Philo's accounts, fate had bequeathed to us only the Alexandrian "chronicle," Isidoros and Lampon would have gone down in history as perfect symbols of civic virtue.

The action begins with a preliminary hearing before the Imperial Council, the *Consilium Caesaris* (*symboulion* in Greek), on the fifth of Pachon, the day before the Calends of May, i.e., April 30; to aid the Alexandrian reader, the Julian date had been converted to Egyptian reckoning. The year has not been conserved but we may assume it was the first of Claudius' reign, 41 CE and not the thirteenth, the year 53, as some modern scholars believed. The object of the hearing is to examine the admissibility of the criminal suit the gymnasiarch Isidoros had brought before the imperial court against the Jewish king Agrippa and, in the king's person, against the Jewish people. The accusation was a weighty one: the Jews and their separatism had been charged with endangering the very foundations of the Roman Empire.

We have already spoken abundantly of the prosecutor. As for the accused, King Agrippa, he is known to us by Philo (*Against Flaccus*) and Josephus (*Jewish Antiquities*), who has described him in elaborate detail. He was the grandson of Herod the Great, friend of Marcus Vipsanius Agrippa, the son-in-law of Augustus, and great-grandson of Antipater the Idumaean, upon whom Julius Caesar had conferred Roman citizenship, and whom he appointed financial administrator of Judea. He had been reared in Rome, where he was the favorite, first of Caligula and then of Claudius, whose bloodless accession to the throne he had facilitated. During his brief reign, the Christians were persecuted in order to reassure the Pharisees: following in the footsteps of his grandfather, Herod, who had given the order for the Massacre of the Innocents, and his uncle Antipas, who had ordered the execution of John the Baptist and mocked Jesus, Agrippa ordered that Peter be imprisoned and James beheaded. He left the traces of a more glorious endeavor in the unfinished construction of a new wall to the north of Jerusalem, which Hadrian completed for the Roman town Aelia Capitolina, built on the ruins of the Holy City; later on, Suleiman the Magnificent was to use it as a foundation for his ramparts. Josephus scrupulously set down in great detail the brief but cruel period of suffering that preceded Agrippa's death at the age of 54, in the year 44 CE.

In the spring of the year 41 Agrippa was in Rome, preparing to take possession of his kingdom, which Claudius had enlarged to the dimensions it had under the reign of Herod the Great. For Isidoros, to indict Agrippa at that time was an act of bravery, if not a deliberate provocation. Claudius was quite unenthusiastic about the accusation and would have gladly postponed the proceedings indefinitely. But Isidoros and his party of "radical" Alexandrians had some supporters in Rome, and two senators, members of the Council, intervened in his favor. One of them drew the Emperor's attention to the "ecumenical" gravity of the charges. He stressed the patriotic character of Isidoros' action and solicited a just hearing. He insisted upon the disadvantages attending the exclusion of the members of the delegation, which included Isidoros, from the proceedings. The Emperor heeded this counsel and announced that he would hear the Alexandrian delegation the next day.

On the sixth of Pachon, the Calends of May, Claudius heard the action brought by the gymnasiarch Isidoros against King Agrippa. The second day of the proceedings can be reconstructed from two concordant papyri. Their combined interpretation affords us an excellent picture of the otherwise little-known workings of the imperial jurisdiction (*Caesariana cognitio*). The hearings took place in the imperial gardens, with the Emperor seated in the midst of his Council. The ladies of the court assisted, as spectators. The dialogue between Claudius and Isidoros rapidly took on a polemic note:

> The sixth day of Pachon: the second day. Claudius Caesar Augustus hears the case of Isidoros, gymnasiarch of Alexandria versus King Agrippa in the . . . gardens. With him sat twenty senators, among which sixteen men of consular rank; the women of the court also attending . . . Isidoros' trial.
>
> Isidoros was the first to speak: "My Lord Caesar, I beseech you to listen to my account of my native city's sufferings."
>
> The emperor: "I shall grant you this day."
>
> All the senators who were sitting as assessors agreed with this, knowing the kind of man Isidoros was.
>
> Claudius Caesar: "Say nothing (may the gods forbid it!) against my friend. You have already done away with two of my friends, Theon the exegetes and Naevius, prefect of Egypt and prefect of the praetorian guard at Rome; and now you prosecute this man [Agrippa]."
>
> Isidoros: "My Lord Caesar, what do you care for a three-penny Jew like Agrippa?"
>
> Claudius Caesar: "What? You are the most insolent of men to speak."
> (BERLIN PAPYRUS II 551 AND LONDON PAPYRUS INV. *2785*; CPJUD. II 156A, COL. 2, AND 156B, COL. 1).

The Emperor reproached the gymnasiarch with having already caused the death of two of Claudius' friends, and accused him of now turning his murderous wrath upon his friend Agrippa. We cannot easily identify Theon the *exegetes*; he is probably a member of the illustrious Alexandrian family of the Tiberii Julii Theones. Naevius Sutorius Macro, prefect of the praetorian guard, is more familiar to us. He had helped Tiberius cede his throne to Caligula by ordering the old man to be suffocated under a pile of blankets; as a reward for this service he was, as we know, appointed to replace Flaccus as prefect of Egypt, but he then had been ordered to commit suicide, along with his wife, before he could take office in Alexandria. Taken at face value, our papyrus affords interesting details regarding the role of Isidoros in the operation by which Caligula had rid himself of this overzealous tutor.

For Isidoros, the Greek-loving Emperor Caligula was the incarnation of "a certain idea of Empire," to paraphrase a celebrated expression of Charles de Gaulle; our gymnasiarch was prepared to defend it by denouncing all its opponents. Besides the two Claudius had mentioned, the list of Isidoros' victims also included A. Avilius Flaccus, prefect of Egypt, whose glorious beginnings and lamentable end we have described. These were recent events, fresh in everyone's memory. Claudius' concern for his friend Agrippa cannot, therefore, be attributed to metaphysical distress. The courtiers knew "what kind of man Isidoros was": this "vicious sycophant" was one to be feared.

Claudius' anxiety only served to bolster the accuser's confidence and encouraged him to smear his opponent. As far as Isidoros was concerned, Agrippa was nothing but a Jewish rascal: why make such a big matter of this "three-penny Jew"? It has been suggested that the word *trioboleios* had an obscene connotation, referring to prostitution fees. It also may have been a reference to the prodigality of the debt-ridden king Agrippa, or merely a derogatory expression (the German "*Dreigroschen-Jude*" is closer to the Greek word than the French "*Juif à quatre sous*").

It appears that Isidoros' insolence brought about a suspension of the session, and the expulsion of the accuser from the court. In the next scene, Isidoros appears once again before the imperial tribunal. Although this part of the text is in a piteous state, we do learn that Isidoros was fifty-six years old at the time of the trial. We also read of "seven temples of the imperial cult" (*sebasteia*)—perhaps a reference to an offense committed against the worship of the emperor's person. Isidoros' veritable offense lay elsewhere, as we shall now see.

In the next act of our judiciary drama, a new character takes the stage: Balbillus (or Barbillus), leader of the Alexandrian delegation to Rome, which included Isidoros. He was the man whose name, Tiberius Claudius Barbillus, heads the list of Alexandrian envoys in Claudius' letter, the epilogue to our trial. Led by Balbillus, the Greek delegation from the city of Alexandria was confronted with a similar delegation of Alexandrian Jews, conveniently present in Rome at the beginning of May 41 CE. The lawsuit against King Agrippa had rapidly turned into a "disputation," as Claudius was later to call it, between the two litigants, each of whom now was both plaintiff and defendant, calling on their respective partisans to appear in turn as witnesses.

The trial was thus no longer a struggle between two persons, but a confrontation between Jews and Greeks. Therefore, it is not surprising to find the familiar topics of Judeo-pagan conflict cropping up, the Jews demanding the restitution of their erstwhile privileges of which they have been unjustly stripped, and the Greeks coming up with their habitual complaint about the Jews' "atheism": there are no statues in their sanctuaries! The pagans, whose religious sentiments were outraged, sought, with the help of Seleucid propaganda, to compensate for this shocking omission by inventing stories about the Temple of Jerusalem being the site of the fable of the ass's head, and the spot where Greek victims of ritual murder were fattened. The prosecutor continued, accusing the Jews of trampling underfoot the symbols of true piety. A half-century later, Tacitus was to formulate an analogous accusation, asserting that the Jews were only too eager to "scorn the gods" (*contemnere deos*). But these grievances were not punishable by the death sentence Isidoros was seeking for the king of Judea, as the standard-bearer of Jewish particularism. The prosecution had a stronger case to plead:

> Isidoros: "My Lord Augustus, with regard to your interests, Balbillus indeed speaks well. But to you, Agrippa, I wish to retort in connection with the points you bring up about the Jews. I accuse them of wishing to stir up the entire world. [To the Emperor:] We must consider every detail in order to judge the whole people. They are not of the same nature as the Alexandrians, but live rather after the fashion of the Egyptians. Are they not on a level with those who pay the poll tax?" (BERLIN PAPYRUS INV. 8877; CPJUD. II 156C, COL. 2)

The Jews were accused of plotting to "destabilize" the Empire and to plunge the world into a state of disorder, endangering the *Pax Romana* and the Roman grip on the *oikoumene*. Isidoros courageously criticized Claudius for not having perceived the threat to the Empire he had been chosen to govern. Because he protected Agrippa, Claudius seemed to approve the sinister connivings of the "most wicked of peoples" (as Seneca called the Jews), who were undermining the integrity of the Roman state. A people, moreover, worthy of scorn since their fiscal status was no better than that of the Egyptian peasants—this last is a most accurate statement, confirmed by our present knowledge of personal status in Roman Egypt. In so many words: yes to the *Pax Romana*—Alexandrian patriotism was certainly compatible with a realistic cosmopolitan viewpoint, each Greek city living "in freedom in its obedience to Caesar"; but no concessions were to be made to the Jews, a people apart, who not only had not subscribed, as had the Alexandrian Greeks, to the idea of a world state, but were clandestinely plotting the destruction of the political structure based on that conception.

To insinuate that the Emperor abetted the anti-Roman plot could be construed as an attempt at intimidation, whose purpose was to have Agrippa condemned in the absence of sufficiently solid proof. The Alexandrian Greeks needed no urging to be convinced of Claudius' complicity, just as the Alexandrian-Jewish readers of Philo's writings were fully convinced of Isidoros' turpitude. Isidoros may have believed in the reality of the Jewish plot, and of Claudius' share in it. By sacrificing Agrippa, Claudius could have cleared himself of suspicion in the eyes of his entourage, within whose ranks many supporters of Isidoros were to be found. But the Emperor, visibly displeased by Isidoros' sarcasm, would not submit to pressure, and decided in favor of Agrippa, to whom he bore a debt of gratitude. This decision was to prove fatal for Isidoros: he was guilty of slander, *crimen calumniae*, equivalent to lèse-majesté in the present case.

Isidoros was doubly guilty. In the first place, he had tried to obtain Agrippa's conviction, thereby running the risk of rendering Claudius guilty of an innocent man's death; on this point, his preceding accusations added the crushing burden of a guilty past to his present crime. Secondly, he was guilty of having supposed that Claudius, by his indulgence toward the authors of a worldwide conspiracy, showed partiality and could even have been lacking in vigilance, a serious shortcoming on the part of the leader of the Empire. It would be difficult to imagine a more grievous insult to imperial dignity. An Alexandrian gymnasiarch was not qualified to give a Roman emperor lessons in the art of government. Isidoros was condemned to death.

But the show is not yet over. In the last act of our spectacle Isidoros is still alive, as is his friend Lampon, who has not yet appeared on the stage. He too had been condemned to death. The tenor of the trial, lively enough in the previous acts, now rises to a paroxysm. The Emperor reminds Isidoros of his earlier victims: Theon, Macro, and perhaps Flaccus. At this point, the discussion curiously turns to the topic of maternal ancestry.

> Claudius Caesar: "Isidoros, you are really the son of a girl-musician."
> Isidoros: "I am neither a slave nor a girl-musician's son, but gymnasiarch of the glorious city of Alexandria. But you are the cast-off son of the Jewess Salome! And therefore. . . ."
> Lampon (to Isidoros:) "We might as well give in to a crazy Emperor."
> (CAIRO PAPYRUS 10448; CPJUD. II 156D)

In Isidoros' opinion, it was more commendable to be the son of a "girl-musician" (read: a prostitute)—a remark that had been addressed to him, putting in doubt his own origin—than to be the despicable offspring of a Jewess, as he suggested was the case for Claudius. It is not too clear which Salome Isidoros had in mind. The most likely candidate would be the paternal grand-aunt of Agrippa, unique sister of Herod the Great. It seems that the legitimacy of Claudius' birth had been a subject of gossip in Alexandria. What counts, of course, is not the supposed identity of his mother, but the statement itself, intended as a slur: for Isidoros, "son of a Jewess" was a greater insult than "son of a bitch."

Finally, the "crazy Emperor" decided he had had his fill of the "frankness," the *parrhesia*, of the two Alexandrians. Since their sentence had already been pronounced, he ordered them to be removed and executed. The curtain falls, and the play is over. We are not invited to the execution, but we can try to reconstitute the measures that accompanied it, through a careful analysis of the letter Claudius sent to the Alexandrians in the autumn of that same year, 41 CE.

Meanwhile, let us return to Alexandria, which was going through a period of stress. Evidence of the strained atmosphere of the city is contained in a private letter, dated early in August of the year 41 CE. The writer, a rich provincial merchant (*emporos*), was in regular correspondence with his partners in Alexandria. He addressed his agent— presumably his slave—who was in the capital at that moment.

Sarapion to our Herakleides, greeting. I have sent you two other letters, one by Nedymos, one by Kronios the policeman. Well, then, I received the letter from the Arab. I read it and I was upset. Keep close to Ptollarion the whole time. He can perhaps put you straight. Tell him: "It is one thing for everyone else and another for me. I am a slave. I sold you my goods for a talent too little. I don't know what my master will do to me. We have many creditors. Don't put us out of business." Ask him every day. Perhaps he may take pity on you. If not, like everyone else, do you too beware of the Jews. It is better to keep close to him and make friends with him, if you can. Or you may, through Diodoros, get the document signed by the wife of the Commander. If you do your part, you are not to blame. My best greetings to Diodoros. Farewell. My greetings to Harpokration.

In the first year of Tiberius Claudius Caesar Augustus Germanicus, the emperor, the eleventh of the month Kaisareios.

[Verso:] To Alexandria to the marketplace of Augustus to the . . . store for Herakleides from Sarapion the son of . . . , the son of Sosipatros.

(BERLIN PAPYRUS IV 1079; CPJUD. II 152)

We shall not attempt to identify the persons mentioned in the letter but shall concentrate our attention on the core of the matter. Certain scholars have interpreted it as evidence of hostility toward Jewish usurers, supposedly widespread in Alexandria. Ulrich Wilcken sees it as "the oldest testimony of a commercial brand of anti-Semitism." This modern fantasy does not, however, take the historical context into account. The letter dates from August 4, 41 CE, first year of the reign of Claudius. Some six months earlier, on January 24, Caligula, as we know, had been assassinated; in February, when the news of his demise reached Alexandria, Josephus informs us that fighting broke out between the Greeks and the Jews, and the Roman army was obliged to intervene (*Jewish Antiquities* 19, 278–79). The Greeks considered the Jews to be dangerous; not as usurers, for there is no proof that they specialized in that activity, but as political adversaries. Sarapion's turn of phrase might very well be understood as an injunction to "keep from seeing the Jews" (in the letter's original Greek: *hos an pantes, kai su blepe sauton apo ton Ioudaion*). He was simply telling his agent that, for the moment, it would be wise to abstain from venturing into the Jewish parts of the town.

The prevalent mood of perpetual tension, which might erupt into open conflict at any time, was detrimental to the interests of the Empire, and the authorities were doing all they could to bring it to an end. On the tenth of November, six months after the execution of Isidoros and Lampon, L. Aemilius Rectus, the prefect of Egypt, issued an edict ordering the letter that Emperor Claudius had just addressed to the Alexandrians to be posted publicly in the city. The well-known text of the letter has provoked a wealth of commentaries. We shall reproduce only the section dealing with the Judeo-pagan dispute.

The "Jewish Question" in Alexandria *Letter of Claudius to the Alexandrians. London Papyrus, vol. VI, no. 1912, col. B (London, British Museum).*

With regard to the responsibility for the disturbances and rioting, or rather, to speak the truth, the war, against the Jews, although your ambassadors, particularly Dionysios the son of Theon, argued vigorously and at length in the disputation, I have not wished to make an exact inquiry, but I harbor within me a store of immutable indignation against those who renewed the conflict. I merely say that, unless you stop this destructive and obstinate mutual enmity, I shall be forced to show what a benevolent ruler can be when he is turned to righteous indignation. Even now, therefore, I conjure the Alexandrians to behave gently and kindly toward the Jews who have inhabited the same city for many years, and not to dishonor any of their customs in their worship of their god, but to allow them to keep their own ways, as they did in the time of the god Augustus and as I too, having heard both sides, have confirmed.

The Jews, on the other hand, I order not to aim at more than they have previously had and not in future to send two embassies as if they lived in two cities, a thing which has never been done before, and not to intrude themselves into the games presided over by the gymnasiarchoi and the kosmetai, since they enjoy what is their own, and in a city which is not their own they possess an abundance of all good things. Nor are they to bring in or invite Jews coming from Syria or Egypt, or I shall be forced to conceive graver suspicions. If they disobey, I shall proceed against them in every way as seeking to spread a sort of public sickness throughout the world.

If you both give up your present ways and are willing to live in gentleness and kindness with one another, I for my part will care for the city as much as I can, as one which has long been closely connected with us. (LONDON PAPYRUS VI 1912; CPJUD. II 153, LINES 73–104)

Isidoros, his indictment of king Agrippa, his conviction and that of his friend Lampon are not mentioned in the body of the letter. The omission is an intentional one. Isidoros and Lampon had not only been convicted of lèse-majesté, condemned to death and executed, but had been sentenced to undergo a supplementary, post-mortem punishment: the condemnation of their memory.

The term of *damnatio memoriae* brings to mind "bad emperors," like Nero or Geta, whose names were hammered off from tablets or stricken from sheets of papyrus (just as Stalin's name was to be removed one day from public monuments, or that of Beria, which was replaced in the Soviet Encyclopaedia by a long article on the Bering Straits). But one should not forget that the *damnatio memoriae* was originally a supplementary punishment inflicted upon all persons convicted of high treason, and carried out by a series of measures designed to eradicate the name of the accused. This was the case for Isidoros and Lampon. And that is why their names are not to be found in the preamble of the letter, listing the members of the Alexandrian delegation, headed by Barbillus.

We know that Isidoros and Lampon were members of the delegation but, since their memory had been condemned, their names were obliterated from all official documents.

There is more. We have referred above to the disturbances which broke out when the news of Caligula's assassination in January 41 CE reached Alexandria: the Jews took their revenge on the Greeks for the pogrom of the year 38. In his letter, Claudius alluded to these troubles. The Alexandrians were not to worry: the Emperor knows who was responsible for rekindling the flames of the "war" which had been raging in Alexandria since Caligula's reign; he knows who the real culprits were: the Jews, of course—for why should Claudius the Emperor be less well informed than Josephus the historian?

For the moment, Claudius would content himself with partial measures: the Jews of Alexandria were forbidden to disturb the games organized by the magistrates of the city and could no longer invite their coreligionists from the Egyptian chora and from Palestine to come to Alexandria (in the last pages of our book, we shall learn how this interdiction has been interpreted). He reprimanded the Jews for having sent him "two delegations" (in other words, they were to work out their problems within their own community before soliciting the Roman government); he reminded them, in passing, that they lived in a city that "was not their own," meaning that they did not have the rank of full citizens, as we already know. However, since he desired that peace reign in the city, the Emperor would momentarily refrain from immediate prosecution, although the Alexandrian delegation had insisted firmly on this point during a "disputation."

What was this disputation? Obviously, the Emperor was referring to the hearing we have just witnessed: the trial of Isidoros, in which the pagan and Jewish delegations from Alexandria defended their respective causes. The ultimate echo of this hearing was the Emperor's reference to a "public sickness" (*koine nosos*) with which the Roman *oikoumene* might be afflicted: the terms of his letter repeat, almost word for word, the accusation brought by Isidoros against King Agrippa and the Jews. Although the name of Isidoros was no longer to be pronounced, the complaints he formulated had been assimilated into the imperial arsenal, to serve as a warning to the "separatists," disturbers of the peace, and enemies of law and order in the Empire.

All in all, Claudius was not more "anti-Semitic" than he was "anti-Alexandrian." In the fulfillment of his imperial duty, he strove with all his might to maintain the *Pax Romana*, perpetually endangered by the lingering Judeo-pagan dispute. But the "gentleness and kindness" prescribed by the Emperor did not prevail for any length of time. After a quarter-century of respite, conflicts were to flare up anew. And this time, for the Jews, their outcome would be fatal.

CHAPTER 9

The Time of Misfortunes

THE SERVICE RECORD OF A BRILLIANT ALEXANDRIAN

The close of Nero's reign marked the beginning of an a ill-fated period for the Jews under Roman rule. A series of great catastrophes befell them during the apogee of the Empire: from the Jewish War, culminating in the fall of the Temple in 70, to the revolt of Bar Kokhba in 132–135, barely fifteen years after the revolt of 115–117, which brought about the tragic annihilation of Hellenized Jewry in Egypt. We shall now call upon a celebrated witness, who lived at the outset of this period of misfortunes.

While the Emperor Tiberius succeeded Augustus in Rome, Tiberius Julius Alexander, the offspring of a rich and illustrious family of Alexandrian Jews, was born in Alexandria, some time between 10 and 16 CE. His father, Gaius Julius Alexander, brother of Philo the philosopher, was one of the most powerful figures in the city. In addition to being charged with managing the financial affairs of Antonia the Younger, the mother of Emperor Claudius, he had an elevated rank in the financial hierarchy of the province, with the title of "alabarch" or "arabarch," probably a sort of inspector-in-chief of customs on the Arabic frontier (Josephus knew of one Demetrios, another Alexandrian-Jewish notable who bore the same title).

His "three names" are to be found in two papyri, dated 26 and 28/9 CE, concerning real estate he owned, or had owned, in Euhemeria, in the Faiyum (today Kasr el-Banat): Alexander the alabarch appears also as an affluent member of the landed gentry. His "second name" (*nomen gentilicium*), Julius, testifies to the fact that his Roman citizenship had been bestowed upon him by Augustus, heir of Julius Caesar. We know, by the correspondence between Pliny the Younger and Trajan, that an inhabitant of Egypt had first to become a citizen of Alexandria before being raised to the level of Roman citizenship. The alabarch's family may have belonged to the lucky few: Jewish notables of Alexandria who, like the father of the unfortunate Helenos, were by exception granted Alexandrian citizenship. This would hold only if the rule referred to by Pliny at the beginning of the second century CE dated from the Augustan epoch, and if it were applicable not only to native Egyptians, but also to educated inhabitants of the city who were not Alexandrian citizens.

Besides Philo, Alexander the alabarch had a second brother, Lysimachos. He also had two sons. Both bore his "nickname" (a Greek name which had become a Roman *cognomen*) Alexander: Marcus Julius Alexander and Tiberius Julius Alexander. The father's nickname, as we see, was transmitted to the sons as if it were a family name. Like his father, Marcus was a businessman, the senior commercial partner of an import-export enterprise, "Nikanor and sons," whose existence we know of by a group of ostraca from Koptos. He married Princess Berenice, daughter of King Agrippa I. After the premature death of Marcus, her first husband, Berenice married her paternal uncle Herod, king of Chalcis, and subsequently married the king of Cilicia, Polemon, who had himself circumcised for the occasion; she abandoned him rather quickly and rejoined her brother Agrippa. The Acts of the Apostles describe her in his company during the trial of Paul of Tarsus; she appears again in Caesarea Philippi, the capital of Agrippa II, where she received Titus after his victory in Galilee. Although Titus was thirteen years younger than Berenice, he was overcome with her irresistible beauty; after the end of the Jewish War she followed him to Rome, where popular opposition prevented the Emperor's son from marrying an oriental princess. Their love affair became the subject of two famous French plays: Racine's *Bérénice* and Corneille's *Tite et Bérénice*.

Marcus' brother Tiberius had chosen another path, turning his efforts to an administrative career in the emperor's service. Like everyone else, he had to begin by serving a term in the armed forces, before taking his first civil position in about 42 CE as the epistrategus of the Thebaid, governor of one of the three great regions into which the Roman province of Egypt was divided. The influence of Alexander the alabarch was certainly helpful in obtaining his nomination by Emperor Claudius. Marcus' affairs also prospered at this time, in the same region.

In 46, Tiberius left Egypt: he had been appointed by Claudius to replace Cuspius Fadus as procurator of Judea, a position he occupied until 48. He dropped out of view for the next fifteen years, before reappearing in 63 as one of the highest-ranking officers in the eastern army, on the general staff of Corbulo, in Armenia. Thanks to a Greek inscription discovered in Tyre, we now know that he was in office in Syria as imperial administrator (*procurator provinciae Syriae*), probably since 59. In 66, Tiberius was back in Alexandria, since Nero had named him prefect of Egypt. He was to conserve this title under five successive emperors, until 69/70, at the beginning of Vespasian's reign. Then, after having accompanied Titus during the Jewish War and taken part in the siege of Jerusalem, he went to Rome. A papyrus from Hibeh (whose interpretation, it is true, has been contested) attests that he attained the summit of his career as praetorian prefect, the second most powerful person in the Empire, after the emperor himself.

What a great success for an Alexandrian Jew! He certainly owed a good deal to his father's wealth and status, but his personal talents were outstanding. In the crisis following Nero's death on June 9, 68 CE, he had managed his own affairs with great skill, successfully conserving his position in Alexandria. Outwardly faithful to Nero, he dealt secretly with Galba, and was so sure of the latter's gratitude that, on July 6 of the year 68 (Nero had died a mere month before), without waiting to be confirmed in his office as prefect of Egypt, he promulgated an edict that was to become famous. The text is known to us by an inscription in the temple of Hibis in the Oasis of Khargeh, and by some other fragments. The prefect hailed Galba's accession to the throne and, responding to the complaints of the provincial population since he had begun his term of office two years ago, published the measures he was taking to better their lot.

The next year, after having officially recognized Othon and then Vitellius, he was already at work preparing the accession of Vespasian, who needed Egyptian support in order to be proclaimed emperor. Our prefect knew this and, on July 1, 69, he had his troops and the people of Alexandria swear allegiance to Vespasian. A mere scrap of papyrus bears witness to the festivities Tiberius organized in honor of Vespasian, whom he greeted personally (Papyrus Fouad 8; CPJud. II 418a). The acclamation in Alexandria was to become the official date of Vespasian's advent (*dies imperii*). The new emperor was greatly indebted to the "cold intelligence of the prefect, who revealed his plans neither to his staff nor to his armies," to quote the incisive words of Claire Préaux.

Since scrupulousness is rarely the key to continued success in politics, we may well ask whether Tiberius was bedeviled with remorseful feelings when his ambitions and his acts came into conflict with his Judaic roots. He may not have been very troubled by the oath he took on assuming his military duties, the first step in his administrative career, which did not exactly correspond to the prescriptions of the Jewish religion: it was this which prompted Josephus to say that Tiberius "did not remain faithful to the customs of his forefathers" (*Jewish Antiquities* 20, 100). The problem became more acute when Nero placed the government of Egypt in the hands of Tiberius at the beginning of 66. In May, King Agrippa II (son of our Agrippa I, the hero of Isidoros' trial) came to Alexandria to congratulate him. Soon afterward, a Jewish uprising broke out in the city, which Tiberius mercilessly crushed. Josephus is our unique source for this episode in the history of Alexandrian Judaism.

> On one occasion, when the Alexandrians were holding a public meeting on the subject of an embassy that they proposed to send to Nero, a large number of Jews flocked into the amphitheatre along with the Greeks; their adversaries, the instant they caught sight of them, raised shouts of "enemies" and "spies," and then rushed forward to lay hands on them. The majority of the Jews took flight and scattered, but three of them were caught by the Alexandrians and dragged off to be burnt alive. Thereupon the whole Jewish colony rose to the rescue; first they hurled stones at the Greeks, and then snatching up torches rushed to the amphitheatre, threatening to consume the assembled citizens in flames to the last man. And they would have actually done this had not Tiberius Alexander, the governor of the city, curbed their fury. He first, however, attempted to recall

Beginning of the edict of **Tiberius Julius Alexander** *Inscription from the Temple of Hibis in el-Khargeh Oasis, 1st century* CE.

them to reason without recourse to arms, quietly sending the principal citizens to them and entreating them to desist and not to provoke the Roman army to take action. But the rioters only ridiculed this exhortation and used abusive language of Tiberius. (JOSEPHUS, THE JEWISH WAR 2, 490–93; ED. H. ST. J. THACKERAY)

In short, the Jews would seem to have been guiltier than the prefect of Egypt, who was only doing his duty. He tried peaceful persuasion, but the Jews remained impervious to his wise and benevolent counsels, only insulting him in return, and he finally had to resign himself to the use of force. As a promoter of Flavian propaganda, Josephus had many good reasons for his indulgence toward Tiberius. His magnanimity is in apparent contradiction with his description of the repression of the Jewish rebellion in Alexandria by the Roman soldiers. But the author was following the laws of the literary genre, throwing into strong relief the cruelty of the avengers.

> Understanding then that nothing but the infliction of a severe lesson would quell the rebels, he let loose upon them the two Roman legions stationed in the city, together with two thousand soldiers, who by chance had just arrived from Libya to complete the ruin of the Jews; permission was given them not merely to kill the rioters but to plunder their property and burn down their houses. The troops, thereupon, rushed to the quarter of the city called "Delta," where the Jews were concentrated, and executed their orders, but not without bloodshed on their own side; for the Jews closing their ranks and putting the best armed among their number in the front offered a prolonged resistance, but when once they gave way, wholesale carnage ensued. Death in every form was theirs; some were caught in the plain, others were driven into their houses, to which the Romans set fire after stripping them of their contents; there was no pity for infancy, no respect for years: all ages fell before their murderous career, until the whole district was deluged with blood and the heaps of corpses numbered fifty thousand; even the remnant would not have escaped, had they not sued for quarter. (JOSEPHUS, THE JEWISH WAR 2, 494–97)

The carnage ended finally when Tiberius, "consumed with compassion" (?) for the Jews, ordered his soldiers to desist. Although the number of dead was most probably less than fifty thousand, the figure put forth by Josephus, the events of the year 66 were nonetheless a terrible trial for the Jews of Alexandria, as bad as the pogrom of 38, if not worse. The only Jews who escaped the general slaughter were the elders, the high-ranking notables Tiberius took under his protection: did "social" solidarity prevail over "racial" solidarity?

Four years later Tiberius was back in Judea, where he had been governor from 42 to 48. Josephus asserts that he governed the country, as had his predecessor, Cuspius Fadus "in the respect of the customs of the land in order to keep the nation in peace" (*The*

Jewish War 2, 220). That "pacification" entailed, among other events, the crucifying of the Jewish rebels, the sons of Judah the Galilean. Tiberius was soon to assist at the siege of Jerusalem and the destruction of the Temple.

Toward the end of 69 or the beginning of 70, Vespasian appointed him to the staff of his son Titus, who was in charge of the war against the Jews. In Josephus' eyes, this was a distinction and a token of gratitude on the emperor's part toward the governor "because he had been the first to welcome the dynasty just arising and with splendid faith had attached himself to its fortunes while they were still uncertain" (*The Jewish War* 5, 46). As military adviser to Titus, he was chief of staff at the time of the council of six generals, who were to decide the fate of the Temple. He voted against its destruction, following in this the wishes of Titus himself who, Josephus pretends, "would not under any circumstances burn down so magnificent a work; for the loss would affect the Romans, inasmuch as it would be an ornament to the Empire if it stood" (*The Jewish War* 6, 241). We know what happened: the Jews renewed their attack on the Romans, who pursued them to their sanctuary where a Roman soldier, without waiting for orders, yielded to panic and threw a firebrand into the Temple, causing the fateful conflagration despite the valiant efforts of Titus to prevent it from spreading. Josephus concluded that the Temple had been destroyed against the wishes of Titus, and that the origin of the fire and its cause were to be attributed to the Jews themselves (*The Jewish War* 6, 251–56).

What did Tiberius Julius Alexander feel as he looked upon the flames destroying the Temple of Jerusalem, the lintels of whose nine portals had been adorned with gold and silver panels through the largess of his own father, Alexander the alabarch (*The Jewish War* 5, 205)? It is true that Tiberius spoke only Greek and Latin; it is also true that he was first and foremost a "Roman citizen of Greek culture," as were a good many other agents of the provincial administration, recruited among the elite of the Greek cities in the East. But the fact that he was an Alexandrian Jew was precisely the reason Tiberius, as a member of this elite, was able to climb the administrative ladder up to its highest rungs. For the "true Romans," this was not enough to make him a full-fledged Roman: Tacitus called him an "Egyptian" (*Histories* 1, 11), a term both insulting and inexact, since Tiberius was a Roman citizen by birth and had never belonged to the category of "Egyptians" we described in a previous chapter.

We shall never know what Philo the philosopher would have thought of his nephew. Philo died in 54 and, fortunately, witnessed neither the Alexandrian massacre of 66 nor the destruction of the Temple of Jerusalem in 70. Would it not have been better if Tiberius had turned his talents to business, like his father and brother, or to literature, like his uncle? At best, he would have been a "Philo II" or, more modestly, another "Alexandrian Rothschild," and his family would have been spared such a sad supplement of celebrity. As for the Jews of Egypt, they were soon to be confronted with perils much graver than an intervention of Roman troops stationed in Alexandria.

A Miracle in Rome

In October of the year 97 CE, Rome lay under the threat of a rebellion of the praetorian guard. Influential counselors persuaded Emperor Nerva—childless at 65—to nominate a co-regent. His choice fell upon the Spaniard Trajan, aged forty-four, born in Italica in the province of Baetica. The nomination took the form of an adoption, a procedure that was rather anomalous in this case, since the chosen son was absent when the act was accomplished. Three months later, at the end of January 98, Nerva died and Trajan remained alone at the helm. He was to wield power for almost twenty years, until his death on August 8, 117. Under his reign, the Roman Empire was to expand its eastern frontier beyond the Euphrates. Trajan was a soldier. He had an authoritarian character, but he never lost his temper. He was an indefatigable worker and a scrupulous administrator, who always had the public welfare at heart, so much so that the Senate conferred upon him the title of *optimus princeps*, "the best of emperors." He died without a natural heir—for us, this is an important detail—and bequeathed the imperial throne to another Spaniard, Hadrian, by the bias of a posthumous or fictive adoption.

Immediately upon his accession to power, Trajan took up the difficult dialogue between the Empire and the proud city of Alexandria, a dialogue that had begun in 30 BCE when Octavianus made his triumphal entry into the spiritual capital of the Greek East. A papyrus from Oxyrhynchos contains the beginning of a letter Trajan addressed to the Alexandrians in the autumn of 98 CE:

> Imperator Caesar Nerva Traianus Augustus Germanicus Pontifex Maximus, invested with tribunician power for the second time, consul, to [the demos of] the Alexandrians, greeting. . . .
>
> [Being well aware of] your city's outstanding loyalty toward the emperors, and having in mind the benefits that my deified father conferred on you since the beginning of his reign, and for my part also, [over and above] these claims [of yours], having a personal feeling of benevolence toward you, I have commended you first of all to myself, then in addition to my friend and prefect Pompeius Planta, so that he can take every care in providing for your undisturbed tranquillity and your food supply and your communal and individual rights. . . . (OXYRHYNCHOS PAPYRUS *XLII, 3022*)

The new sovereign remembers the benevolence with which his adoptive father Nerva treated the Alexandrians; he wishes to show his own benevolence (*idia diathesis*) toward them; he commends them, first to himself, then to his "friend" C. Pompeius Planta, prefect of Egypt between September 98 and February 100 CE, who is known to us by the correspondence between Trajan and Pliny the Younger to which we have already referred, as well as by several papyrological and epigraphical sources. The prefect is to see to it that the city remains in peace, that it receives proper provisions and that its inhabitants continue to enjoy their individual and collective rights. The Emperor's concern for a "durable peace" reminds one of the more or less permanent conflict between the Jews and the Greeks, with which Claudius had dealt at length, a half-century before, in his letter to the Alexandrians. Perhaps Trajan referred to it in the rest of his own letter, which we do not possess. There were latent problems, but the tone of the letter is calm and there is no reason to doubt the "personal feeling of benevolence" of the Emperor toward the Alexandrians.

And the Jews? Still reeling from the effects of the recent catastrophe that had stricken Judea and the Temple at Jerusalem, they were surely appreciative of the promises of civil peace proffered by the new Antonine dynasty. They wanted to show their loyalty to Trajan, the guarantor of these promises. A papyrus from the Berlin collection, whose date corresponds to February 10 of the year 101 CE, furnishes an illustration of this attitude:

> To Isidoros, the royal scribe of the Arsinoite nome, division of Themistos, from Soteles son of Josepos, grandson of Theomnas, his mother being Erotion, of the village of Apollonias. My son Josepos, whose mother is Sarra, being a minor, not yet being enrolled for payment of poll tax, died in the month of Tybi of the present fourth year of the Emperor Trajan. Therefore I request that he be inscribed as dead.
>
> [In another hand:] To the village scribe. If he died, let the man declare as is fitting, under oath with his own signature, and register. The fourth year of the Emperor Nerva Trajan Augustus Germanicus, the sixteenth of Mecheir.
>
> [In a third hand:] Soteles son of Josepos, the one mentioned before, I swear by the Emperor Caesar Nerva Trajan Augustus. . . . (BERLIN PAPYRUS IV 1068; CPJUD. II 427)

This Jewish family of the Faiyum, containing many Greek names (Soteles; Theomnas, short form for Theomnestos; Erotion) as well as Hellenized Hebrew names (Josepos; Sarra), was subject to the poll tax whose workings and political significance we have already explained. Josepos died before attaining the age limit of fourteen, when he would have been subject to taxation. To make sure that he would not be taxed posthumously, his father Soteles accomplished the necessary formalities, which included putting his signature to an oath taken in the name of the emperor. Subscribing to the latter's superhuman nature, by taking an oath in which the emperor's name appeared, is in clear contradiction to the principles of Judaism. Soteles does not appear to have been greatly disturbed by this, either because his fidelity to the emperor overrode his religious scruples, or because he so wished to avoid the tax burden that the means were of secondary importance to him.

Whatever may have been the case, we see that, toward the turn of the century, Trajan entertained good relations with the Alexandrians, as he did with the Jews of Egypt. But it was only the calm before the storm brewing in the West. A few years later, it was to break out over their heads when the Jews of Cyrene rose up against the imperial power, the revolt then spreading to Egypt. The Jews of Egypt, including the Alexandrians, were about to be engulfed in a tragic shipwreck.

On the eve of the tragedy, Trajan had given audience to two Alexandrian deputations, a Jewish one and a Greek, just as Caligula and then Claudius had done in the past. This, at least, is what one can read in a papyrus from Oxyrhynchos, containing a fragment of the *Acts of the Alexandrians*, the collection in which we have been able to read the minutes of the trial of Isidoros. These *Acts of Hermaiskos* are a strange mixture of fact and fiction. But this is precisely why they are interesting, as they provide us with a precious illustration of the prevailing climate before the tempest. Let us begin by making acquaintance with the members of the two deputations.

> Dionysios, who had held many procuratorships, and Salvius, Julius Salvius, Timagenes, Pastor the gymnasiarch, Julius Phanias, Philoxenos the gymnasiarch-elect, Sotion the gymnasiarch, Theon, Athenodoros, and Paulos of Tyre, who offered his services as advocate for the Alexandrians. When the Jews learned this, they too elected envoys from their own nation, and thus were chosen Simon, Glaukon, Theudes, Onias, Kolon, Jakoumbos, with Sopatros of Antiochia as their advocate. (PAPYRUS OXYRHYNCHOS XII 1242; CPJUD. II 157, COL. 1)

The Greek delegation was composed of twelve members, including Hermaiskos, not mentioned here, and Paulos of Tyre. This may seem to be a large number, but it was usual for Alexandria. With its three gymnasiarchs, it was an elite group. Half the members seem to be Roman citizens: this was certainly so for Julius Salvius and Julius Phanias, and probably for Dionysios, first on the list, who may have been the grandson of C. Julius Dionysios, mentioned by Claudius in his letter to the Alexandrians. All in all, these names leave a strong impression of historical authenticity, although their individual identification is debatable.

On the Jewish side, six envoys had been chosen among the "nation" (*ethnos*), plus a *synegoros* (advocate), as for the Greeks: a total of seven persons. Scholars have debated the question of whether this number had some "mystical" value, relating to symbolism of the Sabbath. There are Greek names (Glaukon; Theudes, probably a variant of Theudas; Kolon); Jewish names (Onias and Jakoumbos, a variant of Jakoubos); and one Simon, a "neutral" name, authentically both Greek and Jewish. As for the rhetor Sopatros, the question remains moot as to whether he was a Jew from Antioch or a Greek, engaged for the occasion because of his oratorical talent.

Since two rhetors were confronting one another before the emperor, the meeting tended to take the form of a legal dispute. The term *synegoros* (literally, "who speaks with"), used to describe Paulos of Tyre and Sopatros of Antioch, lends weight to this supposition: it does not simply mean a spokesman, but designates the accuser—or the defender—who assists the party appearing in a trial. Had the Alexandrians brought a lawsuit before the imperial court because of some event that had occurred implicating Jews, who had immediately counterattacked by bringing their own lawsuit? We cannot be entirely sure. We do know that the embassies or trial must have taken place before Trajan left Rome in November 113 CE to make war on the Parthians.

One should not forget that we are dealing here with an account in which the actual proceedings have been transformed for ideological purposes. Had the Alexandrians simply come to complain that Trajan had not kept the promises contained in his letter of the year 98, which we have just examined? And did the Jews, considering themselves concerned by this move, follow on the heels of the Greek delegation, with their own list of complaints? The author of the narrative, in view of the fact that two delegations had been sent to Rome, could have cast their confrontation in the form of a trial, on the model of Isidoros' trial. The date of the account has its importance, in this connection. In the dialogue between Trajan and Hermaiskos, which we shall shortly hear, the term "impious Jews," *anosioi Ioudaioi*, is used, indicating a date of composition after the war of 115–117, during which the term made its appearance as a sort of semi-official name for the rebels. The text, then, must have been brought up to date.

But we are anticipating. For the moment, the two delegations are taking their departure from Alexandria. "They set sail, then, from the city, each party taking along its own gods, the Alexandrians (a bust of Sarapis, the Jews. . .)" (CPJud. II 157, col. 1).

All the commentators have been intrigued by this sentence. Taken literally, it involves us in an inextricable dilemma: either the Alexandrian Jews were guilty of a grave transgression of the biblical commandment against idolatry, or else the author of the account was unpardonably ignorant of one of the fundamental principles of Judaism, known even to the pagans. During the trial of Isidoros, we have seen how they denounced the prevailing "emptiness" in the Jewish houses of prayer. To exonerate the Alexandrians, both pagan and Jewish, from this double accusation, plausible continuations were sought for the text, which unfortunately was broken off at a crucial point.

The nature of the divinity the Greeks brought—a bust of Sarapis—appears clearly in the last part of what we possess of the text. The "divinity" the Jews brought might simply have been a scroll of the Torah, sacred object *par excellence*, or a menorah, a seven-branched candelabrum, of the type to be found in the cemeteries of the period. The wording of the sentence, probably suggested by the symmetrical relation between the two delegations, seems ill-chosen or awkward, but the detail itself is perfectly plausible, even adding credence to the relation. So does the list of ambassadors, or the verb *bastazein*, "to carry in procession," used for both embassies. In those times, it was common practice for an embassy to carry a statue or a sacred object (*aphidryma*), assuring its protection during the voyage. Upon embarking for Ostia, the Jews and the Greeks were both following a widespread practice.

The Menorah of the Temple *Bas-relief on the Arch of Titus in Rome.*

When the winter was over they arrived in Rome. The emperor learned that the Jewish and Alexandrian envoys had arrived, and he appointed the day on which he would hear both parties. And Plotina approached the senators in order that they might oppose the Alexandrians and support the Jews. Now the Jews, who were the first to enter, greeted Emperor Trajan, and the emperor returned their greeting most cordially, having been also won over by Plotina. After them the Alexandrian envoys entered and greeted the emperor. He, however, did not go to meet them, but said, "Do you dare to say 'hail' to me as though you deserved to receive a greeting—after what you have dared to do to the Jews?" *(CPJud. II 157, col. 2)*

Here we have a Trajan who has become philo-Jewish by the good offices of his wife, who had pleaded the cause of the Alexandrian Jews. His reproachful words to the Greeks have aroused some curiosity among historians, who turned to Dio Chrysostom and numismatic testimony in search of an explanation. But in vain. As Victor Tcherikover has aptly observed, all that has been said on this subject is nothing but pure speculation. The *Acts of the Alexandrians* systematically accuse the imperial regime of siding with the Jews in their ongoing quarrel with the Greeks of Alexandria, and the passage quoted here may be a sort of general reference to this theme. The favoritism of Pompeia Plotina toward the Jews nourished this critical attitude, which was only heightened when the empress, soon afterward, was suspected of playing a role in the adoption of Hadrian (and also of having become a Christian). But the imperial couple's sympathy did not end here, as the following dialogue between Trajan and Hermaiskos shows:

> [Trajan said:] "You must be eager to die, having such contempt for death as to answer even me with insolence."
>
> Hermaiskos said: "Why, it grieves us to see your Council filled with impious Jews."
>
> Caesar said: "This is the second time I am telling you, Hermaiskos: you are answering me insolently, taking advantage of your noble birth."
>
> Hermaiskos said: "What do you mean, I answer you insolently, greatest emperor? Explain this to me."
>
> Caesar said: "Pretending that my Council is filled with Jews."
>
> Hermaiskos: "So, then, the word Jew is offensive to you? In that case you ought to help your own people and not play the advocate for the impious Jews." (*CPJUD. II 157*, COL. *3*)

The Imperial Council "filled with Jews"? Were not the Alexandrians carrying their anti-Judaism a bit too far? It would appear materially impossible for the Roman Senate to be the target of their accusations; yet the term employed here, *synedrion* (which appears as "Council" in the English translation of the papyrus), is an equivocal one: it could have referred to the Senate, along with the official Greek denomination *synkletos* (or *synkletos boule*); but it could also have designated the Imperial Council (*consilium principis*), usually called *symboulion*. To be sure, there were no Jewish senators, but a faint trace of Jewish ancestry might be discernible in some members of the Imperial Council, for example, the descendants of Tiberius Julius Alexander. To leap from these premises to the conclusion that the Council was "filled with Jews" was a step the Alexandrian propagandists did not hesitate to take, to the great joy of those who, some eighteen centuries later, triumphantly brandish our text as the antique proof of a "typical" situation: a conspiracy of international Zionism, whose hidden goal, in this instance, was to seize the reins of power from the hands of imperial Rome!

But, if the Imperial Council was thus put into question, why use *synedrion* and not *symboulion*, as in the account of the trial of Isidoros under Claudius, which served as a kind of model for the *Acts of Hermaiskos*? It is easy to conceive of the ill-will Hermaiskos bore to the Senate, as the Senators had been won over to the Jewish cause by the empress Plotina. Hermaiskos heaped abuse upon the Senate, using the flimsy pretext that some of its members agreed to sit down next to a few Jews, on the Imperial Council. Was Hermaiskos, who had openly mocked the "greatest emperor", playing on words? By using *synedrion* in preference to *symboulion*, was he deceitfully suggesting a parallel between the Imperial Council and the Jewish High Court, the Sanhedrin, a name derived from the Greek *synedrion*? *Synedrion* or *symboulion*, small matter; the meaning of Hermaiskos' smear tactics was perfectly clear: the Jews were laying down the law in Rome! Trajan was morally and politically guilty of "playing the advocate" (*synegorein*) for the impious Jews, to the detriment of his "own people," the Alexandrians.

The audacious Alexandrian might have come to a bad end right then and there. Luckily for him, Sarapis, the divine protector, was watching over his flock.

> As Hermaiskos was saying this, the bust of Sarapis that they carried suddenly broke into a sweat, and Trajan was astounded when he saw it. And soon tumultuous crowds gathered in Rome and numerous shouts were heard, and everyone began to flee to the highest part of the hills. (*CPJud.* II 157, COL. 3, IN FINE)

This last passage from the *Acts of Hermaiskos*, as well as the one in which the "travelling divinities" were mentioned, have been considered implausible. To be sure, this is the only case of supernatural interference in the *Acts of the Alexandrians*. Still, a miracle of Sarapis is neither more nor less unlikely at the beginning of the second century in Rome than a miracle of the Virgin in twentieth-century Lourdes. The divine protector of the city of Alexandria had shown his might. The emperor was thunderstruck. For the Romans, a sweating statue was a bad omen, and panic shortly broke out in Rome.

The end of the text (col. 4) is in shreds and cannot tell us how things turned out. In fact, nothing more was ever heard of Hermaiskos. Did he suffer the same fate as his "archetype" Isidoros, who had been condemned and executed for the crime of lèse-majesté? Although no formal proof is available, the idea appears to be quite credible. One undisputed fact remains: the brief idyll between the benevolent imperial couple and the Jews was soon to be shattered by the revolt of 115. The reaction of the Roman government fulfilled the desire of Hermaiskos to see the emperor support his "own people" instead of defending the "impious Jews." And the image of Trajan as friend and protector of the Jews was to give way to that of a Trajan bent on persecution and destruction.

"A SPIRIT OF REBELLION"

In the summer of 115 CE, the Jews of the western and eastern diasporas rose up against the Romans. For more than two years, from the eighteenth year of Trajan's reign to the beginning of the reign of Hadrian in August-September 117, in Cyrenaica, Egypt, Cyprus, Mesopotamia, and perhaps even in Judea itself, a relentless war pitted the Jewish population against the imperial legions. In the turmoil of the general disaster, the Hellenized Jews of Egypt perished, with all their worldly possessions. The war of 66–73 had its historian, but in 115–117 no Josephus was present to spell out the details of the conflict. Today, archaeological evidence concerning Cyrenaica and papyrological data concerning Egypt allow us to reconstitute the events, their causes and their consequences, with a reasonable degree of certainty. These documents can help us interpret the rare literary texts—pagan, Jewish, and Christian—which, until a recent date, had been our sole guide. The most important among these texts is a note by Eusebius of Caesarea, taking up the thread of pagan authors of the second or third century CE, whose identification is difficult.

> In the course of the eighteenth year of the reign of the Emperor [Trajan], a rebellion of the Jews again broke out which led to the destruction of many of their numbers. For both in Alexandria and in the rest of Egypt and especially in Cyrene, as though they had been seized by some terrible spirit of rebellion, they rushed into sedition against their Greek fellow in-habitants, and, increasing the scope of the rebellion in the following year, started a great war while Lupus was governor of all Egypt. In the first engagement they happened to overcome the Greeks, who fled to Alexandria and captured and killed the Jews in the city, but though thus losing the help of the townsmen, the Jews of Cyrene continued to plunder the country of Egypt and to ravage the districts in it under their leader Loukouas.
>
> The Emperor sent against them Marcius Turbo with land and sea forces including cavalry. He waged war vigorously against them in many battles for a considerable time and killed many thousands of Jews and not only those of Cyrene, but also those of Egypt who had rallied to Loukouas their king. The emperor suspected that the Jews in Mesopotamia would also attack the inhabitants and ordered Lusius Quietus to clean them out of the province. He organized a force and murdered a great multitude of the Jews there, and for this success was appointed governor of Judea by the emperor. The Greek authors who chronicle the same period have related the narrative in these very words. (EUSEBIUS, ECCLESIASTICAL HISTORY 4, 2, 1–2; ED. K. LAKE)

Eusebius did not name his source. But, for a fourth century Christian writer, the reference to "Greek authors" is an unmistakable indication of a pagan source, and not, as

Ulrich Wilcken suggested, a traditional Jewish or, at the very least, a pro-Jewish source. The wording suggests that the authors quoted by Eusebius were not writing a "monograph" on the rebellion, but a more extended account of "the period" in which it took place. The revolt of 115–117 had surely aroused the interest of pagan authors prior to Eusebius, such as Arrian of Nicomedia (second century CE, whom we have already quoted on Alexander the Great), whose *Parthika* may have inspired Eusebius. The few fragments that have been conserved make no mention of the Jewish revolt; if Arrian had addressed the subject, he would have dealt principally, if not exclusively, with the Mesopotamian rebellion in the context of the Parthian war waged by Trajan.

Two other authors concern us here: Appian of Alexandria, from the middle of the second century, and Cassius Dio, a Roman historian from the beginning of the third century, who wrote in Greek. In one terse phrase, Appian confirms the total destruction of Alexandrian Jewry under Trajan, corroborating the dramatic mirroring of the rabbinical writings. We shall return to this point. As for Dio, the events that concern us here are treated in the part of his work we possess only in abridged form, whose caricatural nature will soon become apparent. It would seem unlikely, however, that Eusebius employed Dio's original text, lost for us, or one of Dio's own sources. The name of the leader of the revolt may prove decisive, on this point. For Eusebius, he was named Loukouas; in Dio's abridged text, he was Andreas. It is improbable that the author of the abridgment invented this name, as his attention was riveted elsewhere. Andreas, then, already figured in Dio's original text, and Loukouas in Eusebius' source material. We may be dealing with a double name: Loukouas, alias Andreas. Moreover, he was not alone; in Cyprus, according to the author of this same abridgment, a local leader, Artemion, headed the revolt.

Although Eusebius' source remains anonymous for us, it nevertheless appears to have been a perfectly credible one. The information it contains is confirmed by the papyri, which enable us to clarify various points, beginning with the date. Eusebius dates the outbreak of the revolt from the eighteenth year of Trajan, 115 CE (in Egypt, this eighteenth year ran from August 29, 114, to August 29, 115). The papyri indicate the beginning (June–July 115) and even the exact end (August 117) of the struggle, which lasted, according to Eusebius' source, "for a considerable time" (*ouk oligoi chronoi*). The exact spot where the revolt broke out is more difficult to ascertain. Riots occurred in Alexandria and elsewhere in Egypt, as well as in Cyrene; it is hard to determine which Jewish community had given the signal for the general insurrection. Cyrene played a considerable role, since it brought to the fore Andreas-Loukouas, whom the Egyptian Jews seem to have adopted as their leader.

The papyri can help us follow the escalating rebellion, whose progression was sketched out in Eusebius' source. In the traditional manner of Judeo-pagan quarrels, the troubles began with an uprising (*stasis*) of the Jews against their Greek neighbors. The disorders (*thoryboi*) spread throughout the country. Thus, what had begun as a local agitation (*tarachos, tumultus*) soon turned into a veritable war (*polemos*). The emperor named a special envoy, Marcius Turbo, and endowed him with extraordinary powers; he massacred the Jewish rebels by thousands. During his mission, the prefect of Egypt, M. Rutilius Lupus (attested between January 113 and January 117) was probably under his orders. In Mesopotamia, a similar mission had been entrusted to Lusius Quietus, whose name appears in rabbinical texts mentioning "the war of Quietus" (*polemos shel Qitos*).

We shall now call on a few direct witnesses: first of all, Apollonios, strategus of the nome of Apollinopolis Heptakomias, in Upper Egypt, between 113 and 120 CE, who owned some property in the Hermopolite, his native region. He lived in Heptakomia, the "county seat" of the nome, a small town peopled by Egyptians and a few Greeks (today Kom Eshfaht). Apollonios had been mobilized to fight against the Jews during most of the two-year war. Throughout the period of his service, which led him as far away as Memphis, several hundred kilometers from home, he corresponded regularly with his wife, Aline, who was also his sister, and with the couple's mother, Lady Eudaimonis. Some of these letters have survived up to our time, providing much precious information that can help us flesh out the details of Eusebius' account.

On the last day of August or at the beginning of September 115, soon after the beginning of the new year by the Egyptian calendar, Aline wrote to her husband. They had just parted: Apollonios had gone off to fight the rebels, and Aline was filled with anguish.

> Aline to Apollonios her brother many greetings. I am terribly anxious about you because of what they say about what is happening, and because of your sudden departure. I take no pleasure in food or drink, but stay awake continually night and day with one worry, your safety. Only my father's care revives me and, as I hope to see you safe, I would have lain without food on New Year's Day, had my father not come and forced me to eat. I beg you to keep yourself safe, and not to go into danger without a guard. Do the same as the strategus here, who puts the burden on his officers. (GIESSEN PAPYRUS 19; CPJUD. II 436)

This is the oldest document we possess concerning the course of the revolt in Egypt. Apollonios must have left home during August, before the end of the Egyptian year, having barely had the time to send his wife and children to the couple's parents in the large provincial city of Hermopolis. He surely believed they would be safer there than in the tiny village of Heptakomia, as Aline's allusion to the "strategus here" seems to suggest. In the next part of the papyrus, unfortunately quite mutilated, the term "go up" seems to indicate that Apollonios was stationed south of Hermopolis, in the nome for which he was responsible. The mobilization of a civilian official (in this context, his title of "strategus" is misleading) was a rare emergency measure, and Apollonios' sudden departure probably was due to a rapid extension of the revolt, which must have begun in June or July of that same year 115, and had already spread to Upper Egypt.

And what of Alexandria? Eusebius' sources speak of Greeks who fell back upon

Alexandria, where they set upon the Jews of the capital, preventing them from rejoining their fellow rebels in the chora. The following document may have referred to these hostilities. Its numerous lacunae render its exact interpretation problematic; it can, nonetheless, be identified as an edict promulgated by M. Rutilius Lupus, prefect of Egypt, our second witness.

> . . . They are preparing fire and weapons against us. I know that they are few, but they are supported by many more and provided for by the powerful, who pay not to be abused and maltreated. The wickedness of the few can justly be called a reproach to the whole city. I know that most of them are slaves; that is why their masters are blamed.
>
> I therefore bid them all not to simulate anger for the sake of profit. They should recognize that we now know who they are. Let them not trust to my indulgence or (to the entreaties made in the days when I forced myself to protect all I could). If anyone has charges to make, there is a judge sent by the Emperor for this purpose. For not even governors have the power to execute without trial, and there is a proper time for a trial just as there is a proper place and a proper method of punishment.
>
> Let there be an end of those who say, some truly, some falsely, that they have been wounded, and demand justice violently and unjustly; for there was no need to be wounded. Some of these errors could perhaps have had an excuse before the battle between the Romans and the Jews, but now they are purposeless judgments, which have never been permitted.
>
> The nineteenth year of Trajan, Phaophi 16. (*Papyrus Milano Vogliano II 47*; CPJud. II 435, cols. 3–4)

The Egyptian date on the document corresponds to October 14, 115 CE, which seems to fit the facts very well. The prefect was addressing the Greeks of Alexandria, more exactly those who wanted to make the Jews pay for the disorders provoked by their coreligionists of the chora. It seems that they had mobilized commandos of slaves, dangling before them the prospect of unbridled pillaging of Jewish property, thus rendering the entire city responsible for their doings. The prefect reminds them that they were strictly bound to conform to the established norms of justice, and he condemns all lynching. Since his rhetoric is hardly a model of clarity, one may well ask what he meant by "the battle between the Romans and the Jews." Had there already been a battle (*mache*)? Or was Lupus referring to the memory of a past event, such as the intervention, in 66, of the Roman army under the governorship of Tiberius Julius Alexander, in the hope of averting a similar intervention in the present circumstances?

The revolt continued unabated and, although there was a lull in Alexandria, strife reigned in the Egyptian countryside. Eusebius' sources tell us that the expeditionary force under Marcius Turbo waged "many battles" (*pollai machai*) against the Jews. Not only did the Jews have to stand up to the Roman army, but they also had to face the

Greeks and Egyptians who fought alongside it. In the Hermopolite nome, "massed villagers" (*athrooi kometai*) relieved the Greeks after the Jews had won some alarming victories. And the news of the Jews' defeat near Memphis overjoyed the Greeks under Apollonios, who praised the "victory and success" of the Roman forces. In our last chapter we shall learn that, at the very end of the second century CE, the population of Oxyrhynchos still celebrated the memory of the war against the Jews by a commemorative feast.

In this, as in every war, atrocities of all sorts were committed. But one must be quite wary in interpreting the echoes of these events in the few documents we possess. There are two letters from Eudaimonis, the mother of Apollonios and Aline, and a passage from the abridged version of Cassius Dio's account, to which we have already alluded. To begin with, let us call our third witness, Lady Eudaimonis, who sent a message of maternal love to her son upon learning that he was about to leave for the northern front. Only the last part of the letter has been preserved, but it is far from uninteresting:

> . . . with the good will of the gods, above all, Hermes the invincible, may
> they not roast you (*ou me se optesosi*). For the rest, may all be well with
> you and all your men. Heraidous, your daughter, who is free from harm,
> greets you. (*GIESSEN PAPYRUS 24; CPJUD. II 437*)

Who wanted to roast Apollonios the strategus? Some commentators, either spiteful or simply naive, have a ready answer: "The Jews, of course." And they come up with the abridgement of Cassius Dio's text, compiled in the eleventh century (about 1060) by Johanes Xiphilinus of Trapezus, a Byzantine monk.

> Trajan therefore departed thence, and a little later began to fail in health.
> Meanwhile the Jews in the region of Cyrene had put a certain Andreas at
> their head, and were destroying both the Romans and the Greeks. They
> would eat the flesh of their victims, make belts for themselves of their en-
> trails, anoint themselves with their blood and wear their skins for cloth-
> ing; many they sawed in two, from the head downwards; others they gave
> to wild beasts, and still others they forced to fight as gladiators. In all two
> hundred and twenty thousand persons perished. In Egypt, too, they perpe-
> trated many similar outrages, and in Cyprus, under the leadership of a cer-
> tain Artemion. There, also, two hundred and forty thousand perished.
> (*DIO CASSIUS, ROMAN HISTORY, EPITOME OF BOOK 68, 32, 1–2; ED. E. CARY*)

Let us compare this fragment with the one relating the revolt of Bar Kokhba (69, 12, 14). Xiphilinus was so convinced of the uplifting effect this account of the misfortunes of the "perfidious Jews" would have on the Christian soul that he faithfully copied out, in its entirety, Dio's version of the events under the reign of Hadrian. As for those that occurred under Trajan's reign, with which we are at present concerned, he abridged, distorted, and (in a manner of speaking) embellished his remote model in his own inimitable fashion. To give his work a plausible cast, he preserved a few probably authentic details, such as the name of the leaders of the revolt (Andreas, whom we have identified as Loukouas, and Artemion, who appears nowhere else), and then gave free rein to his imagination.

The bad faith of this author can hardly be denied. Eusebius' source spoke of a large number of dead. Here we find nearly half a million. The text does not specify the identity of the victims. We do not know where Xiphilinus sought out these figures. He blames the Jews who "destroyed both the Romans and the Greeks," not once mentioning those Jews who had been massacred by the Roman legions, abetted by the Greco-Egyptian fighters. In his opinion, the rebels had a monopoly on killing. An insurrection is by definition an outburst of violence against the oppressor. But this is not enough to condone Xiphilinus' treatment of the facts. The repression of a rebellion often surpasses in violence the very oppression that was its cause.

The devastating two-year war assuredly left many victims in its wake, on both sides. Documents from the Egyptian records can give a clear idea of their proportionate distribution; our last chapter will tragically confirm that the Jews suffered infinitely more losses than the Greeks. But a body count is hardly necessary to refute the accusation of Jewish cannibalism. On this subject, Xiphilinus' fabrications are variations on a time-worn theme, well known throughout the ancient world and easy to exploit: we are dealing with a new edition of the pagan fable of the ritual murder of a pre-fattened Greek, whose entrails the Jews then gleefully consume. Josephus had already denounced this absurd tale in his *Against Apion*. Likewise, the evocation of the gladiatorial games, and of the practice of offering human beings as victims to be devoured by wild beasts is simply a transposition to a Jewish register of the persecutions of the Christians by the Romans. Decidedly, Xiphilinus is not a trustworthy guide.

Then what are we to make of Eudaimonis' fears? Here is a letter she wrote to her daughter Aline in July 117, a document that gives some measure of the depth of her anguish concerning her son.

> Eudaimonis to her daughter Aline, greeting. I pray above all that you may be delivered of a child in good time and that I shall receive news of a son. You sailed up on the twenty-ninth, and on the next day I began to weave. I at last got the material from the dyer on the tenth of Epeiph. I am working with your slave girls as far as I can. I cannot find girls to work with me, for they are all working for their own mistresses. Our people have been marching all over the city, asking for more pay. Your sister Souerous has been delivered of a child. Teeus wrote to me, expressing her gratitude to you, so I know, lady, that my instructions are being carried out. For she has left all her own people and gone to join you. The little girl sends her greetings, and is persevering with her lessons. Be sure that I shall pay no attention to the god [Hermes] until I get my son back safe. Why did you send me twenty drachmas, when I have no leisure? I already have the vision of being naked when winter starts.

[In another hand:] Farewell, Epeiph 22.

[In the first hand, post script:] The wife of Eudemos has stuck by me and I am grateful to her.

[Verso; in a third hand:] To Aline her daughter. (BREMEN PAPYRUS 63; CPJUD. II 442)

Eudaimonis was quite evidently a courageous, energetic woman, with a strong character, deeply concerned with her children and her grandchildren. She worked hard herself, and supervised the work of her daughter's servants. She was well aware of the world around her and seemed to approve of the public demonstrations by workers claiming raises in salaries (the sentence is not clear; it may refer to her complaint about not being able to find enough workers because they are better paid elsewhere). She braved the local deity, the "invincible" Hermes, refusing to worship at his shrine until her son had returned from the war, safe and sound.

Although she was an active and intelligent woman, Eudaimonis was not above sartorial vanity: on inspecting her wardrobe she decided she had "nothing to wear," and would be "naked when winter starts" (*gymne meno ton cheimona*). Let us hope, for her sake, that her fears in this regard proved as baseless as her fears for her son's safety. In fact, by the autumn of 117 CE, Apollonios the strategus was back home from the wars. And on November 28, he wrote a letter to Q. Rammius Martialis, whom Hadrian, immediately upon acceding to the throne at the beginning of August of the same year (117), had appointed as the new prefect of Egypt. He was asking the prefect for a sixty-day leave, in order to devote himself to his personal affairs in the Hermopolite nome, which had suffered through his long absence (Giessen Papyrus 41; CPJud. II 443).

Apollonios appended a previous unanswered request, in which he had applied for a leave to repair material damage to his personal effects, due to the "invasion of the impious Jews." He hoped then to be able to proceed with his official duties "with a more tranquil mind." Although this first request bore no date, it appears that Apollonios had not waited longer than two months before renewing his demand. In other words, the strategus had returned in September 117. When Hadrian acceded to power, the war had already come to an end. After two years of strife, all was quiet again in Egypt. The Jews had disappeared.

To conclude our chapter, let us attempt to put the uprising into perspective. If the final catastrophe was inevitable, why had the Jews plunged into an enterprise so fraught with danger? The causes of the revolt were manifold; they have not yet been explained in a satisfactory manner, no more than were those of the war of 66–73. Much attention has been paid to the Messianic aspect of the movement. Indeed, since the destruction of the Temple in Jerusalem, the Messianic movement had been steadily gaining ground. The zealots proclaimed the fall of the Temple to be only a premonitory sign. The "end of all times" was near at hand, when the domination of the Romans would give way to a restored Jewish kingdom. Judean zealots who had fled to Alexandria and Cyrene could very well have spread such ideas, inflaming people's minds and hastening the outbreak of the revolt. This could help explain the title of king that Eusebius' source attributed to Andreas-Loukouas, the leader of the rebellion, since the Messiah awaited by the Jews was supposed to belong to the royal lineage of David. According to Hegesippus, an eastern Christian monk from the end of the second century (also quoted by Eusebius), the Roman authorities, from the time of Vespasian up to Trajan, had instituted a sort of manhunt for all of David's descendants; Andreas-Loukouas had managed to slip through the holes in their dragnet.

The presence of a local Messiah, who was, moreover, not the only leader of the revolt, is not a sufficient reason to accredit the Messianic hypothesis as the unique cause of the uprising. Institutional data must also be taken into account. In Egypt, the degraded political status of the Jews was surely a weighty factor, which could have given rise to projects of revenge of an astonishing audacity, although quite plausible in a regional context.

Egypt was an important grain-producing country; once vanquished, it could easily be defended by the conqueror. Tacitus remarks that Augustus had succeeded in "isolating" it (*seposuit*), fearing that "Italy itself could be faced with starvation if an unfriendly power overran the province where, by holding the keys to land and sea, even a weak garrison could resist great armies" (*Annals* 2, 59). To seize Egypt and bring Rome to its knees by depriving it of the deliveries of wheat on which it depended—the enterprise might not have been as suicidal as it appears at first glance. By conquering Egypt, did the rebels hope to achieve their ultimate goal: to oblige the imperial government to accept the reestablishment of a Jewish kingdom in Judea? In any case, to starve Italy and Rome—Rome who had stripped them of their former status of "Hellenes" and abased them to the level of the native peasants—what a magnificent revenge for the destruction of the Temple of Jerusalem and the humiliation of the Egyptian Jews!

Is it entirely unrealistic to read such a project into the minds of the movement's leaders? In any event, its chances of success were practically nil. In Mesopotamia, the Jewish revolt coincided with a general insurrection of the Parthians. In Egypt, the Jews were alone on the battleground. There was no chance whatsoever that their rebellion be the signal for the entire country to rise up against the Roman yoke. For an impartial observer, their courage was nothing but folly. The pagan Greek writer quoted by Eusebius could not understand how an isolated provincial minority would dare to attack the Romans, "masters of the inhabited earth," instead of accepting, like everyone else (or nearly everyone else), the benefits of the *Pax Romana*. He believed that "a terrible spirit of rebellion" had taken hold of the Jews. At the beginning of the fifth century CE, the Christian historian Orosius, taking up the thread of Eusebius' comments, wrote that the Jews had "become wild, as if they had been seized by rabies" (*quasi rabie efferati*). They had pitted themselves, alone, against the Romans, the Egyptians and the Greeks. Alone, they were to pay the price of their folly.

Chapter 10

The Remembrance

Who Destroyed the Great Synagogue of Alexandria?

The revolt of 115–117 led to the obliteration of the Jews from the face of Egypt; various traces of this catastrophe can be perceived in our sources. The emptiness of the Jewish quarters in Egyptian cities and towns is reflected in the documents that have come down to us. Throughout the country, new inhabitants filled the streets of the erstwhile Jewish quarters. The devastated countryside had to be brought back to life, the land had to be tilled, economic order had to be restored. The Greeks, for their part, gave themselves over to joyous victory celebrations. But let us first lend an ear to the sad reminiscences of the glorious past of Alexandrian Judaism, preserved in the Talmud.

We have read the description Rabbi Judah ben Ilai gave in the Jerusalem Talmud of the great synagogue in Alexandria. It ends with a question, immediately followed by its answer: "And who destroyed it? The impious Trogianos." There is no doubt as to the identity of the destroyer: the Emperor Trajan, who had quit his role as "advocate of the Jews" in the *Acts of Hermaiskos*, to become the impious Trajan, more precisely "Trajan the Wicked" (*Trogianos ha-rasha*), a sort of official epithet, later reinforced by the wish that "his bones be ground to powder."

"The best of princes" now ranked among the foremost of Israel's persecutors. The destruction of the great synagogue in Alexandria was a mere episode in the series of disasters that befell Egyptian Jewry in the aftermath of the revolt. The Talmud has its own particular logic when it sets about explaining the reasons for the catastrophe. The explanation was placed under the authority of Rabbi Simeon ben Yohai (second century CE) who, unlike his contemporary Rabbi Judah ben Ilai, was a bitter enemy of Rome.

> It has been taught, Rabbi Simeon ben Yohai said: The Israelites were
> warned at three points not to go back to the Land of Egypt. For it is said:
> "For whereas ye have seen the Egyptians today, ye shall see them again no
> more for ever" (Ex. 14:13). "Forasmuch as the Lord hath said unto you: Ye
> shall henceforth return no more that way" (Deut. 17:16). "And the Lord

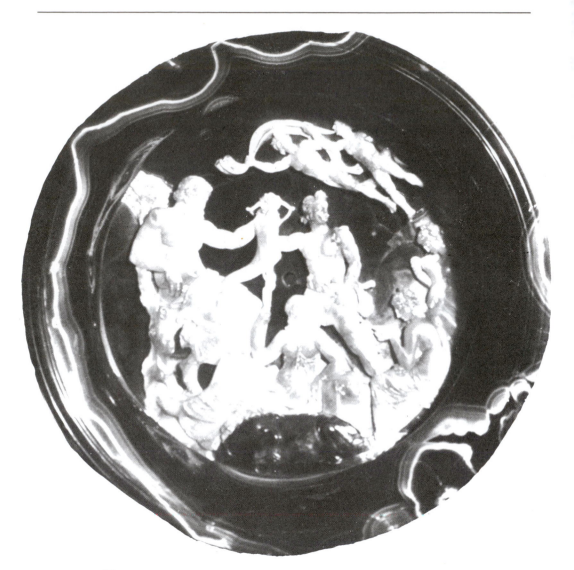

The **Nile with the horn of plenty** *The "Tazza Farnese" (Naples, National Museum).*

shall bring thee back into Egypt in ships, by the way whereof I said unto thee: Thou shalt see it no more again; and there you shall sell yourselves unto your enemies for bondmen and for bondwomen, and no man shall buy you" (Deut. 28:68). In all three instances they did go back, and in those three instances they fell.

Once in the time of Sennacherib, king of Assyria, as it is said: "Woe to them that go down to Egypt for help, and rely on horses, and trust in chariots, because they are many, and in horsemen because they are ex-

ceedingly mighty; but they look not unto the Holy One of Israel, neither
seek the Lord!" (Is. 31:1).

What is written thereafter? "Now the Egyptians are men, and not God,
and their horses flesh, and not spirit; so when the Lord shall stretch out
His hand, both he that helpeth shall stumble, And he that is helped shall
fall, And they all shall perish together" (Is. 31:3).

Once in the time of Johanan ben Qorah: "Then the sword, which you
fear, shall overtake you there in the land of Egypt; and the famine,
whereof ye are afraid, shall follow hard after you there in Egypt; and there
ye shall die" (Jer. 42:16). (JERUSALEM TALMUD, SUKKAH 5:1, 55B)

For the sages of the Talmud, the misfortunes of Israel are to be explained by a metaphysical principle of causation, whereby a celestial punishment was meted out to the
chosen people because of their sins. In this case, a triple warning was followed by a triple
sanction. In the first two cases, the historical record does not bear a clear trace of the
actual accomplishment of the sentences, but the third instance is unmistakably identi-
fiable as the war of 115–117, in which Egyptian Jewry perished. Trajan appears as the
instrument of divine justice. All well and good. But why he and not someone else? The
Talmud goes on to explain this choice:

In the time of Trogianos, the evil one, a son was born to him on the
ninth of Av, and [the Israelites] were fasting.

His daughter died on Hanukkah, and [the Israelites] lit candles.

His wife sent a message to him, saying: "Instead of going out to conquer
the barbarians, come and conquer the Jews, who have rebelled against
you." (JERUSALEM TALMUD, SUKKAH 5:1, 55B)

There was an evident lack of synchronization between the happenings in Emperor
Trajan's family life and the Jewish calendar. A blessed event at the Roman court coincided with the mournful anniversary of the fall of both the first and second Jewish
Temples on the ninth day of the month of Av (Tisha be-Av). While the imperial family was mourning the loss of a daughter, which occurred during the Hannukah holidays, their feelings were injured by the Jews' joyous celebration of the Maccabean victory.

One detail, however, is worthy of mention: according to the official records, Trajan
and Plotina never had children. Is this a good enough reason to declare the talmudic
fragment ahistoric, or should one, on the contrary, try to see whether we have come
upon an authentic fact, unrecorded by the official chroniclers? The frequency, in ancient times, of death in infancy is not a valid excuse for such an omission. If it were
the same child who was born on the ninth of Av (July/August) and died during the
Hanukkah feast (November/December), he would then no longer have been a newborn
infant, but a five-month old prince, whom the ancient historians should have mentioned. Why the birth of a boy was followed by the death of a girl still remained to be

explained. The Midrash subsequently rose to the occasion by changing the sex of one of the children. Aside from this last point, the discrepancy between the seeming certitude of the sages and the silence of the official chroniclers may appear somewhat disconcerting.

One should not, however, reproach the sages of the Talmud for not having been what they never were nor wished to be, namely, professional historians. It is not more convincing to attempt to safeguard the historicity of the account by substituting Marcius Turbo for Trajan. The rabbinical image of an anti-Semitic Trajan is hardly more "unlikely" than the Alexandrian image of a philo-Judaic Trajan. The rabbinical point of view is, after a fashion, a more rational one, since it is an attempt to find an objective reason for the emperor's change of heart toward the Jews. The sages had gone right to the essence of the matter, by insisting upon the fundamental incompatibility between the Jews and the man Trajan, predestined thus by Divine Justice to be cast in the role of scourge.

Let us not forget the Empress Plotina, who played as considerable a part in the talmudic account as in the *Acts of Hermaiskos*, except that she then was on the side of friendship and sympathy, whereas now she was the promoter of hatred and violence. The Midrash recounts that anonymous informers had come to Plotina, complaining of the Jews' insolence. One is led to think of anti-Semites from Alexandria; were they not the counterpart to the "Jewish lobby" and its role in the Imperial Council, as portrayed in Alexandrian propaganda?

One must stress the noteworthy role played by the holiday as a determining factor in the outbreak of hostilities. The Talmud may have wished to point out that the underlying cause of the revolt against Trajan was the Jews' unquenchable thirst for independence, symbolized both by the image of the Temple destroyed by Titus (on the ninth of Av) and by the example of the Maccabees (Hanukkah). The highlighting of the holiday in the talmudic explanations coincides with the privileged status henceforth accorded to the rejoicings and mourning occasioned by family events in the reigning imperial dynasty. This new and important fact is perfectly historical.

Another link to historical truth: in the message Plotina sent her husband, she referred to the war against the barbarians. She could only have been alluding to the war Trajan had launched against the Parthians in the autumn of 113 CE. To check the revolt of the Jews, Trajan had called upon two generals: Marcius Turbo, whom we have spoken of several times, and Lusius Quietus, whose name had become synonymous with the revolt itself in the rabbinical texts ("the war of Quietus"). The Talmud, in recounting the repression of the revolt in Egypt, and the assassination (the word is not too strong) of Egyptian Jewry, assigns the leading role to the master, and not to his servants:

> He thought that the trip would take ten days, but he came in five. He came and found the Israelites occupied in study of the Light [Torah], with the following verse: "The Lord will bring a nation against thee from far,

from the end of the earth, as the vulture swoopeth down; a nation whose tongue thou shalt not understand" (Deut. 28:49).

He said to them: "With what are you occupied?"

They said to him: "With thus-and-so."

He said to them: "That man [Trajan] thought that it would take ten days to make the trip, and I arrived in five days."

"His legions surrounded them and killed them."

(JERUSALEM TALMUD, SUKKAH 5:1, 55B)

The Great Synagogue of Alexandria (*upper left*)   *Mosaic, 5th century* CE (*discovered at Beth Shean, Israel*).

The exact route was not indicated. The context, however, presupposes a maritime journey between Ostia and Alexandria, corresponding to the trip in the opposite direction accomplished by the two delegations in the *Acts of Hermaiskos*. It generally took from six to eight days to sail from Rome (Ostia) to Alexandria; five to ten days is a perfectly plausible figure. The instances described by Pliny the Elder show that an important Roman government official, sailing on a good ship, could easily meet this standard, providing he refrain, as Hermaiskos' companions did, from taking to the sea during the winter period of bad weather.

Although the length of the supposed trip is perfectly plausible, the imperial voyage to Alexandria was purely symbolic; in fact, Trajan never set foot in Egypt, even before the Parthian war, when it would have been easier to do so. He had nonetheless shown undeniable interest in the country, notably by furthering the reopening of the ancient canal between the Nile and the Red Sea. The dialogue between the emperor and the Jews immersed in the study of the Torah was intended to materialize the threat of disaster contained in Deuteronomy (28:49ff.). With the arrival of the Roman legions come to "massacre" (*hargan*) the Jews, we are back in the realm of historical truth. On this crucial point, Appian of Alexandria, a contemporary observer, corroborates the accuracy of the talmudic account.

> Caesar could not bear to look at the head of Pompey when it was brought to him but ordered that it be buried, and he set apart for it a small plot of ground near the city which was dedicated to Nemesis; but in my time, while the Roman emperor Trajan was exterminating the Jewish nation in Egypt, it was devastated by them in the exigencies of the war. (APPIAN OF ALEXANDRIA, CIVIL WARS 2, 90, 380; ED. H. WHITE)

Appian of Alexandria was fleeing war-ravaged Egypt. The sanctuary of Nemesis (*Nemeseos temenos*) is evocative of the duel between Caesar and Pompey in which the latter, after his defeat at Pharsalus in 48 BCE, sought refuge in Egypt, only to be assassinated upon his arrival, by the order of Ptolemy XIV, Cleopatra's brother and co-regent. Egypt does not contain many monuments dedicated to Nemesis. There was one at Krokodilopolis in the Faiyum, which a rich Roman restored in 59 CE. As for the one in Alexandria mentioned here, it might have been situated to the northwest of the city, near the old Jewish quarter. Its destruction during the war of 115–117 is quite credible, but it would be an error to interpret it as a manifestation of the Jewish rebels' iconoclastic fury. Archaeological evidence irrefutably confirms that other pagan temples had been destroyed by the Jews during the revolt in Cyrenaica; this was surely so for Egypt, too. In the present case, as Appian writes, the sanctuary had been demolished "in the exigencies of the war."

The important point in his text is the summary description of Trajan "exterminating the Jewish nation in Egypt" (*exollynto to en Aigyptoi Ioudaion genos*). Appian speaks of the "extermination" as a well-known fact, confirming the mention of "massacre" in the Talmud. For the Greek historian, as well as for the sages of the Talmud, the act and its author have been made to coincide. Even though he was physically absent from the field of battle, the emperor, and not his plenipotentiary, Marcius Turbo, was the veritable exterminator. This convergence lends a sinister aura of historical truth to the last part of the talmudic account.

> [Trajan] said to the women: "Obey my legions, and I shall not kill you."
> They said to him: "What you did to the ones who have fallen, do also to us who are yet standing."
> He mingled their blood with the blood of their men, until the blood flowed into the ocean as far as Cyprus. At that moment the horn of Israel was cut off, and it is not destined to return to its place until the son of David will come. (*JERUSALEM TALMUD, SUKKAH 5:1, 55B*)

The war had thus overflowed the battlefield; the Jewish women shared the fate of their husbands. One remembers the newly-wed girls brutally torn from their bridal chambers and led to the hippodrome in Alexandria, where they were to be subjected to appalling persecutions. The cruelties inflicted upon the Alexandrian Jewesses by the prefect Flaccus also rise to the surface of memory. Whatever may be the actual meaning of the reference to the island of Cyprus, toward which Jewish blood flowed through the sea, the image of a sea of blood is an apt metaphor for the violence of the repression, in whose description the literary sources and papyrological testimony converge.

The sages of the Talmud did not only evoke the memory of the Hellenized Jewry of Egypt and the disaster that engulfed it. They also offered an explanation for the foreordained failure of the revolt. As we have seen at the beginning of this chapter, they pointed out how the Lord punished the infidelity of His people. The three gravest sins: idolatry, debauchery and murder, brought about the destruction of the First Temple. For that of the Second Temple, one sin, "gratuitous hatred" (*sinat hinam*) was sufficient. Upon the third transgression of a triple warning, a third penalty was inflicted upon the Jews of Egypt. The "wicked Trajan," following in the footsteps of Nebuchadnezzar and Titus, set off the machinery of Divine Justice.

A similar logic led the Christians to interpret the same events as did the rabbis, but with their own conception of the nature of the sin entailing the punishment. Eusebius held the Jews guilty for rising up against the historic order willed by God, an order of which Rome was the incarnation, and did not forget to remind them of their cardinal offense, "their iniquity and their impiety in regard to Christ." Before him, Origen, an eminent Christian exegete and theologian (second/third century CE), judged that the Jews had well deserved to suffer the misfortunes that befell them "since they had committed the most abominable of all forfeits by fomenting a plot against the Savior of the human race" (*Against Celsus* 5, 22). The theme of a political conspiracy had a great fortune: we can follow its evolution from the days of Isidoros' trial, when it was the main charge against the Jews, to its Christianized form, presenting the Jews as villainous, justly punishable conspirators. The pagan historians cited by Eusebius simply recorded the succession of events, abstaining from any judgment of the chastisement of Jewish "folly." To the contrary, both the Jewish sages and the Fathers of the Church rose above everyday contingencies to interpret those events as the earthly signs of an immanent justice.

The foregoing explanations of the consequences of the revolt offer a choice only between human folly and divine justice, a choice that may not satisfy all readers. To help us comprehend the magnitude of the disaster, other, more prosaic factors must be taken into account. The very particular "remembrances" contained in financial documents, preserved by Egyptian papyri and ostraca, throw a pitiless light on the events of 115–117.

"JEWISH TAX," "JEWISH ACCOUNTS":
THE TALE OF THE IMPERIAL TAX RECORDS

What was "Jewish Egypt" like, after the defeat of 117 CE? The evidence of tax receipts on ostraca is both objective and appalling. Ever since the year 70, which saw the destruction of the Temple in Jerusalem, any Jew in the Roman Empire was subjected to a special tax. The Emperor Vespasian decreed that, in lieu and stead of the traditional contribution of half a shekel for the upkeep of the Temple, every Jew had henceforth to pay a tax destined to swell the coffers of the Roman rival of YHWH, Jupiter Capitolinus, whose temple had been destroyed by a fire in the year 69. The ancient offering, hallowed by centuries of tradition, had been a symbol of Jewish unity; now it had become a mark of defeat and humiliation. From the times of Domitian onward, this tax was paid into a special account of the Imperial Treasury, the *fiscus Iudaicus*. The entire Jewish population of the Roman Empire was subject to it, but direct evidence of its payment is afforded only for Egypt, by a great number of ostraca that have come down to us.

For one Egyptian town, Apollinopolis Magna (today Edfu), the "Jews' twopence" (*denarii duo Iudaeorum*), soon to be called simply the "Jewish tax" (*Ioudaikon telesma*), appear in a large batch of ostraca, mostly from the Franco-Polish excavations of 1937–39. Every Jew, male and female, from the age of three to sixty or sixty-two, free or slave, was subject to the tax. The annual sum due was eight drachmas and two obols; the eight drachmas represent two denarii and the two obols are a surtax, imposed because it was paid in "native" currency and not in denarii. Yet another supplementary surtax of one drachma had been added, for reasons that remain obscure. Specially appointed officials were to supervise the collection of the payments.

For the period lasting from 71/72 until May of 116 CE, some seventy Greek ostraca list names (Jewish, Greek, Egyptian, and Roman) of the taxpayers and reveal their family relationships. The size of this sample is, of course, due to the hazards of excavations; it represents only a small portion of the Jewish population of Edfu. Not only were the

Jews obliged to pay this tax, but other sums were exacted of them, as shown in other documents in which Jewish names appear, such as demotic ostraca, with native Egyptians apparently acting as tax collectors.

Among the documents we possess, the last receipt for the "Jewish tax" dates from May 18, 116 CE (Ostracon Edfu 159; CPJud. II 229). It concerns a slave, Thermautos, belonging to one Aninios, thought to have been a Roman centurion, which would appear most unlikely for a Jew at the height of the insurrection; in all probability he was simply a man whose father was named Kenturion, a name attested elsewhere in Egypt. Since the year 107, before the outbreak of the war, Aninios had been paying this tax for a slave named Sporos. In Roman Egypt, a slave had the same fiscal status as his owner, and a Jewish slave owner was obliged to pay the "Jewish tax" for his slaves, whether or not they were Jews.

Aninios' case was not at all exceptional, and its only distinguishing feature is that it happens to be the latest of our ostraca, the last of a series relating to the Jewish tax in Edfu. Not that Hadrian abolished it, an absurd notion on the face of it; we shall shortly examine a fresh piece of evidence to the contrary. The truth is much sadder: the Jewish community of Edfu had ceased to exist. As for the other taxes to which the Jews were subject, our last receipt that can be dated with certitude is from April 28, 116. Thenceforth, according to our ostraca, Edfu counted among its inhabitants no more than one family of presumed Jewish origin: some thirty-five years after the revolt, between 151 and 165 CE, three descendants of a Jewish taxpayer from Vespasian's time (69–79 CE) decided to return to their ancestral home; there they dwelt amidst its inhabitants, completely integrated into the local lifestyle, and no longer paid the discriminatory tax.

For the period following the revolt, the only attestation of the Jewish tax is contained in a tax register from Karanis in the Faiyum. It dates from the ninth year of the reign of an emperor, who could have been either Antoninus Pius (corresponding to 145/146 CE) or Marcus Aurelius (corresponding to 168/169). Among others, it lists a payment of nine drachmas and two obols, under the heading of the "Jewish tax." We have seen above that this was the sum exacted from each Jewish taxpayer. In the middle of the second century CE, this large Faiyumic town certainly contained more than one thousand adults; is it possible that its Jewish population had been reduced to a sole survivor, doubtless a returnee who, unlike those of Edfu, had retained his Jewish identity? When one recalls the numbers and the vitality of the Jewish colony in the Faiyum, whose lives we have evoked time and again in foregoing pages, the presence of this unique survivor is in itself a pathetic testimonial to the disaster that had stricken Egyptian Jewry.

Seen in this light, Egypt after 117 had the aspect of a vast cemetery, as did the shtetls of Eastern Europe after the Second World War. Under Hadrian and the Severi, contemporary documents mention "Jewish streets" in Oxyrhynchos and Hermopolis. But there were no longer any Jews in the houses lining these streets. A sorry sight! It was

(Top) **Reform of the Jewish tax** *Sesterce from Emperor Nerva's reign, 97 CE;* (bottom) **The Jewish tax in Egypt** *Receipt on ostracon delivered to a Jewish woman in Apollinopolis-the-Great (Edfu), dated March 31, 116 CE (from the A. Deissmann Collection).*

only at the very end of the third century or the beginning of the fourth that the first new burgeonings of Jewish life were to appear in the provincial cities of Egypt.

A thorough examination of fiscal documents enables us to go a step further, with the discovery of a heretofore unknown aspect of the catastrophe of Egyptian Jewry: its legal dimension. We possess several texts concerning redistribution of landed property after the revolt; they mention parcels of land that had belonged to Greeks who had fallen on the battlefield, and others that had been the property of Jewish rebels. The distinctive treatment accorded these two categories by the provincial administration opens a line of inquiry whose exploration leads to singularly instructive results.

On October 2, 130 CE, the fifteenth Egyptian year of Hadrian, a group of farmers, wishing to take a joint lease on some parcels of state land, addressed a request to the strategus of the Athribite nome, a certain Hierax (Oxyrhynchos Papyrus III 500; CPJud. II 448). Some of these parcels had been designated as "having heretofore belonged" to Greeks and Jews. The Greeks were described as deceased *ab intestato* and without legal heirs (*akleronometoi*). Their property had been allotted to the state in virtue of a rule invented in the days of the Hellenistic monarchy, adopted by the Romans, and which, even today, currently governs the disposition of escheated property.

As for the Jews, another term was employed, whose decipherment is problematic and whose interpretation has been even more so. It was believed at first that it meant people who had been "killed," *aneiremenoi*, who had died during the war. Their property would then have been classified as escheated and thus, like that of the Greeks, attributed to the Imperial Treasury. Actually, the term *aneiremenoi* indicates individuals who had been "assassinated" or "massacred." It would certainly be appropriate in descriptions of wars and their atrocities, such as those of the pagan authors that Eusebius of Caesarea had transcribed, but it would seem singularly out of place in the official administrative vocabulary, and most unlikely to be chosen by Egyptian farmers addressing the public authorities. Another reading, paleographically justifiable, would seem preferable; a reading with the weight of tradition on its side, as it harks back to the Ptolemaic period: instead of Jews who had been "massacred" or simply "killed," it would refer to Jews who had been "stricken by confiscatory measures": *apheiremenoi*. One letter of the Greek alphabet makes all the difference! Now everything falls into place.

A different term was applied to the Jews because their property, although it bordered upon that of the Greeks and was in a similar fiscal situation, did not fall into the same juridical category. Land that had belonged to the Greeks was properly to be considered as escheated, "vacant estates" (*bona vacantia*); under Roman law, if the owner had died without leaving either a will or a legitimate heir, it became state property. This would have been the case for land that had belonged to Greek combatants, single men without children, close cousins, or nephews to claim the succession. Land the Jews had owned, to the contrary, fell into the category of property confiscated from persons condemned to capital punishment (*bona damnatorum*). The state had taken possession of these, too, but on quite other grounds.

Two different administrative registers had been introduced, corresponding to the two distinct legal titles for the two sorts of landed property. In 1971, a papyrus from the Berlin collection, published by the Polish scholar Anna Swiderek, brought to light the existence, in the second century CE, of two special administrative accounts concerning the disposition of public lands after the revolt. One dealt with the "patrimony of heirless deceased Greeks" (*pekoulion Hellenon akleronometon*); the other was the "Jewish account" (*Ioudaikos logos*), whose existence has subsequently been confirmed by other papyrological documents from the same epoch. By the end of the second century, these two registers were no longer in existence.

A clear picture of events now emerges: after two years of warfare, much of the land was no longer being tilled, and immediate emergency measures were necessary. The administration of state land took control of the property of the deceased combatants. Separate registers were established for each region in the country. In the administrative correspondence addressed by his colleague from the Herakleopolite nome to Apollonios, with whom the reader already is acquainted, we hear of a "list of property that had once belonged to Jews" (Oxyrhynchos Papyrus IX 1189; CPJud. II 445). Such a list indicates that appropriate measures had been taken by officials involved in the management of state land. To administrate its newly acquired patrimony, the state had created two special accounts; this was only a transitory phase since, little by little, the lots corresponding to these accounts found their way into other, more permanent categories. The only durable traces of this episode were the expressions designating land that "once had belonged to Jews" (*proteron Ioudaion*) and "once had belonged to Greeks" (*proteron Hellenon*), in lieu of the proper qualifying terms "deceased heirless Greeks" and "Jews whose property had been confiscated."

This temporary solution—it lasted only a half-century, from Hadrian to Commodus—might seem to have little significance other than for matters concerning bookkeeping and administrative terminology. Its historical importance is, in fact, considerable: the documents that unveil the secrets of property accounting in second-century Roman Egypt also provide the measure of the confiscations. In one text, again a Berlin papyrus, ten columns of a long scroll preserve a proportion which may well represent that of the entire country: four plots lost by Greeks against eighteen by Jews. With all proper reserve due to the approximate nature of our data, it would appear that the losses of the rebels represented practically all the property once owned by the Jews of Egypt.

Another, more serious problem, is posed by our documents: that of the legal basis for these massive confiscations. The distinctive categories of property "having once belonged to Greeks" and "having once belonged to Jews" were not due to the inventive genius of the Egyptian fiscal agents, who were simply carrying out orders from above. They were the consequence of a criminal verdict against the Jews who had rendered themselves guilty of the crime of lèse-majesté.

The crime of lèse-majesté had been codified in Roman law in the time of Julius Caesar and Augustus; sedition, or armed uprising against the established authorities, was one

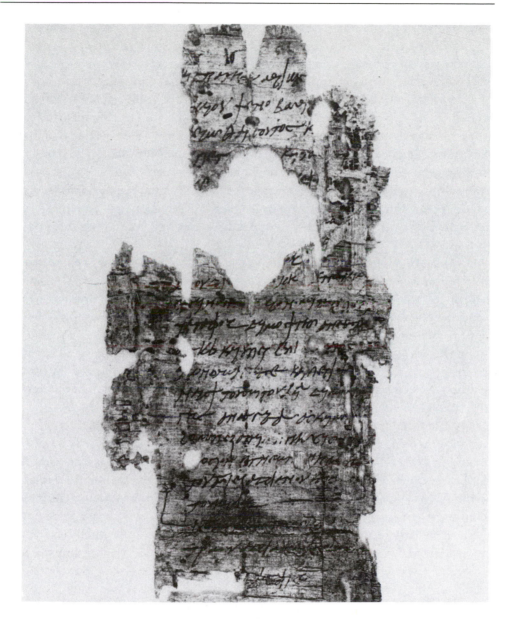

Document of confiscation of Jewish property   *The document reads, "To Hierax, strategus of the Athribite nome, from Horos son of Psenobasthis and from Nekpheros son of Thaisous and . . . Pet [. . .] and the rest . . . [traces of three lines] . . . [parcels] that once belonged to the Jews whose property has been confiscated and to the Greeks who died without heirs, [we will lease] in the district of Tetaphos 24 arouras of public land for 2 artabas of wheat per aroura, with a surcharge of 5 artabas of wheat for the whole, and around Psenarsiesis to the east of the Thostian district, 1 aroura of public land for 3 artabas of wheat, and we will give our mutual security to pay the rent to the public treasury from the new crop of this 15th year of our lord Hadrian Caesar. The 15th year of Imperator Caesar Traianus Hadrianus Augustus, Phaophi 5 [October 2, 130 CE]." Oxyrhynchos Papyrus III 500; CPJud. II 448 (Graz, University Library).*

of the forms it might assume. Defined under Republican law as a danger for the security of the Roman people, it received a later definition in which the majesty of the *princeps* now was substituted for the majesty of the people: any threat to the person of the emperor and the security of the state, of which he was the living incarnation, could be considered as lèse-majesté. Flaccus the prefect, Isidoros and Lampon, *inter alios*, had felt the full force of its weight. It covered a vast field, and could justify various reactions by the Roman government against all sorts of rebellions. The instigators of uprisings and "those who take up arms against the state" were included among the guilty. The Jewish rebels had risen up in arms against Rome, their revolt had become a war, and their guilt was patent. This was the reason they had been dubbed "impious" (*anosioi*), and not because they had pillaged pagan temples. Their impiety was nothing but *impietas in principem*, dereliction of duty toward the emperor, inherent in the crime of lèse-majesté.

Lèse-majesté was a crime against the state punishable by death or deportation and the confiscation of all one's property (*publicatio, confiscatio bonorum*). Isidoros, Lampon, and, before them, Flaccus, found individually guilty, had their worldly goods confiscated after their execution. This punishment was also meted out to the Jews of Egypt, vanquished rebels "stricken with confiscation" (*apheiremenoi*). But, before applying this measure, a trial and a sentencing were necessary. M. Rutilius Lupus, in his message to the Alexandrians at the outbreak of the revolt, insisted on the fact that no governor was empowered to condemn a subject to death without a previous trial and judgment.

It was most unlikely that Trajan had pronounced a judgment of this sort. The emperor was then engaged in a lengthy and laborious campaign against the Parthians and could only have taken military action through his generals, Marcius Turbo in Egypt and Lusius Quietus in Mesopotamia. The revolt had first to be quelled. When, at the beginning of August 117 CE, Hadrian had assumed the reins of government and the country was once more at peace, justice could be handed down. The new emperor took various steps to normalize the situation. In Cyrenaica, he rebuilt the public edifices and restored law and order, earning thereby the flattering titles of "founder, provider, and legislator." He also rebuilt the towns of Egypt, especially the city of Alexandria. But before anything else, he had to see to the basic agricultural underpinning of the economy. The "granary of the Empire" had been seriously damaged. Regular grain shipments had to be resumed from Egypt to Rome and the rest of Italy. The papyri have brought to light several imperial decisions implementing a policy of assistance for the farmers of the Nile Valley. The creation of special accounts and the condemnation of the Jews who were responsible for the damage are to be placed in the same context.

The sentence condemning the Jews has not reached us directly. We have only a distant echo in a note by the Byzantine author George Syncellus (eighth/ninth century), in which he related that "Hadrian had inflicted a chastisement on the Jews who had

Emperor Hadrian *(France, Museum of Vaison-la-Romaine.)*

risen in revolt against Alexandria." The sole interest of this laconic summary lies in its confirmation of the judge's identity. As to the sentence, we can only grasp its substance by its effects. We do not know where it was handed down, nor in what terms. In any case, Hadrian was not obliged to travel to Egypt, as it was not indispensable that the indicted parties appear before the emperor himself, if indeed a fraction of them had survived the slaughter in which thousands of Jews perished, as we learn from Eusebius' source. In lawsuits concerning lèse-majesté, even the deceased could be tried. The extent of the postwar confiscations, and the fact that the Jews of Egypt had participated en masse in the rebellion, point to a penal sentence of the utmost rigor meted out to the bulk of the insurgents as well as their leaders. Their successors also fell within its shadow.

Under these conditions, the Jewish community in Egypt had practically no chance of recovery. The rare survivors, stunned by the harsh verdict of imperial justice, had become totally impoverished. Deprived of their homes and their lands, they could no longer form a nucleus for a possible reconstruction. The accounts of Roman provincial administration in Egypt throw a cold light on the tragic balance sheet of the revolt. In Alexandria and in all the rest of the country, the days of Hellenized Jewry had come to an end.

A Day of Rejoicings in Oxyrhynchos

As the second century drew to a close, in the very last months of 199 or at the beginning of 200 CE, Aurelius Horion, a wealthy Alexandrian who owned a great deal of real estate in the Oxyrhynchite nome, addressed a petition to Emperor Septimius Severus and his son Caracalla. He requested the authorization to establish a cultural fund, by donating a considerable sum of money: 10,000 Attic drachmas (the equivalent of 10,000 Roman denarii), the interest of which was to reward the winner of the annual ephebic games in Oxyrhynchos. The munificent benefactor wished to offer a prestigious gift to this large provincial town, about to become a "city" through an administrative reform that transformed the towns of Egypt into "cities" (*civitates* or *poleis*). He proposed to sponsor prizes for the young men of Oxyrhynchos, following the example of Antinoopolis, the city Hadrian founded in 130, during his visit to Egypt. We do not know the origins of Horion's fortune, but he himself was a member of the local elite. His Roman name (*nomen gentilicium*), Aurelius, attests his promotion by the reigning emperor, very probably in virtue of his high social status, to the dignity of Roman citizen, several years before the generalization of Roman citizenship by Caracalla in 212 CE.

Our benefactor was following a hallowed Hellenic tradition, which furthered the development of Greek and Roman foundations in the period of the Early Roman Empire. In antiquity as in our day, a foundation consists essentially of the apportionment of a sum of money to be spent for a specific purpose, with no temporal limitations. Its perpetuation can apply either to the capital itself or, more frequently, to the interest, as was here the case. To immortalize his memory, it is not sufficient that the founder donate the necessary funds; his project must be ratified by a superior instance, as a guaranty of its fulfillment and its durability. Thus the setting up of a foundation requires the convergence of two acts: the liberality of an individual, in the form of a donation or a will, and an official guaranty; in the Greco-Roman world, a guaranty of this kind was provided by the decree of a city or the decision of a sovereign.

And this is what we find in our document. The request that Horion, former strategus and "chief judge" (*archidikastes*) of the glorious city of Alexandria, had addressed to Septimius Severus and Caracalla, those "most gracious and most human" emperors, "benefactors of humankind," received a favorable answer in the form of a rescript, in which the original petition was also reproduced. The beginning of the request has not been well preserved, but its meaning is clear: Horion praises the Oxyrhynchites, who are to benefit by the games, destined to enhance the prestige of their city. Let us examine the list of exemplary deeds accomplished by the deserving townspeople:

> . . . and more which I pass over, but they also possess the goodwill, faithfulness, and friendship to the Romans which they exhibited in the war against the Jews, giving aid then and even now keeping the day of victory as a festival every year. You yourselves honored them when you came to Egypt, by giving them access to your tribunal first of all after the men of Pelusium. The most illustrious Laetus knows that the city possesses inhabitants of the best and most generous spirit and most just in their dealings with the treasury. For this reason I wished to leave this city in no way inferior to any in our land . . . not less than 10,000 Attic drachmas to be lent and kept according to the former regulations, the accumulated interest to be applied to the ephebic games which they hold annually, in which the inhabitants of Antinoopolis now also compete. And I ask you to forbid the use of this money for any other purpose. (OXYRHYNCHOS PAPYRUS IV 705; CPJUD. II 450)

This is not the first proof of Horion's liberality; he had already shown a lively interest in the ephebic games in Oxyrhynchos. The visit Septimius Severus and his son paid to Egypt, probably in November 199, encouraged our wealthy Alexandrian to renew his efforts. When, in the course of an inspection trip, the prefect of Egypt, Q. Maecius Laetus, stopped off in Oxyrhynchos, Aurelius Horion seized the opportunity to extol the virtues of its inhabitants who, above all by their participation in the "war against the Jews," had given the highest proof of their devotion to the imperial cause. He was referring, of course, to the events of 115–117, and chose a verb that rather pompously suggests a "military alliance" (*symmachia*). Horion's words are to be taken metaphorically since, strictly speaking, there could be no question of the inhabitants of a Roman province being the "allies of Rome." But this is no reason to have any doubts about the fact that the Greeks of Oxyrhynchos (and probably the Egyptians of the Oxyrhynchite nome as well) came to the aid of the Romans in the campaign against the Jews.

Indeed, the Oxyrhynchites were so proud of their exploit that they decided to commemorate the victory of Marcius Turbo's expeditionary force and the active role they themselves had played in the war. Many sorts of holidays were celebrated in Egypt under the Greek and Roman dominations, but this one was quite exceptional. There were religious celebrations, political holidays in honor of sovereigns and their families, and private ceremonies on the occasion of births and marriages. In all the documentation we possess, this papyrus is the only one to mention a public celebration of a "day of victory" (*hemera ton epinikion*). If we lend credence to Horion's words, it would follow that the Oxyrhynchites had been observing it faithfully for a number of years. We do not know how long they continued to do so, no more than we know whether the Oxyrhynchites were alone among the descendants of the "war veterans" to evoke the joyous day when the "impious Jews" were annihilated, or whether similar initiatives had

Young Greek notable from Roman Egypt   *Portrait from the Faiyum, 2nd century* CE *(Paris, Louvre).*

been taken by other Greek towns that had helped the Romans to quell the Jewish rebellion in Egypt.

What we do know is that Horion's project was perfectly successful. The ephebic games of Oxyrhynchos were still attested at the beginning of the fourth century CE, in the age of Constantine. As for the grant that financed them, it was still in operation a quarter-century after its ratification by imperial decision. A papyrus from Oxyrhynchos informs us that, on January 29, 225 CE, a certain Dionysios son of Dionysios, alias Harpokration, and of Theonilla, and grandson of Sarapion, was granted a loan of twelve talents and 1,700 drachmas from the fund instituted by Aurelius Horion, his sons, and Calpurnius Firmus. Thus we learn that the original fund, now under city management, had been swelled by the contributions of Aurelius Horion's sons and another local sponsor. It would be quite reasonable to assume that the "Horion & Sons and Firmus Fund" continued to prosper for many a year, greatly furthering the harmonious development both of Oxyrhynchite youth and local business.

EPILOGUE

While Aurelius Horion was busy setting up his perfectly Hellenic, i.e., perfectly pagan foundation in Oxyrhynchos, the Christian Church of Alexandria began to emerge from the shadows into which it had been plunged until then. In fact, the first Alexandrian bishop of whom we know more than just the name was Demetrios (189–232 CE), a contemporary of Clement of Alexandria and Origen. In writing of Demetrios, Eusebius of Caesarea used the two Fathers of the Church as sources. The same Eusebius had also gathered information concerning the Didaskaleion, the Catechetical School in Alexandria, and the first persecutions of Christians under Septimius Severus, at the onset of the third century. These data have been corroborated by papyrological evidence, attesting the appearance of an Alexandrian and Egyptian Christianity, heretofore of a singularly great discretion. As an epilogue to our book, we shall try to determine the links between the sudden appearance of the Alexandrian Church and the brutal disappearance of Egyptian Jewry.

The silence enveloping the origins and the destinies of Alexandrian Christianity during the first two centuries of the Roman Empire poses a problem for historians. The tradition attributing the foundation of the Alexandrian Church to Peter's disciple, Mark the Evangelist, is based on a legend dating, at the earliest, from the third century and projected backwards in time. No historical confirmation of it is possible, since the traces of a Christian presence in Alexandria during the first and second centuries are too rare and too doubtful to give it solid support. Yet it is difficult to picture that great metropolis, the spiritual capital of the Hellenistic East, as completely impervious to the message that, since the middle of the first century, was spreading out from Jerusalem through the Mediterranean area. Why was it necessary to wait until the advent of the Severi, at the turn of the second century, to see the sudden emergence of a Christian community, sprung up overnight, as if from nowhere, with its well-structured institutions, its leaders, its teachings?

Historians have spent much effort in attempting to explain this enigma. A German theologian, Walter Bauer, suggested in 1934 that it might be explained by a deviation affecting the origins of Egyptian Christianity. In his opinion, the earliest Christianity in Alexandria was heterodoxical or, more precisely, gnostic. It was dominated by the idea confronting the Creator of our material world, reputedly wicked, with the infinite goodness of a transcendent God, source of the spiritual world, the indescribable "Father of all things." He had dispatched a Savior, who would reveal to the chosen the knowledge of the divine attributes, the "gnosis" of salvation. The "orthodox" Christians reproached the Gnostics with preaching "natural" salvation, without moral effort, and condemned their doctrine. When orthodoxy had won the upper hand at the turn of the second century, the first Alexandrian Christianity, whose doctrine had been vitiated by Gnosticism, was retrospectively condemned to oblivion.

The existence of gnostic sects and doctrines at the beginning of the Empire cannot be denied, although, at that period, it is hard to discern the borderline between orthodoxy and heresy. Texts defined as gnostic, quoted by Clement and Origen, had surely been circulating in Egypt. It is equally true that up to the end of the second century, the only two Alexandrian Christians who can be named with certainty are Gnostics: Basilides, under Hadrian, and Valentinus, under Antoninus Pius. The orthodox came from abroad: Pantaenus, Clement's teacher, had come to Alexandria from Sicily, and Clement himself was an Athenian. All this, according to Bauer, was proof that Christianity on the banks of the Nile was born under the auspices of Gnosticism.

This theory provoked a critical reaction among papyrologists, especially on the part of the British scholar, Colin H. Roberts. The study of the papyri effectively shows that, for the two first centuries of the Christian era, gnostic texts of Egyptian origin do not outnumber nongnostic biblical texts. Out of fourteen papyri which date unmistakably from the second century, only one could be labeled as Gnostic. This is as much as to say that we have no better knowledge concerning Gnostics from this period than we have of "orthodox" Christians; therefore, the thesis of the Gnostic origins of Alexandrian Christianity cannot explain the silence surrounding it. Another, more convincing explanation comes to mind: if primitive Christianity had not left any marks on Egyptian soil until the end of the second century, it was because it had been annihilated along with the entire body in which it was immersed—the Jewish community of Egypt.

We are thus brought to consider the second of the two conflicting theses: it propounds the existence of a Judeo-Christianity in Alexandria, which was destroyed during the revolt of 115–117 and replaced by a Greek and Egyptian pagano-Christianity. The true explanation of the haze shrouding the beginnings of Alexandrian Christianity, which Bauer explained as the condemnation of a heterodoxy, would lie in the very strong links which, according to Roberts and his partisans, bound budding Christianity to Alexandrian Jewry. The first Christians in Egypt were Alexandrian Jews who had heeded the "Good News" emanating from Jerusalem. Together with the entire Jewish colony, of which they were a part, they were carried along into the midst of the fatal storm that was to break out some half-century later. Those who managed to survive were absorbed by the new community, recruited among Greek and Egyptian pagans.

In favor of this second thesis, we may quote the rare witnesses of a Christian presence in Alexandria during the first two centuries CE. To begin with, in his famous Letter to the Alexandrians, quoted in a previous chapter in connection with the trial of Isidoros the gymnasiarch, Emperor Claudius addressed the Jews: "Nor are they to bring in or invite Jews coming from Syria or Egypt, or I shall be forced to conceive graver suspicions. If they disobey, I shall proceed against them in every way as seeking to spread a sort of public sickness throughout the world." In a study written in 1924, upon the publication of the Letter of Claudius, Salomon Reinach interpreted these words as an allusion to Christian missionaries who had come to Egypt, causing unrest and dissensions in the Jewish community of Alexandria. Franz Cumont compared this injunction to a passage in the Acts of the Apostles (24:5) dealing with the trial of Paul of Tarsus, in which the leader of the "Nazarean sect" is presented as "a pestilent fellow [literally 'a pestilence'] and a mover of sedition among all the Jews throughout the world." The verbal coincidence between the Letter and the Acts, both of which allude to sickness and to discord, was invoked to support Reinach's idea that the Letter of Claudius might contain the "first allusion to Christianity." Were it so, this reference would also be an indication favoring the hypothesis of a current of Christianity, imported from Jerusalem ("Syria") and implanted in the midst of the Jewish community in Alexandria, as early as the beginning of Claudius' reign (41CE).

Paul himself is our second witness. In a manner of speaking, his case may be classified as one of nonappearance: Paul never came to Alexandria, where he could have spoken his native Greek tongue, although he had envisaged a trip to Spain, for which he would have had to learn Latin, a language he did not know (Epistle to the Romans, 15:24). Was Alexandria less appealing to Paul than Cadiz, Antioch, or Salamis in Cyprus? The partisans of the Judeo-Christian thesis explain this apparent lack of interest for the marvels of Alexandria by the "sharing of the missionary field" defined in the Epistle to the Galatians (2:7–9; see also Acts 15:1–21): Paul, as the "apostle of the Gentiles," and Barnabas were to preach the "Good News" to the pagans (the uncircumcised), leaving the task of preaching to the Jews to Peter, James, and John, the son of Zebadiah. The fact that Paul did not come to Alexandria would thus be a proof that the Alexandrian Christians were Judeo-Christians, falling within the bounds of the Palestinian mission.

Yet another witness from Paul's immediate entourage can be called upon to testify in favor of the Judeo-Christian thesis: a rival of Paul who had become his collaborator, an Alexandrian Jew called Apollos, a convert to Christianity and a zealous missionary (Acts 18:24f.; 1 Cor. 3:4–6; 16:12). A modern scholar may look awry upon his non-Jewish name and consider his Jewishness to be rather lax. In fact, he was following current onomastic practice among the Jews of Egypt, which, as we have seen in the cemetery of El-Ibrahimiya, began in the third century BCE and was perpetuated in the Ptolemaic documents. In regard to our present concern, the only thing we do not know about Apollos is the place where he was baptized. Was it in Ephesus where he began to preach, or was it in Alexandria, "his birthplace," as specified in a manuscript of the Acts of the Apostles from the fifth century? If we follow the latter, the man would then have been a representative of the Alexandrian Judeo-Christian colony in the first century CE.

The Judeo-Christian thesis gives a more satisfactory explanation of the "mystery" of primitive Alexandrian Christianity than does the gnostic thesis. Moreover, the two theses are not mutually exclusive. There are bridges between Gnosticism and Judeo-Christianity which could well justify their coexistence. One should not set aside the idea of a chronological succession. After the catastrophe of 115–117, an initial Judeo-Christianity would have given way to a period of pagano-Christian reconstruction, punctuated by a gnostic crisis; after having successfully overcome all heterodoxical temptations, the pagano-Christian community, at the end of the second century, could have become the basis of the antignostic "Great Church." Likewise, the dominant presence of a Judeo-Christian community in first-century Alexandria did not preclude the parallel existence of some pagano-Christian groups. This situation would tend to explain the mention of two Alexandrian gospels attested, at the latest, at the beginning of the second century: a Judeo-Christian Gospel of the Hebrews and a pagano-Christian Gospel of the Egyptians (these "Egyptians" occasionally were Greeks who did not possess Alexandrian citizenship).

In the troubled career of Egyptian Christianity, the revolt of 115–117 was, clearly, the decisive moment. It launched the irreversible process of separation of Christianity from Judaism, and was simultaneously the nodal point of continuity attaching the former to the latter.

If one accepts the disappearance, in the maelstrom of the revolt, of the Judeo-Christian community of Alexandria together with the rest of the Jewish diaspora in Egypt, then, except for a few surviving Jewish notables, one would search for its rare survivors among the Alexandrian Judeo-Christians. The pagan source of Eusebius of Caesarea recounts how the Jews were viciously attacked by the Greeks who had fallen back upon the capital, after the initial victories of the rebels in the chora. No one then thought of asking them whether they had remained Jews or had become Christians. The Jewish fugitives who had managed to escape from the slaughter joined the insurgents, only to perish by the swords of Marcius Turbo's legionaries. The Judeo-Christians, unlike their non-Christian fellows, were not carried away by the Messianic spirit of the revolt. Their Messiah had already arrived. They were in the same situation as were the Judeo-Christians of Jerusalem during the war of 66–73, who did not take part in the fray; Eusebius says that they had been "divinely informed" and left the city to take refuge in Pella, in Transjordan. We do not know whether the Alexandrian Judeo-Christians had received a similar warning. But a Messianic war had no attraction for them, any more than it had for the Judeo-Christians of Jerusalem. They avoided all involvement in the struggle and were concerned only with saving their lives and their most precious possession: their sacred books.

These considerations may perhaps explain the presence in an Egyptian provincial town, Oxyrhynchos, or in a village of the Faiyum, of the oldest known Christian manuscript, the Papyrus Rylands 457, which dates approximately from 125 CE: a leaf of a codex with a fragment of the Gospel according to John. It may well have belonged to a Judeo-Christian of Alexandria who had taken refuge in the chora. Rather than attesting a "rapid extension of Alexandrian Christianity to the Egyptian chora" (Joseph van Haelst), it would be a mute witness to the tragedy which separated the Judeo-Christians from their Jewish brothers. The salvage of a large part of the spiritual heritage of Alexandrian Judaism may also be interpreted in this light: its survival after the cataclysm is to be credited to the Judeo-Christian survivors.

That heritage was to be bequeathed to the new community of pagano-Christians. They rejected Judaism, but they preserved the masterpieces of Judeo-Alexandrian literature: the Septuagint and the works of Philo the philosopher. Is it proper to employ the terms of "appropriation" or "confiscation," as has sometimes been the case? The question is a delicate one. If the Judeo-Christians had really saved the Alexandrian Bible, then they are irreproachable. This Bible, the Holy Book of their fathers and their brothers who had remained Jewish, was also theirs. Who could blame them for sharing it, thenceforth, with their coreligionists of pagan origin, in a new fraternity?

And thus it came about that the Alexandrian Bible, fashioned by Jews for Jews, was henceforth to serve as a uniquely Christian Bible. This undeniable spiritual continuity renders only more poignant our feelings of distress, when we contemplate the gulf henceforth separating all the components of Hellenized Judaism from Christianity, after the revolt of 115–117. One can well understand the negative attitude of the rabbis toward this translation, as it had been abandoned to the Christians.

Evidence of that rupture can be seen as early as Hadrian's reign, in a text such as the Epistle of Barnabas. Set down in nongnostic circles toward 130–132 CE, it exhibits violent anti-Jewish tendencies in its treatment of the Jewish traditions it conveys. According to this text, very probably of Alexandrian origin, there had never been a Covenant between God and the people of Israel. The Pact of Sinai was broken at the same time as the Tablets of the Law that Moses, enraged by the sight of the Golden Calf, had smashed to pieces at the foot of the mountain. The true Covenant was that of Jesus, sealed in the heart of those who hope and believe in him. Origen, as quoted earlier, spoke of the misfortunes of the Jews as a well-earned punishment for "fomenting a plot against the Savior of the human race." After the disappearance of the Christians of Jewish origin, Judaism was repudiated by those of pagan origin, who soon were to claim that they and they alone were the representatives of the "True Israel." Thus, in the last analysis, the history of Hellenized Judaism in Egypt leads us to ponder the fragility of the foundations of Western civilization, a civilization often referred to as "Judeo-Christian." But that would call for another book.

Chronological Table

Rulers of Egypt and Points of Reference

The Pharaohs

Second Intermediate Period, ca. 1800–1570 BCE:

The Hyksos (Fifteenth and Sixteenth Dynasties), ca. 1730–1530

The Thebans (Seventeenth Dynasty), ca. 1650–1552

New Kingdom (Eighteenth–Twentieth Dynasties) 1552–1069

EIGHTEENTH DYNASTY, 1552–1295:

Ahmosis, ca. 1550: expulsion of the Hyksos

Amenhotep (Amenophis) I, 1526–1506: rapid social and economic development

Thutmosis III (and Queen Hatshepsut), 1479–1425

Amenhotep (Amenophis) III , 1390–1352: zenith of the New Kingdom

Amenhotep (Amenophis) IV, then Akhenaton, 1352–1336: religious reform

Tutenkhamon 1336–1327: decline of the Kingdom

Horemheb, 1323–1295: order restored

NINETEENTH DYNASTY, 1295–1188:

Rameses I, 1295–1294

Sethos I, 1294–1279: temple of Seth at Avaris in the Delta; war against the Hittites

Rameses II, 1279–1212: new capital at Pi-Rameses; departure of the Hebrews from Egypt (ca. 1270?); battle at Qadesh-on-the-Orontes and peace with the Hittites

Mineptah, 1212–1202, fought the Libyans and the Peoples of the Sea; "stele of Israel" (1207)

Amenmesses, Sethos II, Siptah, Queen Twosre, 1202–1188: decline of the Nineteenth Dynasty.

TWENTIETH DYNASTY, 1188–1069:

Sethnakhte, 1188–1186, founder of the Twentieth Dynasty

Rameses III, 1186–1154, saved Egypt from the invasion of the Peoples of the Sea

From Rameses IV to Rameses XI, 1154–1069: internal strife

Third Intermediate Period (Twenty-first–Twenty-fourth Dynasties), 1069–715:

Smendes (Twenty-first Dynasty), 1069–1043: capital at Tanis

Siamun, 978–959: friendly relations with Solomon, king of Israel

Libyan Princes: Shoshenq I (Twenty-second Dynasty) 945–924, pillaged the kingdoms of Israel and Judah and received tribute from Roboam, king of Judah

Bocchoris (Twenty-fourth Dynasty), 720–715

Ethiopians and Saites (Twenty-fifth and Twenty-sixth Dynasties):

Ethiopian rule (Twenty-fifth Dynasty), 747–664

Psammetichus I (Twenty-sixth Dynasty), 664–610: Saitic renaissance; first Judean soldiers in Egypt (?)

Necho II, 610–595: conquered by Nebuchadnezzar at Karkemish, in Syria (605)

Psammetichus II, 595–589: expedition to Nubia (kingdom of Kush)

Apries, 589–570: increasing Greek influence

Amasis, 570–526: founding, in the Delta, of Naucratis, a Greek trading post, afterwards a city

Psammetichus III, 526–525, lost Egypt to the Persians.

Persian Achaemenids (Twenty-seventh Dynasty), 525–405:

Cambyses II, 530–522: conquered Egypt in 525

Darius I, the Great, 522–486: reconstruction of the Temple of Jerusalem (520–515)

Xerxes I, 486–465: birth of Mibtahyah, daughter of Mahseiah, in Elephantine (ca. 480)

Artaxerxes I, 465–424: first mission of Nehemiah in Jerusalem (445); Herodotus in Egypt (ca. 450)

Darius II, 424–405: sack of the Jewish temple in Elephantine (410)

Last indigenous dynasties (Twenty-eighth–Thirtieth), 405–343:

Amyrtaeus (Twenty-eighth Dynasty), 405–399, leader of the rebellion against the Persians

Nepherites I (Twenty-ninth Dynasty), 399–393: last Aramaic document from Elephantine

Nectanebo I (Thirtieth Dynasty), 380–363, repulsed the Persian army (373)

Teos, 363–360

Nectanebo II, 360–343

Second Persian rule, 343–332:

Artaxerxes III, 359–338; reconquered Egypt in 343

Arses, 338–336

Darius III, 336–330: end of the Persian empire

Last indigenous ruler:

Khababash, 333–332.

ALEXANDER AND THE PTOLEMIES, 332–30 BCE

Alexander the Great, 332–323: Alexander in Jerusalem, 332(?); foundation of Alexandria, spring of 331; first Jewish settlements in the new capital

Philip Arrhidaeus, half-brother of Alexander the Great, 323–316

Alexander IV, son of Alexander the Great and Roxana, 316–305

Ptolemy I Soter I, 305–282 (satrap since June 323): Palestine under Ptolemaic hegemony, 320–200

Ptolemy II Philadelphus, son of Ptolemy I and Berenice I, 282–246 (shared power with his father from 285): Greek translation of the Torah in Alexandria

Ptolemy III Euergetes I, son of Ptolemy II and Arsinoe II (sister-wife), "the Brother-and-Sister gods," 246–222: first consecrations of synagogues

Ptolemy IV Philopator, son of Ptolemy III and Berenice II, "the Benefactor gods," 222–205: wars against Antiochus IV; miracle at the hippodrome in Alexandria

Ptolemy V Epiphanes, son of Ptolemy IV and Arsinoe III, "the Father-loving gods," 204–180

Ptolemy VI Philometor, son of Ptolemy V and Cleopatra I, "the Manifest gods," 180–170

Ptolemy VI Philometor, Cleopatra II Philometor and Ptolemy VIII Euergetes II, called Physkon, "The Big-Bellied" (the children of Ptolemy Epiphanes), 170–164: Maccabean crisis (167–164); Onias IV and Jewish temple in Leontopolis (ca. 165?)

Ptolemy VIII Euergetes II alone, 164/163

Ptolemy VI Philometor (restored) and Cleopatra II, 164–146

Ptolemy VII Neos Philopator, son of Ptolemy VI and Cleopatra II, 145 (?)

Ptolemy VIII Euergetes II, restored, with Cleopatra II (his sister) and Cleopatra III (his niece), 145–116

Cleopatra III Euergetes and Ptolemy IX Soter II Lathyros, son of Ptolemy VIII, 116–107

Cleopatra III Euergetes and Ptolemy X Alexander I, son of Ptolemy VIII, 107–101

Ptolemy X Alexander I and Cleopatra Berenice, 101–88

Ptolemy IX Soter II, restored, 88–81

Cleopatra Berenice and Ptolemy XI Alexander II (her son), 80

Ptolemy XII Neos Dionysos (Auletes), 80–58

Berenice IV and Cleopatra VI Tryphaena, daughters of Ptolemy XII, 58–56

Berenice IV and her husband Archelaos, 56–55

Ptolemy XII Neos Dionysos (Auletes), restored, 55–51

Cleopatra VII Philopator, daughter of Ptolemy XII, 51–30: Julius Caesar in Egypt, 48; meeting with Mark Antony, 41; end of the Ptolemaic monarchy, August, 30 BCE.

EARLY ROMAN EMPIRE

The Julio-Claudians:

Augustus, August 30 BCE–August 14 CE: took Alexandria, early in August, 30 BCE

Tiberius, August 14–March 37

Caligula, March 37–January 41: Herod Agrippa I, king of Judea and Samaria (37); massacre of the Jews in Alexandria (summer 38); mission of Alexandrian Jews to Rome

Claudius, January 41–October 54: trial of Isidoros and "Letter to the Alexandrians"

Nero, October 54–June 68

Galba, Othon, Vitellius, June 68–December 69

The Flavians:

Vespasian, July 69–June 79: Jewish war (66–73); capture of Jerusalem by the Romans and destruction of the Second Temple (70); destruction of the Jewish sanctuary at Leontopolis (73)

Titus, June 79–September 81

Domitian, September 81–September 96

The Antonines:

Nerva, September 96–January 98

Trajan, January 98–August 117: Jewish rebellion, 115–117

Hadrian, August 117–July 138: revolt of Bar-Kokhba, 132–135

CALENDAR

The Egyptian year was made up of twelve months of thirty days each, followed by five "epagomenal" (*epagomenai* = supplementary) days for a total of 365. The actual length of the solar year, as we know, is 365 and 1/4 days (more precisely 365 days, 5 hours, 48 minutes and almost 46 seconds). The resulting discrepancy between the calendar reckoning and real time increases at the rate of one day every four years; after 40 years, there is a ten-day gap, after 120 years, a thirty-day gap, and so forth, until the end of a period of 1460 (4 × 365) years, when a new "coincidence" occurs. The Egyptians were able to adjust this mobile (or "vague") year to the solar year, by taking note of a cyclic astronomic phenomenon: once every year (on the nineteenth of July, according to the Julian calendar), the fixed star Sothis (Sirius) becomes visible on the horizon precisely at dawn, just before sunrise (the heliacal rising). Its appearance was considered vital by the Egyptians, as they believed it was the signal for the annual Nile floods, which began about that time. The few documents in our possession, recording the heliacal rising of Sothis, mentioning the day, the month and the year of the reigning monarch, have enabled us to establish, with a four-year margin of error, the chronology of the Egyptian rulers.

The year remained mobile under the Ptolemies; the Greeks promptly adopted the Egyptian calendar. Soon after the Romans conquered Egypt, they stabilized the system. The year, henceforth, began on the twenty-ninth of August (first of Thot), but every fourth year, it began on the thirtieth of August: at the end of each calendar year preceding the Roman leap year, according to the Roman calendar reformed by Julius Caesar (the Julian calendar), a sixth *epagomene* was added; the one-day discrepancy thus inserted disappeared on the first of March, the twenty-ninth of February of the Roman leap year having already been accounted for, as the sixth epagomene of the preceding year of the Egyptian calendar.

In the following table, the twelve months of the Egyptian calendar are given, with their Julian equivalents. The Macedonian names for these months and the one-day difference for the years preceding the Julian leap year (multiples of four) are indicated in parentheses.

1. Thot (Dios): from 29 (30) August to 27 (28) September
2. Phaophi (Apellaios): from 28 (29) September to 27 (28) October
3. Hathyr (Audnaios): from 28 (29) October to 26 (27) November
4. Choiak (Peritios): from 27 (28) November to 26 (27) December
5. Tybi (Dystros): from 27 (28) December to 25 (26) January
6. Mecheir (Xandikos): from 26 (27) January 24 (25) February
7. Phamenoth (Artemisios): from 25 (26) February to 26 March
8. Pharmuthi (Daisios): from 27 March to 25 April
9. Pachon (Panemos): from 26 April to 25 May
10. Payni (Loios): from 26 May to 24 June
11. Epeiph (Gorpiaios): from 25 June to 24 July
12. Mesore (Hyperberetaios): from 25 July to 23 August

Epagomenai (additional days): from 24 to 28 (29) August.

For the Aramaic documents, we list the names of the months in the Babylonian (lunisolar) calendar, adopted by the Jews at the end of the seventh century BCE and still in use today; an important modification was introduced in 344 CE, when the New Year, which formerly began in the spring, was moved to the first day of Tishri, in the autumn:

1. Nisan
2. Iyyar
3. Sivan
4. Tammuz
5. Av
6. Elul
7. Tishri
8. Heshvan (Marheshvan)
9. Kislev
10. Tevet
11. Shevat
12. Adar

Monetary Units and Units of Measure

Money

Persian, Western Semitic, Egyptian:

1 zuz = 1/2 shekel

1 shekel (weights of the king) = 1 kiteh (weights of Ptah)

piece of ten (10 shekels) = 1 karsh.

Greek:

1 obol = 8 chalkoi (bronze coins)

1 silver drachma (ca. 3.6 g) = 6 obols

4 drachmas = 1 tetradrachm (1 denarius)

4 silver drachmas (ca. 14.5 g) = 1 stater

100 drachmas = 1 mina (unit of monetary reckoning)

6,000 drachmas = 1 talent (unit of monetary reckoning).

Measures

Length:

1 foot = ca. 0.30 m

1 cubit = 1 foot and a half = ca. 0.45 m

1 stade = 400 cubits or 600 feet = ca. 180 m

Volume:

1 choenix = ca. 1 liter or 1 quart

1 artaba = 29 to 40 choenices (29 to 40 liters)

Area:

1 aroura = 0.2756 hectares (= 0.681 acres), in the Ptolemaic period, and 0.2025 hectares in the Roman period.

A thicket of papyrus

GLOSSARY

Alabarch (gr. *alabarches* or *arabarches*):   inspector-in-chief of the customs duties collected on the Eastern (Arab) side of the Nile.

Amora (hebr. "scholar"):   term specifying Jewish scholars in Palestine and Babylonia in the third through the sixth centuries CE. The amoraim expounded the Mishnah (see Talmud).

Athlophoros (Gr. "she who bears the prize"):   priestess of the royal Ptolemaic cult.

Calamus (Gr. *kalamos*, "reed," "stubble," "straw"; pl. *calami*):   a sharpened reed for writing on papyrus.

Chora (Gr. "country"):   Egypt, in contrast to Alexandria.

Cleruch (Gr. *kleroukhos*, "who possesses the parcel"):   military colonist, provided with a parcel of land (*kleros*).

Demotic (Gr. "popular"):   cursive Egyptian script in use since the seventh century BCE, corresponding to the state of the language at that time; it was currently employed throughout the Persian, Greek, and Roman periods, in parallel with hieroglyphics, whose use was thenceforth restricted to inscriptions on stone.

Diagramma (Gr.; plur. *diagrammata*):   royal regulation.

Diaspora (Gr. "dispersion"):   Jewish communities settled outside the Land of Israel.

Dioiketes (Gr. "administrator"):   high-ranking Ptolemaic official, a kind of minister of finance and economy.

Epiphanes (Gr. "who shows himself"):   "Visible" or "Manifest," royal epithet.

Epistates (Gr. "officer"):   Ptolemaic civil or military official.

Euergetes (Gr. "benefactor"):   benefactor (patron, sponsor), or "Benefactor," royal epithet.

Gymnasiarch (Gr. *gymnasiarkhos*, "in charge of the gymnasium"): notable charged with the provision of funds for the upkeep of a gymnasium, particularly the provision of oil, and with the management of the gymnastic games; the Alexandrian gymnasiarchs represented their city, whose council (*boule*) was suppressed by Augustus.

Halakhah (Hebr. "rule of conduct"): the body of moral and legal rules governing the comportment of a Jew who is respectful of the Law.

Hanukkah (Hebr. "dedication"): holiday commemorating the purification of the Temple of Jerusalem by Judah Maccabee during the winter (Kislev 25) of 164 BCE.

Hypocoristic (from Gr. *hypokorizomai*: "call by soft names"): diminutive, endearing or pet name.

Kanephoros (Gr. "she who carries the basket"): priestess of the royal Ptolemaic cult.

Kleros (Gr. "parcel"; plur. *kleroi*): parcel of land with which a military colonist (cleruch) was provided.

Kohen (Hebr.; plur. *kohanim*): priest; the kohanim are supposed to be the direct male descendants of Aaron, the elder brother of Moses, who was the first high priest of the Hebrews.

Koine (Gr. "common," scil. *dialexis*, "tongue, speech"): the Greek language spoken and written in Hellenistic times; by analogy, "legal koine": Greek common law practiced at that period.

Kosher (Hebr. "true, in accordance, in keeping with"): food in keeping with Jewish dietary prescriptions.

Menorah (Hebr. "chandelier, candelabrum"): great golden seven-branched candelabrum in the Temple of Jerusalem (in the Temple of Onias at Leontopolis, its place was occupied by a golden lamp); it served as a model for the candelabra of the houses of prayer, tombs, etc; it became the most well-known symbol of Judaism in antiquity; today it is the emblem of the State of Israel.

Midrash (from Hebr. *darash*, "to study, to explain"; plur. midrashim): exegetic explanation of the Oral Law; the principal collections of midrashim were set down between the fourth and the twelfth century CE.

Mishnah (from Hebr. *shana*, "to repeat"): Oral Law taught by the sages and collected at the beginning of the third century CE by Rabbi Judah ha-Nassi ("The Patriarch"); the Mishnah forms the core around which the commentary of the Talmud is wound.

Nome (Gr. *nomós*, "part," "portion"): administrative unit; Egypt was divided into some forty nomes, which were placed under the authority of a strategus (*strategos*) during the Greek and Roman periods.

Nomos (Gr. *nómos*, "rule of conduct," plur. *nomoi*): legal rule or ruling.

Ostracon (Gr. "shell, shard"; plur. ostraca): in Egypt, shards of pottery upon which bills, receipts, etc., were written.

Papyrus (Gr. and Lat.): Egyptian plant of the family of sedges, or *Cyperaceae* (*Cyperus Papyrus*), with a tall triangular stem and a feathery crown. Formed into scrolls or sheets, it was the principal substance for carrying the written word during Antiquity.

Passover (Hebr. *Pesah*): yearly spring feast commemorating the departure of the Hebrews from Egypt.

Philadelphus (Gr. *philadelphos*): "who loves her brother," "who loves his sister," royal epithet.

Philometor (Gr.): "who loves his mother," royal epithet.

Philopator (Gr.): "who loves his father," royal epithet.

Politeuma (Gr. "administration of public affairs"): organization of immigrants of the same (non-Egyptian) ethnic origin; it had a measure of autonomy, but did not possess the status of a body of citizens.

Prefect of Egypt (Lat. *praefectus Alexandreae et Aegypti*): high administrator of equestrian rank, charged with the government of Roman Egypt.

Prostagma (Gr.; plur. *prostagmata*): royal edict.

Purim (Hebr. "lots"): holiday commemorating the deliverance of Jews from annihilation planned by the Persian official Haman (Haman cast lots to fix the date for the massacre of the Jews, thus the name of Purim), as recorded in the Book of Esther (*Megillat Ester*).

Rabbi (Aram. *rabbi*, "my master"): doctor of Law, learned in the interpretation of the Torah, both written and oral (abbreviated R. = Rabbi or Rav), spiritual leader and guide in Jewish communities.

Ribbit (Hebr. "interest"): interest; by extension, prohibition of interest in loans between Jews.

Sabbath: day of rest for the Jews, from sunset Friday to sunset Saturday, consecrated exclusively to prayer and the study of the Torah.

Sages of the Talmud (the rabbis, Wise Men): the tannaim who formulated the rules of the Mishnah during the first and second centuries CE, and the amoraim who commented upon them in the Gemara during the three following centuries.

Sanhedrin (from Gr. *synedrion*, "assembly in session"): assembly of 71 members—priests, elders, and scribes, with political, legal, afterwards religious authority—located in Jerusalem since the first century BCE.

Satrap (Old Pers. *xshasapavan*; Gr. *satrapes*: "overseer of territory"): governor of a province (satrapy) in the Persian Empire.

Second Commonwealth (Second Temple): period of Jewish history in Persian, then in Greco-Roman times, which began with the return from captivity in Babylon at the end of the sixth century BCE, and ended with the great catastrophes of the Flavian period (the destruction of the Temple by Titus in 70 CE) and the period of the Antonines (the revolt of 115–117 and that of Bar Kochba, suppressed by Hadrian in 135 CE).

Seder (Hebr. "order"): family repast held on the first evening of Passover, which follows a traditional order; during the Seder, the Haggadah of Pesah, describing and explaining the meaning of the departure of the Jews from the land of Egypt, is read aloud by the participants.

Soter (Gr. "savior"): "Savior," royal epithet.

Strategus (Gr. *strategos*, leader of a army): military leader, then civic administrator placed at the head of each nome.

Sukkot (Hebr. "tabernacles," "tents"): "feast of Tents" (or "of Booths"), celebrated each autumn by the Jews, who live for seven successive days in small tabernacles made of branches, in remembrance of the sojourn in the desert.

Talmud (Hebr. "teaching," "study"): collection of teachings of the ancient rabbis, in Hebrew and in Aramaic, in two versions: the Talmud of Jerusalem (fifth century CE) and the Talmud of Babylon (sixth century CE), three times as large as the first; the Talmud is composed of a normative part, the Mishnah, divided into six "orders," and an analytic part, the Gemara, a commentary on the Mishnah.

Tanna (from Aram. *teni*, "to teach"; plur. *tannaim*): sage of the Mishnah (first–second centuries CE); the tannaim were the representatives of the Jewish people in their dealings with the Roman authorities.

Targum (Hebr. "translated"): Aramaic paraphrase of the Hebrew Bible.

Tetragrammaton (Gr. "four letters"): the four letters of the Hebrew alphabet forming the Divine Name; since the Name was not to be pronounced, the Hebrew or Greek word meaning "the Lord" was substituted when the Bible was read aloud.

Theophoric (Gr. *theophoros*, "who bears a god"): name of a person, which includes that of a divinity; e.g., Mibtahiah: "The Lord is my assurance," Apollodoros: "gift of Apollo," etc.

Torah (Hebr. "teaching," "doctrine"): the Pentateuch, i.e., the first five books of the biblical canon (Genesis, Exodus, Leviticus, Numbers, Deuteronomy); Jewish tradition distinguishes between the "written Torah" and the "oral Torah," transmitted by the Talmud and other, nonbiblical works.

Tosefta (Aram. "addition"): Tannaitic work that parallels and supplements the Mishnah (second century CE).

BIBLIOGRAPHY

The following list is mainly of titles available in English. Some exceptions are made for works published in other languages, quoted or alluded to in the text, as well as for the writer's previous research.

MANUALS AND GUIDES

GENERAL SURVEYS: L. Finkelstein, ed., *The Jews. Their History, Culture, and Religion*, 2 vols., New York, 1949; 3d ed. 1960; S. W. Baron, *A Social and Religious History of the Jews*, 1–2, revised ed., New York, 1952. More recently, for the general reader: N. de Lange, *Atlas of the Jewish World*, Oxford and New York, 1984; P. Johnson, *A History of the Jews*, New York, 1987.

ANCIENT ISRAEL: J. Rogerson and P. Davies, *The Old Testament World*, Cambridge, 1989; R. E. Clements, ed., *The World of Ancient Israel. Sociological, Anthropological and Political Perspectives*, Cambridge, 1989.

PHARAONIC EGYPT: A. H. Gardiner, *Egypt of the Pharaohs*, Oxford, 1961; N. Grimal, *A History of Ancient Egypt*, Oxford, 1992 (orig. pub. Paris, 1988).

GRECO-ROMAN EGYPT: H. I. Bell, *Egypt from Alexander the Great to the Arab Conquest*, Oxford, 1948; A. K. Bowman, *Egypt after the Pharaohs, 332BC–AD 642. From Alexander to the Arab Conquest*, Berkeley, 1986.

HELLENISTIC WORLD: W. Tarn & G. T. Griffith, *Hellenistic Civilization*, London, 1927; 3d ed. 1952, repr. 1953 and 1974; C. B. Welles, *Alexander and the Hellenistic World*, Toronto, 1970; S. M. Burstein, *The Hellenistic Age from the Battle of Ipsos to the Death of Kleopatra VII*, Cambridge, 1985 (Translated Documents of Greece and Rome, 3).

PAPYROLOGY: E. G. Turner, *Greek Papyri. An Introduction*, Oxford, 1968; 2nd ed. 1980; P. W. Pestman, *The New Papyrological Primer*, Leyden, 1990, 2nd ed., 1994; J. F. Oates, R. S. Bagnall, W. H. Willis, and K. A. Worp, *Checklist of Editions of Greek and Latin Papyri, Ostraca and Tablets*, 4th ed., Atlanta, 1992 (Bulletin of the American Society of Papyrologists, Supplement 7).

JEWISH HISTORY IN THE SECOND TEMPLE PERIOD: Large syntheses: E. Schürer, *The History of the Jewish People in the Age of Jesus Christ (175 BC–AD 135)*, a new English version revised and edited by G. Vermes, F. Millar and M. Goodman, 3 vols., Edinburgh, 1973–87 (based on the 2nd German edition, 1886–90); *Compendia Rerum Iudaicarum ad Novum Testamentum*, Philadelphia, since 1974: I/1–2, S. Safrai and M. Stern, eds., *The Jewish People in the First Century*, 1974–76; II/2, M. Stone, ed., *Jewish Writings of the Second Temple Period*, 1984; II/3a, S. Safrai and P. J. Tomson, *The Literature of the Sages*, 1987; W. D. Davies and L. Finkelstein, eds., *The Cambridge Ancient History of Judaism*, I: *The Persian Period*, and II: *The Hellenistic Age*, Cambridge, 1984 and 1990. For the general reader: E. Bickerman, *From Ezra to the Last Maccabees. Foundations of Postbiblical Judaism*, 7th ed., New York, 1962; Shaye J. D. Cohen, *From the Maccabees to the Mishnah*, Philadelphia, 1987; L. Grabbe, *Judaism from Cyrus to Hadrian*, I–II, Minneapolis, 1992.

JEWS AND GREEKS: V. Tcherikover, *Hellenistic Civilization and the Jews*, Philadelphia and Jerusalem, 1959; 2nd ed., 1961 (English rev. ed. by S. Applebaum of the Hebrew original, Tel Aviv, 1930–31; rev. Hebrew ed. 1963); A. Momigliano, *Alien Wisdom. The Limits of Hellenization*, Cambridge, 1975; M. Hengel, *Jews, Greeks and Barbarians. Aspects of the Hellenization of Judaism in the Pre-Christian Period*, Philadelphia, 1980 (orig. pub. Stuttgart, 1976); E. Bickerman, *Studies in Jewish and Christian History*, I–III, Leyden, 1976–86; idem, *The Jews in the Greek Age*, Cambridge, Mass., and London, 1988; S. Talmon, ed., *Jewish Civilization in the Hellenistic-Roman Period*, Sheffield, 1991 (Journal for the Study of the Pseudepigrapha, Supplement Series, 10); L. H. Feldman, *Jew and Gentile in the Ancient World*, Princeton, NJ, 1993.

JEWISH DIASPORAS IN THE HELLENISTIC AND ROMAN PERIODS: U. Rappaport, "Jews in Egypt," in M. Stern, ed., *The Diaspora in the Hellenistic and Roman World* (Hebrew), Jerusalem, 1983, pp. 21–53; R. J. Coggins, "The Origins of the Jewish Diaspora," in R. E. Clements, ed., *The World of Ancient Israel*, Cambridge, 1989, pp. 163–81; H. Hagermann, "The Diaspora in the Hellenistic Age," in *The Cambridge History of Judaism*, vol. 2, pp. 115–66; J. Lieu, J. North, and T. Rajak, eds., *The Jews among Pagans and Christian in the Roman Empire*, London and New York, 1992; S. J. D. Cohen and E. S. Frerichs, eds., *Diasporas in Antiquity*, Atlanta, 1993 (Brown Judaic Studies, 288).

THE JEWS IN EGYPT: One may still usefully consult the synthesis supplied by Victor Tcherikover in his "Prolegomena" to vol. I (1957) of the *Corpus Papyrorum Judaicarum* (pp. 1–111). A. Kasher, *The Jews in Hellenistic and Roman Egypt. The Struggle for Equal Rights*, Tübingen, 1985 (Texte u. Studien z. Antiken Judentum, 7), English version of a doctoral thesis (Tel Aviv, 1972; orig. pub. Hebrew, 1978), concentrates on the Judeo-pagan conflict in Alexandria under Roman rule. The outlines of the present book have been sketched in J. Mélèze Modrzejewski, "Splendeurs grecques et misères romaines. Les Juifs d'Egypte dans l'Antiquité," in J. Hassoun, ed., *Juifs du Nil*, Paris, 1981, pp. 15–49 (and bibliography, pp. 281–82); 2nd ed., *Histoire des Juifs du Nil*, Paris, 1990, pp. 15–45 (bibliography, pp. 223–29).

SOURCES AND BIBLIOGRAPHIES

BIBLICAL TEXTS are quoted in the version of *The Holy Scriptures According to the Masoretic Text. A New Translation*, Philadelphia, 1917 (and subsequent editions).

ARCHIVES FROM ELEPHANTINE: A. Cowley, *Aramaic Papyri of the Fifth Century* BC, Oxford, 1923, and E. G. Kraeling, *The Brooklyn Museum Aramaic Papyri*, New Haven, 1953 (in the present work citations to Cowley and Kraeling are followed by the number of the document); English translations according to B. Porten and A. Yardeni, *Textbook of Aramaic Documents from Ancient Egypt* (cited here as Textbook), vol. 1–3, Jerusalem, 1986–93 (Hebrew University, Department of the History of Jewish People, Texts and Studies for Students); vol. 4, in preparation, is devoted to ostraca.

GREEK PAPYRI AND INSCRIPTIONS CONCERNING JEWS AND JUDAISM: V. Tcherikover, in collaboration with A. Fuks and M. Stern, *Corpus Papyrorum Judaicarum*, 3 vols., Jerusalem and Cambridge, Mass., 1957–64 (cited here as CPJud.). A special section of this Corpus (vol. 3, Appendix 1), based on vol. 2 of J.-B. Frey's *Corpus Inscriptionum Judaicarum*, Vatican, 1952 (CIJ), is devoted to "The Jewish Inscriptions from Egypt"; a new collection is now available in W. Horbury and D. Noy, *Jewish Inscriptions from Graeco-Roman Egypt. With an Index of Jewish Inscriptions of Cyrenaica*, Cambridge, 1992; in the present work references are given both to CIJ II and to Horbury and Noy.

PAPYROLOGICAL AND EPIGRAPHICAL TEXTS CONCERNING EARLY CHRISTIANITY AND ITS BACKGROUND: G. H. R. Horsley, ed., *New Documents Illustrating Early Christianity, A Review of the Greek Inscriptions and Papyri* (Ancient History Documentary Research Center, Macquarie University, North Ryde, Australia), since 1981.

BIBLICAL PAPYRI: J. van Haelst, *Catalogue des papyrus littéraires juifs et chrétiens*, Paris, 1976.

JEWISH LITERATURE OF THE SECOND TEMPLE PERIOD: J. H. Charlesworth, ed., *The Old Testament Pseudepigrapha*, 2 vols., New York, 1983; C. R. Holladay, *Fragments from Hellenistic Jewish Authors*, I. *The Historians*, Chico, Calif., 1983.

PAGAN AUTHORS: M. Stern, *Greek and Latin Authors on Jews and Judaism*, 3 vols., Jerusalem, 1974–84.

BIBLIOGRAPHIES: R. Marcus, "A Selected Bibliography (1920–1945) on the Jews in the Hellenistic-Roman Period," *Proceedings of the American Academy of Jewish Research* 16, 1946–47, pp. 97–181, continued by U. Rappaport and his collaborators: U. Rappaport, "Bibliography of Works on Jewish History in the Persian, Hellenistic and Roman Periods, 1946–1970," *Studies in the History of the Jewish People and the Land of Israel 2*, Haifa, 1972, pp. 247–321; U. Rappaport and M. Mor, *Bibliography of Works on Jewish History in the Hellenistic and Roman Periods, 1971–1975*, Jerusalem, 1976; M. Mor and U. Rappaport, *Bibliography of Works on Jewish History in the Hellenistic and Roman Periods, 1976–1980*, Jerusalem, 1982; D. Dimant, M. Mor, and U. Rappaport, *Bibliography of Works on Jewish History in the Hellenistic and Roman Periods, Publications of the Years 1981–1985*, Jerusalem, 1987; M. Mor and U. Rappaport, "A Survey of 25 Years (1960–1985) of Israeli Scholarship on Jewish History in the Second Temple Period (539 BCE–135 CE)," *Biblical Theology Bulletin* 16, no. 2, 1986, pp. 56–72.

PHILO: R. Radice and D. T. Runia et al., *Philo of Alexandria. An Annotated Bibliography 1937–1986*, Leyden, 1988 (continuing H. G. Goodhart and E. R. Goodenough, *General Bibliography of Philo Judaeus*, 1938).

JOSEPHUS: L. H. Feldman, *Josephus and Modern Scholarship (1937–1980)*, Berlin and New York, 1984; idem, *Josephus. A Supplementary Bibliography*, New York and London, 1986.

CURRENT BIBLIOGRAPHIES: *Bulletin of Judaeo–Greek Studies*, ed. N. de Lange and J. Humphrey (University of Cambridge, Faculty of Oriental Studies).

PAPYROLOGICAL MATERIAL AND NEW DATA ON JEWS IN EGYPT: J. Mélèze Modrzejewski, papyrological surveys in *Revue historique de droit français et étranger* (Paris), since 1962; in *Archiv für Papyrusforschung und verwandte Gebiete* (Leipzig), 1976–78, for the years 1962–72, and 1985–88, for 1972–82; in *Studia et Documenta Historiae et Iuris* (Rome) 1975–83, for the years 1970–82, continued in *Journal of Juristic Papyrology* (Warsaw), since 1990 (in progress).

The Dawn: Pharaohs and Great Kings

1. Biblical Egypt

JOSEPH AND HIS BROTHERS. *'APIRU-HABIRU*: M. Greenberg, *The Hab/piru*, New Haven, 1955. *APER EL, VIZIR OF AMENOPHIS III*: A. Zivie, *Découverte à Saqqarah. Le vizir oublié*, Paris 1990. *THE SHOSU*: R. Giveon, ed., *Les Bédouins Shosou des documents égyptiens*, Leyden, 1971. *THE HYKSOS*: J. van Sters, *The Hyksos*, New Haven, 1966.

MOSES AND THE PHARAOH. C. Houtman, *Exodus*, Vol. I, Kampen, 1993 (Historical Commentary on the Old Testament). *RAMSES II*: K. A. Kitchen, *Pharaoh Triumphant. The Life and Times of Ramses II*, Warminster, 1982. *THE "PLAGUES"*: L. Schmidt, *Beobachtungen zu der Plagenerzählung in Exodus VII, 14–XI, 10*, Leyden, 1990. *MINEPTAH'S CAMPAIGNS*: F. J. Yurco, "Merneptah's Canaanite Campaign," *Journal of American Research Center in Egypt* 23, 1986, pp. 189–215; idem, "Merneptah, Portrayer of Israel; 3,200 Year-Old Picture of Israelites found in Egypt," *Biblical Archaeological Review*, Oct. 1990, pp. 20–37 (dissociating the Exodus and the "stele of Israel").

THE DESERT ROAD. E. W. Nicholson, *Exodus and Sinai in History and Tradition*, Oxford, 1973. *THE DECALOGUE*: A. Alt, *Die Ursprünge des Israelitischen Rechts*, Leipzig, 1924 (English trans. in *Essays on Old Testament History and Religion*, Oxford, 1966).

2. The Stronghold of Elephantine

A JUDEAN COLONY IN EGYPT. *NUBIAN CAMPAIGN OF PSAMMETICHUS II*: J. Yoyotte and S. Sauneron, "La campagne nubienne de Psammétique II et sa signification historique," *Bulletin de l' Institut français d'Archéologie Orientale* 50, 1952, pp. 195–207. *GRAFFITI IN ABU-SIMBEL*: A. Bernand and O. Masson, "Les inscriptions grecques d'Abou-Simbel," *Revue des études grecques* 70, 1957, pp. 1–20.

MIBTAHIAH AND HER HUSBANDS. B. Porten, *Archives from Elephantine. The Life of an Ancient Jewish Military Colony*, Berkeley, 1968. *CHRONOLOGY*: B. Porten, "The Calendar of Aramaic Texts from Achaemenid and Ptolemaic Egypt," in S. Shaked and A. Netzer, eds., *Irano-Judaica* 2, Jerusalem, 1990, pp. 13–32. *LEGAL PROBLEMS*: R. Yaron, *Introduction to the Law of the Aramaic Papyri*, Oxford, 1961; Y. Muffs, *Studies in the Aramaic Legal Papyri from Elephantine*, Leyden, 1969; 2nd ed. New York, 1973.

"GOD OF HEAVEN" AND GOD OF THE FLOODS. A. Dupont-Sommer, "Les dieux et les hommes en l'île d'Eléphantine, près d'Assouan, au temps de l'Empire des Perses," *Comptes rendus de l'Académie des Inscriptions et Belles-Lettres*, Paris, 1978, pp. 756–72 (with bibliography).

The Zenith: Ptolemaic Egypt

3. Alexandrian Judaism and Its Problems

ALEXANDER AND THE CONQUEST OF THE EAST: W. W. Tarn, *Alexander the Great*, Cambridge, 1948; J. Mélèze Modrzejewski, *Alexander the Macedonian*, Tel Aviv, 1961 (in Hebrew); D. W. Engels, *Alexander the Great and the Logistics of the Macedonian Army*, Berkeley, 1978; A. B. Bosworth,

Conquest and Empire. The Reign of Alexander the Great, Cambridge, 1993. *ALEXANDER AND THE JEWS:* S. J. D. Cohen, "Alexander the Great and Jaddus the High Priest according to Josephus," *Association for Jewish Studies Review* 7/8 (1982/83), 1987, pp. 41–68. *IMAGE OF THE JEW:* J. Mélèze Modrzejewski, "The Image of the Jew in Greek Thought towards 300 BCE," in A. Kasher, G. Fuks, and U. Rappaport, eds., *Greece and Rome in Eretz-Israel. Collected Essays*, Jerusalem, 1989, pp. 3–14 (in Hebrew), and 1990, pp. 105–18 (in French).

CAN ONE BE BOTH JEWISH AND GREEK? *PTOLEMAIC ALEXANDRIA:* P. M. Fraser, *Ptolemaic Alexandria*, 3 vols., Oxford, 1972. *DOSITHEOS SON OF DRIMYLOS:* A. Fuks, "Dositheos Son of Drimylos. A Prosopographical Note," *Journal of Juristic Papyrology* 7/8, 1954, pp. 205–9, and in M. Stern and M. Amit, eds., *Social Conflict in Ancient Greece*, Jerusalem and Leyden, 1984, pp. 307–11; H. Hauben, "A Jewish Shipowner in Third-Century Ptolemaic Egypt," *Ancient Society* 10, 1979, pp. 167–70. *DEMETRIOS THE CHRONOGRAPHER:* E. Bickerman, "The Jewish Historian Demetrios," in J. Neusner, ed., *Christianity, Judaism and Other Greco-Roman Cults. Studies for Morton Smith*, 3, Leyden, 1975, pp. 72–84; rev. ed. in *Studies in Jewish and Christian History*, 2, Leyden, 1980, pp. 347–58; C. R. Holladay, *Fragments from Hellenistic Jewish Authors*, 1, op. cit., pp. 51–91 (text, translation, commentary, and bibliography).

A LOVE STORY. *JUDEO-ALEXANDRIAN LITERATURE AND JEWISH WRITINGS IN GREEK:* M. E. Stone, ed., *Jewish Writings of the Second Temple Period*, op. cit.; G. W. E. Nickelsburg, *Jewish Literature between the Bible and the Mishnah. A Historical and Literary Introduction*, Philadelphia, 1981; rev. ed. 1987; N. de Lange, *Apocrypha. Jewish Literature of the Hellenistic Age*, New York, 1978. *ITS TENDENCIES:* V. Tcherikover, "Jewish Apologetical Literature Reconsidered," *Eos* 48/3 (Symbolae R. Taubenschlag, 3), 1957, pp. 169–93; J. J. Collins, *Between Athens and Jerusalem. Jewish Identity in the Hellenistic Diaspora*, New York, 1983. *ARISTOBOULOS:* A. Y. Collins, "Aristobulus," in J. H. Charlesworth, ed., *The Old Testament Pseudepigrapha*, op. cit., vol. 2, pp. 831–42; N. Walter, *Der Thoraausleger Aristobulos*, Berlin, 1964. *JOSEPH AND ASENATH:* E. W. Brooks, *Joseph and Asenath: The Confession and Prayer of Asenath, Daughter of Pentephres the Priest*, London, 1918; C. Burchard, "Joseph and Aseneth," in J. H. Charlesworth, ed., *The Old Testament Pseudepigrapha*, op. cit., vol. 2, pp. 177–247; M. Philonenko, *Joseph et Aséneth. Introduction, texte critique, traduction et notes*, Leyden, 1968 (Studia Post-Biblica, 13); S. West, "Joseph and Asenath. A Neglected Greek Romance," *Classical Quarterly* 24, 1974, pp. 70–81. *MIXED MARRIAGES IN PTOLEMAIC EGYPT:* J. Mélèze Modrzejewski, "Dryton le Crétois et sa famille: les mariages mixtes dans l'Egypte hellénistique" (1984), in *Statut personnel et liens de famille dans les droits de l'Antiquité*, Aldershot, 1993 (Variorum CS 411), 8.

4. A New Diaspora

AMONG THE "HELLENES." *DEMOGRAPHY:* D. Delia, "The Population of Roman Alexandria," *Transactions of the American Philological Association* 118, 1988, pp. 275–92. *STATUS AND SELF-DEFINITION:* J. Mélèze Modrzejewski, "How to be a Jew in Hellenistic Egypt?," in *Diasporas in Antiquity*, op. cit., Atlanta, 1993, pp. 65–92, and S. Honigman, "The Birth of a Diaspora: The Emergence of a Jewish Self-Definition in Ptolemaic Egypt in the Light of Onomastics," ibid., pp. 93–127; W. Clarysse, "Jews in Trikomia", in A. Bülow-Jacobsen, ed., *Proceeding of the 20th International Congress of Papyrologists* (Copenhagen, August, 1992), Copenhagen, 1994, pp. 193–203. *DISCUSSION ON POLITEUMA:* C. Zuckerman, "Hellenistic politeumata and the Jews. A Reconsideration," *Scripta Classica Israelica*, 8–9 (1985–88), 1989, pp. 171–85; A. Kasher, "The Civic

Status of the Jews in Ptolemaic Egypt," in P. Bilde et al., eds., *Ethnicity in Hellenistic Egypt*, Aarhus, 1992, pp. 100–121; G. Lüderitz, "What is Politeuma?", in J.W. van Henten and P.W. van der Horst, eds., *Studies in Early Jewish Epigraphy*, Leyden, 1994, pp. 183–225. THE "HELLENES": J. Mélèze Modrzejewski, "Le statut des Hellènes dans l'Egypte lagide: bilan et perspectives" (1983), in *Statut personnel et liens de famille dans les droits de l'Antiquité*, op. cit., 3.

SOLDIERS OF THE PTOLEMIES. GREEK SOCIETY: N. Lewis, *Greeks in Ptolemaic Egypt. Case Studies in the Social History of the Hellenistic World*, Oxford, 1986. CLERUCHS: J. Mélèze Modrzejewski, "Régime foncier et statut social dans l'Egypte ptolémaïque" (1979), in *Statut personnel et liens de famille dans les droits de l'Antiquité*, op. cit., 4.

"GOD THE MOST HIGH" AND "SPLENDOR OF ISRAEL." SYNAGOGUES: L. I. Levine, ed., *Ancient Synagogues Revealed*, Jerusalem, 1981; idem, *The Synagogue in Late Antiquity*, Philadelphia, 1987. A list of papyrological and epigraphical sources concerning Jewish synagogues in Egypt is given by E. Bernand, "Au Dieu Très-Haut," in *Hommages à J. Cousin* (Annales littéraires de l'Université de Besançon, 273), Paris, 1983, pp. 107–11. RIGHT OF ASYLUM: J. Bingen, "L'asylie pour une synagogue (CIL Suppl. 6583 = CIJ 1449)," in *Studia P. Naster oblata*, 2, Louvain, 1982, pp. 11–16, and in *Pages d'épigraphie grecque. Attique–Egypte (1952–82)*, Brussels, 1991, pp. 45–50.

5. A Law for the Jews of Egypt

THE GREEK TORAH AND THE DEMOTIC CASE BOOK. LETTER OF ARISTEAS: M. Hadas, *Aristeas to Philocrates*, New York, 1951; R. J. H. Schutt, "Letter of Aristeas," in J. H. Charlesworth, ed., *The Old Testament Pseudepigrapha*, op. cit., vol. 2, pp. 7–34. PAPYROLOGICAL EVIDENCE FOR THE SEPTUAGINT: Z. Aly and L. Koenen, *Three Rolls of the Early Septuagint. Genesis and Deuteronomy, A Photographic Edition*, Bonn, 1980. THE DEMOTIC CASE BOOK: P. W. Pestman, "Remarks on the Legal Manual from Hermopolis," *Enchoria* 12, 1984, pp. 33–42; J. Mélèze Modrzejewski, "'Livres sacrés' et justice lagide," *Acta Universitatis Lodziensis, Folia Juridica* 21 (Symbolae C. Kunderewicz), Lodz, 1986, pp. 11–44; idem, "Law and Justice in Ptolemaic Egypt", in H. Maehler and M. J. Geller, eds., *Legal Documents of the Hellenistic World*, London, 1995, pp. 1–11.

THE LAW OF MOSES AND THE JUSTICE OF THE KING. PTOLEMAIC JUDICIAL SYSTEM: H. J. Wolff, *Das Justizwesen der Ptolemäer*, Munich, 1962, 2nd ed. 1971; J. Mélèze Modrzejewski, "Droit et justice dans le monde hellénistique au IIIe siècle avant notre ère. Expérience lagide," in *Mnêmê G. A. Petropoulou*, Athens, 1984, I, pp. 53-77.

"THE LAW OF THE LAND IS LAW." THE LAW OF RIBBIT: A. Weingort, *Intérêt et crédit dans le droit talmudique*, Paris, 1979 (Bibliothèque d'histoire du droit et de droit romain, 21). LOANS "WITHOUT INTEREST": P. W. Pestman, "Loans Bearing No Interest?" *Journal of Juristic Papyrology* 16/17, 1971, pp. 7–29. JEWISH LAW IN THE PERIOD OF THE SECOND TEMPLE: Z. W. Falk, *Introduction to the Jewish Law of the Second Commonwealth*, 2 vols., Leyden, 1977–78; J. Mélèze Modrzejewski, "Jewish Law and Hellenistic Legal Practice in the Light of Greek Papyri from Egypt", in *An Introduction to the History and Sources of Jewish Law*, Oxford, 1996, pp. 75–97.

6. A Jewish Temple in Ptolemaic Egypt

THE ECHOES OF THE MACCABEAN CRISIS. E. Bickerman, *The God of the Maccabees. Studies on the Meaning and Origin of the Maccabean Revolt*, Leyden, 1979 (orig. pub. in German, Berlin, 1937). A fine analysis of the conflict in its historical and ideological context is proposed by M. Hengel,

Judaism and Hellenism. Studies in their Encounter in Palestine during the Hellenistic Period, Philadelphia, 1974 (orig. pub. in German, Tübingen, 1969; 2nd ed. 1973). *ONIAS IV IN EGYPT:* J. Mélèze Modrzejewski, "L' 'Ordonnance sur les cultures' : droit grec et réalités égyptiennes en matière de bail forcé," *Revue historique de droit français et étranger 72,* 1994, pp. 1-20.

"AN ALTAR OF THE LORD IN THE MIDST OF THE LAND OF EGYPT." M. Delcor, "Le temple d'Onias en Egypte. Réexamen d'un vieux problème," *Revue biblique 75,* 1968, pp. 188–203; A. Zivie, "Onias," in *Lexikon der Ägyptologie* IV/4, Lief. 28, Wiesbaden, 1981, cols. 569–72. *THE GOLDEN LAMP:* R. Hayward, "The Jewish Temple at Leontopolis: A Reconsideration," *Journal of Jewish Studies 33,* 1982, pp. 429–43.

IMAGES OF THE "LAND OF ONIAS." E. Bernand, *Inscriptions métriques de l'Egypte gréco-romaine,* Paris 1969, pp. 196–209. *"HERETIC JUDAISM":* A. Momigliano, "Un documento della spiritualità dei Giudei Leontopolitani," *Aegyptus 12,* 1932, p. 171ff.

7. At the Wellsprings of Pagan Anti-Semitism

MODERN FANTASIES AND ANCIENT MYTHS. *GENERAL VIEW:* L. Poliakov, *History of Anti-Semitism,* London, 1965–85 (orig. pub. Paris, 1955–77; rev. ed. 1981); D. Berger, ed., *History and Hate. The Dimensions of Anti-Semitism,* Philadelphia, 1986. *PAGAN ANTI-SEMITISM:* J. N. Sevenster, *The Roots of Pagan Anti-Semitism in the Ancient World,* Leyden, 1975, and the present writer's remarks on this book: J. Mélèze Modrzejewski, "Sur l'antisémitisme païen," in M. Olender, ed., *Pour Léon Poliakov. Le racisme: Mythes et sciences,* Brussels, 1981, pp. 411–39. *EGYPTIAN ROOTS:* J. Yoyotte, "L'Egypte ancienne et les origines de l'antijudaïsme," *Bulletin de la Socété Ernest Renan* 11, 1962, pp. 11–23; C. Aziza, "L'utilisation polémique du récit de l'Exode chez les écrivains alexandrins (IVe siècle av. J.-C. – Ier siècle ap. J.-C.)," in *Aufstieg und Niedergang der römischen Welt* 20/1, Berlin, 1987, pp. 41–65; H. Heinen, "Ägyptische Grundlagen des Antiken Antijudaismus. Zum Judenexkurs des Tacitus, Historien V 2–13," *Trierer Theologische Zeitschrift* 102/2, 1992, pp. 124–49. *ARTAPANOS:* C. R. Holladay, *Fragments from Hellenistic Jewish Authors,* 1, op. cit., pp. 189–243. *RECENT APPROACHES:* N. de Lange, "The Origins of Anti-Semitism: Ancient Evidence and Modern Interpretations," in S. L. Gilman and S. T. Katz, eds., *Anti-Semitism in Times of Crisis,* New York, 1991, pp. 21–27; Z. Yavetz, "Judaeophobia in Classical Antiquity: A Different Approach," *Journal of Jewish Studies* 44, 1993, pp. 1–22.

THE MIRACLE AT THE HIPPODROME. *3 MACCABEES:* M. Hadas, *The Third and Fourth Books of Maccabees,* New York, 1953; H. Anderson, "3 Maccabees," in J. H. Charlesworth, ed., *The Old Testament Pseudepigrapha,* op. cit., vol. 2, pp. 509–29. *ITS HISTORICAL VALUE:* V. Tcherikover, "The Third Book of Maccabees as a Historical Source," *Scripta Hierosolymitana 7,* 1961, pp. 1–26; M. Z. Kopidakis, *The Third Book of Maccabees and Aeschylus* (in modern Greek), Thessaloniki, 1982. *THE "DIONYSIAC DECREE" OF PTOLEMY PHILOPATOR:* E. G. Turner, "The Ptolemaic Edict BGU VI 1211 is to be dated before 215/14 BC," in *Festschrift zum 100-jährigen Bestehen der Papyrussammlung der Oesterreichischen Nationalbibliothek,* Vienna, 1983, pp. 148–52. THE ELEPHANTS: W. W. Tarn, "Seleucus' 500 Elephants," *Journal of Hellenic Studies* 60, 1940, pp. 84–89.

"THEY LOATHE THE JEWS": R. Rémondon, "Les antisémites de Memphis," *Chronique d'Egypte* 35, 1960, pp. 244–61.

THE TWILIGHT: EGYPT IN THE ROMAN EMPIRE

8. The "Jewish Question" in Alexandria

THE DECLINE. *HISTORICAL CONTEXT:* E. M. Smallwood, *The Jews under Roman Rule*, Leyden, 1976, 2nd ed. 1981; V. Tcherikover, "The Decline of the Jewish Diaspora in Egypt in the Roman Period," *Journal of Jewish Studies* 14, 1963, pp. 1–32; A. Kasher, *The Jews in Hellenistic and Roman Egypt*, op. cit. *THE JEWS AND ALEXANDRIAN CITIZENSHIP:* D. Delia, *Alexandrian Citizenship during the Roman Principate*, Atlanta, 1991. *NEW ORGANIZATION OF THE PROVINCIAL SOCIETY:* J. Mélèze Modrzejewski, "Entre la cité et le fisc. Le statut grec dans l'Egypte romaine" (1985), in *Droit impérial et traditions locales dans l'Egypte romaine*, Aldershot, 1990 (Variorum CS 321), 1.

THE VILE DEEDS OF FLACCUS THE PREFECT. E. R. Goodenough, *The Politics of Philo Judaeus*, New Haven, 1938; E. M. Smallwood, *Philonis Alexandrini Legatio ad Gaium*, 2nd ed., Leyden, 1970; S. Sandmel, *Philo of Alexandria. An Introduction*, London, 1979.

JEWS, ALEXANDRIANS, AND CLAUDIUS THE EMPEROR. *THE "ACTS OF THE PAGAN MARTYRS" OF ALEXANDRIA:* H. Musurillo, ed., *The Acts of the Pagan Martyrs. Acta Alexandrinorum*, Oxford, 1954; idem, *Acta Alexandrinorum*, Leipzig, 1961. *THE TRIAL OF ISIDOROS:* J. Mélèze Modrzejewski, "Le procès d'Isidôros: droit pénal et affrontements idéologiques entre Rome et Alexandrie sous l'empereur Claude," *Praktika tês Akadêmias Athênôn* 61, Athens, 1986, pp. 245–75 (in modern Greek, with French translation of the documents). *KING AGRIPPA:* D. R. Schwarz, *Agrippa I. The Last King of Judaea*, Tübingen, 1990.

9. The Time of Misfortunes

THE SERVICE RECORD OF A BRILLIANT ALEXANDRIAN. *ALEXANDER THE ALABARCH AND HIS SONS:* J. Schwartz, "Note sur la famille de Philon d'Alexandrie," *Annuaire de l'Institut de philolologie et d'histoire orientales et slaves* 13, 1953, pp. 591–602. *TIBERIUS JULIUS ALEXANDER:* G. Chalon, *L'édit de Tiberius Julius Alexander. Etude historique et exégétique*, Olten and Lausanne, 1964; A. Barzano, "Tiberio Giulio Alessandro, Prefetto d'Egitto (66–70)," in *Aufstieg und Niedergang der römischen Welt* 2, 10/1, Berlin, 1988, pp. 518–80. *THE FALL OF THE SECOND TEMPLE:* J. J. Price, *Jerusalem under Siege. The Collapse of the Jewish State, 66–70 CE*, Leyden, 1992 (Brill's Series in Jewish Studies, 3).

A MIRACLE IN ROME. *THE ACTS OF HERMAISKOS:* R. Loewe, "A Jewish Counterpart of the Acts of the Alexandrians," *Journal of Jewish Studies* 12, 1961, pp. 105–22; J. Mélèze Modrzejewski, "Trajan et les Juifs. Propagande alexandrine et contre-propagande rabbinique," *Problèmes d'histoire du christianisme* 17, Brussels, 1988, pp. 7–31.

"A SPIRIT OF REBELLION." A. Fuks, "The Jewish Revolt in Egypt (AD 115–117) in the Light of the Papyri" (1953) and "Aspects of the Jewish Revolt in AD 115–117" (1961), in *Social Conflict in Ancient Greece*, op. cit., pp. 322–56; S. Applebaum, *Jews and Greeks in Ancient Cyrene*, Leyden, 1979; M. Pucci Ben Ze'ev, *La rivolta ebraica al tempo di Traiano*, Pisa, 1981; eadem, "La rivolta ebraica in Egitto (115–117 d.C.) nella storiografia antica," *Aegyptus* 62, 1982, pp. 195–217.

10. The Remembrance

WHO DESTROYED THE GREAT SYNAGOGUE OF ALEXANDRIA? J. Mélèze Modrzejewski, "Trajan et les Juifs," op. cit.; M. Pucci Ben Ze'ev, "Greek Attacks against Alexandrian Jews during Emperor Trajan's Reign," *Journal for the Study of Judaism* 20, 1989, pp. 31–48.

"JEWISH TAX," "JEWISH ACCOUNTS." A. Swiderek, "Ioudaikos Logos," *Journal of Juristic Papyrology* 16/17, 1971, pp. 45–62; J. Mélèze Modrzejewski, "'Ioudaioi apheirêmenoi': la fin de la communauté juive en Egypte (115–117 de n.è.)," *Symposium 1985* (Sixth International Conference on Greek and Hellenistic Legal History, Ringberg, Bavaria, May 1985), Cologne and Vienna, 1989, pp. 337–61. *LÈSE-MAJESTÉ*: R. A. Bauman, *The Crimen Maiestatis in the Roman Republic and Augustan Principate*, 2nd ed., Johannesburg, 1970. *THE SURVIVORS*: J. Schwartz, "Quelques réflexions à propos de trois catastrophes," in G. Dahan, ed., *Les Juifs au regard de l'Histoire. Mélanges en l'honneur de Bernhard Blumenkranz*, Paris, 1985, pp. 21–29; M. Hengel, "Hadrians Politik gegenüber Juden und Christen," in S. J. D. Cohen, ed., *Ancient Studies in Memory of Elias Bickerman*, New York, 1987, pp. 153–82.

A DAY OF REJOICINGS IN OXYRHYNCHOS. *GREEK FOUNDATIONS*: J. Mélèze Modrzejewski, "A propos des fondations en droit grec" (1963), in *Statut personnel et liens de famille dans les droits de l'Antiquité*, op. cit., 9.

Epilogue

ALEXANDRIAN JUDAISM AND THE ORIGINS OF CHRISTIANITY. *GNOSTIC HYPOTHESIS*: W. Bauer, *Orthodoxy and Heresy in Earliest Christianity*, Philadelphia, 1971 (orig. pub. Tübingen, 1934; 2nd ed. 1964). *JUDEO-CHRISTIAN HYPOTHESIS*: C. H. Roberts, *Manuscript, Society and Relief in Early Christian Egypt*, Oxford, 1979. *ALLUSION TO CHRISTIANITY IN THE LETTER OF CLAUDIUS*: S. Reinach, "La première allusion au christianisme dans l'histoire," *Revue de l'histoire des religions* 90, 1924, pp. 108–22; F. Cumont, "La lettre de Claude aux Alexandrins," ibid., 91, 1925, pp. 3–6. *MODERN SYNTHESES*: H. I. Bell, *Cults and Creeds in Graeco-Roman Egypt*, Oxford, 1953; C. W. Griggs, *Early Egyptian Christianity. From its Origins to 451 CE*, 1990; 3rd ed., Leyden, 1993; B. A. Pearson and J. E. Goehring, eds., *The Roots of Egyptian Christianity*, Philadelphia, 1986; B. A. Pearson, *Gnosticism, Judaism, and Egyptian Christianity*, Minneapolis, 1990. *JEWS AND CHRISTIANS*: E. P. Sanders, A. I. Baumgarten, A. Mendelsohn, and B. S. Meyer, eds., *Jewish and Christian Self-Definition*, 3 vols., Philadelphia, 1980–82; J. D. G. Dunn, ed., *Jews and Christians: The Parting of the Ways, AD 70 to 135*, Tübingen, 1993; M. Simon, *Verus Israel. A Study of the Relations between Christians and Jews in the Roman Empire (135–425)*, Oxford, 1986 (orig. pub. Paris, 1964).

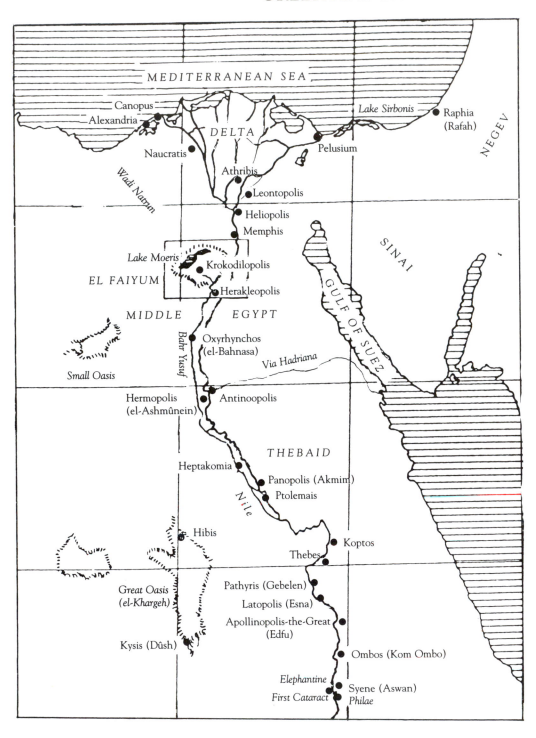

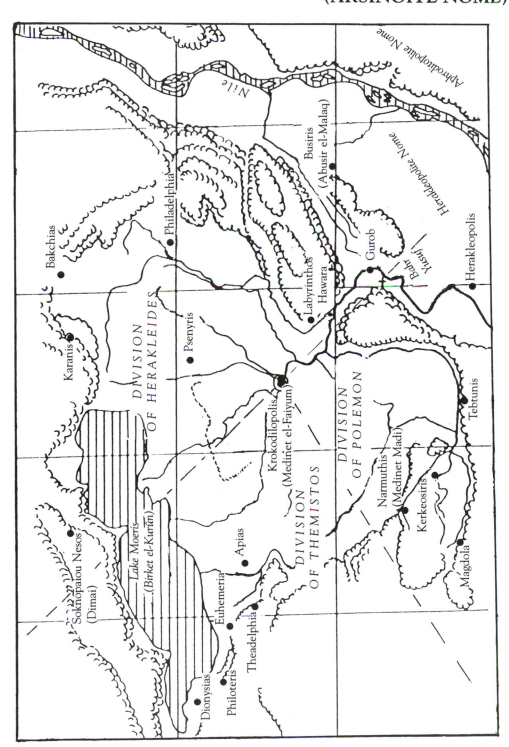

Nile

Aphroditopolite Nome

Busiris
(Abusir el-Malaq)

Herakleopolite Nome

Philadelphia

Bakchias

Labyrinthos
Hawara

Gurob

Bahr

Yusuf

Herakleopolis

DIVISION
OF HERAKLEIDES

Psenyris

Karanis

Krokodilopolis
(Medinet el-Faiyum)

DIVISION
OF POLEMON

Lake Moeris
(Birket el-Kurūn)

DIVISION
OF THEMISTOS

Narmuthis
(Medinet Madi)

Tebtunis

Soknopaiou Nesos
(Dimai)

Euhemeria

Apias

Kerkeosiris

Theadelphia

Magdola

Dionysias

Philoteris

257

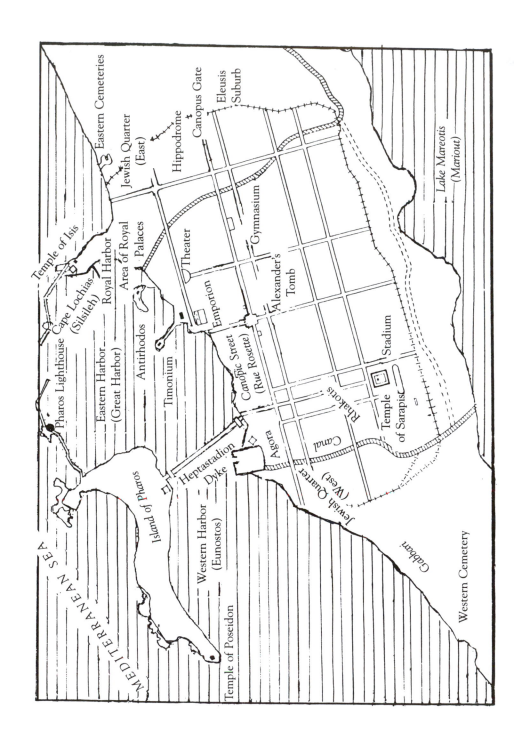

Eastern Cemeteries

Jewish Quarter (East)

Hippodrome

Canopus Gate

Eleusis Suburb

Lake Mareotis (Mariout)

Temple of Isis

Cape Lochias (Silsileh)

Royal Harbor

Area of Royal Palaces

Pharos Lighthouse

Eastern Harbor (Great Harbor)

Antirhodos

Timonium

Theater

Emporion

Gymnasium

Alexander's Tomb

Canopic Sreet (Rue Rosette)

Stadium

Rhakotis

Temple of Sarapis

MEDITERRANEAN SEA

Island of Pharos

Heptastadion Dyke

Western Harbor (Eunostos)

Agora

Canal

Jewish Quarter (West)

Gabbari

Western Cemetery

Temple of Poseidon

Nile boat trip   *Mosaic panel from Tivoli, 2nd century* CE. *(Cardiff, National Museum of Wales.)*

Index of Persons and Places

INDEX OF SOURCES

II. PAPYRI AND OSTRACA

A. EGYPTIAN

IV. BIBLE

DATE DUE